PLANETS IN WORK

PLANETS IN WORK

A Complete Guide to VOCATIONAL ASTROLOGY

Jamie Binder

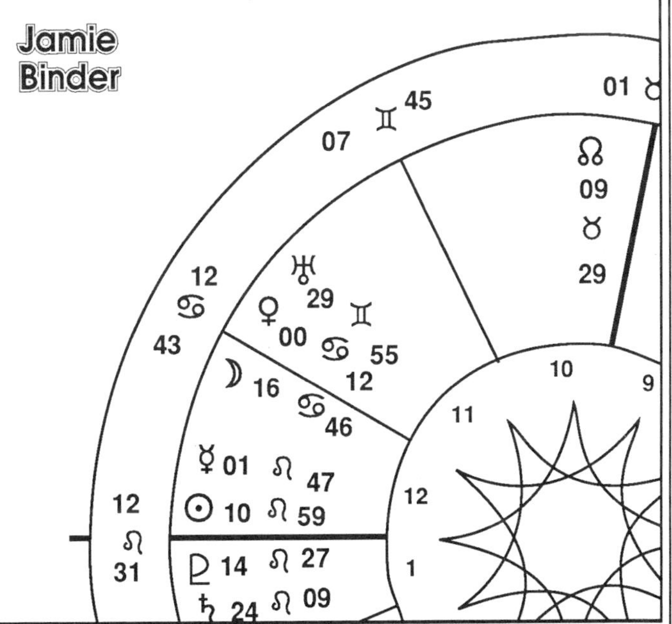

Cover designed by Maria Kay Simms
Author photo by Diane Graham-Henry

International Standard Book Number 0-917086-89-9

Printed in the United States of America

Published by ACS Publications, Inc.
P.O. Box 34487
San Diego, CA 92163-4487

First Printing, October 1989
Second Printing, March 1991

Dedication

This book is dedicated to my father,
Dr. Samuel Binder.

Acknowledgments

I am grateful to:

– my predecessors for their insights and hard work
– Neil Michelsen for recognizing a diamond in the rough
– Maritha Pottenger for helping to polish that diamond and for her conscientiousness, expertise, intelligent criticism, patience and good will.

Contents

Introduction xiii

Chapter One Meaning Motivates, Interests Inspire 1
Interests, Dreams and Vocational choice 4
Meaning and Vocational Choice 13
Type A 14
Type B 15
Type C 17
Type D 21
Type E 25
Planets as Vocational Indicators 26
References 30

Chapter Two Basic Vocational Needs and Traits 31
How to Spot Recurrent Themes and Prominent Tendencies 34
Prominent Traits and Trait Pairs 36
Trait 1 43
Trait 2 47
Trait 3 50
Trait 4 54
Trait 5 57
Trait 6 61
Trait 7 64
Trait 8 68
Trait 9 74
Trait 10 77
Trait 11 80
Trait 12 85
References 89

Chapter Three Applying Personality Drives 90
Hemisphere Emphasis 91
Northern Hemisphere Emphasis 92
Eastern Hemisphere Emphasis 94
Western Hemisphere Emphasis 95
Southern Hemisphere Emphasis 96
Quadrant Focus 97
First Quadrant Focus 98
Second Quadrant Focus 99
Third Quadrant Focus 100

Fourth Quadrant Focus 102
Chart Patterns 103
The Seesaw 106
The Bundle 108
The Bowl 110
The Bucket 112
The Locomotive 115
The Splay 117
The Splash 119
References 121

Chapter Four Pinpointing Personality Needs 122
G-Planets 122
The Singleton 126
Handle and Leading Planets 128
Mars—Trait 1 128
Venus—Traits 2 and 7 131
Mercury—Traits 3 and 6 135
Moon—Trait 4 139
Sun—Trait 5 143
Pluto—Trait 8 147
Jupiter—Trait 9 151
Saturn—Trait 10 154
Uranus—Trait 11 158
Neptune—Trait 12 163
References 167

Chapter Five The Aspects of Personality 169
Major and Minor Aspects 170
Harmonious/Inharmonious Aspects 170
Major Configurations 174
Orbs 174
Retrogradation 175
Intercepted Houses 176
Stations 176
House Rulers 177
Trait Pairs 178
References 244

Chapter Six Developing a Purposeful Identity 246
Ascendant - Trait 1 246
Midheaven - Trait 10 248
Trait 1 on Ascendant or Midheaven 250
Trait 2 on Ascendant or Midheaven 252
Trait 3 on Ascendant or Midheaven 253
Trait 4 on Ascendant or Midheaven 255
Trait 5 on Ascendant or Midheaven 257
Trait 6 on Ascendant or Midheaven 259
Trait 7 on Ascendant or Midheaven 261
Trait 8 on Ascendant or Midheaven 262
Trait 9 on Ascendant or Midheaven 264
Trait 10 on Ascendant or Midheaven 266
Trait 11 on Ascendant or Midheaven 268
Trait 12 on Ascendant or Midheaven 270
The Nodes 272
  Traits 1 & 7 272
  Traits 2 & 8 273
  Traits 3 & 9 275
  Traits 4 & 10 276
  Traits 5 & 11 277
  Traits 6 & 12 278
References 280

Chapter Seven Consciousness and the Job in Life 281
New Phase 283
Crescent Phase 287
First Quarter Phase 291
Gibbous Phase 294
Full Phase 298
Disseminating Phase 301
Last Quarter Phase 305
Balsamic Phase 309
References 315

Chapter Eight The Signs of Consciousness 316
The Qualities 321
  Cardinal 321
  Fixed 324
  Mutable 329
The Elements 333

Fire 333
Earth 336
Air 340
Water 344
References 347

Epilogue 348

Appendix Vocational Needs Analysis Form 349

Bibliograpy 355

Index 356

Introduction

Almost everyone has to face the reality of earning a living. Work, however, can be stimulating and provide a sense of purpose when it is an expression of who you are and what you need. Foggy career directions are symptoms of a lack of self-knowledge. Understanding your needs allows you to create optimal satisfaction in your career and in other areas of life.

Perhaps you are confused about the direction your vocation should take, or feel trapped in a meaningless, routine job. Perhaps you have clients who want more from their work. Or you may simply be interested in a fresh point of view on vocational astrology. Within these pages you will find help and insight.

It is true that some people give no thought to their work; the fact that it pays the bills is enough. However, even they can benefit from knowing what conditions will provide greater satisfaction from the job.

When people do not know who they are, what their needs are or what they truly find interesting to do, it is extremely difficult to select the right job. If their self-image is unclear, they could be advised to pursue an appropriate line of work, based on all the "scientific" evidence in the world, and still be unable to realize its value.

Planets in Work can help determine the kinds of jobs that best fulfill special vocational needs. Self-knowledge is a key to success. Without it, people cannot possibly know what directions their work should take. As a "tool for self-knowledge," astrology can help direct choices.

Although not absolutely necessary, it would be helpful to know the basic principles of astrology. This includes a fundamental grasp of the planets, signs, houses and aspects. Without this, the "Vocational Needs Analysis" available through Astro Computing Services will calculate the career analysis outlined in this book for you. It also cites the appropriate pages in *Planets in Work* designed to enhance your vocational expression.

Astrology, however, is not a hard and fast science. It depends entirely on the interpretive capabilities of the practitioner. Nor does any birthchart "reveal" a destiny, or come equipped with a neon sign flashing "this way to career fulfillment!" Rather the horoscope is a blueprint to needs, tendencies and potentials in all areas of life, not only job- or career-related ones. It does not foretell how anyone will respond or will use the indicated potentials– that is completely up to you. The self-actualization of your potentials is what determines your destiny.

Planets in Work helps you take inventory of the symbolism in your chart or in the charts of your clients. It will suggest occupational outlets that **may** be suitable for individual needs. This will require some work on your part (unless you obtain the "Vocational Needs Analysis" report). But don't worry. You will be guided step-by-step through the process.

Most vocational astrology books ignore personality factors that inhibit an appropriate work-related expression. Here they are highlighted. Our less-than-positive responses to life can account for vocational problems, so antidotes for undermining behavior are provided. Career counseling is not only a matter of knowing appropriate career potentials; it is also a matter of understanding what aspects of self interfere with fulfilling work. Growth stems from acknowledging our "darker" side. If you have enough faith to explore these issues, *Planets in Work* can help you to know yourself more fully, deal with any weakness, and take full advantage of your strengths.

CHAPTER ONE

MEANING MOTIVATES, INTERESTS INSPIRE

Meaning is a fundamental human need. All cultures have developed religious or philosophical perspectives intended to provide a meaningful framework of values by which to live. Despite our society's materialistic trends, "The American Dream" no longer surrounds the mere acquisition of things. More and more people want to be a "somebody" and work has assumed importance beyond just earning a living.

Losing a job is a shock to the system, often as traumatic as divorce. Individuals lose not only financial security, but also self-esteem due to society's current emphasis on money and social standing. Experiencing a job as meaningless, however, can be equally deadly. Comparable to a prison stint, it can slowly drain the life force. But this hollow feeling stems from an inner clamoring to find a satisfying way to earn a living.

A troubled job life often represents a pressing need to make a change. It is an inner signal to reexamine life. Something vital has been overlooked. Individuals may be on the wrong career paths while their inner selves yearn for more fulfilling occupational expressions. Career problems can also represent challenges that test the chosen path. The old adage, "Nothing worth having comes easily," may apply to some people. Others, whose job performance has been faulty, may have to learn the hard way that, when it comes to work, there are few free handouts.

For something new to enter life, what is no longer necessary must be eliminated. An old job or lifestyle may have to be cleared away before anything new can be built in its place, just as a full glass of water cannot hold any fresh water until the old liquid is poured out. Letting go can be a painful, anxiety-ridden process, especially when a new career direction remains unclear. But if job loss or job meaninglessness is faced, dealt with calmly, and recognized for the opportunity it provides, more energy can be available to find satisfying employment.

From Loser to Winner

Paul used to be afraid he was a loser. Unable to complete his first year of college, he later bounced from one job to another. He never experienced a problem getting hired; it was maintaining a job that proved difficult. Because nutrition interested him, he often interviewed for retail positions in small health food establishments. While the concept was meaningful to him, the pay and work were poor. He was never given an opportunity to exercise authority or structure things in his own way. He would end up quitting or being fired. By his last exit, he was growing despondent. What was wrong with him? He seriously questioned his worth, while a lack of funds forced him to accept yet another get-by job.

This time, however, circumstances worked out differently. The initial job transformed into an opportunity which, almost overnight, thoroughly captured his interests. He was placed in charge of organizing, designing, printing and distributing a small, free, new age-related publication. Although publishing was totally foreign to him, new age consciousness was not; it was one reason he gravitated to health foods. Soon he was tapping talents he did not know existed and the magazine, along with his self-esteem, began to grow.

But all did not remain perfect with this job. As with former employers, his boss was a backseat driver. Paul had to fight for every new idea he proposed. Some he lost. As the reins tightened, Paul's developing style became cramped. His wonderful opportunity was assuming a familiar pattern, only this time he hated to leave the most exciting job he had ever had.

In the old days he would have crumbled in defeat, but this time his response was different: why not start his own magazine? In the past, a lack of self-esteem always stood between him and better opportunities; now it was only money. He borrowed enough to move to a different city and get out the first issue. Although it was not easy, he earned enough to pay back a portion of the loan, cover his expenses, and capitalize the next publication. Eight issues later, he was in the black and thoroughly enjoying self-employment. One previous problem was not recognizing this need to be his own boss. Now his work is truly fulfilling because it expresses who he is and what he finds interesting.

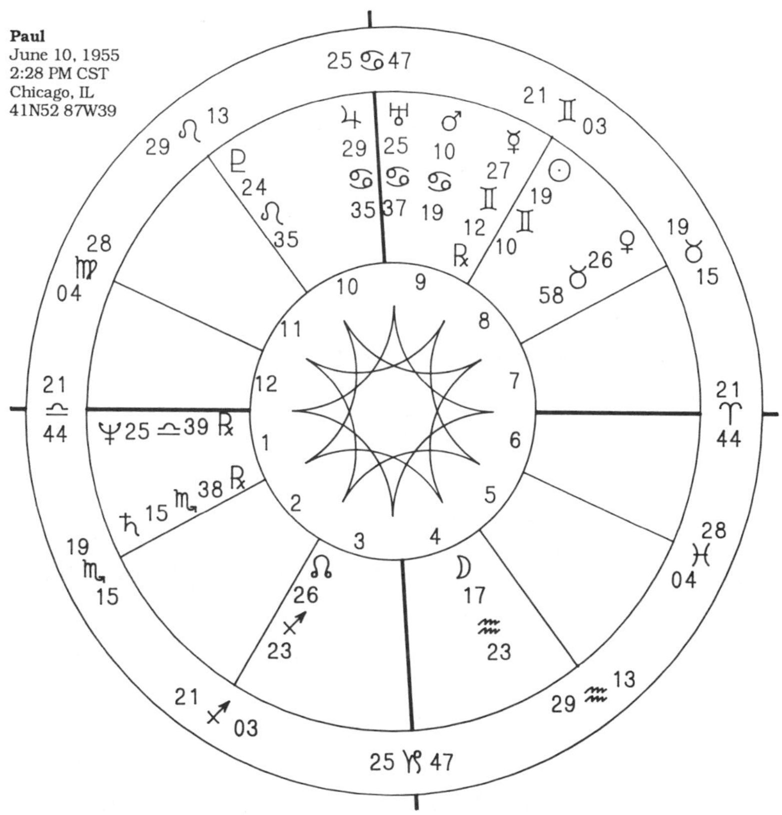

That probably sounds like a fairy tale, but it is a true story. Five years ago even Paul would not have believed it was possible to enjoy working as much as he does. He did not know himself very well then either. His work has become a path to self-discovery and has brought greater meaning and purpose to his life. If it happened to him, it can happen to anybody in the right frame of mind. A very important connection exists between interests, personality needs and rewarding vocational expression.

Interests, Dreams and Vocational Choice

Interests are an expression and manifestation of self. They create a desire to accomplish a task or attain a goal. They are crucial to providing vocational direction. Few things in life are more satisfying than pursuing work that is interesting to do or that fulfills a dream. Responsibilities are easier to bear, even when the effort involved becomes monumental.

People without career directions tend to lack realistic or constructive interests and goals. Without any special interests or hobbies, they tread water in the job world. Like little boats at sea without a rudder, they do not know where to aim themselves. When such people fall prey to a need to be "somebody," career fantasies frequently take the place of reality.

Jean is a thirty-two-year-old high school graduate with a job as a proofreader for a trade magazine. Pinpointing a client's reality quotient is important in career counseling, so I asked Jean "What would you really like to be doing?"

"I have always wanted to be a brain surgeon," she replied sincerely. For the moment I said nothing and took out a piece of paper to calculate how many years it would take a high school graduate to become a brain surgeon. Thirteen to fourteen was the end result, provided she could attend on a full-time basis.

She had never looked at her dream that way and, after a few moments, admitted she was not up to so many years of painstaking effort. She really did not **want** to be a brain surgeon. She wanted to be "somebody," a need her backroom job could not fulfill. The fact she had this fantasy in the first place suggested that she needed a more challenging, visible job. She would have to accept that it was not going to happen while she sat watching "Trapper John" on TV.

FANTASY

A close examination of vocational fantasies reveals threads of important needs not being satisfied in an individual's work life. They leak out of the unconscious as hopes and wishes for a brighter future. Some people only relate to themselves and to others through their vocational fantasies. The actual occupation is nothing more than a bill-paying device; only as much time and energy are devoted to work as are necessary to get through each day. Skills and abilities related to the real world are underdeveloped because only the fantasy is considered important. As a result, these individuals fall behind others who do apply themselves while fantasies balloon to ever greater proportions to ward off feelings of worthlessness.

A classic example is Dan who longed to become wealthy. He went from one psychic to another, anyone who would predict when he would strike it rich. After all, he was born with Jupiter in the second house which, he thought, could only mean one thing: he was destined to make lots of money. Despite the fact he had a prominent Saturn, it never occurred to him that he would have to work for this. Nor did he ever question why he needed to have so much money. Most of his energy was devoted to talking about a $250,000 seat on a stock options exchange that was supposed to drop into his lap and become his path to glory.

Dan, however, is a mail room clerk for a giant law firm. Although bright and college-educated, he is completely insulated behind ego-balming fantasies. At the age of thirty-nine, he is still living with his parents. He hates his job and gets through each day by rehashing his hopeful delusions. He neither applies himself at work nor strives to attain his dreams. He believes, somehow, that luck will see him through. Although he has been fired from his last three jobs, mostly due to negligence and a "prima donna" attitude, he could always shift the blame elsewhere: "they" were out to get him.

Interests and dreams are crucial to determining vocational direction, but not those like Dan's which are no more than fantasies. In a positive sense, dreams are the cornerstones of inspired activity and aspirational drives. What counts is translating those dreams, through an honest application of effort, into a tangible reality. This is what "successful" people do and what Jean and Dan have failed to do as yet.

GAUQUELIN VOCATIONAL RESEARCH
The Gauquelin research, involving the analysis of some 41,000 birth records, indirectly offers insights into the significant roles inspiration and aspiration play in extraordinary achievement. The studies found certain planets tended to appear, far beyond the chance level, in the ninth and twelfth houses of eminent professionals' charts. These are known as the "plus zones."

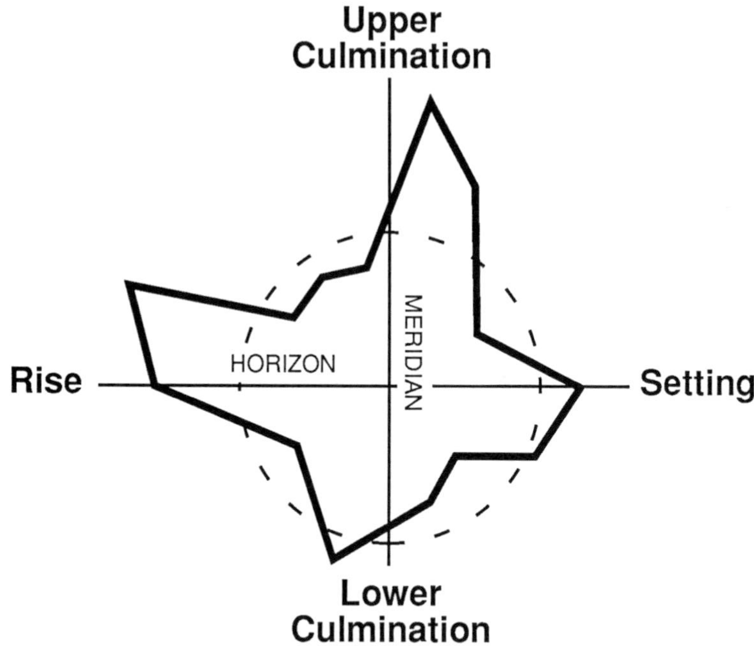

Scientifically replicated, these statistical studies proved that the appearance of Moon, Venus, Mars, Jupiter or Saturn in one of these sectors of the chart has significance in personality and, consequently, vocational choice. The personality precedes the occupation. (See Chapter 4 for a discussion of these studies.)

The results, however, contradicted traditional astrological points of view. Centuries of tradition held that planets located in cadent houses, especially the twelfth, were "weak." The characteristics they symbolize were not supposed to figure strongly in the personality or the career. Angular house placements, especially the first and tenth, traditionally have been considered the "prominent" sectors of the chart. Planets located in these houses received center stage during chart analysis. But the Gauquelin research proved the reverse to be the case, at least about extraordinary achievement. A logical explanation for this discrepancy from tradition exists and it concerns "dreams."

Certain people develop a desire to excel beyond ordinary limits. Their "dreams" and aspirations motivate them to expend the effort required. Interest in the occupation, in addition to a conviction that the goal is attainable, represent necessary fuel. Without a deeply felt interest in or meaning behind the work – an **inspiration or aspiration** – it is difficult to be sufficiently devoted to attain the heights.

This may be a reason why the Gauquelin studies found the inspirational twelfth and aspirational ninth houses significantly occupied in charts of highly successful people. These "fields of experience" (houses) are pertinent to vocational success because they are relevant to faith, confidence and a willingness to try. Tradition was not far off, only limited in its perspective on these sectors of the chart. Both a pipe dreamer and an eminent professional can be born with important planets in the plus zones. The distinction between "dreams" and "pipe dreams" wholly depends on the quality of effort expended to make the dream a reality.

PIPE DREAMS

This brings up a stumbling block common to some career-troubled people. The willingness to "work" can be inadequate when compared to the size of the dream. This was true in Dan's and Jean's cases. They did not wish to look at their fantasies in a realistic light because doing so would require facing features in their own personalities which they preferred to keep hidden. A chart can indicate any number of suitable job outlets, but if an individual prefers to remain unrealistic or is not willing to expend effort, the horoscope is nothing more than an interestingly diagrammed piece of paper. The fault does not lie with the "stars."

This unwillingness to exert effort serves a purpose in life, albeit mostly an unconscious one. A fear of failure often undermines an ability to truly apply oneself. People who strive for a goal place themselves in a position to either win or lose. Any commitment places people "on the line." Pipe dreamers typically balk at committing themselves to anything for long, especially careers. Talking and fantasizing take the place of doing and striving. People who do not apply sustained energy to accomplish goals never confront the limits to their capabilities. They are not placed in a position to be tested. They cannot be accused of failing if they never **really** try. Of course, winning is also denied. Nothing is gained other than the protection of an illusion.

Job-hopping, abandoning careers or being afraid to strike out on a new one can be manifestations of an unconscious fear of failure. Like an invisible chain, fear prevents people from committing to a goal. A faulty self-image usually lies at the root of this problem. Individuals run away from facing themselves. It is easier on the ego to hide behind illusions than to face the truth, so endless, seemingly valid reasons can be invented for not staying with a job.

The mutables are most often accused of this flighty, noncommittal behavior. However, Albert Einstein was a Pisces, Rachel Carson was a Gemini and Andrew Carnegie was a Sagittarian. Besides the fact they all possess mutable Sun signs, what did they have in common? Interests they pursued, a commitment to their fields, a belief in their capabilities and a willingness to exert effort were all displayed. The amount of effort sustained to accomplish a goal is a good barometer of whether a dream or pipe dream is involved. Whatever is unreal is without substance, support and endurance.

CONFIDENCE AND THE EFFORT QUOTIENT

Many career-troubled people lack realistic self-confidence and an effort quotient. Margot is one of them. She unconsciously suffered from a fear of failure while consumed by a need to be a "somebody." Her mother insisted that Margot was destined for greatness and helped her develop unrealistic expectations about life. Bragging and exaggeration became the only way Margot could relate to others. As her life unfolded, she could not understand why her greatness was going unrecognized. To avoid facing the discrepancy between how she viewed herself and the reality of her work life, she became involved with men who represented the ideals she sought.

The first was a wealthy wholesale fish dealer. His money came from "doctoring" poor quality fish. When he was caught, he lost everything, including Margot. The next man was a writer. Although poor, he had promise and she hoped his talent would rub off on her. But he was too absorbed in his own efforts and neglected the relationship. The third man was more willing to share his life. He was involved in a rock band and wanted to make her its lead singer. This was finally it, she thought, her path to glory. She took singing lessons three times a week. But that relationship evaporated when the band failed to get any bookings. Margot continued to move on, first to acting, then dance and then to another sparkling, new career. Each time she dropped a vocation, she had an hour's worth of excuses for why the situation ended and why her most recently chosen path was her "true" career.

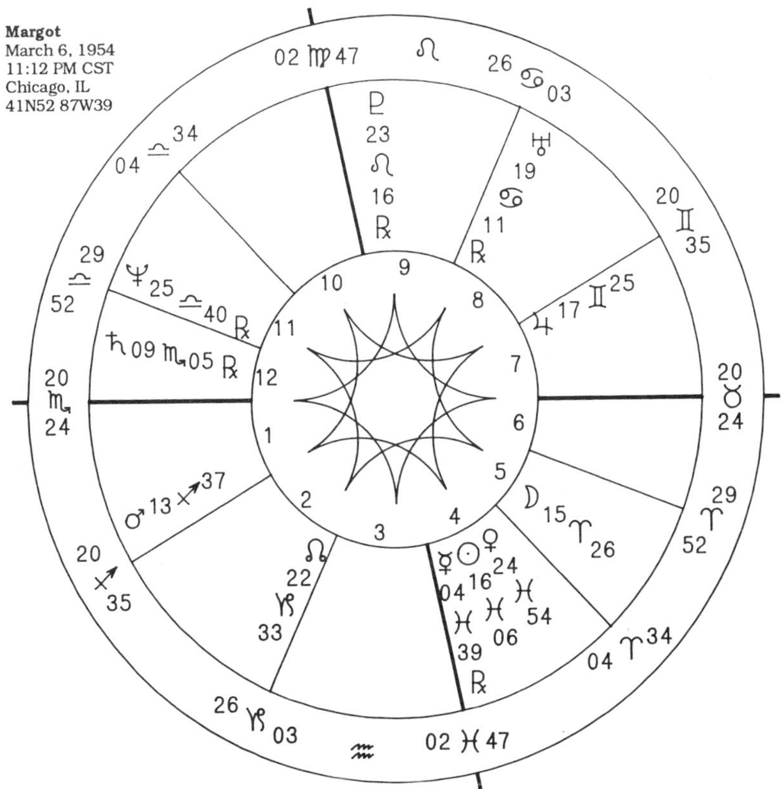

Margot also suffered from an ailment she kept well hidden. She perspired excessively. Her entire wardrobe had to be selected to conceal this annoyance. She insisted it was due to overactive glands and contemplated having an operation. Psychosomatic medicine, though, suggests a different mechanism at work. A tremendous amount of energy is required to consciously maintain a grand self-image when the unconscious is riddled with a fear of failure or worthlessness. In an effort to keep one image from colliding with the other, Margot unwittingly depleted energy which otherwise could have been put to better use: trying to succeed on her own rather than expecting others to do the job for her.

Avoiding sustained effort or commitment and blaming others for failures may enable pipe dreamers to avoid facing the truth. But running away also destroys self-confidence. Skills and confidence develop as a result of testing them and successfully overcoming challenges. This is the role that effort (represented by Saturn) plays in the working world, while interest in work can make effort less of a dirty word.

INTERESTS

But what about people who do not have any interests? From where do interests come?

Interests can spring almost magically from the inner being. They may represent expressive aspects of self that lie dormant until inspiration strikes. Another individual can provide inspiration, directly with support and encouragement, or indirectly through setting an example. It could come from a teacher, a neighbor, a therapist, a lover, anyone, or from a book, TV, a movie or a play. Inspiration, like Cupid, can strike at any time or place. Inspiration plucks a mysterious chord in one's inner being, then swiftly moves on. In the process, one is "touched" and an interest is stimulated. All an individual has to do is be ready, open to it, and sufficiently inspired to pursue it further (as Paul did).

People who do not know who they are frequently cannot decide what interests them. Since there is little connection with the self, there is no awareness of having any interests. Inspiration could strike a million times and still go unnoticed. One's being, or level of consciousness, has to be receptive to the inspiration. Otherwise, the inner chord can only resonate a dull thud.

It is difficult to develop interests or a sound vocation when the self-image is faulty. For most individuals, career problems relate directly to an unrealistic self-image; too much or too little is made out of the capabilities. Sometimes the early home life has a role to play in this.

Whatever the source, some people develop interests and a desire to accomplish. Usually a subject or activity is experienced as being pleasurable and stimulating which creates a motive to pursue it vocationally or avocationally. Some people might pursue an inwardly-felt talent, or perhaps seek knowledge for greater understanding or simply out of "interest." Astrology can help people identify their potential interests.

Peter took the route of following his interests. The oldest of nine children from an Irish Catholic household, Peter was expected to become a priest. Although he never really pictured himself in that role, he played this game until his second year in the seminary when he began to see the reality of a priest's life. Whenever he overheard his mother boast about her son preparing for the priesthood, he experienced a sinking feeling in the middle of his chest. How was he going to get out of this situation without disappointing her or worse? He did the only thing he could do at the time: he acted out to such an extent at school that he was expelled. The priests were grateful to see him go. While his mother cried, Peter financed his way through college and finished with a degree in political science.

Like so many of his peers, Peter did not know what to do after graduating. He took the first job that came along: selling fine wines in a liquor store. Wines fascinated him and the desire to learn more prompted him to study and go to wine tastings. This not only boosted sales and contacts, but further sparked his interest. He decided he needed more hands-on experience and scheduled a trip to France for the next grape harvest. He stayed a year and returned with a wealth of information along with references to upgrade his workplace. He continued to study, collect and catalogue information about grapes, vines, soil, processing, bottling, corks, all aspects of the industry. His apartment looked more like a warehouse than a home.

Then, he began to write about wines. Although he had never studied writing, it came easily to him because he had grown so knowledgeable about his subject. After publishing a few pieces, he submitted a sample article to a major magazine along with a note suggesting he should be hired as its wine columnist. The publisher's agreement was his first big break and he has been with the magazine ever since. The exposure has brought lecture engagements, free worldwide travel, cases of complimentary wine for his classes, and a steadily mounting income from writing and teaching. Recently he opened his own wine school, published a book and created diverse teaching aids for other wine educators, all as an outgrowth of pursuing an initial interest in wine (and eleven years of hard work).

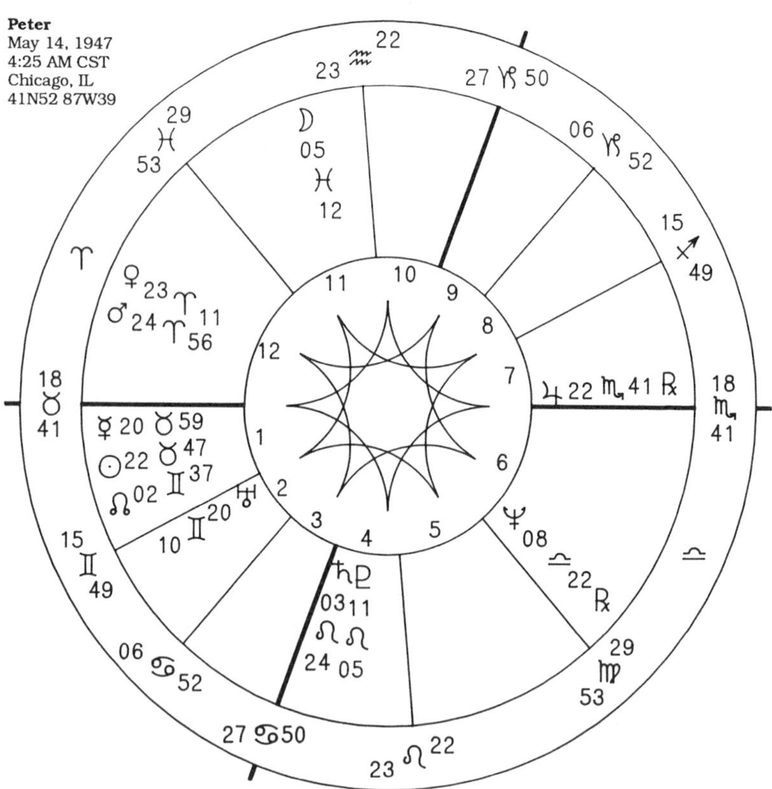

To ask what interests people is to know something about what gives them purpose in life. People without interests tend to lack meaning in their lives. There are many motives behind career choice, but in cases where interests predominate, the selected career provides a greater sense of direction and wholeness. The potential for fulfillment increases. Work is more like fun than effort because it is self-expressive and interesting.

Meaning is an individually-defined experience. What is interesting and brings purpose to one person may be about as stimulating as watching water boil to another. But when people do not know who they are, they cannot know what might be interesting to pursue. Family influence, an inappropriate self-image or the need to be "somebody" typically cloud contact with the inner self and interfere with an ability to determine appropriate career directions.

The world seems to need **all** types of people in **all** walks of life. This includes "misfits" and "losers" as well as conformists and achievers. Unless a sincere and conscious effort is made to find a satisfying vocation, one is likely to land in a job that does not produce purposeful participation in the working world. That is the way life works, so consider it survival of the fit and of the conscious. While it is true that everybody cannot find a thoroughly "meaningful" vocation, "meaning" must be found somewhere in life. It is too vital a need to be overlooked without suffering telltale consequences. Meaning motivates and stimulates a more fulfilling way of life.

Meaning and Vocational Choice

Five types of work personalities can be identified according to interest and meaning derived from the occupation. The more interest a job generates, and the more personality needs it fulfills, the more satisfying is the time spent at work. The job also tends to be maintained for a longer period of time. Effort grows increasingly burdensome as interest and meaning in work diminish. Length of stay also declines.

These classifications should be viewed as a continuum because the borderlines separating them can be very fine in some cases. It is important, nevertheless, to determine in which category one **predominately** belongs, especially with regard to the particular pitfalls mentioned for each. Foggy or troubled career directions result from falling into one of these traps. To understand why helps to navigate a way out.

TYPE A

The individual whose career is based primarily on a deeply-felt interest in or love of the work represents the first category, the type A personality. Something in the **actual doing of the work** is experienced as interesting and meaningful. Type A's may derive physical pleasure or sensation from performing the work or feel a sense of release or satisfaction with the results produced. Peter, the wine connoisseur, is a good example of type A.

These personalities are relatively rare, usually self-employed or they select jobs which permit significant independence. Type A's are the least likely to seek out career counseling because, by an early age, their interests direct them. Some people, however, become type A's after a trial-and-error bout with the vocational world. Paul, the magazine publisher, is a good example here.

Work consumes these people. Their social lives often revolve around it. Work not only becomes an expression of who they are, but adds to a greater sense of selfhood. They are self-motivated, self-disciplined, love doing their work and do not mind investing effort in it. When a career is an all-consuming interest and a self-expressive endeavor, "effort" does not have the same connotation. It is more like fun or an act of devotion. Time flies.

Workaholism

Type A personalities lead an ideal work life, provided they avoid becoming so wrapped up in it that little room is left over for anything else. Important personal relationships can be short-changed. Unless they are type A personalities themselves, partners may feel they come second to the occupation. Social skills or emotional development also may be stunted for some of these people, especially those who established a demanding career course early in life. A "workaholic" devotion to the career can be a way of avoiding relationships or social interaction, or it may cover up an otherwise empty existence. Workaholics can run away, just as vocation hoppers do, only it is not from a fear of failure. They may fear closeness with others or believe they cannot handle social interaction apart from their occupational identities.

Jane was eighteen and already in her third year of college when she decided to become a psychiatrist. She could count the number of dates she had ever had on two fingers. All through grammar and high school, she was known as "The Brain" and she lived up to this reputation through college, medical school, her internship and residency. A prolific writer and researcher, Jane was always able to secure government grants to back her projects. By the age of forty, she was a top psychiatrist, the youngest person and the only woman to be appointed chief of staff of a major metropolitan hospital.

Although Jane loved her work, she was troubled by a gnawing sense that something was missing in her life. The more troubled she became, the more hours she worked until this avoidance practice no longer escaped her attention. She needed someone with whom to share her life, a need she had long denied. Over the years she had learned how to reach out to patients, but not to other people – especially those of the opposite sex. Finally, to experience a more fulfilling way of life, Jane agreed to leave her briefcase at work and venture out to dinner or the movies once in a while. It required some changes, but, most importantly, Jane realized she would have to step down from her pedestal role of physician and learn to relate to others as equals.

TYPE B

The next category contains more well-rounded personalities, called type B's. Work and activities outside of the job are experienced as meaningful pursuits. While the job is interesting and self-expressive, it is not so all-consuming as it is for the predominantly A type. For type B's, a portion of the meaning derived from work can be traced to the **tangible things** they are able to purchase or do as a consequence of the paycheck. The ability to build up and sustain a certain standard of living is important to this type. Leisure activities, education, family, hobbies, sports, travel, creative endeavors, social, club or volunteer work may have significance equal to a career. A productive work ethic also exists.

Due to the work ethic and the need to express self through the occupation, type B's become troubled when their work lacks meaning. They are likely to seek out career counseling if the need arises. Sometimes important vocational needs have been overlooked which can be satisfied by a change in job or in some aspect of the job. Sometimes an avocation has been disregarded as a potential vocational outlet. This could be due to inhibiting family responsibilities, lack of confidence, or the inability of the avocation to generate a living. Perhaps if converted to a full-time endeavor the enjoyed activity would require too much effort and thus become less meaningful. Still, type B personalities often transform into A types when avocations become income-producing and self-sustaining.

From nine to five Jack is an executive for a national health

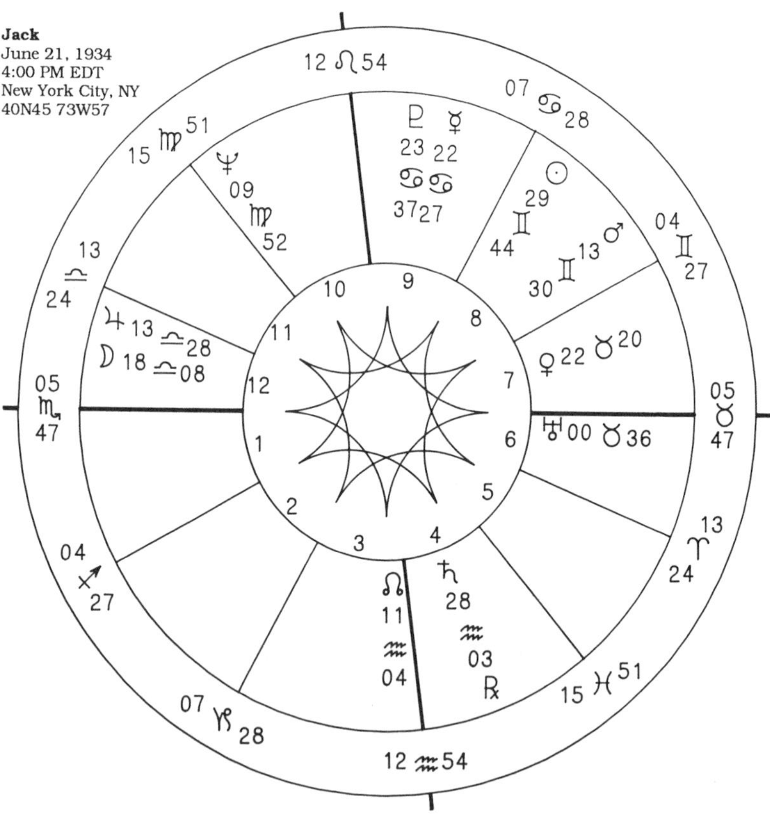

care association. After hours he is a family man and a playwright. One of his plays has been produced off Broadway in New York while another awaits finishing touches. As a type B personality, Jack enjoys his job for various reasons (not necessarily in this order). The salary is adequate to sustain a family of five comfortably, including college educations for the three children. His job allows him to travel, write policies and make speeches on issues that matter to him, and to act with authority and influence through his advisory role. He also enjoys the people with whom he routinely works. For Jack, the job is appealing because it satisfies many of his interests and needs.

TYPE C

The next work personality, type C, is motivated to pursue a particular occupation primarily for its **less tangible rewards**. This type selects a vocational role to play. When the personality matches the role, sufficient ambition, realistic effort and competence exist to fulfill the dream. When the personality does not match the dream role, this type encounters career obstacles.

Intangible rewards include, but are not limited to, status, fame, power, influence, approval, or freedom from authority. A desire to "prove" something also can underlie an attraction for an occupation, although this type is usually unaware of it. For example, the type C individual might be driven to make a large sum of money, not for the things it can buy, but for the power and influence it can bestow. A choice to become a doctor or lawyer might be made initially to achieve status or fulfill family expectations rather than due to interest in the work. This is not to suggest that interest in the occupation cannot develop over time. For many, it does, but usually only after some degree of success has been achieved.

For the C type, work can become interesting and an expression of self, but it is initially selected to attain an intangible reward. This intangible reward represents the most important aspect of the endeavor. If interest in the work develops, this type might shift to A or B. How realistic the goal is depends on how closely the occupation matches the individual's other personality needs and the effort put forth. Most intangible rewards require an unwavering commitment because the type C personality often must face many years of preparation and stiff competition to achieve the dream. Striving toward excellence can be as much a fact of life for the C type as it is for type A. However, problems can arise for the C type whenever aspirations overshadow interest in the work. When the occupation cannot sustain interest, or does not reflect true self-expressive needs, the work situation can turn sour. It is important to fairly assess one's true capabilities and the amount of effort needed to fulfill such dreams. **Unrealistic goal expectations** stem from an unrealistic self-appraisal and an illusionary inventory of one's true capabilities. The need to be a "somebody" could be overshadowing an acceptance of one's personal reality.

Individuals striving toward intangible rewards place themselves in precarious positions, especially when apparently meaningful goals turn out to be beyond their abilities no matter how much effort is expended. However, it can be difficult to know if such people are failing due to a lack of talent and ability or due to an insincere application of effort. Running into a vocational brick wall could be a signal that the wrong path or approach has been taken. It could also indicate that more effort is needed. Only the level of commitment to overcome the obstacle, in addition to the interest generated in the work, can determine the answer.

Diane, an aspiring photo journalist, once remarked that,

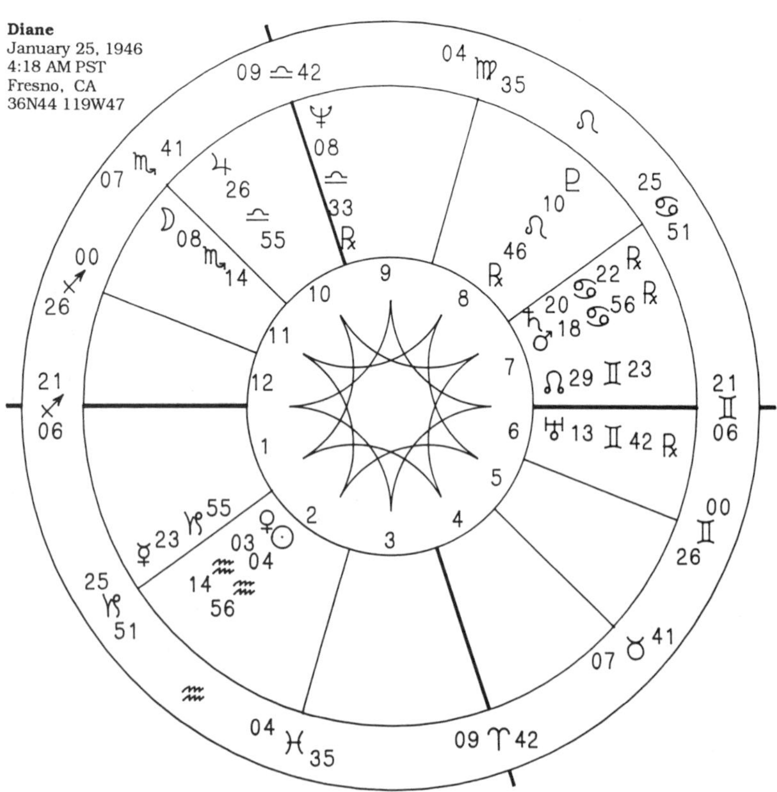

"People cannot call themselves writers until they can plaster a wall with rejection notices." Her belief in herself, the fact she grew to enjoy her work and her total commitment to succeed always managed to help her over the tallest hurdle. Besides, as a child, nobody paid any attention to her. It was assumed her older brother would carry on the family's success image. More parental energy was devoted to assuring his vocational success. Ironically, all the support undermined his career drive while the lack of support fueled Diane's. She developed an insatiable need to prove herself and will beat down an editor's door until he or she finally agrees to review Diane's portfolio. She knows that once she gets her foot in the door, her work will have to rest on its own laurels and Diane is willing to face life under those terms.

By contrast, Les, who had a similar childhood experience, was tearing himself apart because he had not become a household name by the age of forty. He had staked his happiness on becoming famous. He tried acting, astrology, writing, radio broadcasting, but never stayed with anything. Whenever he ran into a roadblock, he simply changed roads. Without interest, the work held no meaning for him, only the notoriety that was supposed to result. Les suffered from a delusion common to some type C personalities: he believed success should materialize quickly because success was all that he wanted.

After four months of hunting for a new job, he found himself paralyzed. His savings account was running out and panic was setting in. A paralysis of this nature is often a clue that the unconscious, inner self is at odds with the outer, conscious intentions. It was difficult for Les to accept the possibility that his unrealistic goal was based on a deeper, albeit repressed, problem in his life: a compulsive need to prove himself to his millionaire father. His quest for that "magic" profession which would bring him fame was actually a quest for the attention he felt his father never gave him. But that was not what he came to an astrologer to hear.

A basic pitfall for certain C types concerns this investment in factors lying outside of the self. Interest in the work vanishes when the intangible reward loses its meaning or when an unrealistic goal is recognized for what it is: a pipe dream or someone else's dream. At such a juncture, this C type may find

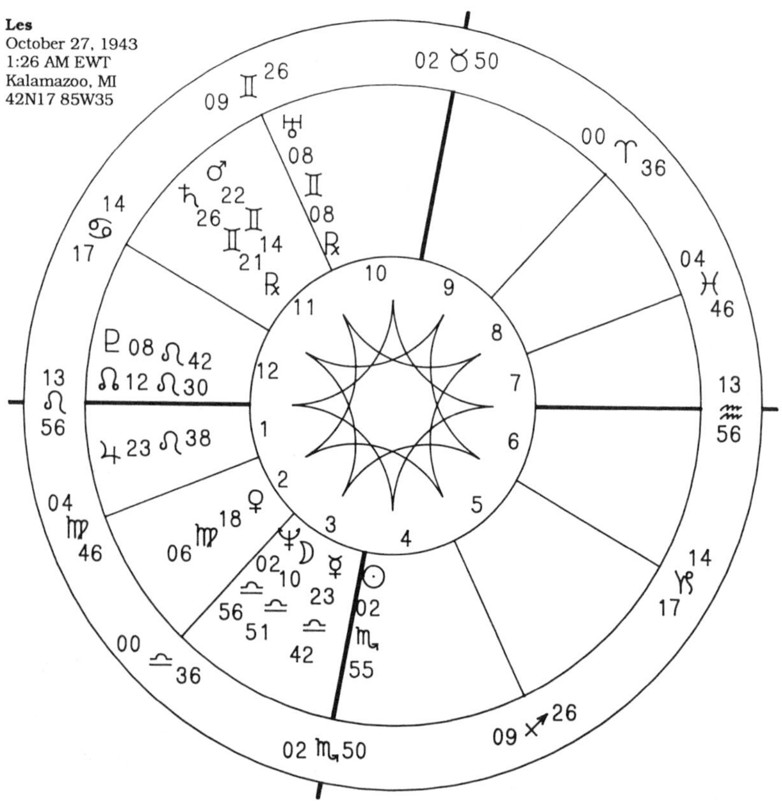

life directions evaporating because everything has been staked on the intangible reward, including the individual's sense of identity. That is why job loss, when it strikes, can hit this personality most fiercely. Not only has the intangible reward disappeared, but the individual may now be faced with an identity crisis. However, whenever intangible rewards are at stake, bigger, better and more may never be enough. It may be difficult to achieve contentment from **any** accomplishment.

It can be easy to confuse a C type with an A since both are interested in their work, but for different reasons. The distinction between them is an important one. The enjoyment A types derive from their work sustains them through the rough times. Of course they want to be successful, but for the predominantly A type, the work process can be as important as the end result. For certain C types, the ends justify the means;

the intangible reward counts the most. This attitude can undermine the work performance. An individual focused only on future results may not pay sufficient attention to how well the job is being performed in the present. This was Les's problem. Shortcuts, buck-passing or using others may help the person get to the top, but the "victory" is likely to be hollow. On an inner level, the individual may never be certain of competency and, therefore, becomes easily threatened or quick to give up.

TYPE D

Still another group of people choose or retain their jobs for only one reason: they have to pay the bills. This is the type D personality, who finds **nothing intrinsically meaningful** in the occupation. Work is pursued for survival reasons and is neither considered interesting nor an expression of self. Aspirations, skill, talent, education or a desire to expend effort may be lacking. This is not to say that all D types are untalented. Many are very talented. For various reasons, however, they do not choose to express those aspects of their personalities. Once they do, and there is talent to be mined, they shift to a higher work category. Paul, the new age magazine publisher, began his career as a D type.

Ed is beginning to shift from the D to the B category. The primary interest in his job had always been the tangible rewards it produced. He has an exceptionally well-paying office job with the city government. While **he** does not consider his work to be "interesting," it does satisfy his basic vocational needs, a reason he has maintained the job for so long. He likes being left in charge whenever the boss is away from the office. A witty and lively personality, he enjoys the constant banter that volleys back and forth from desk to desk. He also is considered a reliable jack-of-all-trades and is often sent out on assignments that change the work pace and require him to make spontaneous, independent judgments. Other stimulating activities and people populate his job and keep it from getting boring. Most appealing to **him** is the fact the work day ends at 3:30 in the afternoon, leaving him time for his hobby: drag racing and working on race cars. He considers himself fortunate to have a job that not only takes care of his living expenses, but supports such an expensive avocation.

Recently he developed an interest in calligraphy. He took a course and then practiced when he was recruited to reorganize the filing system at the office. With hundreds of files to relabel, he became quite good. Much to his surprise, the fancy, perfectly-drawn lettering drew a clamor of attention. In no time, his reputation was established as a sign maker and he began receiving requests for this aspect of his "work" from all quarters. Accustomed to getting by with as little effort as possible, Ed initially was leery of this change in circumstances. He secretly hoped to win the lottery so he could "retire" from the work force, not get dragged more deeply into it. Then, one request came from a highly ranked city official who now calls Ed for advice on other matters. The job does not seem quite so bad anymore.

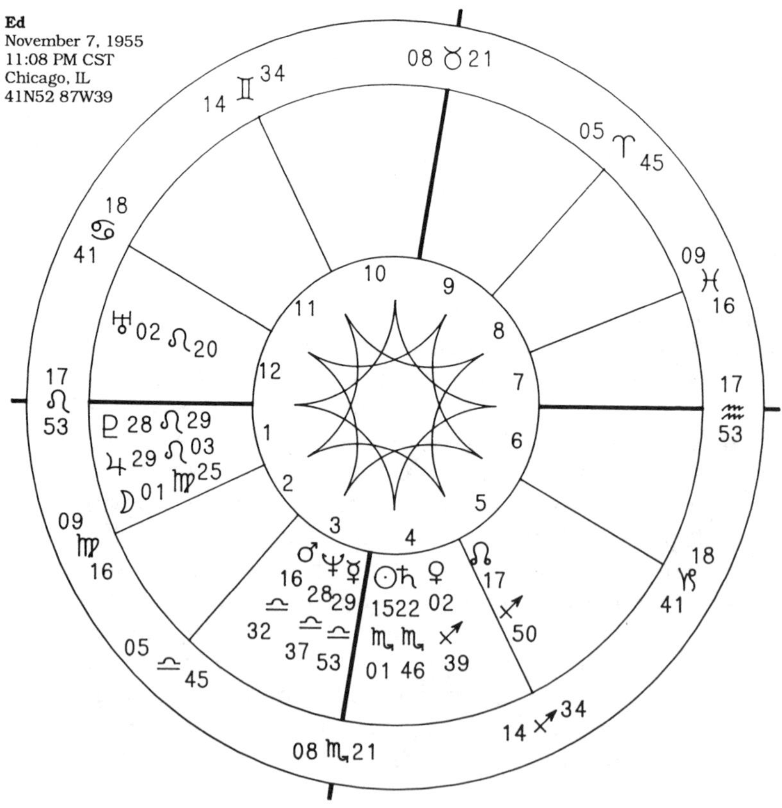

Ed's approach to life and work illustrates something important. Not everybody has to be thoroughly enamored of work, provided basic vocational needs are fulfilled. It also illustrates something else: a little inspiration can go a long way. Ed's motivation to pursue calligraphy was the step he needed to change his perspective on work, although he was unaware of this. Work can be a self-expressive and more meaningful endeavor, provided one is open to the possibility.

Other D types view their work as a disdainful waste of energy and just "get by" as Ed used to do. These personalities often lack interest in anything. Dan, who dreamed of becoming wealthy, is a good example of this type. Many avoid relationships and spend an excessive amount of time alone. Television, drugs, drink, sleep, fantasies or sex fill empty hours. They may blame their existence on a boring job when, more to the point, they suffer from a lack of purpose and willingness to exert the effort needed to instigate a change. Life itself may seem empty and not always worth the trouble. An altered perspective on life, not merely work, is needed in such cases. Not all people have to aspire to something grand in this world, but living without interests and goals makes life seem hollow.

Anyone can experience the plight of a D type personality at any time. But individuals without an education or a marketable skill, those who lack a religious/philosophical framework, who are not in touch with a true sense of identity, who find it difficult to sustain effort, or whose parents lacked job or religious outlets are the most vulnerable.

Peggy was such a person. She graduated from a top law school because her parents wanted her to become an attorney. She entered the career world as a type C due to this cajoling. After only four short years, she began to slip into the D category. It almost seemed to happen overnight. Work became increasingly boring while she helplessly watched the little details slip through her fingers. The intangible reward underlying her occupational choice was beginning to lose its meaning because the parental approval no longer seemed quite so necessary. Peggy was growing up and could see her job for what it was: an expression of parental needs which only confused her about her own needs. She was faced with a decision: to keep the job that made her parents happy – but not Peggy – or change directions in pursuit of greater satisfaction.

Saturn Return

Type C personalities often come to such a juncture during the Saturn Return period, which occurs between ages 28 to 32. Not only they, but other people at this time become motivated to change their work situations. The Saturn Return represents the beginning of a new career cycle (which lasts approximately twenty-nine and one-half years) and is the point in time when people enter full-fledged adulthood. For certain C types, however, the period can be a lesson in tightrope walking. Realistically grounded, individuals, who have laid a proper foundation, strengthen and solidify their careers, or start on a fresh, new, more stimulating path. In Peggy's case, once she liberated herself from parental expectations, she chose as suggested in Robert Frost's poem – the road less traveled. Initially it horrified her parents, but after a while they got used to the fact that their pretty, well-educated daughter had become an astrologer.

The pipe dreamer often runs into a real problem during a Saturn Return. The trouble is a signal that something underlying the vocational choice or performance has been faulty. The chance to make a change and get on a more realistic course is disguised as a menacing obstacle which forces a reevaluation of the career path.

The Saturn Return can be a very crucial or rewarding period in any career life. For people who have been applying themselves realistically, it can represent a time of increased responsibility, authority or even advancement and recognition. Other individuals question their paths and make significant changes. However, a word of caution is needed here. In many cases, switching careers or changing a job at this time is fine, but only if there is a tangible alternative. Too many people thoughtlessly drop a line of work with nothing more than an ill-defined dream to pursue.

Nick decided to reevaluate his career at the time of his Saturn Return. After nine years, he had worked his way up to an administrative position in a large hospital, but lately the bureaucracy was "getting" to him. Although his salary and authority were well above those of other high school graduates like himself, he wanted to walk away from his job and pursue a college education in New Mexico. Why New Mexico? He thought he could "spiritually elevate" himself there because it was the stomping ground for Carlos Casteneda's Don Juan. What he would study or do with a degree once obtained was obscured by his "spiritual quest."

Quests of this nature can be viable goals for many people. For others they are good excuses for running away. This was true in Nick's case. He was tempted to run away from something more than to strive toward a real goal. That is why it is important for people to be thoroughly honest with themselves should a desire to change careers arise during the Saturn Return. Individuals who unconsciously choose to run away are childishly attempting to play dodge ball with life.

TYPE E

For the unaware personality, the Saturn Return can represent a time when the urge to run away overtakes a need to grow and face life with a mature attitude. This is the greatest pitfall for type E personalities, the final category which contains all nonworkers, such as dropouts, drifters, criminals, those who choose not to work and those whose condition prevents work. In all cases, they **need** or **want** to be taken care of by others or society.

Certain C and D types slip into this category temporarily or for longer periods when unrealistic goal expectations are finally recognized as mere illusions. At such times the self-image and directions in life need to be reshaped. It usually takes one to three or more years to undergo this process and to establish a new, more realistic direction.

Type E personalities are those who slip in, but do not come out of this nonworking lifestyle: pipe dreamers and excuse addicts populate this category. They are unwilling to work or to assume responsibility for their actions. Illusions may have kept them in the work force until they had to face reality; then the bubble bursts and they prefer to drop out. Facing reality was a problem for Margot. (See chart page 9.) She did not wish to truly work, to develop her competency or to face her inadequacies – which only meant they could never be overcome.

Anyone at any time in life can shift from one category to another, as a couple of examples have demonstrated. A change in the work-related personality is always traceable to the influx of new interests, which create new needs and directions, or to the loss of old ones, by choice or circumstance (job loss, retirement, illness).

The best way to derive meaning from work is to follow interests. Pursuing interests is not always possible vocationally. However, avocations, volunteer work, a family or other relationships can fill in where a career is lacking and make a significant contribution to life.

Career directions come as a result of meaning, and meaning springs from interests. Some C and D types and all in the E category suffer from a lack of constructive interests and direction. Without direction, contact with self is lost; individuals feel undefined and alienated from the mainstream of society. The reverse also applies. Without a sense of self, determining a direction in life is difficult because interests and purpose are unknown factors. But here is where astrology can help by facilitating self-awareness and suggesting potential interests which can lead to gaining a sense of direction (see Chapter 6).

Planets as Vocational Indicators

Traditional vocational astrology views the planets as corresponding to vocations. This approach is a holdover from astrology's ancient past, when a proliferation of job possibilities did not exist. Since there are only ten planets and over a thousand times that many jobs in the world today, each planet logically would have to encompass approximately one thousand occupations.

A number of different approaches are currently in use on this "planet as vocation" theory. Some astrologers see the "vocational indicator" as the first planet to rise ahead of the Sun (using only five possible planets). Others look to the planet in the chart which receives the greatest number of favorable aspects. Some practitioners exclusively use the sign on the Midheaven to establish vocational direction. All of these approaches to vocational analysis make three common assumptions: (1) that vocational aptitude is somehow separate from the rest of the personality, (2) that there exists a single, "true" occupation for every human being and (3) that each planet can specify an **exact** profession.

H. Baron Von Klocker[1] has this to say:

> I consider it impossible to make a satisfactory interpretation on the basis of any single planet and its position. There is really no such thing as a 'Saturn vocation' or a 'Jupiter vocation', or a 'Mars vocation', although, for example, astrological tradition states that Mars rules butchers, doctors, soldiers, and smiths, etc., but the length of this list, even as it is, shows that specific judgments cannot be obtained in this way. Of course, Mars plays a role in these professions, but always as part of a larger configuration, and this configuration is the important thing. Besides, we know that a Mars component is important or even necessary in other vocational areas as well, and traditional astrology has little to say about this. Of what value then is the concept of a 'Mars vocation?'

How can Von Klocker's logic be denied? With so many occupations from which to choose, the "planet or sign as vocation" approach is too simplistic nowadays and only infrequently reveals an appropriate direction. Many occupations represent a combination of several "jobs" and require a person to be self-expressive along a number of different channels. Peter, for example, is a wine connoisseur, a teacher, a lecturer, a writer and the owner of a small business. He is a complicated, multitalented personality with a wide variety of vocational needs and skills. Which "job" is his true vocation and which planet or sign would be used to depict it? The theory, when viewed against reality, does not "work" because the premise has grown faulty.

One line of work can lay the foundation for a completely different field later in life. Human beings are not stagnant. People grow, develop and change. New interests, directions and occupational pursuits become possible over time. The traditional approach to vocational astrology does not take these issues into account because it is based on too simplistic a view of vocational aptitude and of human behavior. More importantly, it ignores personality factors which can interfere with establishing a sound line of work. A chart is expressive of both positive and negative potentials. Negative personality characteristics, such as a faulty self-image and a lack of willingness to work, can be as much responsible for career-related difficulties as failure to determine what lines of work might be worthwhile to pursue.

PROFESSIONS ALIGN WITH PERSONALITY

If the "planet as vocation approach" does not suffice, what can be used? Michel Gauquelin wrote about athletes in *Your Personality and the Planets*:

> The position of Mars gives us a clue not so much to a person's profession but rather to their personality. **The planet is related to profession only because the profession you succeed at reflects your personality.**[2]

The boldfaced sentence represents the central theme underlying this book. Human beings derive satisfaction and achieve a sense of wholeness when personality needs are met and interests are pursued. People devote more energy to interesting jobs than to unself-expressive work. Obviously, the higher the quality of energy input, the greater the chance for "success."

Types A, B and many in the C category pursue work that is a reflection not only of their interests, but also of their personalities. Job motivation and satisfaction are highest among these categories (provided the aspirations of the C type match interest in the work). For D type personalities, job dissatisfaction can be traced to work which is not a reflection of self-expressive needs. Some D personalities and the nonworking E types express **negative** personality characteristics, such as lack of willingness to work or failure to be responsible for oneself.

The Gauquelin findings bear out the remarks Von Klocker made 45 years earlier. The planets do **not** primarily represent occupations. They symbolize personality traits which **tend** to express best **through** certain occupations. For this reason the traditional rulerships designated for each planet can appear to be valid at times. However, a planet can just as readily represent a suitable vocational **approach** as it can suggest a suitable occupation. The personality precedes the occupation and they are linked on levels that are often difficult to detect without the aid of astrological symbolism. There is no way to know which possibility of a given planet or sign is being represented. That is why analyzing a chart from the standpoint of overall personality traits represents a more productive way to assess vocational aptitude. Appropriate directions can be deduced, rather than divined, especially when the educational level and prior work experience are taken into consideration.

Many people who turn to astrology for a vocational assessment mistakenly look for magic, as if education and the work history were not important employer considerations. They want the astrologer to pinpoint the one and only vocation that is right for them, and to provide the assurance that they will be successful at it. They do not realize their charts may reveal why they are experiencing career-related difficulties and that these factors must be cleared up before a fulfilling career can be recognized.

Remember Paul? Six years ago if an astrologer, or any career counselor, had told him to pursue publishing as a self-employed venture, the advice would have gone in one ear and out the other because his poor self-image could not have sustained the proposition. No matter what the vocational indications in his chart may be, he **had** to undergo certain experiences before publishing could be recognized as an appropriate occupation. That is why a career setback can be a blessing in disguise. The discomfort is a signal that inner needs are not being met.

When the personality meshes with job-related duties, a comfortable working arrangement exists. Natural abilities flow easily. People can take up a new occupation and quickly master it. One of the most challenging aspects of career counseling is not pinpointing appropriate career paths for individuals, but getting them to recognize the benefits of a particular occupation. Some people can be in an appropriate line of work, but feel they **should** be doing something else. For reasons such as a need to be special or influential, they fail to see the "rightness" of their jobs - given the effort they are willing to invest.

Here is a formula for this book's vocational process:

Contact with **self** and **interests** stimulates **meaning** and **direction** which in turn gives **purpose** and a **potential for fulfillment. Inspiration, aspiration, effort, talent** and **luck** play interdependent roles.

Luck, by the way, is generating positive opportunities through constructive visualization, applied effort and intelligent recognition of prospects. Job loss or meaninglessness presents an opportunity to search within for alternatives. Astrology can be an extremely helpful tool as a guide to looking inward. The birthchart blueprints personality needs, tendencies and potentials which, when analyzed as a whole, suggest vocational aptitudes, appropriate directions and difficulties which may interfere with identifying satisfying employment.

References

1. Von Klocker, H.B., *Astrology and Vocational Aptitude*, Tempe, Arizona: American Federation of Astrologers, 1974, p. 6
2. Gauquelin, Michel, *Your Personality and the Planets*, New York: Stein and Day, 1980, p. 19

CHAPTER TWO

BASIC VOCATIONAL NEEDS AND TRAITS

Any number of ways exist to synthesize a chart. No two are exactly alike and no two practitioners agree on precisely the same way to conduct an analysis. It is comparable to learning to write the alphabet: once basic principles are learned, each person develops a unique style.

Astrology, however, is more complicated than memorizing what the various glyphs symbolize. Quite a few schools of thought are in vogue, and agreement over basic chart factors, such as house systems, is not universal. Astrologer Noel Tyl once remarked, "It is not a matter of how much astrology an individual knows as it is what that individual knows about life."

Astrology is a symbolic language of human behavior whose use becomes enhanced according to the knowledge about that behavior. The horoscope is a diagram of each person's "cosmic clock" and the individual's relationship to the universe. When utilizing astrology for vocational analysis, it also is important to know the pertinent components of any career.

Still, the main obstacle to learning the language of astrology is understanding why a particular feature in a chart might manifest in one way and not in another. How does the astrologer know which to pick from all of the possible meanings symbolized by a planet, house or sign? Students can be baffled by the choices and how to narrow them down. This book offers assistance to help put the chart into perspective.

Recurrent Themes Are Most Significant

Synthesis is a matter of knowing what the symbols represent, which carry more weight and how these factors relate to one another in real life, not merely according to textbooks. As with any foreign language, it takes time and practice to learn how to sort out the details. The system which follows is not intended to reflect any hard and fast rules on chart synthesis. It is a method of taking inventory of a chart for its prominent tendencies to determine what occupational outlets would be suitable.

Due to Sun sign newspaper columns and magazines, astrology publicly has been watered down to a single factor, the almighty sign. But **one chart factor does not a tendency make.** The Sun in Capricorn, for example, does not mean an individual automatically will be good in business. Other factors have to be taken into consideration, for example, the Sun's aspects, its house position and how it fits into the overall structure of the chart. Everything in a chart relates to everything else and the trick is to discover which features "rise above the noise." The more something is repeated in a chart, the more prominent a vocational need it represents. **Recurrent themes represent important life issues and personality characteristics** which pinpoint appropriate vocational directions.

The brilliantly simple **astrological alphabet**, originated by Dr. Zipporah Dobyns, offers a marvelous tool for spotting recurrent themes.[1]

For those unfamiliar with the technique, the following represents an illustration. The word "trait" has been substituted for the term "letter." The astrological symbols associated with each personality trait are not exhausted below; other factors new to this technique assist the synthesis process and are identified in later chapters.

Mars, Aries, first house, Ascendant ....Trait 1
Venus, Taurus, second house ....Trait 2
Mercury, Gemini, third house ....Trait 3
Moon, Cancer, fourth house ....Trait 4

Sun, Leo, fifth house ....Trait 5
Mercury, Virgo, sixth house ....Trait 6
Venus, Libra, seventh house ....Trait 7
Mars, Pluto, Scorpio, eighth house ....Trait 8
Jupiter, Sagittarius, ninth house..........................Trait 9
Saturn, Capricorn, tenth house, Midheaven ....Trait 10
Saturn, Uranus, Aquarius, eleventh house ....Trait 11
Jupiter, Neptune, Pisces, twelfth house ....Trait 12

To illustrate, Mars in Aries in the first house represents a triple dose of trait 1, written 1/1/1. It suggests a need to apply oneself in a direct, self-determined and energetic fashion. Saturn in Aries becomes 10/1; if also located in the first house, it would read 10/1/1. The abbreviation shows how strongly trait 1 is associated with trait 10. If Saturn also rules the first house or is conjunct Mars, for example, the chart's 10/1 tendencies escalate. (The order followed in these abbreviations is planet/house/sign.)

This symbolism suggests a number of possibilities due to self-projection (trait 1) and competence or authority (trait 10) being linked in the personality. This promotes self-expression (trait 1) through a career (trait 10). It could represent an individual who must strive (trait 1) for the competency to become an authority (trait 10), one who can apply (trait 1) disciplined effort (trait 10) or one who experiences blocks (trait 10) to self-assertive drives (trait 1).

Charles Carter[2] has this to say about the language of astrology:

> We have already warned the reader against the common statement that "signs affect the 'soul' (or disposition); houses affect the environment (or 'destiny')." There is no ground for this rule in practical astrology. Saturn afflicted in Leo will show trouble through children as much as Saturn in the 5th house.

What Carter means is that a 10/5 "theme" correlates with a certain range of possibilities (not exclusively or necessarily trouble with offspring) whether it appears as Saturn (10) in Leo (5), Saturn (10) in the fifth house (5), Sun (5) square Saturn (10), Sun (5) in the tenth house (10), or Sun (5) in Capricorn (10). That's quite a list, but the possibilities are still not exhausted. These same themes repeat in a chart when **any** ruler of the tenth house (10) is in the fifth house (5), in Leo (5), aspecting the Sun (5) or aspecting a ruler of the fifth house (5); when any ruler of the fifth house (5) is in the tenth house (10), in Capricorn (10), or aspecting the Sun (5) or any fifth house ruler (5). The latter combinations merely represent less prominent tendencies. The **astrological alphabet** is an indispensable tool for chart synthesis. Like shorthand, the alphabet pinpoints how many times a personality trait (or need) recurs and, as stated before, recurrent themes are important to an analysis. (A demonstration follows that will allow the reader to easily spot recurrent themes.)

How to Spot Recurrent Themes and Prominent Tendencies

Though the above factors are relatively interchangeable, it is important to keep separate the distinctions between a planet, a house and a sign. Planets symbolize the predominant energy in the personality and always are the most significant representatives of a trait. For this reason, the traits associated with the planets appear first in the thematic structure (e.g., the Moon in Taurus in the eleventh house would be 4/11/2). Houses and signs correspond to less dynamic features and appear in second and last order in a thematic structure. It is helpful to use this sequence of prominence when analyzing the horoscope in the following manner.

Astrology would be more readily "scientific" if a chart factor always manifested in only one way. However, astrology as a symbolic language does not function that way. Why? Because all people do not respond to the same features in their personalities or life experiences in an identical fashion. A good case in point is the Gauquelin research. As mentioned earlier, the twelfth house area proved significant in the charts of eminent professionals. This outcome was so contrary to orthodox thinking that many practitioners chose to believe all of the (41,000) birth records used were off by approximately one hour. This possibility has been dismissed.[3]

Still, any competent astrologer knows that twelfth house placements **sometimes** correlate with a confusing, if not difficult, life path. However, astrologers most often see troubled people. Given this nature of clientele, and the fact that few astrologers conduct "scientific" research, it is easy to understand why the traditional interpretation of this sector (weak, ego-denying, sorrowful, etc.) has predominated.

But all people do not respond to twelfth house issues in the same fashion. One individual with Mars there might demonstrate an inspired (trait 12) enterprisingness (trait 1) with self-motivated energy (trait 1) that knows no bounds (trait 12), while another might repress (trait 12) self-assertive drives (trait 1) and be in a fog (trait 12) over how to direct oneself (trait 1). Either interpretation is valid and is not only possible in a given chart, but is possible at any time in an individual's life.

Astrology is a symbolic language and each symbol encompasses a broad range of possibilities – both positive and negative ones. That is why it is **not possible to know from the chart alone** that it belongs to an alcoholic, for instance. While an intuitive sense may uncover this, the chart itself does not specify in what exact direction the personality will gravitate. The very same factors indicative of an alcoholic also correlate with intuitive capabilities, an interest in meditation, certain imaginative or assisting qualities or a number of other possibilities, provided the energy represented is constructively channeled.

The horoscope describes **issues** with which an individual must deal. It does not depict the **details** of how those issues will be confronted. We create our own realities. An ability to constructively channel drives and tap higher potentials are among the many factors, such as sex, race, IQ and consciousness, that are not specified in a chart. How a person responds to the indicated potentials entirely depends on the individual human being – and choices can change over time.

A chart can demonstrate any number of "themes" or vocational needs, even conflicting ones. How important a need will be depends on what planets are involved, where in the chart they are located and how often a theme repeats itself. Some planets carry more weight and some sectors of the chart are more "prominent" than others. For this reason, three levels of the career analysis exist and a "trait grid" has been devised which, when completed, will show how often traits repeat themselves in a chart.

PROMINENT TRAITS AND TRAIT PAIRS

1	2	3	4	5	6	7	8	9	10	11	12
1/1	1/2	1/3	1/4	1/5	1/6	1/7	1/8	1/9	1/10	1/11	1/12
	2/2	2/3	2/4	2/5	2/6	2/7	2/8	2/9	2/10	2/11	2/12
		3/3	3/4	3/5	3/6	3/7	3/8	3/9	3/10	3/11	3/12
			4/4	4/5	4/6	4/7	4/8	4/9	4/10	4/11	4/12
				5/5	5/6	5/7	5/8	5/9	5/10	5/11	5/12
					6/6	6/7	6/8	6/9	6/10	6/11	6/12
						7/7	7/8	7/9	7/10	7/11	7/12
							8/8	8/9	8/10	8/11	8/12
								9/9	9/10	9/11	9/12
									10/10	10/11	10/12
										11/11	11/12
											12/12

Note the first line, numbered one through twelve. This represents the traits for the "prominent" (Level I) planets which are described in Chapter 4. A demonstration follows which will easily guide the reader step-by-step through the process. Do not attempt to grasp the entirety of this new format until the demonstration chart has been walked through. Be patient.

The paired numbers represent the numerous possible "themes" or trait pairs which can be present in a given horoscope. To help spot recurrent themes, not only each planet, but every factor discussed in this text is assigned to one or more traits from the astrological alphabet. For example, an eastern hemisphere emphasis represents trait 1 (Chapter 3). The quadrants are assigned specific trait pairs (Chapter 5) according to the hemispheres which they encompass. For example, a first quadrant focus is a 1/4 blend. Similarly, the chart patterns, Sun/Moon phases and the other factors discussed herein are assigned to a trait or trait pair. As inventory of a chart is taken, the corresponding trait or trait pairs should be circled on the "trait grid" portion of the needs analysis form at the end of the book according to the level of analysis to which they have been assigned. Use a different colored pen for each level.

At this point, it is only important to understand what chart features belong to which level of the analysis, according to their corresponding significance in the personality and vocational expression.

Level I = traits related to Gauquelin planets (referred to here as G-planets, see Chapter 4), leading and handle planets (Chapter 3) and other planets located within six degrees of the angles; trait pairs for major (orb five degrees) and minor (orb one degree) aspects (Chapter 5); traits for stationary planets (Chapter 5) and singletons by hemisphere (Chapter 4). The major aspects include conjunctions, sextiles, squares, trines and oppositions. The minor aspects include semisextiles, noviles, semisquares, septiles, quintiles, sesquiquadrates, bi-quintiles and the quincunx. Also included is the 22.5 degree aspect.

When a chart factor is repeated on the trait grid in "Level I," a highly pronounced personality trait is represented. It needs to be expressed constructively through the vocation, although **all Level I factors are vocationally significant**. In the following sample chart, circles represent Level I. Because it is important to distinguish major from minor aspects (for reasons specified in Chapter 5), trait pairs associated with minor aspects are noted in broken circles.

Level II = traits or trait pairs associated with the Sun/Moon phase (Chapter 7), Ascendant, Midheaven, their rulers by house position (Chapter 6); the Sun, Moon, Mars, Saturn and the Ascendant/Midheaven rulers each by house and sign; the trait or trait pairs associated with a diminished representation or preponderance of a quality or element (Chapter 8).

Factors in "Level II" represent less prominent characteristics. However, when two or more are repeated in a chart, especially with one or more from "Level I," that trait or pair needs to be expressed through the vocation. In the following sample chart, squares represent Level II chart factors.

Level III = traits or trait pairs associated with hemisphere emphasis, quadrant focus, chart pattern (Chapter 3), the remaining planets (other than the Sun, Moon, Mars and Saturn) by house and sign, the signs on the remaining house cusps (including interceptions), double cusped houses, houses ruled by Taurus and Libra, houses ruled by Gemini and Virgo (chapter 5), each node (Chapter 6) by house and sign; the remaining house ruler positions by house only.

Level III factors are the least important and tend to be vocationally significant only when they repeat a trait or trait pair three times or fortify indications from Level I or II. In the sample demonstration, triangles represent Level III.

Using the chart of an eminent ophthalmologist and researching scientist, Perry, here is a sample demonstration. Again, this technique is not intended to represent the one and only way to synthesize a chart. In the back of this book, a complete form is provided for vocational analysis. (If you want a computer to do the detailed work, you can order "Vocational Needs Analysis" through Astro Computing Services.)

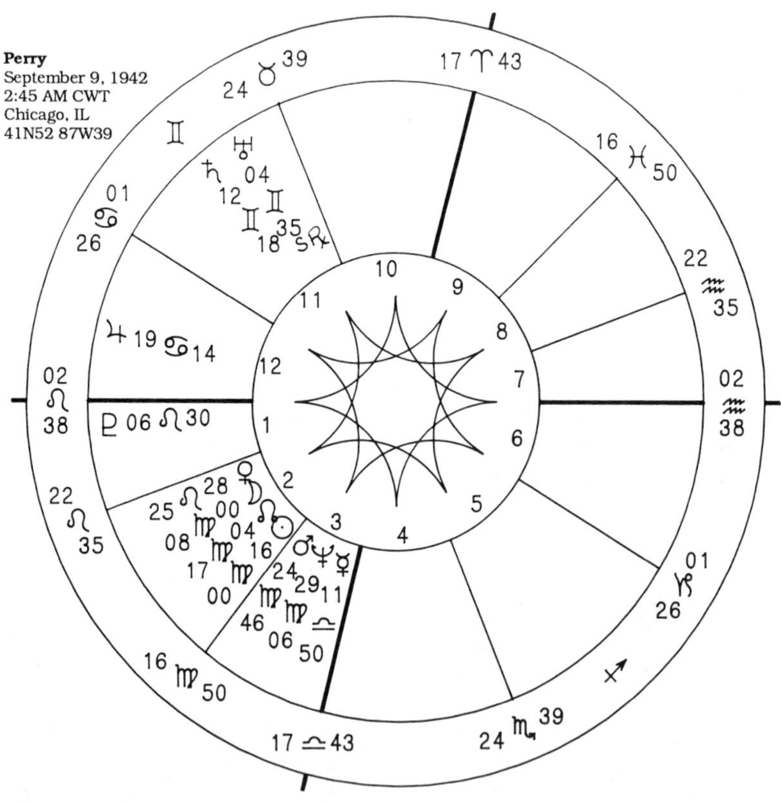

Level I (indicated by circles)

- O trait 9 (Jupiter as G-planet)
- O trait 11 (Uranus as leading planet/bundle pattern)
- O trait 8 (Pluto near the Ascendant)
- O traits 3 and 6 (Mercury near the IC)
- O trait 11 (Uranus as stationary retrograde planet)

Trait pairs related to major aspects within five degrees:

- O 5/9 (Sun sextile Jupiter)

- O 5/10 (Sun square Saturn)
- O 2/4 and 4/7 (Moon conjunct Venus)
- O 4/11 (Moon square Uranus)
- O 3/10 and 6/10 (Mercury trine Saturn)
- O 1/12 (Mars conjunct Neptune)
- O 9/10 (Jupiter square Midheaven)
- O 8/11 (Uranus sextile Pluto)
- O 11/1 (Uranus sextile Ascendant, same as 1/11)
- O 12/1 (Neptune sextile Ascendant, same as 1/12)
- O 8/1 (Pluto conjunct Ascendant, same as 1/8)

Trait pairs related to minor aspects within 1 degree (indicated by broken circles):

- ◌ 5/8 (Sun novile Pluto)
- ◌ 4/9 (Moon novile Jupiter)
- ◌ 2/8 and 7/8 (Venus 22.5 degrees from Pluto)
- ◌ 2/9 and 7/9 (Venus novile Jupiter)
- ◌ 2/12 and 7/12 (Venus semisextile Neptune)
- ◌ 1/1 (Mars septile Ascendant)
- ◌ 9/11 (Jupiter semisquare Uranus)

Level II (indicated by squares)

- ☐ 11/12 (balsamic Moon phase)
- ☐ 1/5 (Leo Ascendant)
- ☐ 1/10 (Aries Midheaven)
- ☐ 1/3 (Ascendant ruler, Sun, conjunct third house cusp)
- ☐ 10/3 (MC ruler, Mars, in third house, same as 3/10)
- ☐ 5/3 (Sun in third house, same as 3/5)
- ☐ 5/6 (Sun in Virgo)
- ☐ 4/2 (Moon in second house, same as 2/4)
- ☐ 4/6 (Moon in Virgo)
- ☐ 1/3 (Mars in third house)
- ☐ 1/6 (Mars in Virgo)
- ☐ 10/11 (Saturn in eleventh house)
- ☐ 10/3 (Saturn in Gemini, same as 3/10)
- ☐ 5/3 (Ascendant ruler, Sun, in third house)
- ☐ 5/6 (Ascendant ruler, Sun, in Virgo)
- ☐ 1/3 (MC ruler, Mars, in third house)
- ☐ 1/6 (MC ruler, Mars, in Virgo)
- ☐ Trait 4 (diminished water element)
- ☐ Trait pair 3/6 (preponderance of mutable element)
- ☐ Trait 1 (diminished fire element)
- ☐ Trait 1 (diminished cardinal quality)

Level III (indicated by triangles)

△ Trait 1 (eastern hemisphere emphasis)
△ 1/4 (first quadrant focus)
△ Traits 3 and 6 (bundle pattern)

Remaining planets by house and sign:

△ 3/3 and 3/6 (Mercury in third house)
△ 3/7 and 6/7 (Mercury in Libra)
△ 2/2 and 7/2 (Venus in second house)
△ 2/5 and 7/5 (Venus in Leo)
△ 9/12 (Jupiter in twelfth house)
△ 9/4 (Jupiter in Cancer, same as 4/9)
△ 11/11 (Uranus in eleventh house)
△ 11/3 (Uranus in Gemini)
△ 12/3 (Neptune in third house, same as 3/12)
△ 12/6 (Neptune in Virgo, same as 6/12)
△ 8/1 (Pluto in first house, same as 1/8)
△ 8/5 (Pluto in Leo, same as 5/8)

Remaining house cusps:

△ 2/5 (second house Leo)
△ 3/6 (third house Virgo)
△ 4/7 (fourth house Libra)
△ 5/8 (fifth house Scorpio)
△ 5/9 (fifth house Sagittarius)
△ 6/10 (sixth house Capricorn)
△ 7/11 (seventh house Aquarius)
△ 8/11 (eighth house Aquarius)
△ 9/12 (ninth house Pisces)
△ 2/11 (eleventh house Taurus)
△ 3/11 (eleventh house Gemini)
△ 4/12 (twelfth house Cancer)

Double cusp houses:

△ 1/2 (Leo rules first and second houses)
△ 7/8 (Aquarius rules seventh and eighth houses)
△ 4/11 (houses ruled by Taurus and Libra)
△ 3/11 (houses ruled by Gemini and Virgo)
△ 2/6 (North Node in second house in Virgo)
△ 8/12 (South Node in eighth house in Pisces)

Remaining house rulers by house only:

△ 2/3 (ruler second, Sun, on third house cusp)
△ 3/3 (ruler third, Mercury, in third house)
△ 2/4 (ruler fourth, Venus, in second house)

△ 3/5 (ruler fifth, Mars, in third house)
△ 1/5 (co-ruler fifth, Pluto, in first house)
△ 5/12 (co-ruler fifth, Jupiter, in twelfth house)
△ 6/11 (ruler sixth, Saturn, in eleventh house)
△ 7/11 (ruler seventh, Saturn, in eleventh house)
△ 7/11 (co-ruler seventh, Uranus, in eleventh house)
△ 8/11 (ruler eighth, Saturn, in eleventh house)
△ 8/11 (co-ruler eighth, Uranus, in eleventh house)
△ 9/12 (ruler ninth, Jupiter, in twelfth house)
△ 3/9 (co-ruler ninth, Neptune, in third house)
△ 2/11 (ruler eleventh, Venus, in second house)
△ 3/11 (co-ruler eleventh, Mercury, in third house)
△ 2/12 (ruler twelfth, Moon, in second house)

(See trait grid next page)

Should the reader feel overwhelmed, keep in mind the most important task is to uncover repeated traits and pairs according to their levels. Although all Level I factors are significant, the doctor's "prominent" trait is 11 because it is circled twice in Level I and is fortified in Level III (11/11 is identical to trait 11). His analysis would begin here. A vocationally rewarding trait 11 expression is contingent on a well-developed Saturn function. Without discipline, hard work, competence and responsibility, chances for success diminish. Because Perry demonstrated healthy Saturnian capacities, a rewarding Uranian occupation was available to him (see trait 11 in this chapter).

The analysis would proceed to trait 1 because it is fortified from Levels II and III. Next, needs for traits 3, 6, 8 and 9 would be included. These prominent features are discussed in Chapter 4 and each is reflected in his multifaceted career which is detailed later in this chapter. His outstanding trait pairs (Chapter 5) are: 1/3, 1/8, 1/12, 2/4, 3/5, 3/10, 3/11, 4/7, 4/9, 4/11, 5/8, 5/9, 6/10, 7/8 and 8/11. These pairs and above mentioned traits are most significant to Perry's vocational expression. It is not necessary to analyze every little piece of the horoscope. That will result in confusion and a mass of contradictions. It is essential to note the repeated features according to their levels and thereby distinguish what is meaningful from "background noise."

Astrology is **not** simple, and synthesizing a chart is like piecing together a jigsaw puzzle. It takes practice, thought,

PROMINENT TRAITS AND TRAIT PAIRS

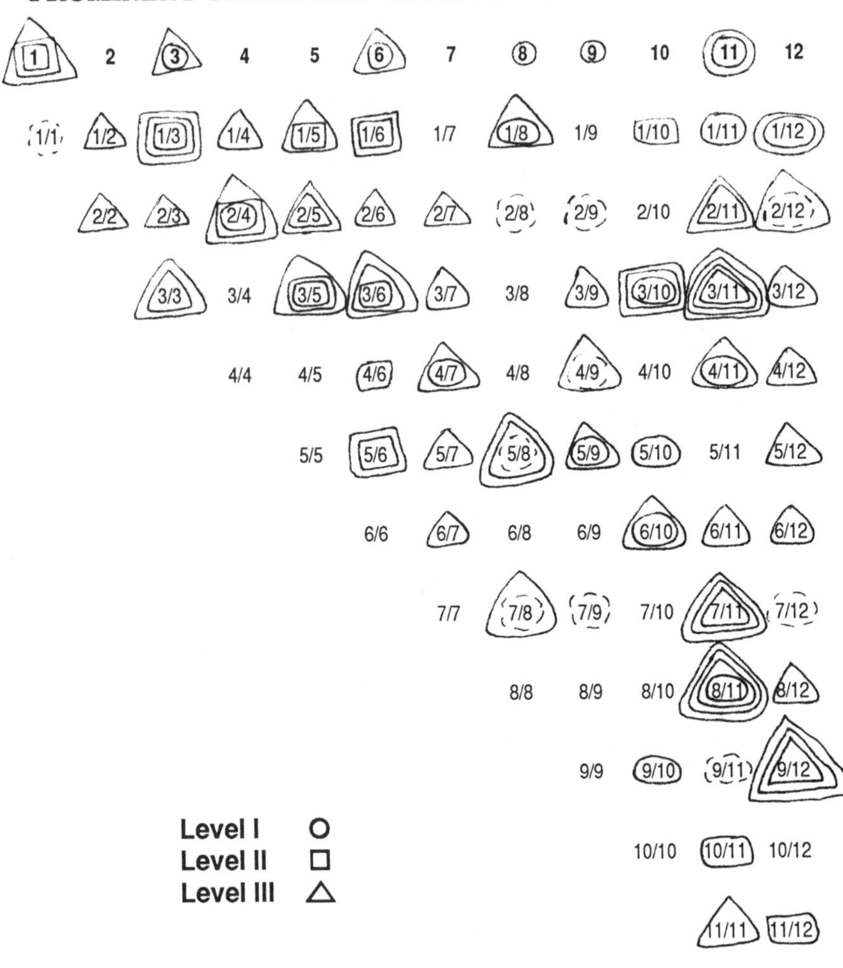

knowledge of the symbolism and understanding of life to put a chart into perspective. If astrology were simple, it could not reflect the complexities of life or the diversity of job possibilities that exists today. But astrology is also inherently logical and organized. The astrological alphabet, when formatted on the trait grid, allows one to "put the pieces together" much more easily than might be suspected.

The remainder of this chapter outlines twelve personality traits according to their vocational needs and approaches and suggests suitable occupations. Always refer to this chapter for the most complete analysis of a trait. In subsequent chapters examples of famous people are included, most of which were supplied from *The American Book of Charts*[4] for its highly legible horoscopes and the brief biographical sketches it provides. It would be beneficial to use it in conjunction with this book.

Trait 1:

Self-Assertive Drives, Sense of Identity, Physical Stamina, Initiative, Leadership, Courage, Independence, Competitive Qualities, Enterprise, Achievement Needs, Striving Tendencies, Mechanically Inclined

ASTROLOGICAL CORRESPONDENCES :

- Mars as G-planet, singleton, handle, leading or stationary planet
- Sun, Moon, Mars, Saturn, Ascendant-ruler or MC-ruler in Aries, in first house (especially Mars in first), or aspected by Mars
- Ascendant or MC in Aries or in aspect to Mars
- Mars in conjunction aspect to Ascendant, its ruler, first house or Aries
- Mars in or ruling the sixth house or in the tenth
- Planets in the first house or an Aries stellium
- Preponderance or diminished representation of fire or the cardinal quality
- Eastern hemisphere emphasis or first quadrant focus
- New Moon
- Locomotive pattern
- Singleton, handle or leading planet in Aries or in the first house
- Conjunction aspects involving Mars, Ascendant, its ruler, first house or Aries
- Ruler of the sixth in the first house
- Either node in Aries or in the first house

Trait 1 can appear in a number of different ways, as the astrological correspondences show. Although each facet is described in subsequent chapters, this trait is prominent when it appears in Level I, is involved in a number of close aspects or when it is repeated through the layers of the chart. It functions best through two different vocations: those requiring **entrepreneurial spirit, leadership, competitive drives or initiative** or those involving physical prowess, manual labor and out of doors activity. As an approach to any occupation, the trait requires one to be active, assertive, enterprising and to come out on top.

Trait 1 functions best in occupations that demand striving, self-motivation, nerve or leadership; that allow one to be free of supervision, to break new ground, to have outlets for winning, risk-taking, recognition and making independent decisions. Personality types A, B and many in the C category (see Chapter 1) tend to have well developed trait 1 features to their make-up. But for anyone with this trait in Level I, the job and work environment should be fast-paced, frequently with competitive edges, and include a series of short-term goals, deadlines or projects. Opportunities should be given to act directly on situations, to take charge, to think on one's feet, to do the best job possible, and to face immediate challenges.

The disposition can be self-involved, self-promoting, achievement-oriented, dynamic or executive (depending on what other traits are emphasized). A need exists to take risks, to push, be bold or daring. These characteristics are likely to be most apparent when Mars is focalized as a G-planet (Chapter 4).

Depending on their level of consciousness, however, pronounced trait 1 individuals may need to learn the difference between self-assertion and impulsive, thoughtless action. They must understand how their desire to win out over others can influence their behavior. Competitive qualities can be a plus in the working world, provided they are constructively channeled. Otherwise, such competition degenerates into caustic remarks and argumentativeness due to a desire to have the last word.

When they fail to grasp their limits, some trait 1 types can be foolish and naive to the extreme. They suffer from hubris and can overstep their bounds. (See New Moon in Chapter 7.) Because many are dominated by their **ego drives** they find it difficult to understand another's position. They learn by doing and by freely discharging energy into the world, but they also need to learn from their mistakes and not to step on other people's toes. Some also tend to rush through projects without adequately covering their bases, but this depends on how they respond to drives shown by trait 10 in their charts.

For the robust individual, vocations involving **physical activity, manual labor, bodily exertion** or **physical daring** could be suitable, for example, sports, physical education, dance or marital arts, racing, fire fighting and construction work. This trait also can manifest through any occupation associated with the use of **machinery, guns, instruments** or **tools** due to the ancient connection Mars (the trait 1 planet), the war god, has with sharp, metallic objects. It frequently correlates with a facility for such things which includes for many a capacity to be **mechanically inclined.**

Many occupations relate heavily to trait 1 in ways even the ancients could not foresee. **Self-employment** or any occupation involving a commission or freelance income is an expression of trait 1 because such jobs require initiative, independent action and risk-taking. As Von Klocker notes, there is no such thing as a "Mars vocation." Every occupation requires some demonstration of this trait simply because it symbolizes the capacity to direct oneself.

Some occupations, however, require more trait 1 drives than others. Individuals whose charts highlight this trait express themselves best through such occupations (balanced with the other traits that must be considered in the analysis). Peter, for example, has a G-planet (Chapter 4) Mars, among other prominent planets, and trait 1 consistently reappears throughout his chart (page 12). He recognized his self-employment needs early in life and an interest in wine brought it all about.

Charts demonstrating an abundance of trait 1 symbolism, however, are not automatically guaranteed to correspond to dynamic, physically active, mechanically inclined, or achievement-oriented people. Before trait 1 drives can be adequately expressed, contact with a **sense of identity** must be made. This is essential to trait 1 and its formation is vital to adequate vocational expression (see Chapter 3). For some people, identity awareness comes easily while for others, identity formation can be delayed (Chapter 6). This can be true for many D or E types. In these cases, an accent on trait 1 can indicate a need to first develop proper self-assertive, self-directing characteristics before an appropriate occupational expression can be achieved. A sense of identity precedes fulfillment.

This was Paul's initial difficulty (chart page 3). Although he was born with a G-planet Mars, early problems between his parents forced him to live with a grandmother who was ill-equipped to respond to his self-expressive needs. As time went on, he lost track of who he really was and did not learn how to adequately assert himself until after a six-year stint in the national guard (a trait 1-related outlet).

When trait 1 is emphasized in a chart but is not vocationally expressed, the work life becomes unsatisfactory because it does not express what the individual needs. Crises arise due to dammed-up drives which are not adequately demonstrated (see cardinality in Chapter 8). When an individual is surrounded by overly aggressive coworkers or domineering supervisors, it is an indication that self-assertive drives may be blocked. Whatever is not expressed of one's own nature is attracted **in excess** from others until the light finally dawns. Avoiding challenges, especially those of a confrontational nature, denies opportunities to clarify identity boundaries. One fails to understand what situations can be handled. Remember Dan who longed to be wealthy? He has pronounced trait 1 features, but because his goals are pipe dreams, he does not apply himself and constantly runs into nasty bosses, pushy coworkers and termination notices. This is classic for inadequately expressed trait 1 vocational needs.

The option for this problem is to acknowledge the desire for recognition, achievement, leadership and independence on the job. A course in assertiveness training or an aggressively competitive sport or some other trait 1-related endeavor could be taken up to get in better touch with this trait. Like Paul, whole new career vistas can open.

Some **possible outlets for trait 1 drives** might include –

- being the "head" of anything: administrator, department head, foreman (woman), supervisor, manager, director, commander, owner, president
- the military or national guard
- athletics: athlete, coach, trainer, physical education instructor, stunt person, sports writer/commentator
- physical movement or exertion: dance, martial arts, steel worker, laborer
- work conducted out of doors: construction worker, forestry, lumberjack, firefighter

- the use of tools or instruments (could be mechanically inclined): machinist, mechanic, manufacturer or dealer of instruments, industrial work, auto parts dealer, auto painter, dentist, barber, physician, assembler, meat cutter
- the use of guns: police officer, security guard, soldier
- nerve, courage, a pioneering spirit or daring risk: surgeon, reporter, professional athlete, explorer, astronaut, self-employment, sales, business executive, daredevil, race car driver, leader, inventor

Trait 2:

Sense of Self-Worth, Rewarding Talents, Stability, Practical Necessities, Aesthetic Qualities, Sensual Pleasures, Art, Finance, Beautiful Objects, Beautifying

ASTROLOGICAL CORRESPONDENCES :

- Venus as G-planet, singleton, handle, leading or stationary planet
- Sun, Moon, Venus, Mars, Saturn, Ascendant-ruler or MC-ruler in Taurus, in or ruling the second house (especially Venus in second), or aspected by Venus
- Ascendant or MC in Taurus or in aspect to Venus
- Planets in the second house or a Taurus stellium
- Venus in or ruling the sixth house or in the tenth
- Preponderance or diminished representation of earth or the fixed quality
- Crescent Moon phase
- Seesaw pattern
- Singleton, handle or leading planet in Taurus or in the second house
- New phase semi-sextile aspects, especially including Venus, the second house or Taurus
- Taurus in or ruling the second house
- Ruler of second house in the second house
- Ruler of the sixth house in the second house
- Either node in Taurus or in the second house

Trait 2 can appear in a number of different ways, as the astrological correspondences show. Although each facet is described in subsequent chapters, this trait is prominent when it appears in Level I, is involved in a number of aspects or when it is repeated through the layers of the chart. It manifests through entirely different vocational outlets: those associated with **stability and practicality** and those demonstrating **rewarding talents**. The person can be torn between a safe, financially secure, practical approach to earning a living, and an aesthetic, artistic or otherwise satisfying one.

When financial security issues predominate, trait 2 types seek jobs which provide a **stable paycheck,** regardless of interest in the work. When none exists, the type D approach to earning a living takes hold. Reliable, easy work routines are preferred. Such individuals function best in pleasant, comfortable surroundings and often take jobs which are involved in finance, the **exchange of cash, practical necessities** of everyday living, or those catering to the **physical senses, sensual pleasures** or **indulgences.** Agriculture and all other occupations associated with **products of the earth** also can be suitable.

Because many trait 2 people are concerned with tangible realities, like paying the bills, they can maintain jobs for lengthy periods. They are disinclined to change jobs, unless a major boost of income is entailed. Even then they can be reluctant to face new horizons and give up familiar routines. Forced career or job changes can be particularly disturbing. (Other traits in the chart may offset this.)

For those more aesthetically inclined, only occupations expressive of **rewarding talents, abilities or interests** are going to be suitable. Often, these will be of an **artistic or sense/pleasure-related** nature, but this is not always true. Different people value different things. Still, an occupation must sustain a reasonable livelihood. Although these types possess an amazing ability to live modestly until significant work can accommodate a higher standard of living, they must have determination of purpose and know when to set limits on self-indulgent behavior. Otherwise, it will interfere with productivity and advancement or lead to expecting others to support them.

Frequently, pronounced trait 2 factors correlate with a need to produce a **finished, tangible product,** so this trait is connected to all **arts, crafts and design-related occupations.** Such individuals need to produce something tangible, be it a a book, a business, a painting, or a compilation of research findings. For some people, cash and the lovely things it can buy fulfill the need for tangible production. However, aesthetic trait 2 types require more personal results from the exercise of their gifts, talents or abilities.

Diane has fairly pronounced trait 2 needs (chart page 18). To support herself through graduate school, she mastered the art of key-line paste-up which she continues to do on a part-time basis for a small advertising agency while she is trying to establish herself as a photo journalist. Although she could readily obtain a full-time paste-up position, she chooses not to because her limited funds force her out and about in search of photo assignments. Peter also has trait 2 pronounced in his chart (page 12) and, for a while, worked part-time in a bank (trait 2) to make ends meet. Both of these individuals have had to pinch pennies and make do with meager incomes, although Peter, who once gave serious thought to abandoning his wine career for this reason, is now seeing the material fruits of his labors.

Before trait 2 aesthetic needs are recognized, **a sense of self-worth** must be firmly established. This is a keynote to trait 2. When people do not feel they have something of value to offer the working world, it is unlikely they will develop potential talents. This is why easy, financially secure occupations can be selected. People are unsure of their creative worth, although with trait 2, **laziness** could be at fault. While they may yearn for a satisfying career, they may not be sufficiently motivated to apply themselves. Workers D and E are prone to this type of trait 2 response.

Whenever work becomes intolerable, it is a safe bet that repressed talents yearn for expression. They may not be developed due to doubts about their value. In such cases, the individuals' early lives were filled with accusations about being inept, clumsy or stupid. Recriminations often can be traced to parental jealousy or an unconscious fear the child would surpass parental ability. Self-doubts first must be overcome before a **need to exhibit important capabilities** can be realized. Once this issue has been soundly dealt with, and self-doubts lose their grip, talents and abilities usually emerge. Financial security concerns take a second seat and the work personality shifts to higher levels. All one has to do is be willing to work for it. (In many regards, trait 7 individuals share similar foibles.)

Some **possible outlets for trait 2** might include –

- money: cashier, bank teller or representative, retail sales person, collection worker, credit manager, comptroller, economist
- an artistic aptitude or flair: artist, performing artist, designer, singer, musician, dancer, wedding planner, building or landscape architect, art therapist, layout artist, writer, advertising copywriter, window trimmer
- anything personally rewarding
- agriculture or products of the earth: farming, soil scientist, flower arranging, plant shop worker/owner, geologist, conservationist, agricultural engineer, farm equipment sales
- beautiful objects or beautifying: gift shop owner/worker; beautician, potter, sculptor, fabric designer, weaver, buyer, purchasing agent
- the physical senses or self-indulgences: wine connoisseur, gourmet, physical/massage therapist, food/liquor sales, candy sales
- the practical necessities of everyday living: grocery store owner/worker, food server, cook or chef, dishwasher

Trait 3:

Factual Knowledge, Exchange of Information, Skilled Use of Hands, Use of Voice, Objective Reasoning, Physical Movement, Transportation, Communication, Paperwork

ASTROLOGICAL CORRESPONDENCES :

- Sun, Moon, Mercury, Mars, Saturn, Ascendant-ruler or MC-ruler in Gemini, in or ruling the third house (especially Mercury in third) or aspected by Mercury
- Ascendant or MC in Gemini or in aspect to Mercury
- Mercury as singleton, handle, leading or stationary planet, or located within six degrees of the angles
- Planets in the third house or a Gemini stellium
- Mercury in or ruling the sixth house or in the tenth
- Crescent Moon phase
- Bundle pattern
- Preponderance or diminished representation of air or the mutable quality
- Singleton, handle or leading planet in Gemini or in the

third house
- Crescent phase sextile aspects involving Mercury, third house or Gemini
- Gemini in or ruling the third house
- Ruler of third house in the third house
- Ruler of the sixth house in the third house
- Either node in Gemini or in the third house

Trait 3 can appear in a number of different ways, as the astrological correspondences show. Although each facet is described in subsequent chapters, this trait is prominent when it appears in Level I, is involved in a number of close aspects, or when it is repeated through the layers of the chart. It manifests in two directions depending on the interest in developing the mental faculties and powers of evaluative judgment.

An emphasis on this trait does not always equate with a high IQ or even an intellectual form of vocational expression. In many cases, pronounced trait 3 indicates people who gravitate to less serious, less intellectually challenging vocations. Still, fundamental to trait 3 types is a need to be **physically, mentally or verbally active** on the job. A gossip uses as much mental energy as a scientist; what differs is the quality of that energy, and a birthchart alone cannot make that distinction. All a focus on trait 3 demonstrates is that mental/verbal/dexterity factors are likely to be an issue in life.

Trait 3 people function best in occupations which offer diversity, incorporate busy schedules and require one to be on the go or to travel. Loads of paperwork, mail, phone calls or figure work tend to be involved. Because trait 3 individuals bore easily, **active communication**, interpersonal exchanges, changes of scenery or faces and a reasonable amount of space in which to move around at work are required. Busy office practices or other beehive environments fill this bill, but so do those requiring a great deal of walking, talking, thinking or driving. Trait 3 people may have so many interests that they never seem to have enough time for them all. When motivation to develop their minds is lacking, important interests are likely to lie outside of the work arena.

When interest in obtaining an education exists, the person tends to be more studious and serious about career-related matters, although some prefer to remain perpetual students with a stockpile of various advanced degrees. Knowledge, speech patterns, language or writing skills are developed along with an ability to make sound judgments based on facts and procedures. They often rely on books, reference material and other printed information in their jobs. Any occupation related to the **accumulation, utilization or dispersal of facts and information** can be suitable. However, some need to understand how prone they are to living solely through their intellectual considerations. They may need to better develop their emotional, feeling sides to experience fuller lives.

This trait also can represent an aptitude for occupations requiring manual dexterity or a **skilled use of the hands.** Depending on interests, education and the aspirational drives, these can range from typing to calligraphy to surgery.

Almost every occupation involves some component of this trait because it represents a supportive function in the personality necessary to carrying out other vocational duties (see Mercury in Chapter 4).

The importance placed on learning and education in the early home plays a vital role behind the career direction a trait 3 person takes. In families where such assets are prized, trait 3 tends to express through developed mental faculties and any one of the professions can prove suitable. When the family atmosphere does not value these qualities, or the individual lacks interest in them, occupational needs tend to be of a less mentally taxing nature and more conventional jobs are selected. The work personality could be a type D, especially when a lack of focus and a profusion of interests exist. Some of these individuals can be described best as "scattered." They often job-hop until constructive interests evolve and bring focus into their lives. (Refer also to trait 6; many of the occupations listed there are appropriate for trait 3.)

The prominent eye surgeon and scientist, Perry, who has his own fully equipped research laboratory, has trait 3 pronounced (chart page 38). Because he did not decide to become a physician until his senior year in college, when it was too late to apply to medical school for the next term, he stayed to complete a Master's degree in microbiology before moving on. Now he is known throughout the field of ophthalmology because he publishes more papers and research findings than any two top physicians combined. Although he participates in a busy group practice and supports a family, he is invited all around the world to deliver his findings and demonstrate his specialized techniques.

Ed never developed an interest in his education, but also has trait 3 pronounced (see chart, page 22). During high school he studied drafting which he pursued after graduation while enrolled in a junior college. After two years, he not only dropped out of college but also gave up drafting because it could not support his drag racing hobby. Because he knew so much about mechanics, he started with the city government as a truck driver and soon was promoted to truck inspector, a job which requires a great deal of paperwork and takes him out of the office much of the time. He loves that. Because he is such a natural with his hands, drafting, calligraphy and sign painting came easily to him.

Ed and Perry illustrate trait 3's divergent occupational expressions. The difference between these men involves interest in developing their intellectual capabilities which influenced the career directions each chose to take.

Some **possible outlets for trait 3** might include –

- trait 6 (because Mercury rules Gemini – trait 3 and Virgo – trait 6) occupations
- the accumulation and distribution of facts or information; any of the "professions" (especially teaching), tour guide, information specialist, librarian, newspaper delivery, editor, reporter, translator, lecturer
- a reliance on the telephone: switchboard operator, telephone solicitor or marketing, customer service, claims representative, reservation or ticket agent, telephone installer
- the analysis of facts or figures: accountant, bookkeeper, analyst, mathematician, billing clerk, statistician, insurance actuary, scientist, lab technician, technical consultant, numerologist
- office practices: secretary, mail room/inventory or file clerk, shipping and receiving, messenger, runner, receptionist, office manager
- manual dexterity: typist, surgeon, calligrapher, sign painter, sculptor, musician, draftsperson, typesetter, palmist

- travel or the transportation of objects or people: chauffeur, mover, flight attendant, pilot, travel representative, bellhop, cab driver, truck driver, delivery person, railroad conductor or engineer, bus driver
- being "on the go": waiter/waitress, mail carrier, fast food service, gas station attendant

Trait 4:

Sense of Adequacy, Caring Instincts, Assisting Nature, Intuition, Imagination, Emotional Sensitivities, Intellectual Qualities, Family Influence, The Home

ASTROLOGICAL CORRESPONDENCES :

- Moon as G-planet, singleton, handle or leading planet
- Sun, Moon, Mars, Saturn, Ascendant-ruler or MC-ruler in Cancer, in or ruling the fourth house (especially the Moon in fourth) or aspected by the Moon
- Ascendant or MC in Cancer or in aspect to the Moon
- Planets in the fourth house or a Cancer stellium
- Moon in or ruling the sixth house or in the tenth
- Bowl pattern
- First Quarter Moon phase
- Preponderance or diminished representation of water
- Northern hemisphere emphasis or second quadrant focus
- Singleton, handle or leading planet in Cancer or in the fourth house
- First quarter square aspects involving the Moon, fourth house or Cancer
- Cancer in or ruling the fourth house
- Ruler of fourth house in the fourth house
- Ruler of the sixth house in the fourth house
- Either node in Cancer or in the fourth house

Trait 4 can appear in a number of different ways, as the astrological correspondences show. Although each facet is described in subsequent chapters, this trait is prominent when it appears in Level I, is involved in a number of close aspects or when it is repeated through the layers of the chart. It encompasses several different occupational possibilities.

For some people, trait 4 indicates an attraction to occupations which **assist others by attending to their various**

needs and are defined by their reliance on intuition, sensitivities or caring instincts, for example, the helping professions or the metaphysical/psychic arts. Lunar types love to be needed. In many instances, a warm, caring or intuitive approach to the job can be a forté.

Others with trait 4 pronounced gravitate to the world of the imagination and utilize sensitivities along different lines. They choose **creative occupations,** especially writing. However, advertising, the performing arts, painting, or any occupation which makes use of the creative imagination can be suitable. Trait 4 is similar to traits 2, 7 and 12. All share artistic proclivities. However, with trait 4 (or 12), an intellectual bent to the creative output often exists.

For many a desire to **build a business** or a professional practice is evident. Work conducted **out of the home** is not only prevalent, but also favorable. Competitive or hostile work environments can be emotionally draining and are better avoided, unless trait 1 or 8 also is highlighted. **Closeness, belonging or attachment** to the place of employment or to the others who populate the work environment is needed. For this reason, trait 4 people could be happiest working with a family member, for a family-owned business or in a warm, family-like atmosphere. However, a word of caution is needed here. The desire for closeness and belonging can prompt some to go beyond the call of duty. The need to be needed can be overstimulated and lead to taking on additional work. While it may make the boss happy, it makes trait 4 workers vulnerable to being taken advantage of.

The family background tends to influence their career choices and/or the heights they expect or wish to attain. An accent on this trait can represent a C type of worker, but not exclusively. It is important for trait 4 individuals to understand exactly how their childhoods impacted them. Parental influences can range from following in the vocational footsteps of a parent (more or less) to working for the family's business. In some cases, parents can be supportive of the selected vocation, by providing emotional or financial assistance, or they can represent positive role models. In other cases, parental expectations or an inaccurate self-image create problems which must be dealt with and overcome.

These people may be influenced in ways that are not immediately apparent. A diminished self-image frequently represents the crux of their employment dissatisfaction. Because they do not perceive themselves accurately, they do not select appropriate careers. Low ceilings are placed on the job outlets they feel adequate to perform. A poor self-image also accounts for their being slack on the job. They may not work as hard as they could because they do not believe their efforts could amount to anything.

At some time, most trait 4 people need to develop a **sense of adequacy, inner security and healthy self-image.** This represents a vital capacity related to trait 4 and a viable vocational expression (see Chapter 3). The sense of identity must be separated from the family influence, especially when early experiences of nurturing were inadequate. Unconscious habit patterns and emotional responses formulated in childhood could be governing their lives (see First Quarter Moon in Chapter 7). Some form of **self-development or psychological repair** may be necessary. **Unconscious dependency needs,** moodiness and vulnerability must be acknowledged so individuals can learn appropriate ways to check their feeling states. When they do not develop themselves, such people can slip into the E category of worker and experience difficulty getting out.

Once the introspection process has been faced, and the self-image escalates, trait 4 individuals are better equipped to determine appropriate vocational directions. Ambitions emerge and they tend to be more sociable and intellectually conversant. They may even take up writing or public speaking as part of the occupational expression. It is a mistake to assume that trait 4 always is passive or necessarily domestic. Jack, the executive for the health care association, is a very lunar personality (see chart, page 16). He needs to feel close to his staff and is a natural as a speaker and policy writer. His avocation as a playwright provides outlets for his imagination and intellectual aspirations not available from his job.

Some **possible outlets for trait 4** might include –

- following in parental footsteps, working for a family-owned business or in a family-like atmosphere
- having a business or a professional practice
- the caring instincts/feeling nature/use of intuition or catering to the important needs of others: health or mental

health care professional, personnel director/recruiter, nursery/grammar school teacher, day care center owner/ worker, psychic, counselor, nurse
- the creative imagination or intellectual processes: novel-ist/author, poet, songwriter, playwright, painter, advertising copywriter, artist, performing artist, metaphysician
- the home, products for the home or work conducted from the home: domestic services, housekeeper, real estate sales, housewife, janitor, house painter/plasterer, interior designer, rental agent, building manager, cottage industry
- trait 2 or 7 occupations

Trait 5:

Self-Expressive Drives, Fun, Spontaneity, Business Management, Leadership, Self-Esteem, Hobbies, Recreation, Children

ASTROLOGICAL CORRESPONDENCES :
- Sun, Moon, Mars, Saturn, Ascendant-ruler or MC-ruler in Leo, in or ruling the fifth house (especially Sun in fifth) or aspected by the Sun
- Ascendant or MC in Leo or in aspect to the Sun
- Sun as singleton, handle or leading planet or located within six degrees of the angles
- Planets in the fifth house or a Leo stellium
- Sun in or ruling the sixth house or in the tenth
- Gibbous Moon phase
- Bucket pattern
- Singleton, handle or leading planet in Leo or in the fifth house
- First quarter trine aspects involving the Sun, Leo or fifth house
- Leo in or ruling the fifth house
- Ruler of fifth house in the fifth house
- Ruler of the sixth house in the fifth house
- Either node in Leo or in the fifth house

Trait 5 can appear in a number of different ways, as the astrological correspondences show. Although each facet is described in subsequent chapters, this trait is prominent when it appears in Level I, is involved in a number of close aspects or when it is repeated through the layers of the chart. It manifests in several different ways.

As a member of the fire family, trait 5 shares many occupational drives with trait 1, such as a need to think on one's feet, to exhibit independent decision-making, advancement, recognition, popularity or prominence. Trait 5 types need to be accomplishment-oriented as doers, speculators, creators or managers. Many are drawn to occupations which are **self-involving** or entail **self-promotion.**

However, most important to this trait is the need to enjoy the occupation, to experience it as fun and as self-expressive on an intimate level. For these reasons, work involving a **special loved one,** fun-loving coworkers, children, sports, creative outlets, amusements or recreational activities can be suitable employment avenues. Speculative ventures of any nature also belong to trait 5, for example, stock options or any risk-taking ventures. Many need to have an audience or to be a performer, usually along off-the-cuff, extemporaneous lines. Not only the entertainment industry, but other occupations call for a performance at times, for example, lecturing, teaching, sales presentations or promotional campaigns.

Trait 5 is not especially creative in a strict artistic sense, but is creative in terms of an ability to bring to life what has been conceptualized in the mind. It is not that such people merely have to "prove" themselves through their work, although this is true in many instances. They seek to **discover** and define themselves, and thereby tap inner resources to gain self-confidence, through the results of their creative projects. Hence, the occupation must be expressive of self. They often prefer to call the shots of projects with minimum input from others. That way, when the results are in, they can feel it is their "baby." Humor and fortitude tend to be their higher qualities. At their best, they are responsible example-setters and are naturals as job trainers, teachers, account executives and business managers.

Trait 5 individuals need to feel appreciated, if not applauded, for their contributions and to feel they offer something important or special to the job or the boss. For this reason, the relationship to superiors can be highly significant to job satisfaction. Trait 5 people need to take **healthy** pride in themselves, their creations and their places of employment. Recognition from others often is important to validating their sense of worth.

However, depending **too** much on the recognition of others can be problematical and is often cloaked behind a seeming arrogance. They can be touchy about respect and more inclined to **notice** seeming disrespect due to a marked need for praise and the assurance of being liked. Although the desire for respect and to be considered special are human qualities (because everyone has the Sun located somewhere in the chart), it is prominent in trait 5 people. Jobs which expose them to any maltreatment are emotionally unhealthy because the loss of self-esteem can be overwhelming. However, when the need to be special goes too far, it creates problems, especially in getting along with bosses and coworkers.

An **underlying sense of inadequacy** prompts many to strive for achievement, recognition and center stage. They are most likely to reflect a C type of work personality in a healthy sense, provided their hearts are in what they are doing and their effort and reality quotients are intact. Otherwise, an excessive need to have fun or to be **special** creates vocational difficulties. Rather than being achievement-oriented, such individuals may not strive on the job. This could be a D or E type personality who develops a preference for not working because skills and abilities are inadequate to land that "important" job. The pride factor and image consciousness associated with trait 5 prompts some to refuse suitable work because it is not considered significant enough.

The problem is often traceable to the family background, especially the relationship to the father. This can be true when the Sun is highlighted in the chart (Chapter 4). Strong ties of a positive or negative nature can exist. Trait 5 persons tend to be approval-seeking of "father" and must be careful not to select an occupation on the unconscious expectation of gaining approval. For the trait 5 C type of worker, approval-seeking without a sufficient demonstration of skill and effort is like fishing without a reel at the end of the rod; nothing gets caught. "Fivers" can be strivers or boring malcontents, depending on how they handle this issue of self-esteem and proving themselves.

Les suffers from an unconscious need to win his father's approval. It has developed to the point that his happiness is staked on becoming famous (chart page 20). As if this were not enough of a problem, Les does not work that hard to achieve anything. Unconsciously, he is so sure he will fail that he does not stay with anything long enough for the expected failure to occur. Studying astrology did not help matters. Once he learned Jupiter was in his first house, he was convinced that all he had to do was sit back and wait for fame. He neglected to take seriously what the rest of his chart indicated.

Because **fun and self-expression** are so important to a satisfying way of life, trait 5 also can represent fulfillment through important hobbies, especially when skills or education limit job possibilities to less prestigious outlets. Sometimes hobbies develop into income-producing endeavors and recognition can be gained from them. With trait 5, however, it is important to bring an intimate aspect of self to bear during the work process, be it intellectual, creative or entrepreneurial. This is what will bring a sense of contentment from a career.

Some **possible outlets for trait 5** might include –

- promoting one's special talents or interests
- catering to an audience, especially along extemporaneous lines: product demonstrator, public/community relations, advertising promotions, lecturer, teacher, entertainer, comedian, improvisational performer
- a speculative, risk-taking or entrepreneurial nature: stock options/commodity trader, promoter, business owner
- recreation, amusements or children: the toy industry, cartoonist, summer camp counselor/owner, amusement park owner/worker, recreational vehicle sales, greeting card designer/sales, gym teacher, child psychologist, hobby shop or video arcade owner/worker, cruise or sports director, children's clothes, school principal, sporting goods
- business management or job training
- working with a special loved one or working with fun-loving, amusing coworkers
- trait 1 occupations

Trait 6:
Work, Analysis, Attention to Detail, Diligence, Service, Technical Skill, Craft or Talent

ASTROLOGICAL CORRESPONDENCES :
- Sun, Moon, Mercury, Mars, Saturn, Ascendant-ruler or MC-ruler in Virgo, in or ruling the sixth house (especially Mercury in sixth)
- Ascendant or MC in Virgo
- Mercury as singleton, handle, leading or stationary planet, or located within six degrees of the angles
- Planets in the sixth house or a Virgo stellium
- Bundle pattern
- Gibbous Moon phase
- Mercury in or ruling the tenth house
- Singleton, handle or leading planet in Virgo or in the sixth house
- Quincunx aspects involving Mercury, sixth house or Virgo
- Virgo in or ruling the sixth house
- Ruler of sixth house in the sixth
- Either node in Virgo or in the sixth house

Trait 6 can appear in a number of different ways, as the astrological correspondences show. Although each facet is described in subsequent chapters, this trait is prominent when it appears in Level I, is involved in a number of close aspects or when it is repeated through the layers of the chart. It represents a need to fulfill ego drives in the service of others – the boss, clients, customers, students, patients, a group or a company.

Work and one's skills must be elevated to significant forms of self-expression. This is especially true when trait 1 or 5 is connected to trait 6 or 10 or when the Gibbous Moon phase (Chapter 7) is present. Such people often define themselves by what they do for a living. Their emotional equilibrium and sense of self-worth revolve around work in ways that baffle others. Unless the paycheck is sizeable, a get-by job can undermine health as well as self-confidence. Minor ailments can arise due to frustration from a lack of satisfying employment. Trait 6 D type workers often get sick as an unconscious way to escape from a job they detest. When they resist their need to work or to develop skills, illness becomes an unconscious excuse not to work. They may even abandon the work force altogether, as do type E workers.

Whenever this trait is accented, it is imperative to develop a marketable skill, craft, talent or service to perform. It could manifest as a **technical expertise** – a skilled use of the hands, office practice occupations, crafts, any of the trades, analytical or mathematical capabilities, or an aptitude for details. Individuals with trait 6 accented often are adept at uncovering flaws and improving conditions. Many enjoy taking things apart and putting them back together again, so any form of repair or research work can be suitable. Any occupation that relies on trait 6 qualities can be satisfying, including many of those associated with trait 3.

A need to **act in an advisory capacity,** with others relying on the skills or knowledge one has acquired, is especially important to trait 6. Unless fire traits are strong, this personality can be satisfied being the power behind the throne. The **need to be useful** and considered indispensable for one's abilities is also paramount. For this reason, trait 6 people can be attracted to all forms of health care, where the sick and helpless depend on one's capabilities and authority.

When work is important to them, trait 6 people continually hone their skills. They represent the best of work types A, B or C, although if the need to be useful and indispensable goes to extremes, workaholism results. They might get sick as the only way the body can get them to take a "vacation." Their impeccable, diligent natures may stem from the early home where a role model was a perfectionist along similar lines. Criticism could have played strong parts during family discussions. Feeling that they must somehow "measure up" influences how they participate in the job force. Some trait 6 people are like "Mr. Spock" – pragmatic and serious about occupational matters; they gain security through their ability to perform well on the job. Others experience stress over applying themselves due to the early criticisms which have become internalized and serve as constant reminders of real or imagined inadequacies. Like an invisible chain, self-criticism holds them back. It becomes their "job" to eliminate the dysfunction to gain greater satisfaction from work.

Linda has fairly pronounced trait 6 needs. She is a topnotch legal secretary for a railroad. With a typing speed and

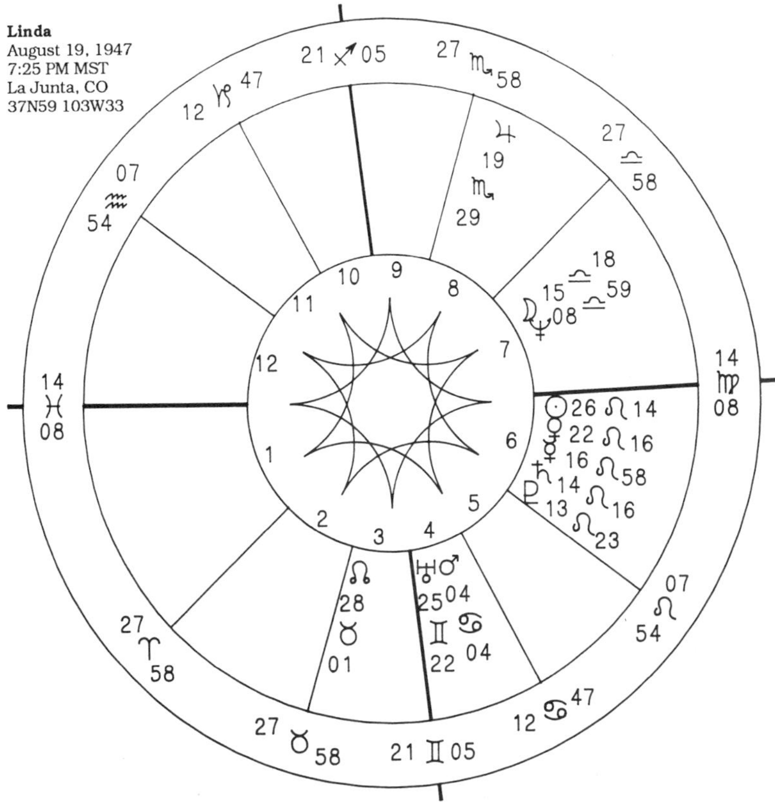

matching shorthand skills of over 120 words a minute, plus an amazing capacity to keep track of details and legal proceedings, she is always requested to attend the company's most important meetings. Even during a hard-earned vacation she can expect to receive a few calls from the office because her boss does not trust anyone else's judgment. She enjoys her job because it fulfills many needs, although, due to a trait 5 component in her personality, she feels secretarial work is not significant enough. Determined to elevate her position, Linda has plowed through five years of evening courses and soon will receive her B.A. Next comes graduate school and, eventually, a high-level management spot.

Some **possible outlets for trait 6** might include –

- a technical service, craft or skill or the need to accumulate and distribute facts or information: any of the "professions" but especially teaching, social service, health care and law, any of the "trades," tour guide, information specialist, librarian, translator, lecturer, programmer, lab technician, technical consultant, health inspector
- the analysis of facts or figures: accountant, bookkeeper, analyst, mathematician, billing clerk, scientist
- office practices or services which back up another individual or a larger structure: secretary, mail room/inventory or file clerk, messenger, runner, receptionist, office manager, advisor, waiter/waitress, delivery person, mail carrier, fast food service
- the health care industry and related services: nurse, doctor, nutritionist, dental assistant/hygienist, dental lab technician, optometrist, veterinarian, technician
- attention to detail or manual dexterity: typist, surgeon, calligrapher, sign painter, dentist, sculptor, musician, draftsperson, editor
- any kind of repair work: appliance, television, radio, watch repair, surgery, etc.
- trait 3 occupations

Trait 7:

Interpersonal Skills, Aesthetic Appreciation, Art, Diplomacy, Cooperation, Partnership, Teamwork

ASTROLOGICAL CORRESPONDENCES :

- Venus as G-planet, singleton, handle, leading or stationary planet
- Sun, Moon, Venus, Mars, Saturn, Ascendant-MC rulers in Libra, in or ruling the seventh house (especially Venus in seventh), or aspected by Venus
- Ascendant or MC in Libra or in aspect to Venus
- Planets in the seventh house or a Libra stellium
- Venus in or ruling the sixth house or in the tenth
- Seesaw pattern
- Full Moon phase
- Western hemisphere emphasis or third quadrant focus

- Singleton, handle or leading planet in Libra or in the seventh house
- Opposition aspects involving Venus, seventh house or Libra
- Libra in or ruling the seventh house
- Ruler of seventh house in the seventh house
- Ruler of the sixth house in the seventh house
- Either node in Libra or in the seventh house

Trait 7 can appear in a number of different ways, as the astrological correspondences show. Although each facet is described in subsequent chapters, this trait is prominent when it appears in Level I, is involved in a number of close aspects or when it is repeated through the layers of the chart. It functions in two distinct directions: through aesthetic outlets or through occupations which focus on relating to others. Aesthetically expressed, an aptitude for any of the **artistically-related professions** or performing arts may emerge in a fashion similar to trait 2 (or 4). A distinction exists: trait 2 aesthetic outlets lean toward those appealing to the physical, tactile senses, with an emphasis on products of the earth, whereas trait 7 suggests refinements of the mind and a visual appreciation of form and beauty.

Traits 7 and 2 share a great deal in common, including a proclivity to allow the practical, remunerative aspects of a job to overshadow all other factors. The desire to work in attractive, comfortable surroundings is shared, but it tends to be more compelling for the trait 7 type.

An accent on this trait also can encompass a **need to work with or through others** and partnership arrangements, teamwork, or the one-to-one interrelating process can represent fulfilling vocational expressions. How well the trait 7 person fares in the working world rotates around an ability to interrelate well. The individual relies on **interrelating skills** as a primary job function, or the development of these skills is essential to success. This is another personality function vital to adequate vocational expression (see Chapter 3).

Sales, politics, interviewing, all forms of therapy or public relations, for example, are diverse occupations which rely on interpersonal relating skills. They also incorporate a need for charm, diplomacy, graciousness, interest in others or good looks, factors often associated with trait 7. Any job which routinely relies on such abilities or requires one-to-one interaction with others can be suitable. This includes personal forms, as in counseling or private tutoring, or impersonal ones, such as retail sales, customer service, or jobs which entail **face-to-face dealings with the public** as opposed to business conducted over the telephone (trait 3). When interrelating skills are well developed, an accent on trait 7 can suggest an aptitude for handling people, a valuable asset for any job.

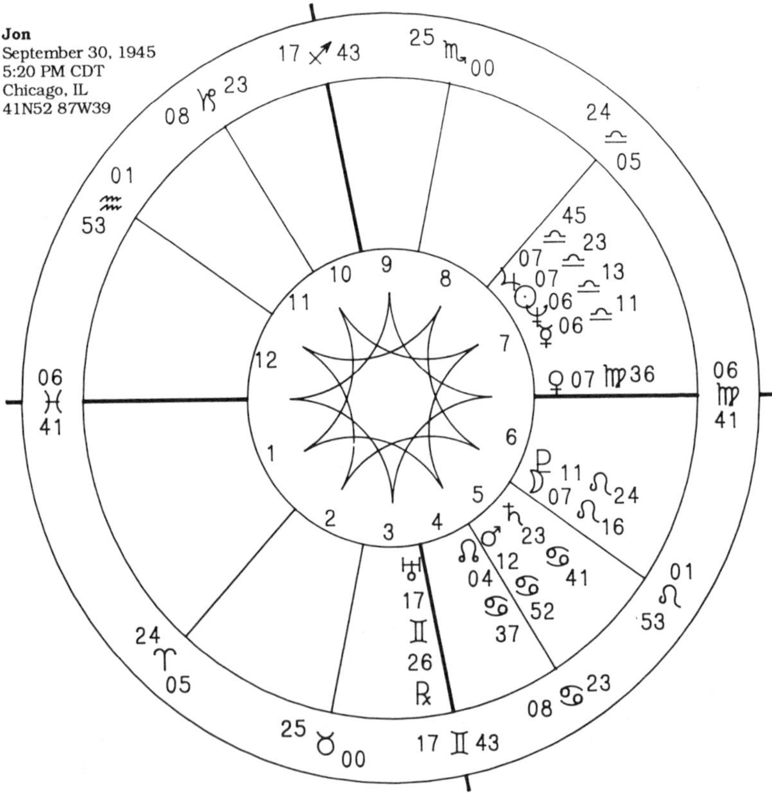

Jon had a poor grasp of his identity and, consequently, his vocational needs were a complete mystery to him. Not until he began to study astrology did it even occur to him that perhaps he was in the wrong line of work. For most of his adult life he was employed by the government in a dingy office pushing papers and shuffling numbers. It was a living and he was raised to believe a job is a job. The more he studied astrology, the more disenchanted he became with his job. With a strong accent on trait 7 in his chart, it was obvious that people, rather than paper, would make his vocational life more rewarding. Previously unaware of his hidden potentials as a counselor, Jon is discovering new horizons through astrology.

It is most important to the fulfillment of trait 7 to work with people whose presence contributes to a successful occupational expression. Job satisfaction largely depends on it. In some cases, working with a **business partner(s) or the spouse** can be more profitable than working alone. Teamwork could enhance one's opportunities by contributing resources, talents or abilities which broaden one's own scope of action. An assistant, agent, editor or trainer serves a similar function. Becoming a partner, for example, in a law or accounting firm, or in any professional group practice, also can represent an important goal. In such cases, the partnership actually signifies an elevation of the work status and a reward for a job well done.

When interrelating skills are inadequately developed, the individual experiences difficulty maneuvering in the job world. It is a place where others rarely fail to be present, even if one has the good fortune to be self-employed. Many a promotion or job can be lost due to a failure to relate well to those above or below one on the job ladder. Job interviews can turn out poorly because the person appears too passive and weak, or the reverse - too forceful. Obtaining a desirable job may require proper development or toning down of self-assertive drives. Since "others" represent a vital aspect of the vocational experience, inadequate interrelating skills undermine advancement opportunities. The issue boils down to self-worth (trait 2). It is difficult to get ahead in the job world when one is unsure of one's value or how to present oneself in the best light. And that often includes one's physical appearance and manner of dress.

Although mixing work and relationships comes naturally to trait 7, it can create difficulties. Relationships in or outside of the work arena can dilute career drives if they deflect attention away from pressing career goals. If trait 7 people wish to get ahead, relationships must not be placed far above their work responsibilities. A balance needs to be struck between the two, which is why trait 7 people may be happiest sharing work with a loved one.

Some **possible outlets for trait 7** might include –

- partnership, teamwork or a staff
- the interrelating process, especially face-to-face dealings with the public: sales person, guidance counselor, therapist, teacher, recruiter, interviewer, customer service, bank representative, tutor, cashier, teller
- an artistic aptitude or flair: artist, performing artist, designer, singer, musician, window trimmer, dancer, wedding/party planner, architect, flower arranger
- charm, diplomacy, refinement or good looks: diplomat, receptionist, model, restaurant hostess, maitre d', politician, golfer, a leading lady or man, public or community relations, advertising, hotel manager
- trait 2 or 4 occupations

Trait 8:

Power, Commitment, Deep Involvement, Fascination, Intense Interaction, Hidden Elements, Research, Physical Exertion

ASTROLOGICAL CORRESPONDENCES :

- Sun, Moon, Mars, Saturn, Pluto, Ascendant-MC rulers in Scorpio, in or ruling the eighth house or aspected by Pluto (especially Pluto in eighth)
- Ascendant or MC in Scorpio or in aspect to Pluto
- Pluto as singleton, handle, leading or stationary planet or located within six degrees of the angles
- Planets in the eighth house or a Scorpio stellium
- Pluto in or ruling the sixth house or in the tenth
- Preponderance or lack of the fixed quality
- Disseminating Moon phase
- Locomotive pattern
- Singleton, handle or leading planet in Scorpio or in the eighth house
- Disseminating phase quincunx aspects involving Pluto, the eighth house or Scorpio
- Ruler of the eighth house in the eighth house
- Ruler of the sixth house in the eighth house
- Either node in Scorpio or in the eighth house

Trait 8 can appear in a number of different ways, as the astrological correspondences show. Although each facet is described in subsequent chapters, this trait is prominent when it appears in Level I, is involved in a number of close aspects or is repeated through the layers of the chart. The **use or abuse of power,** by oneself or others, often becomes a significant career issue.

Power manifests in many ways; occupations call for physical power, healing power, intellectual power, political power, psychological power, psychic power, sexual power, inner power, creative power or financial power. Although any job incorporating these various "powers" can be suitable, trait 8 tends to signify an approach to a career rather than specifying appropriate occupations. A deep sense of **commitment** to and total immersion in the occupation is especially important. One's drives must be passionately applied.

When the personality is self-secure, trait 8 people enjoy mastering an occupation and through it exercising one of these forms of power. A daring, determined, self-driving, do-or-die quality often surfaces. Occupations associated with trait 1, especially those encompassing leadership drives, can be appropriate. However, while trait 1 acts in a more open manner, if only at times out of complete naiveté, trait 8 is more secretive, vulnerable, self-protective, doubting, cautious and security-oriented. A back door approach to accomplishing most goals is likely and situations are pondered long before taking action. In many instances, trait 4-related occupations can be equally suitable as this trait shares a security orientation with trait 8.

Due to a need for control and independent decision-making, some trait 8 types prefer to work alone or under their own direction as much as possible. For others, the **corporate world** and the arena of **office politics** are fascinating places to exercise power. Other outlets could be of a sexual or occult nature, that influence the masses or that involve **physical exertion or an element of danger and risk.**

Occupations involving the hidden or unknown aspects of existence, life or death matters, the "underworld" or socially taboo activities also can be enthralling. Any job entailing decay or rebuilding, deep emotional probing or intense interaction with others applies. The demolition aspects of the construction industry and the trades related to factors necessary to building, but which are not visible on the surface of a structure (e.g., pipe fitting), are apropos.

When individuals are not self-secure, an emphasis on trait 8 coincides with a need to develop a more **powerful, resourceful or charismatic personality** to succeed at interesting jobs. Some trait 8 individuals are timid, disturbingly withdrawn or appear threatening. Such behavior interferes with obtaining or maintaining satisfying employment. The sense of inner power or fortitude to stand on their own feet is lacking and must to be developed. Upheavals and horrendous encounters often materialize with competitors, coworkers or authority figures. These circumstances arise from the projection of the trait 8 person's fears of inadequacy and denied inner power. The corporate world, which attracts this type, tends to stir up old childhood **persecution complexes** due to its similarity to the family structure. Involvements with coworkers often are a replay of the early relationship to siblings, while superiors are commonly experienced as limiting parental figures.

This personality often approaches life like a lamb thrown in a wolf pack, as if an attack could be launched from any corner. Psychotherapy or some form of personal growth may be needed to eliminate **convoluted perceptions** of others before efforts can be directed successfully in the job world. The individual may be blocked by irrational fears belonging more to the past than to the present and must understand what is being repressed to move toward a fuller life.

Kathy is a financially successful sales representative for a computer systems company. She also is a tortured human being who can talk for hours about what this or that one at the office is doing to her, including her boss. Although she is the top rep for her territory, word from on high mysteriously instructed a reduction in her base salary. None of the others received this slap in the face, even though they generated less sales than she did. She also was turned down for a more lucrative spot and later, some of her best clients were turned over to a rookie. She thought it was because her boss enjoyed torturing her and did not wish to see her get ahead. It never occurred to her that he wanted her to quit.

No doubt events at the office transpired as she said. Kathy was unaware that she threatens people in a way that attracts

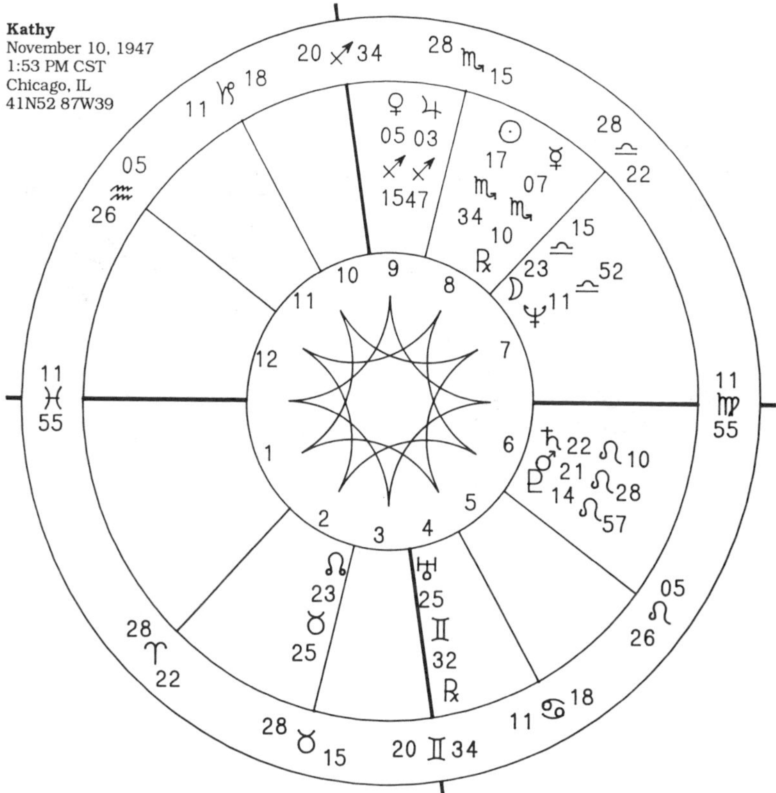

these problems to her. It was difficult to get her to stop focusing on "them" and, instead, to look at what was going on in "her."

The power player is another face of trait 8, the one most popularly recognized. It is the type who masks an unconscious dread of inferiority by maliciously attempting to out-power, control or suppress others. Excessively dominating or timid behavior on the surface of the personality often belies its opposite nature locked away and hidden on the inside. When trait 8 is strongly accented, some form of control, domination or manipulation often was experienced as part of the upbringing. Timid passivity or power playing can become a habitual response to others. These types mirror each other, which is why they often are drawn together in a sadomasochistic ritual. A third Plutonian type was aware, even if only subliminally, of what was going on in the childhood home and learned how to adapt without losing the sense of self.

Domination can come in many forms. At one extreme, an emphasis on trait 8 can correlate with having endured physical, sexual or emotional abuse. But a **smother-love** family atmosphere also can sap a child so that a true sense of self and individual effectiveness are not readily achieved. Often such parents do this in the name of love, although controlling the child's self-expression is more to the point. They do not let the child "be." Under such circumstances, dependency needs and the ability to trust go unfulfilled in the early life. Honest give-and-take relationships, in addition to a self-expressive career, become difficult to develop later. The early domination is carried over and projected onto others in adult life. It prompts some to seek safety through minimal contact with other people. Others learn by parental example to assume power and total control in their interactions, usually by relating to weaker people.

Sometimes parents can be experienced as being grossly ineffectual. Children of such personalities may later develop a need for power, or grow to imitate the passive parental behavior. Still another type may be more "conscious" and learn what **not** to do from the negative example set by the parents. These individuals develop early **self-mastery** and self-control. They respect the rights and needs of others and are able to share "power" in ways their parents are not likely to comprehend.

In addition to overt domination, smothering and timidity, other forms of manipulation exist. The passive variety includes overkilling kindness and the overgiving of material things as an unconscious way to control others through obligation. This behavior often suggests an underlying lack of self-worth which prompts individuals to "buy" others. Constant joking and an ingratiating personality are other tricks to covertly influence people. Who wants to take anything out on a cheerleader or a clown? Sickness, manipulation by guilt, **mind games**, jealousy, brooding, silence, withdrawal and sex appeal also serve similar ends. The trait 8 personality is often expert at one or more of these control tactics, having previously learned them from other masters of the art.

Denied inner power or the willful use of others eventually comes back to haunt a person. In the latter instance, thrones can be toppled from stepping on one too many toes. When inner power is suppressed, one may be drawn to powerful occupations, but lack inner stamina to see them through. Or, a boring wallflower job may be selected due to suppressed factors of self. Powerful boss figures or coworkers will pop up, make life miserable and serve as reminders of one's own denied inner power. Inner fortitude must be developed so that control can be taken in the proper areas to create a more satisfying life.

Some **possible outlets for trait 8** might include –

- a giant corporation or a corporate structure, office politics
- the construction industry, especially "trades" which cannot be seen on the surface of structures: plumbing, pipe fitting
- work underground: miner, mining engineer
- decay: sewer workers, garbage collector, sewage plant operator, dentist
- life and death matters, hidden or unknown aspects of life, deep emotional probing or intense encounters with others: past life regression therapist, funeral director, psychologist, psychiatrist, the occult arts, space exploration, boxer, ambulance driver, insurance agent, pest control, FBI/CIA agent, detective
- bringing about a transformation in others: the healing arts, pharmacist, chiropractor, hypnotist, hairdresser, crisis intervention, emergency room nurse/doctor
- influencing the masses: television commentator, advertising director, political writer
- research: marketing or medical researcher, occult research
- social taboos: sex magazine editor, adult bookstore owner/worker
- one of the "powers" or anything that is experienced as being fascinating, intense
- physical exertion involving an element of danger or risk: steel or construction worker, lumberjack, firefighter, daredevil, race car driver, stunt person
- trait 1 or 4 occupations

Trait 9:
Aspirational Drives, Influence, Important Ideologies, Travel, Fame, Dissemination of Knowledge

ASTROLOGICAL CORRESPONDENCES :
- Jupiter as G-planet, singleton, handle, leading or stationary planet
- Sun, Moon, Mars, Jupiter, Saturn, Ascendant-MC rulers in Sagittarius, in or ruling the ninth house (especially Jupiter in ninth) or aspected by Jupiter
- Ascendant or MC in Sagittarius or in aspect to Jupiter
- Planets in the ninth house or a Sagittarius stellium
- Jupiter in or ruling the sixth house or in the tenth
- Splay pattern
- Disseminating Moon phase
- Singleton, handle or leading planet in Sagittarius or in the ninth house
- Disseminating trine aspects involving Jupiter, ninth house or Sagittarius
- Sagittarius in or ruling the ninth house
- Ruler of the ninth house in the ninth house
- Ruler of the sixth house in the ninth house
- Either node in Sagittarius or in the ninth house

Trait 9 can appear in a number of different ways, as the astrological correspondences show. Although each facet is described in subsequent chapters, this trait is prominent when it appears in Level I, is involved in a number of close aspects or when it is repeated through the layers of the chart. It correlates with aspirational drives which prompt people to **reach beyond present limits.** Such drives are integral to successful vocational expression (see Chapter 3). For many people, aspirations surround notoriety, recognition, influence or wealth. An accent on this trait can be the mark of an accomplishment-oriented A, B or C worker who is realistically optimistic about an ability to succeed. Others express this trait differently.

On one level, trait 9 can represent a desire for **travel and adventure** as a way to reach out and discover the world. Many occupations fulfill this yen, for example, jobs involving faraway places or foreign cultures. Such occupations "take one places" and expand horizons in a direct or indirect manner. Sometimes the connection to distant places as part of the job is sufficient to satisfy these yearnings.

But the urge to reach out might manifest in another individual as a desire to **expand mental horizons** and to understand human existence. That is why Jupiter, Sagittarius and the ninth house traditionally have been associated with philosophy, religious ideologies and higher education. Any of these outlets can be important to a fulfilling trait 9 vocational expression. An advanced education is a plus in the job world and a stepping stone to higher-paying positions. Trait 9 individuals may need to obtain a degree, or some other form of advanced training, to land an interesting job.

This urge to reach out could become a desire to share or spread important beliefs and perspectives. Teaching, lecturing, preaching, writing, publishing or any occupation which relies on a system of thought, theory or belief can be fulfilling. Paul, the new age publisher, has this trait consistently represented throughout his chart.

Aspirational drives also can surface as an urge to have **greater influence** and manifest vocationally in the form of acting, politics or the broadcasting industry. These and related occupations serve as vehicles to spread one's name, face or ideas to broader segments of society. The eminent eye surgeon has this trait focalized. As a high school youth, he acted in quite a few plays. Before going into private group practice, he was in academic medicine as an associate professor at a major university and teaching hospital.

Trait 9 individuals need independent decision making and freedom on the job. Their work must provide advancement potential, adventure or entail travel. To be fulfilling, important ideologies and perspectives on the meaning of life may require on the job expression.

But aspirational drives do not function properly when **unrealistic expectations** about life and one's capabilities exist. Pipe dreamers and unproductive type C, D or E workers suffer from this problem, particularly when a preponderance of fire (Chapter 8) or trait 12 also exists. The need for success could be overwhelming and so intimately connected to the sense of identity that individuals cannot envision life without it. Fabricated successes and exaggerated expectations of achievement serve as insulation. They assume that success will materialize without effort and that the **big break** is just around the corner. An inner need to believe in their innate "specialness" has grown to unrealistic proportions. Dan has this trait pronounced in his chart.

Some trait 9 individuals go to the opposite extreme and set vocational sights too low. They cannot relate to their own aspirations due to a diminished self-image and fears of failure. Denied aspirations gnaw at these people until acknowledged. Nervous ailments or other problems develop and undermine the physical or mental health. Chronic, low grade depressions are common. Steps must be taken to eliminate the restrictive self-image and free the personality to fulfill unacknowledged aspirations.

Some **possible outlets for trait 9** might include –

- fame, making a name for oneself or having influence: the entertainment field, acting, politics, radio or television broadcaster, advertising director, being an important influence in or through one's vocation, all aspects of the advertising, broadcasting and publishing industries
- adventure: explorer, safari leader, astronaut
- making a great deal of money: wheeler/dealer business person, financial investor, stock options or commodity trader
- going places in person or otherwise: worker in the travel industry, pilot, flight attendant, air traffic controller, travel agent, all aspects of the telecommunications industry
- foreign places or cultures: foreign trade, import/export business, cruise director, ambassador
- a university or college: professor, registrar, admission clerk
- disseminating important ideas: author, teacher, lecturer, magazine publisher, advertising copywriter
- a particular ideology, system of thought or religion: psychologist, astrologer, metaphysician, lawyer, philosopher, judge, theorist, minister, priest, nun, etc.
- trait 12 occupations

Trait 10:

Sense of Competence, Effort, Tangible Achievement, Professionalism, Authority, Expertise, Discipline, Academic or Diligent Approach

ASTROLOGICAL CORRESPONDENCES :

- Saturn as G-planet, singleton, handle, leading or stationary planet
- Sun, Moon, Mars, Saturn, Ascendant-MC rulers in Capricorn, tenth house (especially Saturn in tenth) or aspected by Saturn
- Ascendant or MC in Capricorn or in aspect to Saturn
- Planets in the tenth house or a Capricorn stellium
- Saturn in or ruling the sixth house
- Last quarter Moon phase
- Southern hemisphere emphasis or fourth quadrant focus
- Singleton, handle or leading planet in Capricorn or in the tenth house
- Last quarter square aspects involving Saturn, MC ruler or Capricorn
- Ruler of the tenth house in the tenth house
- Ruler of the sixth house in the tenth house
- Either node in Capricorn or in the tenth house

Trait 10 can appear in a number of different ways, as the astrological correspondences show. Although each facet is described in subsequent chapters, this trait is prominent when it appears in Level I, is involved in a number of close aspects or when it is repeated through the layers of the chart. It is fundamental to occupational expression because it symbolizes the need to grow into responsible adulthood and make contributions to society.

Trait 10 represents the sense of reality and the limitations of earthly existence. Unlike trait 9, which seeks to broaden the scope of action, trait 10 represents focus and concentration for the purposes of tangible production. A balance between traits 9 and 10 is essential to employment success. The best of worker types A, B and C know how to strike this balance.

Vocationally, trait 10 manifests most profitably through a yen for tangible achievement, distinction and authority through an **academic or a diligent approach.** As a member of the earth family, measurable rewards can be important to job selection and satisfaction. Some trait 10 people build their own businesses and typically a tangible service or product emerges from the work effort. Any occupation of a detail-oriented nature which relies on the painstaking development of expertise or technical skill can be suitable. Most of the "professions" encompass these factors, especially science and research-oriented vocations. Most "trade" occupations similarly rely on technical know-how or skill, although an advanced education is not usually required. However, at bottom line, it is how one works and deals with the issue of limits that counts. One must be thorough and patient because the fruits of one's labors typically take time to ripen. A mature, serious and realistic approach is absolutely vital. Authority and competence do not develop out of thin air.

When it comes to limits and trait 10, three responses are possible. (1) People can be realistic, diligently apply themselves, develop their skills and earn the authority they crave. (2) They can see more limits than realistically exist, and block themselves from what they might otherwise achieve. (3) They can refuse to face realistic limits, not develop true competence, and attempt more than is possible by wanting too much, too fast, without "paying their dues."

The role effort plays in skill development should be obvious, and effort is necessary when this trait appears in Level I. Without effort, solid skills cannot be developed and without skill development, one cannot be sure of one's competence to **accept responsibility** for decision making. A **fear of failure** or a fear of exercising authority can develop. Easy, pay-the-bills occupations tend to result and the need to express oneself as a person of distinction goes unacknowledged due to unnecessarily low job expectations. Type D and E personalities often have trait 10 pronounced in their charts. Their inadequate response to it accounts for their employment dissatisfaction or their lack of willingness to work.

Trait 10 people must inwardly sense themselves as competent to assume responsible jobs before they can recognize their need for tangible achievement, prestige and authority. A sense of capability prompts individuals to act on their aspirations. With trait 9, a "dream" of assuming a certain role in society exists. With trait 10, this dream must be followed up with the **discipline and effort** to develop skills and earn the desired position. The ceilings placed on career attainments depend on the degree to which aspirations and a sense of competence complement each other. When aspirations and competence are low, the job ceiling also is going to be low.

Some trait 10 people are eager to assume authority without realistically developing their capabilities. For them, short cuts take on tantalizing qualities. Rather than indicating where work must be done, obstacles become an affront to their achievement. Sorry consequences eventually emerge from the diminished work ethic as Saturnian setbacks, roadblocks, losses or depression. These are warnings that something about the career path or performance is faulty. Trait 10 can be deadly in this regard for pronounced fire or trait 12 personalities. The ability to accept responsibility is an essential trait 10 issue and the expenditure of quality, sustained effort is required when this trait is accented in a chart. Effort is a reality of the job world and both are a reality of life. Trait 10 people who do "work" and develop true competence make long-lasting, valuable contributions to their fields of endeavor.

Some **possible outlets for trait 10** might include –

- authority, professionalism or the painstaking development of an expertise: any of the "professions," any of the "trades"
- being "the boss" or in charge
- becoming an expert, an authority or a prestigious person
- business administration, advisor
- technical or academic skills: lab technician, technical writer, consultant, scientist, professor, science teacher, researcher, any type of intellectual work
- a detail orientation or precision: watch repair, surgeon
- any hard work or labor: cement finisher, brick layer

Trait 11:

Group Participation, Independent Contribution, Colleague Recognition, Technical Know-How, Mental Mastery, Consulting, Electronics, Cause Orientation, Stimulation, Excitement, Sudden Changes

ASTROLOGICAL CORRESPONDENCES :

- Sun, Moon, Mars, Saturn, Uranus, Ascendant-MC rulers in Aquarius, in or ruling the eleventh house (especially Uranus in eleventh) or aspected by Uranus
- Ascendant or MC in Aquarius or in aspect to Uranus
- Uranus as singleton, handle, leading or stationary planet or located within six degrees of the angles
- Planets in the eleventh house or an Aquarius stellium
- Uranus in or ruling the sixth house or in the tenth
- Balsamic Moon phase
- Splash pattern
- Singleton, handle or leading planet in Aquarius or in the eleventh house
- Last quarter sextile aspects involving Uranus, eleventh house or Aquarius
- Ruler of eleventh house in the eleventh house
- Ruler of the sixth house in the eleventh house
- Either node in Aquarius or in the eleventh house

Trait 11 can appear in a number of different ways, as the astrological correspondences show. Although each facet is described in subsequent chapters, this trait is prominent when it appears in Level I, is involved in a number of close aspects or when it is repeated through the layers of the chart. It points to many different vocational possibilities because Aquarius, the trait 11 sign, is co-ruled by Saturn and Uranus. Their contrasting personality factors (see Chapter 4) account for the divergent occupational expressions of this trait.

One of its fundamental expressions includes the need to be part of a group and yet participate as an **independent contributor.** Trait 11 individuals prefer congenial, intermittent contact with stimulating people who share similar goals or interests. Sometimes the group involvement is political in nature or a cause underlies its purpose, such as fan clubs, humanitarian causes, professional societies, associations or charitable organizations. Membership in a group practice is yet another way for trait 11 individuals to band together while working independently of each other.

Consulting or outside sales-related occupations are also appropriate because individuals represent a group/company while remaining independent of it. They act as their own boss. For trait 11, the less hands-on supervision the better. Trait 11 is pronounced in the self-employed due to this need for independence and freedom.

Frequently, but not always, trait 11 occupations entail **technical know-how,** clients, students, patients or customers. Interest may be shown in mastering a subject or activity. Any of the professions could prove suitable, but especially those which rely on a logical system of thought or theory, for example, any of the sciences, the legal field, psychology, astrology or the computer field. Such "professional" outlets, however, require trait 10 to be well developed. It takes a tremendous amount of discipline, effort and commitment to "master" anything. To be innovative, inventive or original – the characteristics typically associated with trait 11 – it is necessary to have a thorough grasp of the field's basic "laws" so they can be exceeded. For these reasons, trait 10 must be highly functional before this type of Uranian occupational expression can be achieved.

For other personalities, an **offbeat, new age or out of the ordinary** occupation is more suitable. They experience a needed sense of exhilaration from being "different" or from functioning through occupations which are outside the mainstream of the working world. Many flaunt the conventions of society, whether it is through their appearance, demeanor or vocation. While some may offer society worthwhile alternative lifestyles, others simply disdain living by the rules of the game. The latter types need to be careful in case their disdain represents a cover-up for unconscious fears of not being accepted or of failing.

Others achieve this needed sense of exhilaration through occupations catering to **innovation and new technology,** such as the electronics industry, engineering, television and other aspects of the broadcast media. The eye surgeon's research revolves around computers. He has three in his laboratory and two in his den at home, just in case the mood strikes him there. He once remarked that if he had his career to live over again, he would have gone into the computer field instead. As it is, his proclivity for electronic equipment has enabled him to perform the most delicate surgery under electron microscopes.

Since trait 11 belongs to the air element, the relationship to others populating the work environment can be important to job satisfaction. This includes how one feels about clients, customers or patients as well as coworkers, colleagues and peers. An outgrowth of this need is a desire to gain recognition from members of the group or profession to which one belongs. Awards dinners, chapter presidencies, highest sales quota awards or employee of the month are some ways **colleague recognition** is shown in the working world. Many trait 11 people are drawn to occupations which provide such outlets.

FEARS OF CLOSENESS

Stimulation or excitement is vital to trait 11 need fulfillment, so these types are open to making career changes or innovations. Due to its intellectual tendencies, and depending on how the more emotionally sensitive chart factors are represented, people with a focus on this trait often prefer to avoid issues of closeness on the job as well as outside of it. They can take a cool, logical approach when a hug or other forms of comforting may be called for, but they also can be counted on to take a detached and reasoned viewpoint. A descriptive term for this behavior is **humanitarian.** While they might not always be "nurturing," they do care about the human condition and seek to make contributions that benefit a greater whole. For this reason, the trait can be highlighted in the charts of those who work for charitable institutions, not-for-profit organizations or humanitarian causes.

Sometimes **emotional foibles** can be traced to a distant or cold early home, populated with separate beings independently going their own way. Perhaps parental separations occurred or the individual felt lost amidst a crowd of siblings with insufficient love to go around. Possibly the parents were older or were experienced as cold, aloof or too intellectual to relate adequately to the needs of a child. It may have seemed as difficult to receive attention from them as it is to squeeze toothpaste from an empty tube. Such individuals may never have learned how to be close and, as adults, choose places to work where emotional factors do not become an issue. Some turn to the world of the mind. However, when Uranian intellectualizations go to extremes, they represent a capacity to fly above the crowd to such an extent that interrelating capabilities may be deadened. As the song from *Hair* – "Easy to be Hard" – describes it, theoretical considerations can become more important than actual people or the realities of practical, everyday living.

This does not mean that all trait 11 types are emotionally cold fish who came from such backgrounds. Quite the contrary. The early home could have been an exceptionally exciting place by average standards. Parents could have been unusually stimulating, avant-garde types who enjoyed being surrounded by lively, arousing friends. This trait 11 type is accustomed to such goings-on, one reason why boredom on the job can be deadly.

When the **desire for authority** is not a strong personality drive, the commitment to advance in a career also diminishes in importance. Work in such cases is not considered an important form of self-expression. Life tends to rotate around other interests, mostly hobbies or activities with a small circle of friends. Still, to be reasonably attractive, the job has to meet certain requirements, including relative independence from supervision, a stimulating environment and an element of excitement during the course of the day.

Ed's chart (page 22) focalizes trait 11 in Level I. As an employee of the City of Chicago his job is rarely devoid of excitement, television exposes or political intrigues which get his blood boiling. Jack, the association (trait 11) executive, also has this trait accented. So does Paul, whose interests are along new age (trait 11) lines.

Trait 11 can point to still other possibilities. It can represent such a desire to break from authority and the establishment that the entire concept of the nine-to-five working world generates dread. Out of the ordinary, offbeat occupations or work conducted at unusual hours can maneuver around this problem. Otherwise, these trait 11 types are likely to experience difficulty maintaining jobs. Because excitement and change are their focal needs, a couple of different part-time jobs might fill the bill (although probably not their bank accounts). These individuals have a facility for suddenly changing jobs, especially when supervisors start breathing down their necks. They can quit faster than a speeding bullet, or – due to boredom – unconsciously set themselves up to be fired. That way they do not feel guilty about leaving and can face new job prospects with an air of excitement. For them, leaving one job for another can be the most exciting part of their work.

Another problematical expression of trait 11 arises from not recognizing the need for an exhilarating work life. These trait 11 types appear more Saturnian in temperament and are likely to select relatively routine jobs. Hopefully, interests exist for them outside of the work arena so that important needs for **excitement and stimulation** have some avenue of release. Otherwise, buried trait 11 needs build up in the psyche and unconsciously bring about sudden changes of an undesirable nature. The job could become obsolete, a new supervisor could come aboard who ruins things or the company could relocate to a different state. The possibilities are unpredictable because it is the nature of trait 11 to be unpredictable. When such circumstances arise, however, they often point to a need to make important changes. The purpose is to keep life fresh and exhilarating. When the vocational rug is suddenly pulled out in this manner, it can be a blessing in disguise. All people have to do is to be open to the needed changes they have unconsciously drawn to themselves.

Some **possible outlets for trait 11** might include –

- new technology, any aspect of the electronics industry, engineering, mathematics, science and the computer fields, the record industry, radio, television or other aspects of the broadcast media, electrician
- inventiveness: inventor, promoter, hobbyist, model maker, scientific invention
- being a consultant or a representative of a company/group
- not-for-profit organizations, charitable institutions or associations formed for the protection and advancement of a profession, that espouse a certain political bent or cause/humanitarian concern, fan clubs, societies
- the new age/consciousness-raising movement
- all group-related functions: seminars, workshops, conventions, professional group practice, musical group, particularly a rock band, any team sports
- the out of the ordinary, offbeat or "out of this world": astrologer, metaphysician, aerospace engineer, psychic, space explorer, technologist, science fiction writer,

astronomer, astronaut
- self- or part-time employment
- trait 3 (share air) or 10 (Saturn rules Aquarius and Capricorn) occupations

Trait 12:
Inspiration, Committed Beliefs, Intuition, Creative Imagination, Aesthetic Abilities, Other Worldliness, Caring Instincts, Scholarly Pursuits, Visionary Proclivities

ASTROLOGICAL CORRESPONDENCES :
- Sun, Moon, Mars, Saturn, Neptune, Ascendant-MC rulers in Pisces, in or ruling the twelfth house (especially Neptune in twelfth) or aspected by Neptune
- Ascendant or MC in Pisces or in aspect to Neptune
- Neptune as singleton, handle, leading or stationary planet or located six degrees from the angles
- Planets in the twelfth house or a Pisces stellium
- Neptune in or ruling the sixth house or in the tenth
- Balsamic Moon phase
- Void of Course Moon
- Splay pattern
- Singleton, handle or leading planet in Pisces or in the twelfth house
- Ruler of the twelfth in the twelfth house
- Ruler of the sixth in the twelfth house
- Either node in Pisces or in the twelfth house
- Intercepted planets
- Retrograde planets

Vocationally, trait 12 correlates with a yen to pursue **inspired, artistic or idealistic** goals based on strong, committed beliefs. It can appear in a number of different ways, as the astrological correspondences show. Although each facet is described in subsequent chapters, this trait is prominent when it appears in Level I, is involved in close aspects or when it is repeated through the layers of the chart.

Similar to trait 9, an accent on trait 12 can be the mark of the **accomplishing dreamer, genius or visionary.** A belief in self, the capabilities and the fortitude to act on one's dreams in a realistic fashion are vital to a grounded expression of this trait.

The everyday world does not tend to be openly supportive or convinced of the value of what one aspires to accomplish, or else in one's ability to do so. A need exists to be inner-directed, to stand alone, and to be alone, at times, to retreat and make repair from the world.

But an equal need exists to possess a sound reality quotient and to establish a firm emotional foundation through a strong sense of personal adequacy. Otherwise, one feels weak, inferior and helpless, or gets lost in hopes and wishes of how life "should" be. As with trait 9, **unreasonable goal expectations** can undermine what individuals might realistically achieve. When reality, effort and inner vision are not wholeheartedly combined, this trait can mark the **pipe dreamer**, the know-it-all **dilettante**, the con artist or the type D "lost soul." Menial, illicit or get-by employment may be the only work available because skills have not been developed. Job-hopping also can become standard due to being dissatisfied with common aspects of the work place. Some individuals prefer not working and choose (consciously or unconsciously) to be taken care of by others or by society. This is the E type personality.

Without **inner definition and commitment,** a spongy sense of self is left to soak in the most prevailing influences. Today, this often represents a need to become a "somebody." The ordinary nine-to-five working world can appear to be an abysmal waste of energy. Of all the traits, this one is the most dependent on the adequate functioning of what Saturn symbolizes: reality and effort. Without practicality, aspirational drives become diluted and evaporate into fantasies or other forms of escapism.

This is what has happened to Margot (see chart page 9). Although Saturn appears in Level I, suggesting her need for authority and distinction, trait 12 is pronounced in her chart. Because she fooled herself into believing that success should develop out of thin air, the need to develop competence did not seem reasonable to her. Besides, a commitment to accomplish something places people face-to-face with the potential to fail. Many ungrounded trait 12 types prefer to maintain the illusion that success can be theirs, as long as they avoid confronting their limitations. It is what keeps them on the run in the job world.

Because trait 12 is part of the water family, occupations

relying on the **creative imagination, the sensitivities, caring instincts or psychic skills** can represent suitable expressions. Traits 4 and 12 share many of the same vocational outlets. Additionally, the capacity for creative visualization can be quite strong, something which can be a blessing or a curse depending on how it is used. Because it is easy for trait 12 types, like Margot, to literally "see" themselves in any occupational role that strikes their fancy, it can be difficult to comprehend why their dreams do not become instant realities. Fantasies appear so plausible that it seems reasonable to wait for the opportunity to come knocking at their doors. Realistic trait 12 types utilize dreams, in conjunction with effort, commitment and developed competence, to get where they want to go. They feel connected to a higher plan, to God or whatever they define as a Higher Power in life. This connection stimulates belief in themselves, their devotion to good works and an awareness that they are never alone. They feel comforted by the knowledge that help will be there when it is needed. Their career potentials can be limitless.

An accent on trait 12 in a chart often indicates a sickly or disturbed relative in the early life over whom a great deal of sorrow or guilt was consciously, or more often unconsciously, experienced. The pain or guilt can remain hidden and drive some people to find solace in the heights of the limelight while others wish to make amends by attending to the needs of others. A third type unconsciously wants to escape from it all, which is why trait 12 can job-hop and fears a confrontation with self.

Many trait 12 people yearn for the heights of intellectual expression and **scholarly accomplishment.** Writing or lecturing can become desirable avenues through which to disseminate important ideas. For the trained and grounded mind, an accent on this trait can be indicative of an uncanny perceptual sense and an ability to synthesize facts in a manner that completely baffles the less astute personality. Neptune in Level I, in close aspect to personal planets or the Balsamic Moon phase could highlight these qualities. Again, the handling of the trait 10 function will be telltale about what can be accomplished. When the reality quotient is inadequate, opinions readily are confused with facts. While such individuals may be able to demonstrate insight, it will be fleeting with a catch-as-catch-can quality. These trait 12 persons imagine they know more or can do more than is the case. They get in over their heads occupationally. When they realize what is happening, they are likely to lay blame elsewhere or turn tail and run, rather than face failure.

Trait 12 is the most illusive factor in the chart and can be completely entangled in longings, yearnings and vague aspirational desires. The seemingly unreal can appear more real than reality and, certainly, more interesting.

Some **possible outlets for trait 12** might include –

- the caring instincts or catering to the important needs of (often downtrodden) others: health/mental health care, any hospital or nursing home work, radiologist, anesthesiologist, orderly, nurses' aide, dietician, psychotherapist, social worker, day care center worker/owner, worker for the elderly, poor or children
- art, performing arts, creative imagination or intellectual processes: romance or mystery novelist, poet, songwriter, playwright, painter, advertising copywriter, musician, dancer, philosopher, scientist, mathematician, physicist, chemist, biologist, historian
- the glamor industry or the making of illusions: fashion designer, entertainer, make-up artist, magician, actor, film producer, photographer, female impersonator, cosmetic/perfume sales, mirror manufacturer
- the use of the intuition: psychic, tarot reader, astrologer, palmist, therapist, etc.
- religious, spiritual or metaphysical pursuits: eastern philosophies, yoga, martial arts, Salvation Army, nun, priest, etc.
- small things: microbiology, miniatures, model making
- the otherworldly or infinitely boundless: oceanography, space exploration, science fiction
- the unconscious mind: psychologist, meditation, dream analysis, hypnosis, past life regression
- escapist activities: drug/alcohol rehabilitation counselor, bartender, liquor or wine sales, counselor for eating disorders
- trait 2, 4, 7 (shared aesthetic quality) or 9 (Jupiter and Neptune rule Pisces) occupations

References

1. Dobyns, Zipporah, *The Astrologer's Casebook*, Los Angeles, California: TIA Publications, 1973
2. Carter, Charles E.O., *The Principles of Astrology*, Wheaton, Illinois: Theosophical Publishing House, 1963, p. 92-3
3. Dean, Geoffrey, editor, *Recent Advances in Natal Astrology*, Western Australia: Analogic, 1977, p. 386-8
4. Rodden, Lois M., *The American Book of Charts*, San Diego, California: ACS Publications, Inc., 1980

CHAPTER THREE

APPLYING PERSONALITY DRIVES

Career-troubled people often have an identifiable problem underlying their vocational dissatisfaction, stemming from an inadequate or unclear self-image. But its ramifications may be unclear in their lives. Hemisphere emphasis and quadrant focus, when reduced to trait form, indicate fundamental life issues that must be faced before a purposeful career can be established. Although these traits are universally significant to appropriate vocational expression, they pertain to one's specific dilemmas.

In practice, these chart factors have been prone to misuse because they are mistakenly regarded as "quick and easy" synthesis techniques. They are not intended as such here. Hemisphere emphasis and quadrant focus do not represent prominent trends, except when their associated traits are repeated in the chart. Because everything in a chart modifies everything else, there are no cut and dried interpretations for any hemisphere orientation. Only a general frame of reference can be suggested.

The chart pattern, when reduced to its corresponding trait,

suggests an appropriate approach to the career and how to channel drives to obtain fulfilling results. The practical uses of chart patterns will be demonstrated later in this chapter.

Hemisphere Emphasis

Five interdependent personality functions underlie successful vocational expression. These are:

Mars-trait 1	(**initiative and identity**)-Eastern Hemisphere
Moon-trait 4	(**sense of personal adequacy and comfort with self**)-Northern Hemisphere
Venus-trait 7	(**rewarding talent and interpersonal relationship**)-Western Hemisphere
Saturn-trait 10	(**sense of competence, discipline and effort**)-Southern Hemisphere
Jupiter-trait 9	(**aspirational drives**)

Jupiter-trait 9 functions realistically **only** when the four primary functions have been adequately developed. These five personality functions are universally pertinent to rewarding vocational expression. They are the same planets the Gauquelins discovered as significant in the charts of highly successful professionals. A hemisphere emphasis, when reduced to trait form, suggests which one of the four primary functions requires attention. The trait represents the foundation to vocational expression. A failure to adequately develop this trait points to a flaw in the personality which underlies vocational difficulties or dissatisfaction. For example, an eastern hemisphere emphasis is assigned to trait 1. Career satisfaction rests on the degree to which the sense of identity, initiative, enterprise and self-assertive drives are operative in the personality. When trait 1 is not functionally developed, employment dissatisfaction will be experienced.

Hemisphere emphasis is determined by the number of planets occupying each of the four hemispheres. The nodes and other points in the chart are not counted because they do not represent energy in the psyche as do the planets. Six or more planets in a sphere constitutes an emphasis, the more planets, the greater the emphasis.

In some charts a house may contain several planets and its emphasized trait may appear to contradict a hemisphere orientation. For example, the sixth house could be filled in a chart with a western hemisphere focus. Typically trait 6 is more interested in working efficiently than in working with people. However, because this sphere is emphasized, the person tends to work closely with others and must have a developed interrelating capacity to function optimally. An overly pragmatic approach to others may not get the job done.

Should an equal number of planets occupy two spheres, use the following system to ascertain which contains the greater significance: Sun and Moon are given four points; Mercury, Venus and Mars are given three points each; Jupiter, Saturn and the Ascendant ruler each receive two while each outer planet is assigned one point. The less "personal" and consciously available is the energy symbolized by a planet, the less weight is given to that planet.

NORTHERN HEMISPHERE EMPHASIS – TRAIT 4 (LEVEL III)

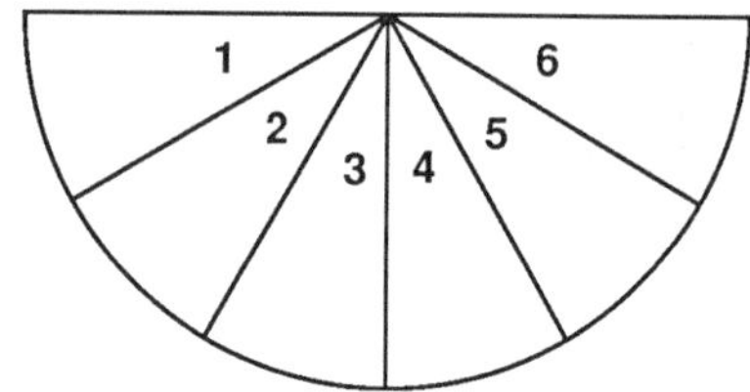

Inner security and a positive self-image are the foundation to vocational success. A northern emphasis suggests that these issues must be faced to pave the way for a fulfilling career. This is due, initially in life, to an uncertainty many feel over how to orient themselves to the outer world. The inclination is to be a bit self-limiting. Feelings of having something to "bear" or of being held back are not uncommon. The need to develop a sense of personal adequacy and self-image often exists. As soon as personal problems or a sense of inadequacy are overcome, the self-image escalates and the career ceiling elevates. This takes place earlier in life for some people than for others.

Positive or negative tendencies *vis à vis* the working world can be traced to the early home life. All trait 4 chart factors suggest this possibility. The more pronounced this trait is, the higher the probability that the family background has played a strong role in the career expression. The more healthy the family experience, and the more inspiring parental role models were, the more likely the career will reflect a positive family influence.

However, some northerners experienced their early lives as fraught with deep emotional rifts or bereavements not always dealt with in a constructive manner. They were thrown back on themselves with no one to depend on in childhood. How life unfolds for these adults depends on the individual response to this situation – how much constructive energy is generated to become a self-sufficient, responsible and self-directing human being. Uninspiring role models could have influenced these people to "get by" in the world of work. They may not push beyond safe, familiar limits. It is similar to owning a big house and choosing to live in only two rooms, never caring about what the rest of the place might have to offer. Potentials may not be tapped because these individuals are inclined to remain child-like or trapped by an inadequate self-image.

No feature in a chart condemns one to anything and the northern sphere is just as "good" or "bad" as the others. In its most productive expression, once personal adequacy is established, a sense of inner direction emerges. The person acts on life (trait 1) in a more self-expressive manner. The five vocationally significant traits are interdependent. Initiative and identity (associated with trait 1) rest on attaining a sense of personal adequacy and comfort with self (associated with trait 4). With inner security established, rewarding career goals become evident and contribute to advancement in work.

Famous northerners: Jim Arness, Marlon Brando, Carol Burnett, Albert Camus, Zsa Zsa Gabor, Michel Gauquelin, Jim Jones, Vivien Leigh, Jack Nicklaus, Pat Nixon, Leontyne Price, Barbra Streisand

EASTERN HEMISPHERE EMPHASIS – TRAIT 1 (LEVEL III)

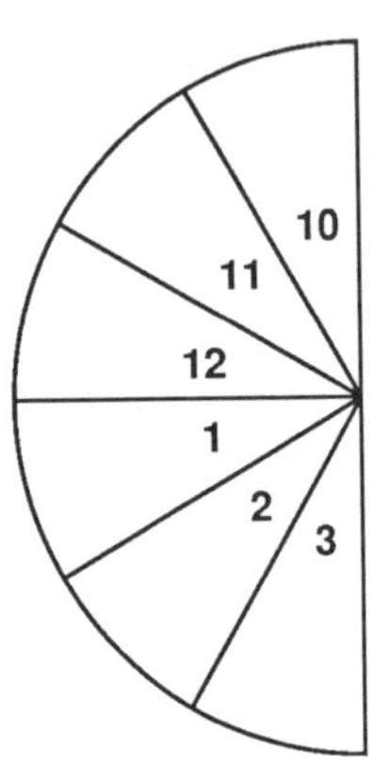

An emphasis in the eastern sphere suggests that an appropriate career expression rests on the sense of identity and initiative that can be exhibited by the person. One must act on life, take charge of it and develop a self-determined approach to an occupation. Drives must be aimed somewhere and striving is required at work, art or love. A sense of self solidifies from asserting energy out into the world and from the accomplishments which result. Demonstrating leadership, executive qualities or enterprise is important to vocational fulfillment. Accepting responsibility and standing on one's own two feet are imperative. Dependency issues or feelings of inadequacy undermine the needed "take charge" approach to life.

In well-directed striver types, who have developed a sense of identity (and adequacy), career building takes place steadily, usually through self-promoting occupations. These individuals want to make a mark in life and are often absorbed in their activities and goals.

Before this assault on life takes place, however, a fundamental belief in self must exist. The initiative of trait 1 rests on the grounding process associated with trait 4. Without internal comfort with self (trait 4), the external expression of identity (trait 1) is not likely to be thoroughly self-expressive. An individual must connect with a sense of identity and perceive that identity as being under one's control to identify a goal worth pursuing. Without an appropriate identity, how can people know what to "goal" for or where to aim themselves?

For easterners, lack of interests, striving or purpose in life wears like a mismatched suit. Dissatisfaction with work results whenever trait 1 characteristics are not adequately expressed. The problem stems from a diminished self-image and an overly self-protective attitude (trait 4). Steps must be taken to overcome this problem so that career striving can take place. When a firm sense of identity has been established, confidence, energy and the ability to act become marked in work.

Famous easterners: Ellen Burstyn, Johnny Carson, Chris Chubbuck, Ram Dass, Phyllis Diller, Francoise Gauquelin, Uri Geller, Diane Keaton, Caroline Kennedy, Jean Claude Killy, Guglielmo Marconi, Phoebe Snow

WESTERN HEMISPHERE EMPHASIS – TRAIT 7 (LEVEL III)

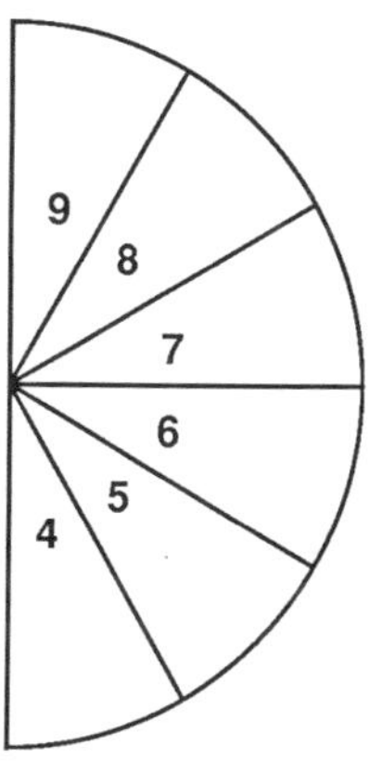

With a predominantly western orientation, the ability to functionally interrelate, if not to enjoy the company of others with whom one works, is important to a fulfilling vocational expression. This is because career motivation often comes **from the promptings, assistance or support of others, or one works closely with or through other people.**

Some westerners, however, perceive their lives as conditioned by others. They can lose the sense of self by living up to other people's expectations. This is not uncommon in charts featuring trait 7. Such individuals have failed to adequately develop the trait 1 and 4 functions in their personalities. It is difficult to relate to others appropriately when one is unsure of who one is or what one has to offer. Before proper career functioning can take place, and before sound relationships can be established, the self-image would have to be repaired and self-assertive drives would have to be developed. The fulfillment of trait 7 is dependent on the adequate formation of traits 1 and 4.

Another facet to the western hemisphere emphasis exists. Instead of being passive and easily imposed on, one acts **on** people, sometimes in a manipulative or dictatorial fashion. Other people may be expected to support one's endeavors and are often blamed when plans do not turn out as anticipated. The real problem may lie in one-sided habits of relating; give-and-take could be absent. Certain western-oriented individuals can be blind to their unreasonable expectations of others. If the career potential is to be realized, these types must develop a better interrelating capacity and learn how to be more cooperative with and considerate of others. Balanced interrelating skills contribute to vocational success.

Famous westerners: Jack Anderson, Fred Astaire, Warren Beatty, Ingrid Bergman, Clint Eastwood, Dorothy Hamill, Dustin Hoffman, Jean Houston, R.D. Laing, Isabelle Pagan, Helen Reddy, Suzanne Somers

SOUTHERN HEMISPHERE EMPHASIS – TRAIT 10 (LEVEL III)

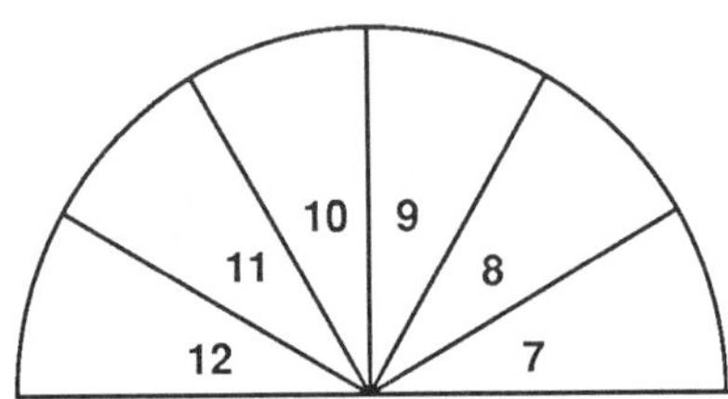

A sense of competence is integral to vocational expression. In charts with a southern emphasis, however, the issue is an imperative one. This hemisphere focus correlates with an awareness of having a place in society. Purpose is found through a **practical, achievement orientation to life.**

Such awareness can stimulate advancement needs to pull the self up by the bootstraps. For many southerners, a prestige-seeking nature emerges, through a desire for authority or distinction. The positive response is to acknowledge that diligent, persistent effort is required to earn prestige.

A less constructive response is to hope status will materialize without having to earn it. While such people consider themselves competent, they fail to apply sufficient effort to get the job done. They not only lack a realistic sense of their limits, but tend to be "out in left field" when it comes to understanding the "rules" of the working world. A lack of sustained, quality effort is the primary source of their career-related difficulties.

For other southerners, career difficulties stem from an inability to experience themselves as being competent. Because they see more limits to their capabilities or the career world than realistically exist, they do not develop themselves. The fulfillment of trait 10 is utterly dependent on the adequate formation of traits 1 and 4. People cannot experience themselves as competent to assume responsible roles when the sense of adequacy is faulty or when self-assertive drives are inadequately expressed.

When the self-image is diminished, low ceilings to career attainments are established. The need to be a person of distinction goes unfulfilled, unless one marries into it. When the self-image is grandiose, the person tends to be foolishly impatient and gives up on a field too quickly. Aspirational drives (trait 9) cannot be responded to adequately when one is riddled with a fear of failure or when insufficient effort is applied to fulfill goals. The willingness to be disciplined, practical and to work hard contributes greatly to eventual success.

Famous southerners: Muhammad Ali, Steve Allen, Arthur Ashe, Jacques Cousteau, Albert Einstein, Edna Ferber, Nina Foch, Morgana King, Princess Anne, Brooke Shields, Lotte Von Strahl, Natalie Wood

Quadrant Focus

This is determined by the quadrant which holds the most planets. When quadrants contain an equal number, use the point system to determine which possesses the greater significance. Nodes and the other non-planets are not counted.

Each quadrant also has been assigned to a trait pair. The combined drives are universal in their application: all people must express such drives to succeed vocationally. However, the individual quadrant focus suggests which of these universal themes is most significant to one's personal career development.

FIRST QUADRANT - TRAIT PAIR 1/4 (LEVEL III)

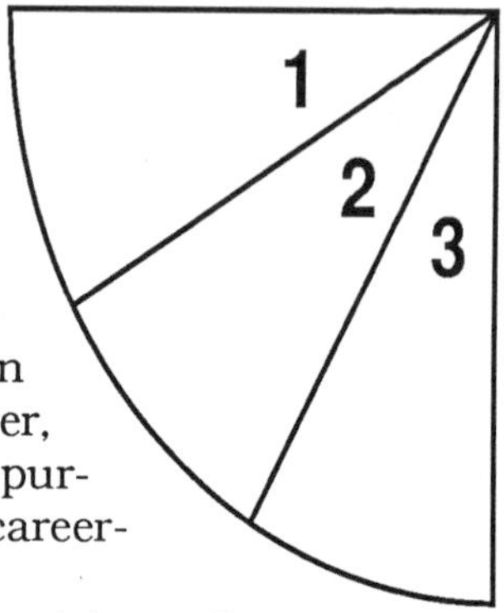

The first quadrant symbolizes achieving a sense of identity. It encompasses an eastern (trait 1) and northern (trait 4) orientation to a career. A focus here correlates with a need to discover who one is: "who am I, what am I worth." It accounts for the high degree of self-absorption which often accompanies this emphasis. However, one must focus in on self because purpose is found through developing career-related abilities.

For the self-secure first quadrant type, the more self-involving, "on the line," daring and emotionally charged the occupation or place of employment is, the better. Ambitions are stirred, one reason this quadrant focus is common to self-made people. An initial sense of adequacy (trait 4) prompts many to reach for the heights (trait 1).

Self-motivation (trait 1) and a positive self-image (trait 4) are essential. Otherwise, daring displays of talents do not materialize. In cases where the 1/4 theme is not functionally operative, one tends to lead a cocoon life of over self-protection which undermines aspirational drives and fosters a "get-by" approach to work. The view of self and what can be achieved tends to be limited. Therapy or personal development may be needed before appropriate career directions can be ascertained. This frees up the personality so that drives can be channeled more productively in the outer world. A firm sense of inner security (trait 4) and an ability to assert oneself (trait 1) cannot help but pay dividends in the work arena. (Refer to Chapter 5 for further discussion of this trait pair.)

Famous first quads: Jim Arness, Carol Burnett, Ellen Burstyn, Albert Camus, Johnny Carson, Chris Chubbuck, Phyllis Diller, Uri Geller, Jim Jones, Diane Keaton, Vivien Leigh, Pat Nixon, Leontyne Price, Phoebe Snow, Barbra Streisand

SECOND QUADRANT FOCUS – TRAIT PAIR 4/7 (LEVEL III)

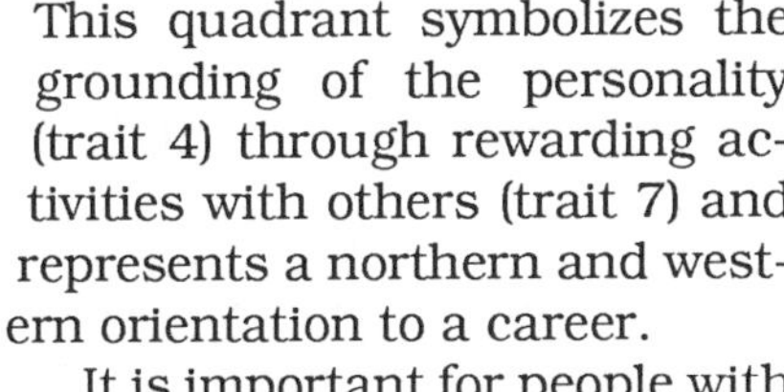

This quadrant symbolizes the grounding of the personality (trait 4) through rewarding activities with others (trait 7) and represents a northern and western orientation to a career.

It is important for people with a second quad focus, or the 4/7 theme repeated in their charts, to find work pleasurable. They often work best with a partner or loved one who shares the same interests or others may support their efforts, for example, as a trainer, secretary, editor or agent. The company of those with whom they work is vital to job satisfaction. The trust factor has to be high. Dissatisfaction with work may have little to do with job duties, but rather may stem from uncomfortable interactions there.

For other second quad types, dependency issues are problematic and someone else may be leaned on too much for motivation, direction or assistance. This can degenerate into "serving" the other party as a way to maintain support. It might lead to not working, sometimes due to laziness, a lack of ambition or illness. The reverse holds true for a third type who serves other people in the highest sense of the term.

Some of the best counselors and skilled technical types can be found with this quadrant focused. Anyone who is willing to expend vast amounts of energy in the service of others may have this emphasis. Instead of looking for support, they **provide** support, often of an emotional nature or a highly talented skill. These people express the highest potentials of a 4/7 theme. (Refer to Chapter 5 for further discussion of this trait pair.)

How the early home was experienced is perhaps most crucial when this quadrant focus exists. Second quad types are highly susceptible to family issues and role models, especially when trait 4 is otherwise represented in their charts. The more difficult the home was perceived as being, the higher the probability that psychological repair will have to take place before career satisfaction can be achieved. Some individuals can be held up when a strong sense of inner security (trait 4) has not been developed. The poor self-image creates low job ceilings and forecloses on satisfying relationship outlets which are significant to these people.

When inner security needs have been met, highly personal talents or interests (4/7) are pursued with all the force and gusto of a linebacker. This second quadrant type tends to be strongly absorbed in work precisely due to the interest in it or the pleasure (4/7) derived from it, thus creating a fulfilling vocational experience.

Famous second quads: Jack Anderson, Fred Astaire, Marlon Brando, Zsa Zsa Gabor, Michel Gauquelin, Dorothy Hamill, Rob Hand, Victor Hugo, Jack Nicklaus, Isabelle Pagan, Suzanne Somers

THIRD QUADRANT FOCUS – TRAIT PAIR 7/10 (LEVEL III)

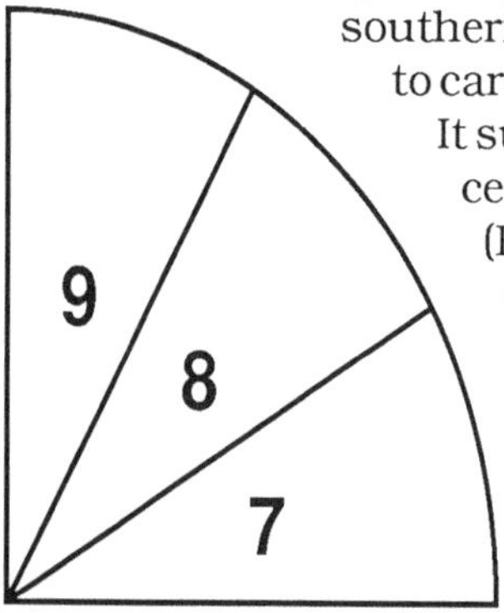

This quadrant overlaps the western (trait 7) and southern hemispheres (trait 10) and points to career activities involving close others. It suggests that a rewarding career necessitates developing the 7/10 theme. (Refer to Chapter 5 for further discussion of this trait pair.) It rotates around the "Golden Rule" and requires one to be responsible toward others and to understand that talent (trait 7) takes time and effort (trait 10) to develop.

A need exists to have (or be) a partner, but not for reasons of identity grounding as in the second quadrant. In some instances, a third quadrant focus can represent the person who is married to the career. In other cases, the issues become confused and one can instigate relationships for money, status or reasons other than love. The relationship may be used to enhance the public image or to assist vocational endeavors. This approach muddles up the career. Too much emphasis may be placed on expecting people to help one get ahead, even to the extent of using them.

When the 7/10 theme is not adequately incorporated into

the career expression, damage to the reputation and abandonment by even the heartiest of supporters is at risk. This can be true whenever the 7/10 theme is highlighted in a chart. Because "getting ahead" can be a strong need, give-and-take may be absent. People could be so wrapped up in getting somewhere that the work process does not receive proper attention. Blaming others is easier on the ego than accepting responsibility for work efforts that have not been up to par.

In most other cases, healthy interpersonal concerns are as important as self-establishment in society. Efforts are joined more equally with a business partner or spouse. Such teamwork often makes the occupation more enjoyable or more profitable. Creative flair, artistic expression or dealings with the public also may figure into work.

For still another third quadrant type, relying on others goes to extremes. One needs people to create the structure through which work takes place. This is a less constructive expression of the 7/10 theme. Self-motivation tends to be lacking. Close supervision by superiors may be required because the person has failed to adequately develop career-related abilities and/or interrelating skills. But shyness in interpersonal affairs is about as helpful to career advancement as drinking a bottle of poison. Steps must be taken to clear up the problem before a career can flourish.

Feelings of being used sometimes surface. How much recognition for one's job contributions is received from those above can affect such feelings. Resentment for work, or for those in authority, can develop from a lack of recognition or when the individual is given insufficient opportunity to exercise independent decision-making. Rather than blaming the boss, it would be advisable for the person to look within for the source of the difficulty. Work efforts might not have been up to snuff or interrelating skills could be deficient. Once responsibility has been assumed for enhancing career abilities and the interrelating capacity, this person can look forward to a more fulfilling occupational experience.

Famous third quads: Steve Allen, Warren Beatty, Ingrid Bergman, Sean Connery, Jacques Cousteau, Clint Eastwood, Dustin Hoffman, Jean Houston, R.D. Laing, Helen Reddy, Brooke Shields

FOURTH QUADRANT FOCUS – TRAIT PAIR 1/10 (LEVEL III)

The fourth quadrant combines the eastern and southern hemispheres. It relates to striving (trait 1) for a place in society (trait 10) so that contributions can be made to a greater whole – a company, community, profession or humanity at large. When this quadrant is emphasized, a purposeful, self-expressive career, not merely a job, is an important need. Most fourth quadrant types long for recognition and want to have impact. When drives are productively channeled, and the 1/10 theme is well developed, the determination to make a mark in life exists. These people can be accomplishing dreamers who tackle obstacles and know no career boundaries. Something avant garde, inventive or out of the ordinary can be executed through the career, provided ability and effort are in evidence. (Refer to Chapter 5 for further discussion of this trait pair.)

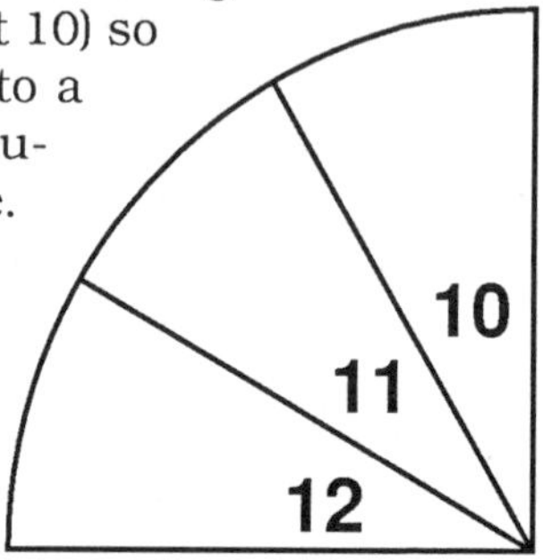

10
11
12

In addition to disciplined effort and a practical view of reality, an undying belief in self and in the capabilities must exist. Without these qualities, fourth quadrant types float through life and a career. Fear of failure and unrealistic goal expectations are factors that most undermine the work effort. Without positive striving and a sensible goal (1/10), meaninglessness surfaces because the need to have impact is so strong. It can drive some people to the verge of a nervous breakdown when the desire to be "somebody" collides with a less than fulfilling work life.

The reality quotient and willingness to exert **quality** effort (1/10) separate a dreamer from a pipe dreamer. The fourth quadrant person has to be careful that the occupation sustains a reasonable livelihood and that the proper abilities and discipline exist to make the dream come true. It is easy to fool oneself about career goals here. When expectations exceed reality, or when effort is not truly applied, the fourth quadrant type can turn into a dilettante or live-off-others-type; job-hopping can be problematical.

A sense of purpose and contribution to a greater whole is vitally important to this quadrant focus (or 1/10 type). For some people a cause orientation emerges through the occupation or they work for an organization formed for the protection of a certain field or profession. For others, only more lofty causes can contribute to their elevated need fulfillment. This is why discipline, effort and unrelenting striving are so necessary. It takes a well developed 1/10 component to the personality to turn vocational dreams into reality.

Famous fourth quads: Muhammad Ali, Ram Dass, Albert Einstein, Nina Foch, Pancho Gonzales, Jimi Hendrix, Caroline Kennedy, Morgana King, Princess Anne, Lotte Von Strahl, Natalie Wood

The hemisphere emphasis and quadrant focus represent personality traits which must be functionally operative before a viable career is likely to be established. How personality **drives** need to be **applied** for the best vocational results is the domain of the chart pattern, originated by Marc Edmund Jones.[1] Although Jones did not classify patterns according to personality traits, they have been so classified here.

Chart Patterns

Jones grouped charts according to seven different patterns. (The nodes and other points in a chart are excluded when defining a pattern.) The trait associated with a pattern suggests ways in which personality drives must be applied on the job, or through a career, for it to be rewarding. This trait is significant of a suitable occupation only when it is repeated through the layers of the chart. When the five vocationally significant traits are not thoroughly developed, interpretations for less constructive applications of the chart pattern traits are presented. Pay attention to the famous examples provided. Most tend to express through their occupations the higher potentials of the traits symbolized by the chart patterns.

To better conceptualize how hemisphere emphasis, quadrant focus and the chart pattern interrelate, consider Cher's chart. It has an eastern hemisphere emphasis (trait 1), fourth quadrant focus (1/10) and a bucket pattern (trait 5). Only general career needs and drives will be indicated at this stage of the analysis.

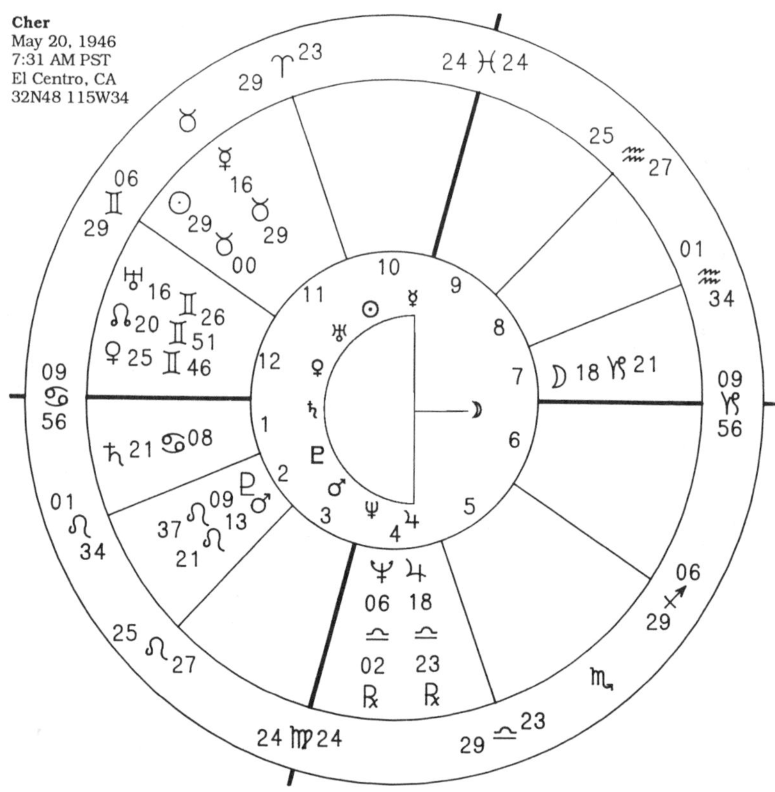

This individual must have traits 1 and 10 well developed in her personality before her career potentials can be realized fully. She must work hard to establish a self-expressive, self-promoting career. A mere job is not likely to be sufficiently rewarding due to an elevated need to make a name for herself and to impact her profession. Her ability to demonstrate initiative, effort, competence, executive-like qualities, leadership and to strive to be the best represent the foundation to her vocational fulfillment (traits 1 and 10).

As part of her overall career game plan, she must also channel her drives through trait 5, representing the bucket pattern. For Cher, this took place through her impressive capacities as a singer, entertainer, commedienne and, later, as a highly gifted dramatic actress. Few women have achieved the heights of success along such divergent lines. Playing to an audience (trait 5) must be in her blood, although playing second fiddle (to Sonny) was not. She has become a “star” (trait 5) through a combination of executive ability (trait 1) and the bootstrap approach (trait pair 1/10).

Some patterns are structured in such a way as to highlight a planet or planets and thereby pinpoint certain personality needs and drives. These pattern focal points are referred to as “handle” and “leading” planets. The traits they symbolize are among the primary vocational need factors a chart can demonstrate and, therefore, are included in Level I of the analysis (see Chapter 4). In Cher’s chart the Moon represents the handle of the bucket while Mercury holds the leading position.

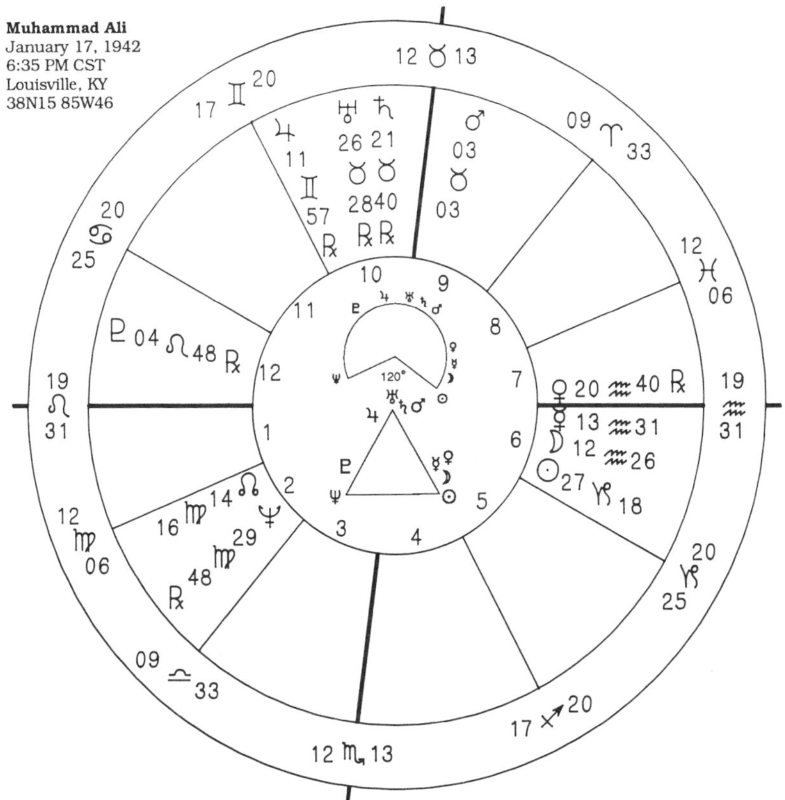

Some charts can be classified as two or more patterns. For example, Muhammad Ali’s chart could be a locomotive (focalizing the Sun in the leading position) or a splay (focalizing Neptune), depending on the size allowed for gaps.

With careful thought, it is possible to realistically classify most charts by one of the seven patterns, although there will be exceptions. In such cases, it is better to forego in the analysis the trait(s) associated with the chart pattern.

THE SEESAW – TRAITS 2 AND 7 (LEVEL III)

This pattern is present whenever planets appear in two groups roughly positioned opposite each other. Ideally, there should be at least one opposition aspect between the two groups with an open space of 90 degrees separating them on one side and 60 degrees on the other. The grouping can be as few as two planets on one side versus eight on the other, or a more even distribution. Ordinarily it does not possess a "focalized" planet. However, a planet can be focalized when it is the only one outside the boundaries of the encompassing oppositions and is separated by 15 or more degrees. The trait(s) associated with that planet

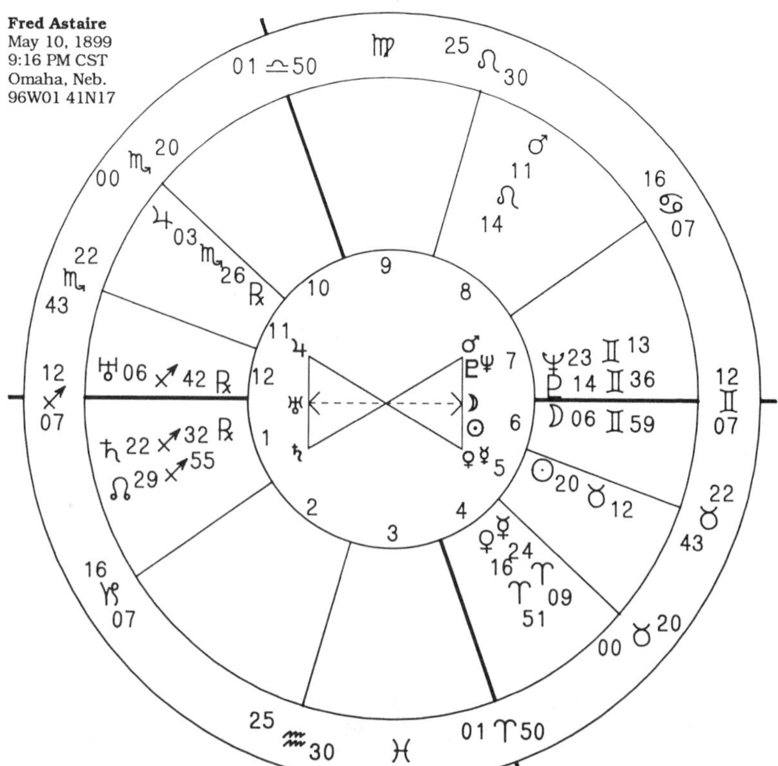

would be circled under Level I, indicating the planet's significance in the analysis.

Although Fred Astaire's chart does not display a focalized planet, this beloved star made entertaining use of the seesaw pattern throughout his long-enduring career. He and his sister became a famous dance team from their first hit in 1916. Later he paired up with Ginger Rogers.

The seesaw pattern correlates with trait 7 vocational drives, but equally exhibits those belonging to trait 2 (see Chapter 5). Conducting vocational activities cooperatively with or through others is one constructive use of these drives. The personality often is gracious, refined or sociable. Should a western orientation exist in this chart, trait 7 vocational needs and drives would begin to grow in importance, but would have to be confirmed elsewhere in the chart to establish a firm trend. Venus, for example, as a G-planet or focalized in this pattern would be sufficient evidence. The occupation may need to encompass close or intermittent one-to-one encounters, a partnership arrangement, dealings with the public or it could be enhanced by good looks and charm.

Depending on interests and abilities, artistic talents, the performing arts, beautiful objects or the handling of cash could play a role. However, whenever trait 2 or 7 is sufficiently emphasized in a chart, the ease and remunerative aspects of the work can figure strongly into vocational choice. Individuals who are uncertain of their creative worth are tempted to sell out to such factors and get by on the job. This is not the most rewarding use of trait 2 or 7.

Some people act kindly, motherly or fatherly. Being "nice," cheerful or thoughtful can be their way of life. But they lose a sense of identity when this behavior is insincere. Some individuals with seesaws or trait 7 prominent in their charts easily slip into being nice, especially those who experienced early family dissensions or separations – also not uncommon to this trait. Some found themselves caught in the squeeze and had to take sides or act the diplomat amidst parental differences. Acting nice or cheerful was a way to stay out of the line of fire, and helped to soothe an already tense environment. This habit of relating could become second nature and persist into adulthood until it is changed. Although it could well equip them for occupations which require a diplomatic approach to others,

false role playing diminishes effectiveness in the working world.

In a different family atmosphere, one more reflective of the trait 2 side of the pattern, parents might have "acted" nice on the surface, simply suppressing conflicts, and the person might grow up to do the same. This does not mean that all individuals with a seesaw pattern respond in kind to parental disputes. People can learn from parental example exactly how not to act as much as they can imitate inappropriate behavior. Still, normal, healthy interrelating skills may not have been adequately learned and may have to be developed later. A "nice" seesaw person may not really be all that nice, but may have grown into the habit of acting that way for fear of what **not** being nice might do. Underneath the behavior is an individual caught in a bind between acting sweet on the surface versus expressing aggression (not uncommon to trait 2 or 7). This is why the person may appear "torn" or struggle over how to project the self at times.

Whenever one side of the personality has taken over exclusive expression to the neglect of the other, seesaws may find themselves torn by guilt or second guessing. It is advisable to eliminate the role-playing tendencies. Otherwise, coworkers who appear more self-assured are likely to step ahead when promotions are given. Achieving a balanced sense of identity comes in time, provided the aggressive versus the complacent features are acknowledged and integrated. People then become strongly directed with an ability to work closely with others and/or to express rewarding talents.

Famous seesaws: Fred Astaire, Ingrid Bergman, Albert Camus, Zsa Zsa Gabor, Françoise Gauquelin, Andre Gide, R.D.Laing, Henry Cabot Lodge, Rip Torn, Lotte Von Strahl

THE BUNDLE – TRAITS 3 AND 6 (LEVEL III)

This pattern manifests as a self-contained bundle of energy, but how people choose to apply their busy bee drives is dependent on the commitment to developing the mental faculties and communicative skills. Two different approaches to work can be seen, depending on these factors.

Ideally, all ten planets should be contained within a span of approximately 120 degrees (anywhere from 0 to 150 degrees).

It is the least common chart pattern. Look for the planet in the group which would be first to rise and cross the Ascendant. It is the "leading" planet. The trait it symbolizes plays a significant role in the career and suggests activities or approaches through which bundle drives best can be fulfilled. Note the eye surgeon's chart on page 38. It displays an ideal bundle pattern with Uranus in the leading position.

Bundle people tend to be busy all the time with endless plans, schedules and things that must be done. Space and freedom to come and go almost as they please are needed as part of the daily work routine. The mind also tends to be preoccupied. The thinking, analyzing or figuring things out that transpires would make most heads spin. Bundles also have busy hands which often are engaged in important work-related tasks, or else they need to do a great deal of talking or walking on the job. Life is commonly filled with many interests, people and activities, including meetings, telephone conversations, errands and driving or traveling. Boredom easily results whenever work routines fail to incorporate such diverse trait 3 or 6 activities (see Chapter 2).

Some people with bundle charts are compact, tidy parcels; efficiency and a detail orientation can become a way of life for those who reflect the trait 6 side of this pattern. They specialize in a field and readily attract clients, students, patients or customers. Occupations catering to them can be especially profitable. They are serious about their work and perfect their abilities, analytical skills or whatever service they perform. Work becomes important to their self-expression.

The pattern's trait 3 tendencies are completely different. People who reflect this side of the pattern find interests outside of work more rewarding. Some can be described as hyper, nervous or scattered, mostly when air or mutability predominates (Chapter 8). They are less serious about their work and more inclined to "get by" with a job. Although these bundles may be constantly busy doing "things," they do not necessarily have to be constructive. Purpose in life would depend on what their outside activities entailed.

Famous bundles: Chris Chubbuck, Anatole France, Mick Jagger, Tom Jones, Rockwell Kent, Jean Claude Killy, Benito Mussolini, Ringo Starr, Igor Stravinsky, Billy Joe Thomas

THE BOWL – TRAIT 4 (LEVEL III)

With this pattern, all planets should occupy a span of approximately 180 degrees (anywhere from 150 to 210 degrees) preferably without any gaps separating them by more than 67 degrees. Look for the leading planet. It is the first in the grouping to rise and cross the Ascendant in its diurnal motion. The trait it symbolizes plays a significant role in the career and suggests activities or approaches through which trait 4 drives can be productively channeled. Ideally, the leading planet should be in opposition to another planet, the aspect between them representing the "rim" of the bowl structure, but this is not always found.

The bowl suggests that the career game plan should include sensitivities, intuition, creative imagination or a service that assists others. Work conducted out of the home, or close to it, is another suitable outlet for sensitive bowl drives (see Chapter 2 for additional outlets). Depending on how trait 1 is situated in the chart, face-to-face, competitive occupations may not be the most rewarding. Additionally, the pattern may be a clue that the early family, or the most influential parental figure, has had an influence on the career choice and achievement ceiling, usually as a positive or negative role model. The sense of personal adequacy also is pertinent to how this individual functions; the higher this sense, the higher the career ceiling.

Orson Welles' chart is a good example of the bowl pattern, although the rim opposition is not displayed. (Notice the structure spans less than 180 degrees.) Uranus is in the leading position and suggests his need to channel career drives through an inventive, original, sometimes avant garde or brilliant (trait 11) creative imagination (trait 4) which might include writing or the performing arts. He pursued both, in addition to being a director and producer. He managed to "shock" the nation with his 1938 radio broadcast of *War of the Worlds*.

If his interests had been different, he might have turned his attention to assisting occupations and utilized his sensitivities along different lines. For example, he could have become an astrologer or used a capacity for public speaking (trait 4) to head conferences, seminars or organizations (trait 11) designed to assist others. Traits 4 and 11 also suggest that emotional fulfillment (trait 4) could come about through colleague recognition (trait 11), such as Welles earned from his peers when he

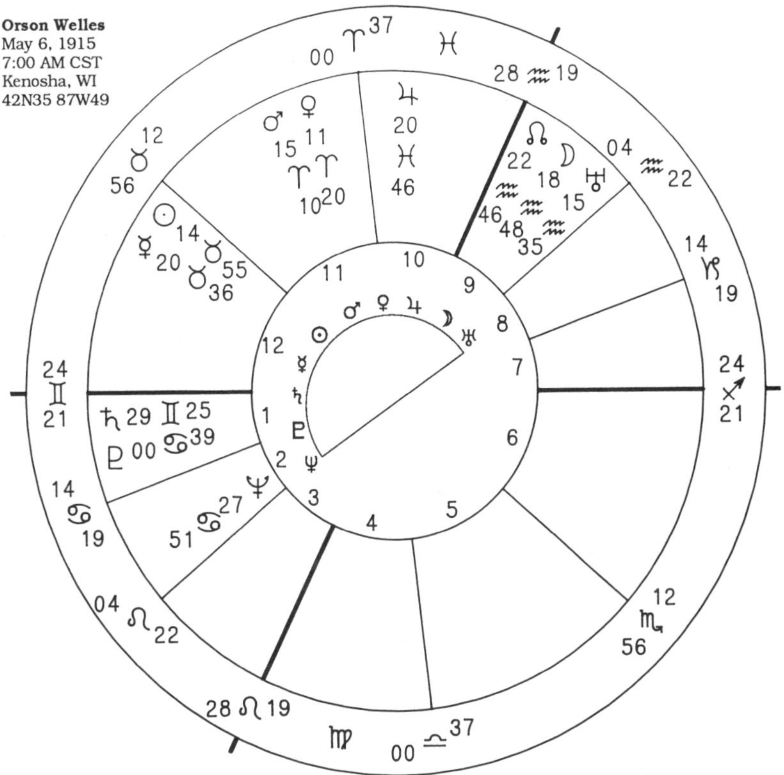

was an Oscar nominee for best actor in his film classic, *Citizen Kane.*

Bowl drives function least adequately when people are locked in a self-limiting shell. They feel different, inadequate or like strangers in a strange land. Attaining a sense of belonging to the early home frequently has been hampered. They may have felt held back or pushed to the sidelines as children. Some believe they harbor a secret talent, a special skill or mission to perform. They need to feel needed even when that can be achieved only through imaginary outlets.

As Jones[2] writes, this pattern correlates with the person who has something to give to others. It can come in the form of a special talent (like Welles), emotional support, knowledge or other forms of assisting. However, until a solid self-image has been established, that special talent may not be discovered or put to best use. The self-limiting bowl person can entrench along safe, familiar job courses, when breaking out of the shell may be needed to experience a fuller vocational life. Learning to face fears, especially a fear of failure, can be a top priority. Once an appropriate self-image is established, the person is likely to be more self-directing. Drives are free to channel more constructively through trait 4 vocational approaches (see Chapter 2). A solid sense of adequacy opens up career potentials to more elevated possibilities.

Famous bowlers: Arthur Ashe, Edna Ferber, Uri Geller, Ernest Hemingway, Jimi Hendrix, Caroline Kennedy, Fritz Perls, Suzanne Somers, Barbra Streisand, Orson Welles

THE BUCKET – TRAIT 5 (4) (LEVEL III)

This structure is identical to the bowl, and trait 4 overtones are present, except one planet, called the "handle", adds an extra, dynamic feature. Ideally, this planet should be separate from the grouping by at least 67 degrees. The drives and personality needs symbolized significantly relate to career directions, needs and objectives. For example, a Jupiter (trait 9) handle would emphasize a need to conduct bucket drives through occupations which bring advancement, spread one's influence or reflect important beliefs. The bowl grouping can span anywhere from less than 90 degrees to 210 degrees and still conform to the bucket definition.

The leading planet in the bucket pattern (the first planet in the bowl grouping to rise and cross the Ascendant) also must be included in the analysis. For example, Mars and Jupiter represent similar extroverted drives which, if not constructively channeled by the individual, could push bucket drives to overly aggressive or overblown extremes. Saturn in one of these positions indicates toned down drives. The individual could be more serious, committed and inclined to seek tangible achievement through a trait 5 endeavor.

As opposed to the more held-in or self-contained manner of the bowl pattern, bucket people must strive toward goals that bring recognition and rely on spontaneous creativity, impromptu self-expression or leadership abilities. The occupation **must** be experienced as fun and interesting, and represent an intimate expression of self. Without such outlets, the vocation is not likely to be experienced as thoroughly fulfilling. The underlying bowl structure also correlates with trait 4's anxiety over the sense of personal adequacy, a factor not unknown to trait 5 consciousness. When the sense of adequacy has not been established, self-help programs or therapy may be needed to enhance the career expression. When this issue is properly dealt with, a determined goal orientation and executive drive are likely to exist, especially if trait 1 or 9 also is accented in the chart. This type tends to push to the forefront of an occupation and become the star, numero uno, the boss or the leader of the pack. Playing second fiddle may be difficult and close supervision chokes the creative output. Besides, bucket types may never believe the boss's ideas are as good as their own.

Apart from the business community, bucket drives can be successfully directed through a service, creative/aesthetic outlets, or having an audience as part of the job or outside of the work arena. Creative hobbies or sports can contribute to a greater sense of enjoyment or perhaps children (including preteen or teenaged) can figure into the work, as in teaching or counseling. Everything depends on individual interests. Other outlets suitable to trait 5 are covered in Chapter 2.

When feelings of inadequacy are not overcome, insecurity mixes with leadership needs and touchy, overly sensitive, unreasonable personalities can result. These individuals may have had parental figures who overly praised or dismissed and laughed at the self-expressive needs of their child. Under such circumstances, people later grow to crave attention or repress this need. The latter is the least productive response because energies bottle up to the explosion point or are turned in on the self. Appropriate careers may be out of reach until the sense of adequacy is established (but this is frequently true of trait 5). Career challenges are met with a defeatist attitude or frustration and anger arise whenever roadblocks appear.

At certain extremes, controlling the temper can be a problem, while others report feeling "tired." The tired feeling, however, may be an unconscious attempt to avoid facing challenges so that individuals can remain safe within the confines of a shell. Because bucket drives must be channeled through trait 5 approaches, these types should take the necessary steps to enhance their self-esteem. Once this happens, trait 5 drives can be successfully applied in a manner that makes work a more fulfilling experience.

Johnny Carson's chart is an excellent example of the bucket type. A tight rim opposition exists between Jupiter and Pluto and no gaps greater than 67 degrees exist. Uranus, in the fifth house, represents the handle planet. Notice the important repetition of trait 5 which encompasses the entertainment industry or occupations which rely on extemporaneous self-expression. Pluto represents the leading planet and suggests Carson's desire to throw himself into his work, something he has been doing since 1957 when he became the quizmaster of the TV (trait 11) game show (trait 5) *Who Do You Trust*. Later he became the long-enduring host for NBC's *Tonight Show*.

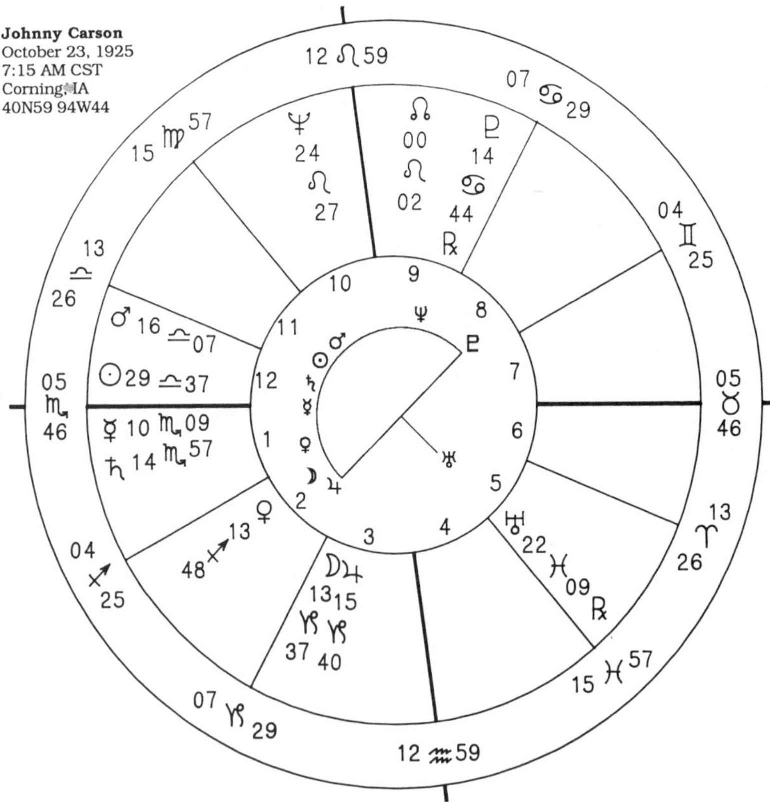

Famous buckets: Carol Burnett, Johnny Carson, Cher, Jacques Cousteau, Albert Einstein, Morgana King, Robert Mathias, Pat Nixon, Leontyne Price, Vincent Price, Ira Progoff, Marcel Proost

THE LOCOMOTIVE - TRAITS 1 AND 8 (LEVEL III)

In this pattern all ten planets ideally should be distributed evenly throughout a span of roughly 240 degrees (anywhere from 210 to 270 degrees), leaving an open space of approximately 120 degrees. The leading planet is the first in the group to rise and cross the Ascendant. The trait associated with it figures prominently into the career. Ideally, the pattern should contain a grand trine configuration and no other open spaces greater than 67 degrees, although the latter is the least significant and the former is not always present.

When locomotive types are self-secure, they prefer to work under their own direction, in their own way, and the ability to compromise may not always exist (partially depending on trait 7 features of the chart). They would rather be in charge of others or in charge of themselves. They are independent-minded and display a self-driving, do-or-die quality with a passionate desire to leave their mark. They throw themselves into their work, often appearing to obsess over it. If employed by others, very independent jobs are essential. Otherwise, dissatisfaction is likely to result. Depending on how pronounced a trait it is, trait 1 or 8 occupations may be suitable (see Chapter 2). However, the job is likely to be satisfying when it can be approached in a passionate trait 8 fashion.

Although a gap of more than 67 degrees exists between the Sun and Pluto, Jean Houston's chart can be considered a locomotive type. Mars in Capricorn is the leading planet for this top humanistic psychologist, author and researcher. Here is an individual who needs to pour every ounce of her being (trait 8) into her work with an unrelenting commitment (trait 8) to break new ground and do the best job she knows how to do (trait 1). Because she also has a loaded eighth house, the trait 8 quality to her personality should be quite strong. It is no wonder that psychology, research and the need to delve deeply into human behavior (trait 8) represent important facets of her occupational expression.

This pattern (or trait 8) also suggests that power tends to become a major career issue and often a bottom line motivation for the career choice. Many locomotives wish to have power and set out on a career course to acquire it. Although power can surface as a desire for wealth, it can appear in many other forms, as discussed in Chapter 2. The job must actively

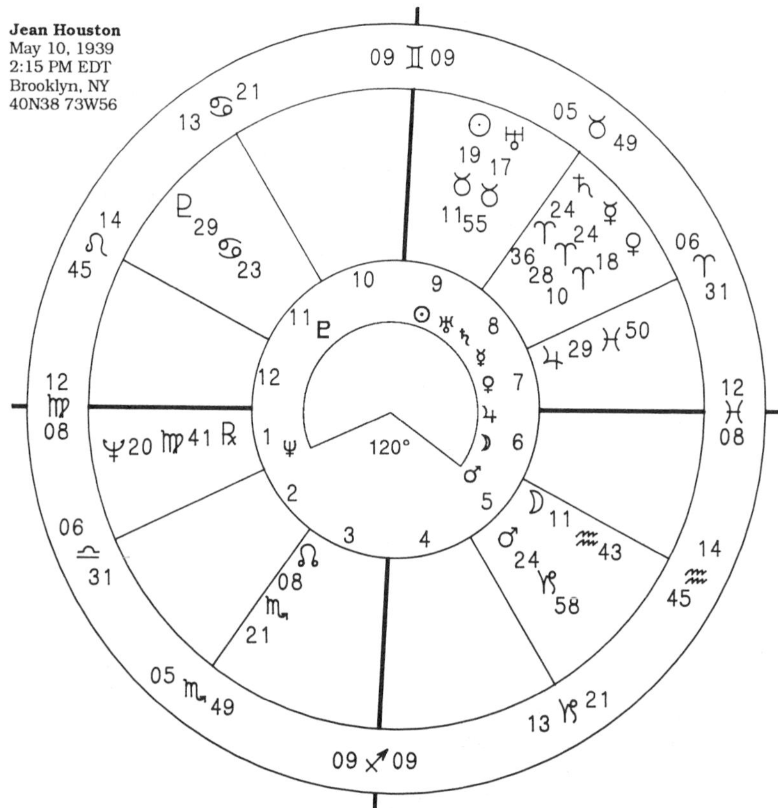

demonstrate some form of power to be rewarding. In many instances, the corporate, executive world is ideal for locomotive types, however, other trait 8 occupations can be equally suitable.

Safe, boring, noncommittal jobs are all wrong for locomotives. Power and passion need to be displayed somewhere. When suppressed in the personality, power haunts people in the form of horrendous relationship run-ins, mean, uncaring bosses, romantic obsessions with charismatic personalities or feelings of dread and of being overwhelmed. In such cases the locomotive pattern can indicate individuals who must develop a more powerful, determined or resourceful approach to their careers. They often appear disturbingly reticent, which does not inspire the confidence of superiors or job interviewers. They need counseling or assertiveness training before appropriate job expressions can be established (see Chapter 2). Once inner power is tapped, new approaches and new career vistas become available.

Famous locomotives: Muhammad Ali (could be a splay), Steve Allen, Jack Anderson, Jim Arness, Jean Houston, Diane Keaton, Jack Nicklaus, Isabelle Pagan, Ronald Reagan, Helen Reddy

THE SPLAY - TRAITS 9 AND 12 (LEVEL III)

This can be a difficult pattern to identify because it is easy to mistake it for others, mostly the seesaw or locomotive. In the splay pattern, planets are supposed to cluster in three separate, distinct groups of roughly 60 degrees each. Ideally a grand trine configuration should be present to link them, although this is not always found. A planet can be focalized when it is the only one to represent one of the legs of the grand trine, but this is rarely present. The pattern correlates with trait 9 vocational drives or outlets, but it also encompasses those belonging to trait 12 because Jupiter co-rules Sagittarius and Pisces. Refer to Chapter 2 for the discussions on these traits.

Splays often seek fame or excellence, although few become sure of themselves until their talents gain exposure in the world. But their reality quotients and self-images must be firmly intact to attain the heights. An occupation built on a house of cards never lasts long.

Warren Beatty's chart provides a good example of the splay type. Notice the close grand water trine and how each of the three groupings of planets is contained within a span of approximately 60 degrees. From an early age, Beatty has been involved in the performing arts. He is an accomplished pianist, a fine director and was nominated for an Oscar as best actor for his role in *Bonnie and Clyde.*

Splays often select a career course early in life and do not deviate from it. A dream captures their interests and they nurture it over time. An urge exists to make a mark, to become known or to promulgate a certain point of view about the profession or life in general. Beliefs or aspirations, sometimes of a spiritual, religious or otherworldly nature, become the breath of life to these people, and tend to be apparent through their vocations. Some suddenly switch to an entirely different field or create a totally new approach to the current one. The

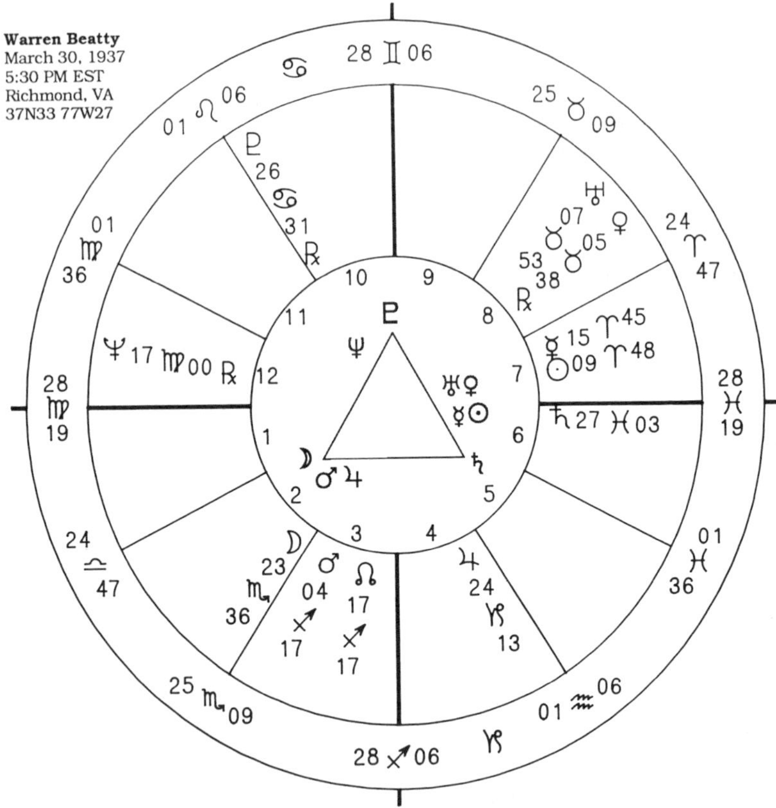

change usually results from a yen to promote their ideas or to experience greater purpose than what the old occupation permitted. The desire to always accomplish more, to grow in consciousness, to have more influence or to become famous exists as an internalized longing. Traits 9 and 12, in a constructive sense, represent accomplishing dreamers who know no career bounds.

However, traits 9 and 12 also can correlate with pipe dreamers. Everything depends on the expenditure of quality effort, a factor which relates to the reality quotient and trait 10. Difficulty selecting an appropriate career or an inability to function adequately in the job world results when splays lack constructive interests, beliefs, effort quotients or possess false self-images. A longing for glamor, wealth or a fantasy success emerge in their place. They spend more time talking about lofty futures than applying effort. This typically leads to job-hopping or to fizzling out in a career. They may never settle on a constructive path for long. Foundations are what hold up a structure, but for these types, there is not enough "support" from within to fortify lasting achievements.

The accomplishing dreamers of the group are distinguished by their ability to persist, maintain their principles and to have enough faith in a Higher Power to trust that things will work out. They believe in the value of what they are doing and in their capacity to fulfill their dreams.

Famous splays: Warren Beatty, Harry Belafonte, Michel Gauquelin, Jackie Gleason, Henry Miller, Robert Redford, Franklin Roosevelt, Babe Ruth, Auturo Toscannini, Lee Trevino, H.G. Wells

THE SPLASH - TRAIT 11 (10) (LEVEL III)

In this pattern, planets should be distributed fairly evenly throughout the chart and, ideally, it should not contain more than one conjunction. It does not possess a focalizing planet. Because planets are spread out and scattered, the pattern can symbolize innate competency for a number of different occupations. The individual must be stimulated by special interests or, better yet, intellectual activities. Otherwise, the scattering effect takes hold. Drives release in different directions which make it difficult to ascertain appropriate career paths.

The pattern correlates with trait 11 vocational drives, but also exhibits trait 10 overtones. A sense of contribution and shared activity bring purpose into life. While "others" may be needed, it is not for reasons of emotional closeness. One can be an independent worker, a leader or an authoritative boss, but a need exists to be a part of a process involving group cohesion. (Refer to the discussion on this trait in Chapter 2.)

This splasher makes commitments to an occupation. Stimulating interests often surround a "cause" orientation with humanitarian or political inclinations. Activities involving organizations, associations or societies can play meaningful roles in the career or outside of it. In many instances, academic, scientific or intellectual groups or achievements are sought when trait 10 accomplishment-oriented drives are activated. The potential is to become a consultant or an expert within the structure of a group, for example, a group practice, professional organization, society or club. Colleague recognition becomes integral to vocational need fulfillment in such cases.

These types bore easily, another reason vocations must be interesting, diverse and stimulating. An element of excitement is required as part of the occupational process. This is true whenever trait 11 is repeated throughout a chart (see Chapter 2).

When constructive vocational attributes or interests are not developed, roadblocks, setbacks or boredom result. Some splashers mistakenly prefer the noncommittal job over any other due to an inability to experience themselves as competent. Work is not interesting or stimulating to them and they "get by" with a bill-paying job. These splashers must wake up to their needs for excitement, authority and independence. If trait 11 is otherwise present in their charts, they may find that secure vocational rug suddenly pulled out from under them – as the psyche's way of

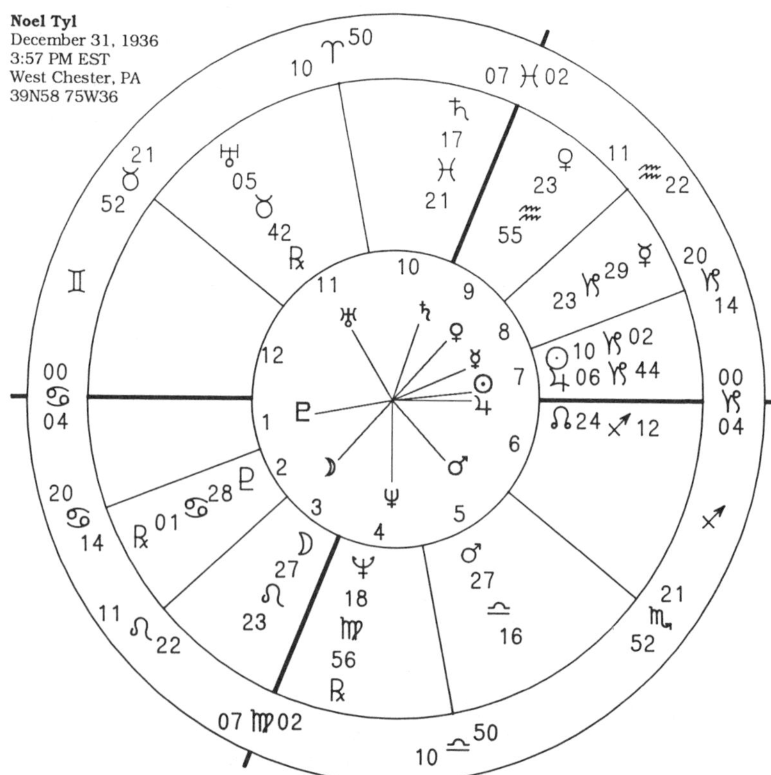

bringing to life the needed elements of excitement and change. Once stimulation needs are consciously acknowledged, and a commitment is made to enhance competence, these people can look forward to a complete change in their work lives.

Noel Tyl, astrologer, author, Wagnerian opera singer and business consultant, offers an excellent example of the multifaceted splasher. Only one conjunction appears in his chart (Sun conjunct Jupiter), while the remaining planets are spread evenly throughout the horoscope. Only three houses are unoccupied, the first, sixth and twelfth. Tyl has achieved competence in quite a few diverse occupations. Several factors are repeated in his chart. Uranus (trait 11) stands out by being located in its own house. Saturn (trait 10), Venus (traits 2 and 7) and the Moon (trait 4), significant of hard work, expertise, writing, counseling and the performing arts, are more pertinently highlighted as will be explained in the next chapter.

Famous splashers: Garth Allen, Marlon Brando, Ram Dass, John Denver, Nina Foch, Elton John, Henry Mancini, Burt Reynolds, Theodore Roosevelt, Noel Tyl

References

1. Jones, Marc Edmund, *The Guide to Horoscope Interpretation*, Wheaton, Illinois: Theosophical Publishing House, 1974
2. Jones, p. 60

CHAPTER FOUR

PINPOINTING PERSONALITY NEEDS

Because people are most likely to succeed at occupations which reflect their personalities, specific vocational needs and traits must be explored. These Level I chart factors include any Gauquelin planets in the plus zones (referred to as G-planets), any planets located within six degrees of the angles, singletons, stationary planets, handle and leading planets. In addition to the aspects, which are discussed in the next chapter, Level I features focus a career analysis by pinpointing personality traits significant to satisfying vocational expression. The more Level I factors that appear in a chart, the more complex the vocational need picture becomes. (Note Perry's chart on page 38.) Such people require occupational outlets able to sustain a wide variety of needs and skills.

G-Planets

The research of French psychologist Dr. Michel Gauquelin, who was later joined by his wife, Françoise (degreed in both statistics and psychology), represents the most significant findings on vocational astrology to date. This text relies on their results because they have convincingly passed a number of reality tests. While the Gauquelins originally hoped to disprove astrology, they produced stunning evidence which supports many of astrology's most basic tenets but refutes others.

They collected approximately 16,000 birth certificates of "eminent" European professionals in ten different occupational categories. These included actors, athletes, artists, business executives, doctors, journalists, politicians, scientists, soldiers and writers. Registered births of 25,000 "average" professionals in the same well-defined categories were collected for comparison as a control group. Most of the births took place between 1850 and 1910, the most recent being 1945. Because France, Germany, Italy, Belgium and Holland register birth times, these countries were selected. England does not record time of birth.

Information on the eminent professionals was painstakingly gathered from some 200 professional biographical dictionaries, news and magazine accounts and many other "objective," nonastrologically originated, sources. Data on personality factors and vocational success was converted into abbreviated biographical sketches on 41,000 index cards also containing the positions of the planets to the horizon and meridian of the Earth. This monumental effort took nine years, from 1949 to 1958, and all the birth information had to be obtained by writing to the individual registry offices, a costly and time-consuming chore. I refer you to Dean[1] and books by Michel Gauquelin for further details on the design of this massive undertaking.

The findings focus on the Moon, Venus, Mars, Jupiter and Saturn occupying the "plus zones." (See page 124 for a representation of these areas in the chart.) No significant results were detected for the remaining planets. However, only ten occupations were examined and mostly male professionals were used. The five primary planets correlated significantly with distinctive personality characteristics which, in turn, are related to vocational aptitude and choice when they are found **rising** (roughly ten degrees under the Ascendant– or one-third of the first house– to roughly thirty degrees into the twelfth house); or **culminating** (roughly ten degrees on the tenth house side of the MC– or one-third of the tenth house– to roughly thirty degrees into the ninth house). These are the **primary plus zones** which most closely approximate Placidus cadent houses.

The less prominent, or **secondary plus zones**, are located roughly ten degrees under the Descendant, or one-third of the sixth house, and approximately ten degrees behind the IC, or one-third of the third house. These positions are called **setting** and **anticulminating**. Personality characteristics and the vocational aptitude associated with a planet, though still significant, tend to be less pronounced when the planet occupies a secondary zone. (The exception to this rule is Mars.)

A G-planet neither insures a related occupation will be entered, nor guarantees success in it; it only highlights personality traits significant of those who are successful in the related occupations.

A very skeptical Belgium Committee for the Scientific Study of Paranormal Phenomena, composed of leading scientists, conducted an independent analysis of 535 Belgium athletes. Much to its eyebrow-raising surprise, the Committee duplicated the Gauquelin findings for Mars and, thus, "...the results appear to be beyond question."[2]

The findings contradict long-held views regarding the cadent houses; they are not the characterless sectors previously thought. However, planets located near the angles have always prominently figured into the personality and this was upheld for half of the planets.

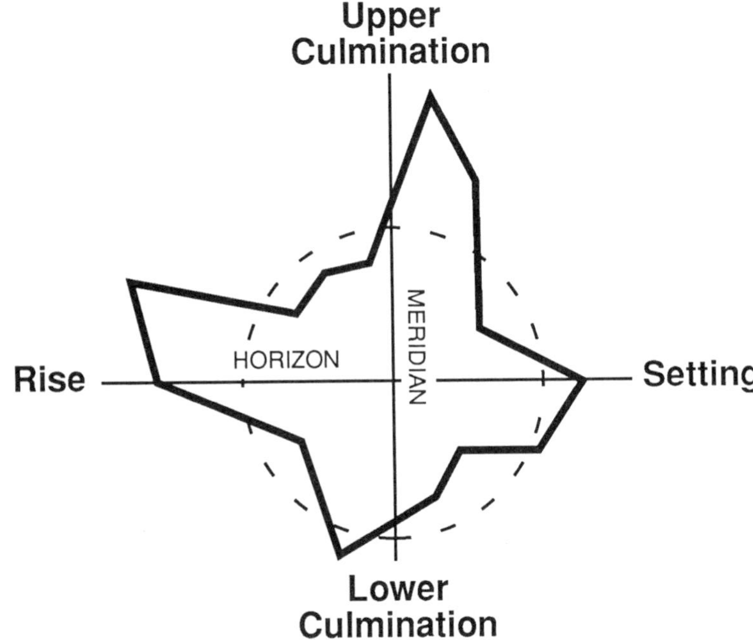

When any of the G-planets appear in the indented sectors of a chart, the corresponding traits are **statistically** less likely to influence the personality and the vocation. However, statistical trends do not always apply in individual cases. A consistently repeated trait reveals a definite trend even when the corresponding planet does not appear in a plus zone.

Not all people respond to their needs nor are they always in touch with a firm sense of identity. Some individuals are "neurotic" and cannot be anticipated to manifest the usually focal G-planets, especially those found in the twelfth house, in the same fashion as eminent professionals. People who attain the heights are special individuals who are strongly motivated (related to traits 1 and 4), talented (traits 2 and 7), aspire to goals (trait 9) and do not balk at effort (trait 10). Even if the talent factor is removed from this list, most people possessing the remaining qualities are likely to be successful at what they do.

Frequently more than one G-planet will appear in a plus zone, a factor which complicates the career analysis. Depending on the needs and drives each planet represents, a situation can arise where one planetary trait functions well with another, as a kind of backup trait, or seems to overshadow the other's expression. For example, Mars and Jupiter functionally relate because they are both fire planets associated with basic, extroverted drives. Located in a plus zone, they could suggest a highly dynamic personality drive which would be an advantage in the working world, provided these drives are realistically channeled. Moon and Venus also share similar natures and occupations. They tend to highlight creative or assisting vocational aptitudes, provided the personality is not otherwise inclined to passivity.

However, Moon/Mars, Moon/Saturn, Venus/Mars, Venus/Saturn, Jupiter/Saturn and Mars/Saturn are dissimilar. These pairings can represent divergent or conflicting needs which can make pinpointing appropriate career outlets more difficult due to the more complex nature of the individual's make-up. Some people can combine such divergent drives without apparent difficulty.

In Muhammad Ali's chart (page 105), Mars and Saturn appear in a primary plus zone. Typically the traits to which these planets correspond gravitate to the business community. However, for this world heavyweight boxing champion, the trait

1 factor predominates his vocational expression. Trait 10 blends in and represents the discipline required to train and endure through such a gruelling sport to become an "expert." Why did trait 1 "win out" when trait 10 (in the form of Saturn) usually represents the more "weighty" factor? The answer lies in the trait 1 repetition shown in Level II of Ali's analysis. He was born under the New Moon phase (Chapter 7) which correlates with trait 1 drives. This fortifies Mars as the primary G-planet and the trait which indicates his most important vocational needs.

This does not mean that all people will manifest a similar repetition in the identical manner. Besides, having access to the single most reliable chart synthesis technique ever known to astrologers – the hindsight technique – the author could hardly go wrong. Still, the reader should be advised that an individual possesses both positive and negative potentials when integrating contradictory needs. It is a good idea to review the resume to determine how career drives have been utilized in the past. Conducting a vocational analysis without this minimal reference to the client is like brushing one's teeth without toothpaste; the job rarely gets done satisfactorily.

The Singleton

A singleton is an isolated planet solely occupying a hemisphere. Because it can be determined only when the birth time is known, it is significant to individual vocational analysis. Jones[3] writes that a singleton represents a special capacity or gift for a related activity. Its trait could represent a vocational approach or outlet or, just as readily, can symbolize a special interest that seeks fulfillment avocationally.

Sometimes a singleton will be highlighted in another fashion, for example, as a handle or leading planet. This adds to that planet's vocational significance, as Barbra Streisand's chart exemplifies. She was born with a singleton Venus (south) intercepted in Pisces located in the (Placidus) twelfth house. Note how strongly trait 12 is associated with the planet. Venus (2 and 7) also is the leading planet in a bowl pattern (4) and, most significant to her career expression, it is located in a Gauquelin primary plus zone. Level I of her analysis would show traits 2 and 7 circled three times indicating their vocational significance over the Mars G-planet which must be incorporated into her occupational expression to experience work as fulfilling.

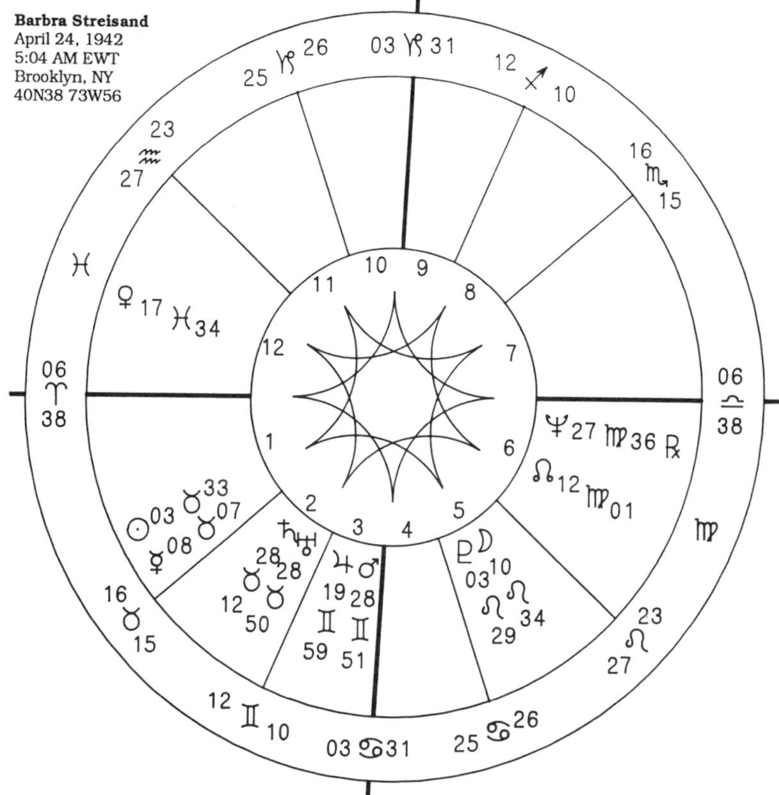

Sensitive, possibly aesthetically-inclined vocational drives are suggested by the chart pattern (4) and the combined focus on Venus. Because traits 2, 4 and 7 are related to the arts or counseling (see Chapter 2), this person could be suitable for an artistically-related vocation or one providing nurturing assistance to others. Venus as a G-planet, however, highlights an artistic aptitude according to the Gauquelins and, therefore, this occupational direction would be the author's first choice.

A session with the client might start out something like this:

"Well, Barbra, there seem to be some indications that you might possess an aptitude for the arts, especially the performing arts, although other suitable possibilities exist for you.

Do you have any interests along these lines?"

"Yes, I love to sing. I've been singing ever since I can remember and know I have an interesting voice. I'd love to be an actress, but I'm not certain my looks could see me through...."

Of course this is an imaginary dialogue intended to illustrate a point. Why did music, film and acting surface as opposed to some other occupation? Why did she not become a photographer for instance? That is a good question, one a chart alone does not answer; **the horoscope only suggests general aptitudes which are acted on according to the individual's interests in life**. She could have become a photographer if her interests had inclined her in that direction.

Handle and Leading Planets

Jones[4] considered the handle and leading planets in a pattern to be among the most outstanding features in a chart. To him, they represented a characteristic and important direction of interest. But the traits associated with such planets also need to be visible occupationally, something he overlooked. They represent prominent personality needs and activities which shape the drives symbolized by the pattern in which they appear (see Chapter 3).

The remainder of this chapter examines the personality characteristics and needs appropriate to the planets. Refer to Chapter 2 for their corresponding vocational outlets and approaches to work. However, whether the occupation directly relates to a Level I planet is secondary to the **need** for the occupation to reflect appropriate outlets for that planet's symbolized personality drives. This is especially true when several Level I planets appear in a chart. The occupation must be sufficiently broad to include the needed expressions and approaches of each planet.

Mars - Trait 1 (Level I)

Mars is the vanguard of all trait 1 chart factors. As a personality function, it represents directable ego energies, self-assertive drives, competitive qualities, striving tendencies, physical stamina, courage, initiative and that urge within the human being to "win." All personally motivated drives, including sexual ones, are associated with this planet. The "cosmic state" of Mars (a term coined by Rob Hand to include the house, sign, aspects, retrogradation, interception, etc., of a planet) indicates how and where ego drives need to be directed. Because it represents one of the primary vocational functions, Mars is always pertinent to occupational expression no matter where it is located in a chart. However, it is especially pertinent to work when it appears in Level I or when it is associated with the sixth or tenth houses or traits.

Gauquelin[5] found Mars appearing in plus zones of eminent athletes, soldiers, physicians and business executives significantly beyond the chance level. Personality traits statistically confirmed by the Gauquelins as typical of Martian expression date back hundreds of years in astrological literature. Such dynamism is needed to achieve in the above-mentioned occupations. However, trait 1 plays a significant role in other occupations (see Chapter 2). Unlike the remaining G-planets, Mars traits are not less pronounced when the planet occupies a secondary zone.[6]

Mars as a handle or leading planet represents another Level I factor. It implies that vocational drives need to be highly dynamic, goal-oriented and that an executive, self-determined or aggressive thrust must be applied. When Mars receives or makes a number of close aspects, much the same holds true. As a **singleton**, the planet represents another Level I factor which could denote an ability for or avocational interest in trait 1 outlets (see Chapter 2). For example, the person could be mechanically or athletically inclined or possess a capacity to pioneer in the field of interest.

Trait 1 occupations may be suitable when Mars appears in Level I, especially when as a trait it is repeated. But what is most important is that the occupation permit a sound expression of trait 1 personality drives. Similar themes apply to any handle or leading planet in the first house or in Aries, but to a much reduced extent.

Even if Mars appears in Level I, there is no guarantee trait 1 will be recognized or expressed adequately. Some people are not aware of their leadership, striving needs, most likely due to interference with the development of self-directed assertiveness (see Chapter 6). This situation does not change the need, only its outward expression. It is a safe bet that an undeveloped Mars function with an emphasis on trait 1 will correlate with feeling weak, nervous or ineffectual. Job selection, the achievement ceiling or work performance can be inappropriate because the individual fails to present the self in a "real" fashion. (Refer to Chapter 2 for remedies to this problem.)

In or ruling the sixth house (or in Virgo), Mars suggests that work must become an important form of self-expression because a significant portion of one's drives are directed toward the job. The trait pair associated with these placements is 1/6 (Chapter 5). A useful skill, craft or talent must be put to work in an independent, self-directed manner by providing a service to others. The constructive potential is to work hard, to have an active full day, to strive to be a leader on the job or to seek self-employment. Mars colors the atmosphere of the work environment, the job-related duties, and one's experience of coworkers or employees in a trait 1 light.

Mars in or ruling the tenth house (or in Capricorn) is similar to a fourth quadrant focus because it encompasses trait pair 1/10. Realistic striving must be demonstrated to establish a place in society. It signals a need to develop trait 1 characteristics to get ahead and/or to exercise these drives as part of one's expression of authority. Tangible achievement results from taking initiative, facing career challenges and applying steady effort; a lackadaisical attitude or short cuts undermine opportunities. Because the tenth house also represents people in authority, superiors can exhibit trait 1 characteristics and some may not like to make room at the top for anyone else. They might prefer underlings who can be pushed to any extreme.

If such authority figures are attracted, it is an indication that one's own Martian side has not been dealt with constructively. The 1/10 blend (see Chapter 5) indicates the need to combine self-will with the limits of the world --what one can and cannot accomplish within the confines of a physical reality. The person with 1/10 highlighted in the chart could give up "the fight" too soon, experiencing more limits than truly exist, or try to accomplish more than is realistically possible and end up fighting authority figures until the lesson is learned. The middle ground is energetic accomplishment within the structure of the individual's current reality. When the reality quotient is solid and positive striving is in evidence, Mars associated with trait 10 can represent self-employment as a desirable outlet because the need to be in charge, especially of oneself, is quite strong.

When Mars falls into the indented sectors of the chart, is not focalized or tied into the sixth or tenth houses, it is a suggestion that certain occupations may not be natural to the person. One would **tend** to shy away from those calling for initiative, competition and direct confrontation with others, or one **could** fall short when such drives were required, unless other important factors, such as close aspects to Mars, were present. However, this does not mean that a competitively-oriented vocation should be avoided. Weaker personality traits can be developed. The person merely has to be alerted to better develop trait 1 characteristics before adequate functioning in related occupations is likely to occur.

Famous personalities with Mars Singleton: Bob Dylan (east, bucket handle), Sigmund Freud (east, bucket handle), Pierre Renoir (east, leading bowl)

Mars leading: Arthur Ashe (bowl), Paul Cezanne (locomotive), Leonardo Da Vinci (locomotive), Herman Hesse (bucket), Jean Houston (locomotive), Mick Jagger (bundle), Jean Claude Killy (bundle), Ryan O'Neal (locomotive), Jack Parr (bucket), Helen Reddy (locomotive, G-planet)

Mars Bucket Handle: William Jennings Bryan, Richard De Mont, Alan Leo, Karl Marx, George Bernard Shaw (singleton west)

Mars G-Planet: Muhammad Ali, Lenny Bruce, Johnny Carson, Rennie Davis, Morgana King, Henry Kissinger, Rollo May, Walter Mondale, Friedrich Nietzsche, Leontyne Price, Princess Anne, Brooke Shields, Barbra Streisand

Venus - Traits 2 and 7 (Level I)

Quite apart from Mars, Venus represents the receptive, yin aspects of being: the need for love, affection, harmony, relationships with others, beauty and refinement. Venus often signals a need for satisfying interpersonal outlets, partnership or work involving the interrelating process (see Chapter 2). Attractive, comfortable surroundings also enhance job satisfaction; dirty back rooms are not for the Venusian type.

Tradition has implied that a prominent Venus (Taurus or Libra) often correlates with being beautiful or handsome. More to the point, beauty can be an issue in life. This is not to say that one must necessarily be beautiful. Different people experience this issue differently. Some people are beautiful, which is a marketable asset in our society. Attractive people have the upper hand in the job world, especially during the interviewing process. They immediately elicit a positive response from others. Others create beauty through art, or enjoy being surrounded by it through their homes, furnishings and art objects. Still other people aspire to become beautiful or suffer from a lack of beauty in their lives.

Traditionally, Venus also symbolizes what has personal value as well as one's resources, talents, "self worth," artistic, creative interests, financial matters, beautiful objects and sensual pleasures. Such factors correlate with Venus' fixed earth nature through its rulership of Taurus. Whenever trait 2 or 7 is accented in a chart, any of these outlets can play a role at work. Art, as used here, refers to making or doing anything of a creative nature that has form and beauty. What is "Art" to one person might appear as something altogether different to someone else.

Michel Gauquelin[7] confirmed that **Venus in a plus zone correlates with an aptitude for the arts** because it appeared in plus zones of eminent artists, actors, poets, musicians and writers beyond the chance level. Success in these related occupations, however, and the corresponding personality characteristics, were not as clearly definable for Venus as for the other G-planets.

> The essential elements of the Venus personality are charm, friendliness, gentleness, courtesy and a pleasant kind of extraversion...a tendency to be diplomatic and very cunning with people...has a passive side to it so that individuals...can suffer problems in achieving their full potential. It is very easy for them to be slack. A certain talent for compromise also exists...[8].

This talent for compromise and slackness can extend to the vocation when Venus appears as a G-planet (or when its related traits are emphasized in the horoscope). Without self-motivation and value placed in the job, the Venus person often is tempted to "get-by" at work. Financial security concerns frequently compromise artistic outlets, or other interests, as a career. The risk involved in earning a viable income from them and self-doubts about their worth can play a role in choosing to just get-by with an easy, secure job. Trait 2 especially, but trait 7 also can be very "stay put" and safety-oriented. Others with these traits highlighted require vocations or avocations through which to satisfy aesthetic or artistically-related needs and interests.

Because Venus travels in close proximity to the Sun and Mercury, these "planets" cannot represent the handle of a chart pattern. In the leading or otherwise focalized position, Venus represents another Level I factor, but it does not necessarily show a softening or passivity to the drives symbolized by the pattern. The trait drives associated with the pattern could take on "artsy" or more refined characteristics. Similar themes apply to any leading or handle planet that appears in the second or seventh houses or in Taurus or Libra, but to a greatly modified extent.

Consider the bowl pattern (trait 4) with Venus leading. These factors are pertinent to Barbra Streisand's chart (on page 127). Traits 2, 4 and 7 relate to each other and correspond to similar occupational outlets. In this case, high-powered motivational factors need to be present in the chart. (Streisand has Mars in a secondary plus zone symbolizing dynamic leadership needs which she satisfies through directing and producing.) Otherwise, there might be a tendency toward passivity.

In the case of the locomotive, a leading Venus could correspond to the individual who has a compulsive, turbulent or passionate urge to write, dance or act. Traits 2, 7 and 8 also could combine to represent a drive to have power or influence over others, for example through politics. The combination also could indicate one who pursues art through a trait 8 occupation, for example, a police artist.

Venus as a singleton represents another Level I factor which could suggest ability or interest in trait 2 or 7 vocations (see Chapter 2). For instance, the person might possess creative talents, an ability to work with others or a special interest in art objects.

In or ruling the sixth house (or in Virgo), Venus implies 2/6 and 6/7 themes (Chapter 5) which suggest a need to enjoy (value) work and the people (or things) with whom one works. One could work closely with others, for example, as an editor, trainer or secretary, or require such services from others.

Friendships and other relationships frequently are formed on the job and working with a spouse or partner could prove satisfying. Venus here also can represent the coming and going of clients, students, patients or customers as part of the daily routine or indicate a potential to be talented at technical jobs or detail-oriented work. Job dissatisfaction could stem from unsatisfying interpersonal relationships rather than a dislike of work duties, although insufficient effort on the job is another trait 2 or 7 potentiality. See Chapter 2 for other suitable trait 2 or 7 occupational outlets, but consider them within the context of a sixth house setting.

In or ruling the tenth house (or in Capricorn), Venus can represent many of the same needs, interests and career-related outlets. It is similar to a third quadrant focus in that both encompass a 7/10 theme, although a 2/10 theme (see Chapter 5) also applies here. One could have a talent for business administration, a flair for the arts and/or experience periods when the cash flow is tight. Money may be recycled into the business or is spent to enhance career opportunities. Interrelating skills, diplomacy, partnership, good looks or a special talent may need to be developed or exercised as part of the vocational expression. Work also must reflect one's own brand of creativity or interests; otherwise, one tends to job hop or maintains an emotionally unrewarding line of work. In the tenth, one could be known for having or being a partner. An impressive partner, who confers status or enhances the career, could be sought. One can attract the positive attention of superiors, form any variety of relationship to them or be taken advantage of by them if the interrelating capacity is deficient. The possible manifestations of these themes are extensive and are not limited to the above considerations.

Famous personalities with Venus Singleton: Phyllis Diller (east), Barbra Streisand (south, leading/bowl, G-planet)

Venus Leading: Ada Byron (bowl), Georges Clemenceau (locomotive), Jean Cocteau (bucket, G-planet), Gustave Paul Dore (bucket), Tom McLoughlin (bucket), Friedrich Nietzsche (locomotive, G-planet), Ira Progoff (bucket), Giacamo Puccini (locomotive), Phoebe Snow (bucket, G-planet), Earl Warren (locomotive)

Venus G-Planet: Alan Alda, Ingrid Bergman, Otto Von Bismark, Marlon Brando, Paul Cezanne, Cher, Ram Dass, John Dean, Merle Haggard, Herman Melville, Walter Mondale, Paul Newman, Princess Anne, Jack Nicklaus, Brooke Shields, Lotte Von Strahl, Natalie Wood

Mercury - Traits 3 and 6 (Level I)

Mercury has long been associated with how a person thinks, communicates and makes observations based on the five physical senses. Tradition has connected it to the intellect and writing always headed the occupational list. When the Gauquelins aimed a kilobyte computer in its direction, however, Mercury failed the reality test. It did not produce any significant results in writers' charts or in any of the occupations examined. This ruffled a few astrological feathers. In a separate study, Hyneck[9] concluded the same result. Vocationally, where does that leave the tiny planet?

Mercury represents a **vehicle** for communication rather than having any relationship to the **quality** of what is being transmitted. In mythology, he was the messenger of the gods, not the one responsible for the content of their messages. Additionally, a chart does not specify the IQ of its owner or if brain power will be adequately used.[10] Because intelligence is so basic to determining suitable career directions, it is not possible to "know" from the chart alone what that person should do for a living. In Level I, or in or ruling the sixth or tenth houses, Mercury predominantly represents a fundamental vocational need to be **mentally or verbally/vocally active**. This includes the extremes of a gossip, a wit, jokester or a genius, depending on the individual.

Mercury poses a difficulty to vocational analysis because it can express on divergent levels directly related to the mental faculties, evaluative judgment or communicative skills. When such interests exist, a Level I Mercury correlates with a more "serious" approach to the career, with a need to develop skills, abilities and often factual knowledge. This is the mutable earth (trait 6) side of the planet. When such interests do not exist, a casual, less strenuous way to earn a living tends to be preferred. Jobs entailing increased decision-making responsibilities are not always desirable. This correlates with the mutable air (trait

3) side of Mercury. Vocational matters are taken lightly, even to the extent of being flip and noninvolved at work. When carried to extremes, the attitude can lead to carelessness or job-hopping. One of these vocational approaches is likely when Mercury appears in Level I, although without access to information outside of the chart, it is not possible to determine which approach predominates.

A prominent Mercury coincides with job functions surrounding the transmission of information, facts, ideas or the transportation of objects. If earth-related traits are represented, writing could be suitable, but it is likely to be technical or fact-oriented rather than fictional. To be satisfying, the job has to keep the person's mouth, hands or legs busy. Mercury represents a very "busy" energy, in the sense of needing to be "on the go" with a hectic schedule. One also tends to maintain a youthful air and a hyper buoyancy that gets others hopping. Wit and verve could be a potential forté. People who drive, talk, walk or who experience frequent changes of places, faces or scenery on the job tend to have a prominent Mercury or trait 3 accented in their charts. (For a complete list of common job duties, refer to traits 3 and 6 in Chapter 2.)

In terms of vocational correspondences, Mercury may relate to "conventional" occupations. This may be one reason the planet failed to show significance in the Gauquelin studies where only professional categories were examined. A highlighted Mercury especially can relate to office practice occupations or work conducted in a busy beehive-type setting. It also might relate to food service or any service-related occupation that assists or acts as a backup in, or for, a larger structure.

An accented Mercury also represents other vocational possibilities (see Chapter 2). Considering all of its possible manifestations, it is easy to see how large a role Mercury plays in the working world. Its divergent needs and drives are exercised through any occupation listed by the Department of Labor. Everyone relies on these functions whether employed as a messenger, secretary or president of General Motors. The planet represents an essential backup function which allows one to proceed with other job responsibilities or represents the individual who occupationally serves in this backup capacity so that others may proceed with their work.

Because this planet represents the fundamentals of thought

and speech, logically it should correspond to a primary vocational function even more basic than the other five G-planets. It represents the capacity to reach inside of self through thought channels, and to convey qualities of self to others through the verbal capacity. How well one relates to the world depends on it. Try working without access to Mercury's functions: sight, hearing, speech, mental processes, the ability to use one's hand and legs. Handicapped individuals have a dysfunction in one or more of these capacities, which is why conventional employment is often difficult for them. These functions are required in all work, although some jobs rely more heavily on certain functions than on others. For this reason, six personality functions can be considered fundamental to adequate vocational expression (related to the five G-planets and Mercury).

In or ruling the sixth house (or in Virgo) Mercury suggests that communicative abilities, factual knowledge or another Mercurial function is relied on as part of the daily routine or needs to be honed to experience a fuller vocational expression. These placements correspond to trait pairs 3/6 or 6/6 (see Chapter 5), which suggest the importance of skill development and that interesting work could involve technical skills, analytical capabilities, a needed service or craft.

Much the same applies to **Mercury in or ruling the tenth house (or in Capricorn).** Here Mercurial abilities may be especially "on the line" as part of the expression of authority or must be developed to obtain satisfying employment. It corresponds to a 3/10 or 6/10 blend (see Chapter 5). The 3/10 trait pair suggests one who needs to be taken seriously and/or who may experience blocks about this personality function. Saturn in close aspect with Mercury indicates similar potentials. The person can choose to elevate these factors, through additional training or school, or refuse to "enter the fight." The 6/10 blend suggests the potential for hard work, especially of a research, health or detail-oriented nature. However, meaningful skills have to exist, otherwise a preference for not working can arise. It is difficult to be taken seriously on the job when one has failed to develop competence at one's tasks; hence the desire to avoid the work arena.

Mercury as a singleton is somewhat rare, but corresponds to a Level I factor. It might suggest a propensity for work in trait 3 or 6 occupations. For example, the person might possess skill for the analysis of facts or figures, teaching, a capacity to deal with myriad details or represent the fastest, most efficient waitperson to ever grace a restaurant.

Because Mercury travels closely to the Sun and Venus, it **cannot represent the handle of a pattern**. When leading or otherwise focalized, Mercury represents a Level I factor and suggests that trait 3 or 6 outlets tend to be suitable employment avenues. When any handle or leading planet appears in these related houses or signs, similar themes apply, but to a much reduced extent.

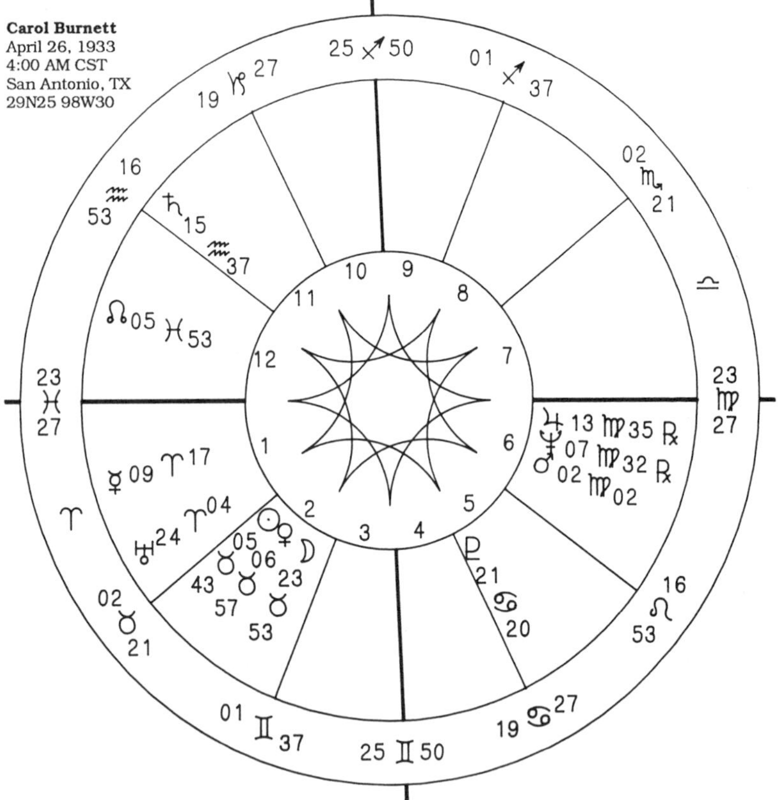

Carol Burnett is a good example of the witty potentials Mercury can symbolize, especially when it leads in a bucket pattern. (Cher shares these features.) The bucket implies that drives should be channeled through trait 5 outlets or approaches, among which is the entertainment field. But these same factors could also represent the teaching profession or science as a suitable outlet, especially since Saturn represents a singleton handle planet in the southern sphere. Saturn and Mercury are her only Level I factors. For Burnett, however, Mercury prevailed vocationally while Saturn represents the diligent, professional approach this comedienne takes to organizing and perfecting the television skits for which she is so famous.

Famous personalities with Mercury leading: Carol Burnett (bucket, near angles), Benvenuto Cellini (locomotive), Cher (bucket), Charles Gordon (bucket), Herbert Von Karajan (bucket), Jack Nicklaus (locomotive), Louis Pasteur (bowl), Edmond Rostand (bucket), Leopold Stokowski (bowl)

Mercury Near Angles: Honore de Balzac, Alexander Graham Bell, Lenny Bruce, John Cage, David Carradine, Johnny Carson, Billy Carter, Michel Gauquelin, Caroline Kennedy, Morgana King, Liberace, Burt Reynolds, Phoebe Snow, Lotte Von Strahl

Moon - Trait 4 (Level I)

The Moon symbolizes inner feelings, caring instincts, emotional sensitivities and imaginative qualities. As one of the vocationally significant personality functions, the Moon encompasses the sense of adequacy and comfort with self on an unconscious level. Each of these is shaped by the early experience of nurturing. The Moon's prominence in the chart indicates how apparent these factors may be in the vocation and how much the early family may have influenced career ceilings or choices (see Chapter 2). Lunar types are often grateful to parents or blame them (or their heritage) for their problems.

The basis of all success relates to the "cosmic state" (house, sign, aspects, etc.) of the Moon. The entire structure and foundation to life, and a sense of belonging in the world, are tied to it and other trait 4 chart features. The Moon always is important vocationally, even if it is not located in Level I because it symbolizes emotional contentment. For some people, stressed lunar factors can represent poor self-images which undermine career abilities. These individuals experience difficulty sustaining themselves in the workplace. Trait 4 can correlate with a need to undergo self-development or counseling to repair the self-image. For others, stressed lunar factors, or early life problems, spur achievement needs and the desire to establish a solid career.

It is a mistake to assume the Moon (or Cancer) always is symbolic of passive or domestic people. As the ruler of Cancer, it represents a combination of cardinality and water (defined in Chapter 8). While the Moon is commonly accepted as being a water planet, its cardinal quality is less often recognized. However, once adequacy has been established, lunar types can be highly ambitious and goal-oriented. The passivity associated with the Moon arises from a failure to establish personal adequacy.

Because mother has tended to represent the primary caregiver and nurturer, the relationship to her is intimately connected to where her offspring eventually land in the career world. Perhaps this is why many astrologers, Liz Greene included, assign mother to the Saturn-ruled tenth house, the calling in life, as opposed to the Moon-ruled fourth house. However, in different households, different roles are played. Ever since Pluto and Uranus transited their way through Cancer, the family structure has been changing; more single parent families have emerged. Motherhood seems to be losing its standing among the various callings women can pursue, most likely due to the expanding roles now available to them. For many women, however, this is an exceptionally confusing affair and double messages surround their function in society.

The Gauquelins have shed new light on the vocational properties of the Moon. It significantly appeared in the **plus zones of eminent novelists and poets**, completely overshadowing Mercury in this capacity. Creative writers are lunar, or "dreamy," personalities who bring imagination and sensitivity to bear during the creative process.

> The essential characteristics that go with the Moon are, on the one hand, good humor, sociability and tolerance and, on the other, a certain love of discord. Moon people are easily distracted and easily influenced. They also tend to share less pleasant characteristics, which include snobbery and very worldly vanity[11].

When the Moon appears in a plus zone, it does not automatically signal the chart of a writer or snob. It signifies a tendency to possess personality traits which match those belonging to writers, or anyone who participates in a "dreamy" occupation, such as the performing arts. Still other occupations require a similar brand of sensitivity, or intellectual expression, which manifests as assisting or supporting people in the fulfillment of their personal needs. (See Chapter 2 for trait 4 occupational outlets.)

The atmosphere in which a strongly lunar type works also is significant to job satisfaction. The work arena needs to be a place to which one can feel "attached" and very much a part of what is going on. One might prefer to work out of the home, as most creative writers do, or in a friendly, supportive family-type atmosphere. (Refer to Chapter 2 for additional job conditions.) Lunar types also often experience highs and lows in terms of workload or feast/famine periods. One's bank account and emotional equilibrium should be reasonably prepared for these fluctuations.

In or ruling the sixth house (or in Virgo), the Moon suggests that work must become an important basis to life. Each represents a 4/6 blend (see Chapter 5) which could suggest a flair for the healing arts or an interesting combination of intuitive and technical capacities. Day-to-day job functioning tends to reflect trait 4 needs and outlets. Emotional security is derived from honing a needed skill, craft, talent or service which can be put to work in fulfilling ways. Without a rewarding daily routine, the basis to life grows faulty. Depression or emotional fragility result. Because sensitivities are focused here, it is easy to become "worked up" over job issues or changes and to experience an overload of worry or anxiety. One also needs to be needed and useful. When carried to extremes, one tends to be a "mother of the world" type, overworked and underpaid. The need to be needed, in such cases, would have to be tempered.

In or ruling the tenth house (or in Capricorn), the Moon suggests that assisting, imaginative, intuitive or intellectual qualities must be developed or exercised as part of one's expression of authority. A 4/10 blend is represented here (see Chapter 5). One may prefer to work closely with the boss or may end up with one who needs to be babied. The Moon here also might imply that developing the sense of self as being competent, or a professional, is necessary for gratification. The same applies when the Moon closely aspects Saturn. Emotional rewards and a sense of grounding in life are likely to result only from a steady application of effort and taking one's authority needs seriously. It also can signal the person who needs to have a family and a career.

The Moon in the tenth frequently coincides with those who are sensitive about their reputations. More than a few report feeling demeaned by a parent or some other relative in childhood. The response to this situation can result in strong or weak career drives. Being the boss, or having their own businesses, is the only suitable vocational path for some people. Others need to be taken care of, more or less, and lean on others for support, sustenance or guidance. They lack an appropriate sense of adequacy and are self-limiting due to fears of failure. They avoid assuming responsibility on the job and place low ceilings on achievement possibilities.

The Moon as a singleton represents another Level I factor and highlights trait 4 emotional and/or creative sensitivities as pertinent to vocational expression, depending on the state of personal adequacy.

As a Level I handle, leading or otherwise focalized planet, the Moon suggests that the entire range of trait 4 activities or approaches would be suitable channels through which to demonstrate the drives symbolized by the pattern. This is especially true when leading a bowl, bundle or locomotive structure, again depending on the state of personal adequacy. One's heritage, country or family needs and issues also tend to run high. The same applies when the Moon leads or appears as a handle in the bucket pattern or makes a number of close aspects. The emotions, sensitivities and/or intellectual needs tend to be highly charged, although they are not likely to find constructive expression when this personality function is not reasonably developed. Similar themes are likely to apply, although to a diminished extent, when any handle or leading planet appears in the fourth house or in Cancer.

Famous personalities with Moon Singleton: Charles Baudelaire (east), Alexander Graham Bell (west), Joe Chambers (north, bucket handle), Martin Luther (south, bucket handle), Tyrone Power (east)

Moon Bucket Handle: Alexander Graham Bell, Joe Chambers, Cher, Robert De Niro (G-planet), Sir Alexander Fleming, Edouard Lalo, Andre Maurois (G-Planet), Amadeo Modigliani (G-planet), John Ruskin, O.J. Simpson, Walt Whitman

Moon Leading: Prince Charles (locomotive), Edgar Degas (locomotive), Albert Einstein (bucket), F. Scott Fitzgerald (bowl), Alfred E. Houseman (bowl), Jim Jones (bucket), Mahara Ji (bowl), John J. O'Neill (bucket), Fritz Perls (bowl), Troy Perry (bowl), Arthur Rimbaud (locomotive), Roy Rogers (bucket), Charlie Tuna (locomotive)

Moon G-Planet: Harry Belafonte, William Blake, Chris Chubbuck, Edgar Degas, Jack Kerouac, Mario Lanza, Vivien Leigh, Liberace, Abraham Lincoln, Isabelle Pagan, Helen Reddy, Brooke Shields, Suzanne Somers

Sun - Trait 5 (Level I)

The Gauquelin findings failed to uncover any significance for the Sun in eminent professionals' charts. If big Sol correlated with success or greatness, as tradition suggests, it should have been apparent in comparison to the "average" professionals used in the study as a control group. It was not. However, since only ten professional categories were examined, this may be of limited significance. In another study, Françoise Gauquelin[12] compared a whole host of astrologers' keywords to Sun positions in plus zones; again, no results. This held true for other research.[13]

The situation is ironic because so much has been written about the importance of the almighty "Sun sign." Why characteristics traditionally attributed to it cannot be detected by researchers is difficult to comprehend. In another of her comparative studies, Françoise noted that the traits traditionally ascribed to the Sun significantly corresponded to Mars and Jupiter.[14] Because all three share the fire element in common (Chapter 8), this is not surprising.

As a psychological function, Sol has been associated with general vitality, the basic approach to life and the will, or urge, to exist. Is this not symbolically a more basic, all-pervasive energy than Mars or Jupiter represents? This definition for the Sun does not suggest a pinpointed "personality" drive as much as it suggests a fundamental life drive (the **most** fundamental because no person or thing on Earth could live without the

Sun). This drive stimulates and operates **through** the personality functions symbolized by the planets and could encompass varying need-sets to be a special or distinct personality. This need to be "special" may be pronounced when the Sun (or trait 5) is accented in a chart, but the need does not represent the "fuel" to become great, successful or eminent. In many instances, the reverse is the case.

FATHER IMAGE

Astrologers also have connected the Sun to the early experience of father. When it appears in Level I, the fathering aspects of the early home environment stand out in personality development and need to be examined. In a psychological sense, "father" is responsible, through his example, for making the child aware of the outer world. From the attention and experience of him, his child develops notions about self regarding a place in society apart from the mother. In this sense, the relationship to father is as much connected to where an individual lands in life as is the mother's role of protector and nurturer. The Sun and Moon represent basic grounding factors related to the sense of support in life: the Moon on an interior level of being, and the Sun on a more exterior level of expression.

The Sun could represent a **psychic state** related to the sense of self developed from the early experience of father, or the fatherlike, directing qualities which pervaded the early home. It encompasses a basic human need for positive attention, love and acknowledgment. A Sun stressed by aspect might correlate with stress surrounding those needs. The Sun relates to "directions" in life due to this symbolic tie to the father image. The experience of father, however, includes spoken or unspoken "shoulds" or conditions. A feeling of having something special to offer him (or some other paternal figure) in childhood, and the ability to live up to those conditions, later develops into confidence to move out into life, knowing one has something to offer the career world.

When the father image has been disturbed for whatever reasons, the basic psychic state symbolized by the Sun may not be able initially in life to adequately generate the needed confidence to support personality drives in a "wholehearted" fashion. One might attempt to "prove" the self and live up to parental expectations when these may have nothing to do with one's needs. Another individual might shy away from hard work until this confidence is gained. Still a third type might bluster the way through, or turn to crime for that "get rich quick" boost.

Whenever the Sun appears in Level I, the experience of father and the ramifications of his presence (or absence) must be clearly understood. They have impacted the person on a level which can affect innate confidence to meet the challenges of the working world. When this confidence has been gained, which happens earlier in life for some than it does for others, exceptionally gratifying, self-expressive occupations through which talents or managerial capabilities can be expressed tend to be selected. Individuals pour their hearts into their work because they seek to discover themselves through their creations and accomplishments. (For a more complete listing of trait 5 occupational approaches and outlets, see Chapter 2.)

No matter where it is positioned in a chart, the Sun represents fundamental needs related to a satisfying occupational expression. **In or ruling the sixth house (or in Virgo)**, a special technical skill, craft, talent or service is vital to a purposeful way of life. It highlights a 5/6 blend (Chapter 5) in a fashion similar to the Gibbous Moon phase (Chapter 7). Managerial ability or analysis of facts, figures or people may play a role on the job, although trait 6 factors equally could be involved (see Chapter 2). There also is a need to feel proud of one's work, appreciated and needed, if not thoroughly indispensable. These factors cannot be ignored without creating discomfort, discouragement, or the desire to quit or become a rabble rouser on the job. Being equals with the boss, or having some independent authority is a must and problems with superiors can arise when they do not view the situation the same way. Self-employment can be an appropriate direction for those who have developed their special skills.

Difficulties emerge when a marketable skill, craft, service or talent has not been developed. Illness or feelings of insignificance surface due to the lack of satisfying work and the fact that a vital personality dimension is not being expressed. Withdrawing from the work force, however, is not the answer; it will not contribute to positive personality development and emotional stability.

In or ruling the tenth house (or in Capricorn), the Sun represents a need to work hard, to succeed on one's own, and to set an example through one's persistent efforts and earned reputation. Trait pair 5/10 (Chapter 5) is represented here. Self-conscious about the standing in the community, this individual desires positions of responsibility, authority or respect; the same applies when the Sun closely aspects Saturn. One person might work hard to earn distinction, while another, unconsciously fearing failure, might abandon the attempt. Again, because a vital dimension of self is not being expressed, the latter personality is not likely to attain a sense of purpose and may drift through the job world. Work efforts tend to be diluted with short cuts insufficient to create a lasting career. This person needs to wake up to important 5/10 career needs, and those necessitate hard work.

Because Venus and Mercury are close companions to the Sun, it cannot represent a handle planet. **As a singleton**, it is on the rare side and must be located near one of the angles, representing a double emphasis on trait 5 in Level I of the analysis. This highlights the above discussion related to the father principle and tends to suggest a special interest in or need for trait 5 vocational activities or approaches. Remember Jean who fantasized about becoming a brain surgeon? The Sun is a southern singleton in her chart located opposite the Ascendant in the seventh house. Les, who wished to become famous in an unconscious attempt to win his father's love (see chart page 20), has a singleton (western) Sun conjunct the fourth house cusp. Because he has Leo rising, the Sun also represents his Ascendant ruler.

Leading any pattern, the Sun suggests needs for an audience, doing things on a grand scale, a capacity for business or an ability to work with children (more fundamental to the bucket). Any trait 5 occupation or approach could prove suitable. The same applies to any handle or leading planet appearing in the fifth house or in Leo, but to a greatly reduced extent. When the Sun shines in Level I, the need to be special, almost magically so, can be counted on to exist. This can have positive or negative ramifications. Some push forward in a career, while others, like Les, give up on a field too soon, when recognition is not forthcoming, or they can fail to recognize suitable work due to overblown needs to be distinctive.

In the more innately confident types, a humorous cheeriness often can be detected. Feeling "special" for this person is more a state of being than an overt need and it is connected to a deeper quality of selfhood – innate self-love. What many people fail to understand is that one does not have to **do** anything special to **be** special. People with the Sun highlighted or in Leo may be here to learn that lesson. Purpose in life is fulfilled by simply being oneself and doing vocationally what one loves to do.

Without this inner feeling, gratifying skill development may not take place. People cannot share the best of what they have to offer. From the standpoint of the psyche (or the soul?), this is disquieting. The more conscious driver of self – the ego – is not able to fulfill its "job in life" (see Chapter 7). Typically this state of discomfort is misinterpreted as the need to be famous or honored. Exaggerated bragging or overly humble shyness (which are two sides of the same coin) may be demonstrated. When the Sun appears in Level I, attaining a sense of contentment from accomplishments may not be easy. Bigger, better and more may not suffice when healthy self-love has not been fostered.

Famous personalities with Sun Singleton: Gustave Coubert (north)

Sun Leading: Muhammad Ali (locomotive, although could be a splay), Richard De Mont (bucket), Hugh Downs (locomotive), Galileo (bucket), Sir William Rowan Hamilton (bucket), Leontyne Price (bucket, near angles), Harry Truman (bowl)

Sun Focalized in a Seesaw: Enrico Fermi

Sun Near Angles: Hugo Black, Willy Brandt, Lenny Bruce, Johnny Carson, Nina Foch, Peter Fonda, Caroline Kennedy, Bruce Lee, Vivien Leigh, Abraham Lincoln, Phoebe Snow, Lotte Von Strahl

Pluto - Trait 8 (Level I)

Most astrological literature about Pluto relates it to power and describes this symbol as ruthless, manipulative and desirous of influencing the masses. This description, however pertinent, represents only one side of the Plutonian coin. While these characteristics can exist when the planet appears in Level I, or when it receives a number of close aspects, Pluto also can correspond to a fear of power. Self-repressiveness, passivity, passive aggression or timidity can consume the person because some aspect of self has been suppressed (see Chapter 2). Such a response tends to correlate with low career ceilings or with a blocked ability to obtain more desirable positions. It signals a need to develop "inner" power and a more resourceful, resilient personality. A third type of Plutonian character can be demonstrated by those who have positively developed and channeled their inner power. They have learned to master themselves and to share power for constructive purposes.

Arroyo[15] relates Pluto to the principle of transformation, a personality function not yet acknowledged by science. Transformative urges eliminate outworn behavior and attitudes to experience a rebirth of consciousness. Wherever Pluto is located or rules in the chart, an imperative need exists to eliminate fears and self-doubts and usher in a new self-image. The more highlighted trait 8 is in the chart, the more pronounced the need becomes to confront denied aspects of self and early life experiences which may have contributed to the problem. The potential is to change from one state of being into another (i.e., the high school nerd who becomes a highly renowned professional). This tends to be particularly true when Pluto appears in Level I.

Confronting denied qualities of self can be exceptionally disturbing. It tends to be fought by the ego due to the fears and dread associated with it. The conflict is shown symbolically by Pluto's fixed, water nature. Fixity and water cannot exist together for long. Without change and new input, one nature (water) conflicts with the other (fixity); hence turbulence (see Chapter 8). A highlighted Pluto, or close aspects with the personal planets, can represent deep-seated emotional disturbances which, if not squarely faced, can flare up and disrupt the vocational expression.

The Gauquelins were unable to significantly verify any Plutonian occupations or characteristics. Only a slight tendency to show positive correlations after its rise and culmination was noted.[16]

But Pluto represents a personality function as far removed from consciousness as the planet is from the Earth. All three of the outer planets relate to the hidden depths of the unconscious and represent transpersonal forces for change and growth. For most people, the symbolic energies of these planets extend beyond personal control and everyday comprehension. (Refer to

Chapter 2 for a complete list of Pluto's vocational outlets and approaches.)

PLUTO PASSIONS

Many Plutonian (trait 8) types want to stand for something and often display "passions" or obsessive qualities about their work - which appears to others as workaholism. All of the outer planets highlight a basic need for commitment to work, especially good works. Otherwise, their disruptive themes might undermine the occupational process. For power players, thrones can be toppled as a result of stepping on too many toes. When their tactics go to ruthless extremes, they often are being used by power, instead of utilizing power.

Individuals who are more conscious and considerate of their power also are likely to be those who have adequately developed the vocationally significant personality functions. Self-repressive types and power players, on the other hand, tend to be deficient in the Moon and Venus areas. The sense of personal adequacy, comfort with self and ability to relate in a give-and-take manner tend to be faulty. This accounts for the control issues that dominate their lives, their lack of trust and their interrelating problems.

More developed Pluto types do not experience this, and throw themselves into their work with an unrelenting commitment to master the subject or activity. They often possess a capacity for getting to the bottom line of events or other people's behavior. This is why some are so suited for the field of psychology, while others conduct research as an important facet of their work. They focus a conscious eye on sharing power by benefitting a greater whole, not merely themselves. This is why they wish to stand for something or influence the standards of practice in their chosen fields. They often pulsate from a dark mysteriousness or sexual allure that immediately attracts the attention of others. Additionally, they can function in many different occupations without limit to trait 1 or 8 outlets. The advertising and television industries "influence the masses" and are passionately involved in their own, high-powered corporate structures (trait 8). Writing and the performing arts (trait 2, 4 or 7) also are ways to influence society.

In or ruling the sixth house, Pluto suggests a 6/8 blend (see Chapter 5) and a capacity for grueling, corporate or "dirty" work, for a healing-oriented occupation or for immersing oneself in the job. Any occupation associated with the recycling of goods also could prove suitable. Power needs to be exercised daily and fortitude may be required to deal with office politics. Much the same applies to the 6/10 blend (see Chapter 5) which exists **when Pluto is in or rules the tenth house**. One of the forms of power needs to be exercised as part of the expression of authority or inner power needs to be developed to attain a fuller vocational expression.

Pluto as a singleton is a Level I factor perhaps indicative of a special trait 8 interest or capacity, for example, to influence the course of a profession or to passionately stand for something. This may be one reason Pluto is said to correspond to the "revolutionary," although the nature of the revolution does not have to be violent. As a singleton these days it is rare.

When it is focalized in a chart pattern, Pluto represents another Level I factor which tends to intensify, or make more turbulent, the drives symbolized by the pattern in which it is found. The capacity to become embroiled in or impassioned by the vocation escalates, in addition to one's charisma (or emotional problems). To experience work as fulfilling, vocational drives need to be unrelenting, possibly probing, risky, research-oriented or they need to demonstrate one of the forms of "power" (see Chapter 2). Similar situations apply, to a diminished extent, when any handle or leading planet appears in the eighth house or in Scorpio.

Famous personalities with Pluto Singleton: Sir William Rowan Hamilton (south/east, bucket handle), Edouard Manet (south)

Pluto Leading: Steve Allen (locomotive), Jack Anderson (locomotive), Philip Berrigan (bucket), Johnny Carson (bucket), Montgomery Clift (bucket), Ernest Hemingway (bowl), Heinrich Himmler (bucket), Walter Koch (bowl), Martin Luther (bucket), Gary Middlecoff (locomotive), Mickey Rooney (locomotive), Dr. Sam Sheppard (locomotive)

Pluto Bucket Handle: Hector Berlioz, Alexander Dumas, Stephen Foster

Pluto Near Angles: Hector Berlioz, Willy Brandt, Edmund G. Brown, Albert Camus, Jimmy Carter, Chris Chubbuck, Ram Dass, Zsa Zsa Gabor, Evel Knievel, Christopher Reeves, Brooke Shields

Jupiter - Trait 9 (Level I)

Jupiter symbolizes the extroverted, aspiring side of the personality and represents an urge to broaden horizons. This can encompass a desire to learn more about life or one's profession. When Jupiter appears in Level I, it is imperative to have an interesting, productive vocation which offers advancement, travel or notoriety. As one of the vocationally significant planets, however, Jupiter always is important to vocational expression because it symbolizes what is needed to experience a growth in understanding.

Traditionally, the planet has been called the "greater benefic" and has been associated with luck. But luck is what people make out of their opportunities. Some individuals with Jupiter in Level I get more out of their opportunities than others, depending on the trait 10 component to their personalities.

Tradition also has associated Jupiter with long distance travel, foreign places, philosophy, religion, higher education, publishing and the law. Although not typically related to astrology, it often is significant in such practitioner's charts. These vocations are suitable outlets for Level I Jupiter because they encompass activities connected to broader aspects of life, society and the physical universe.

Jupiter also represents the urge to spread one's name, influence or important beliefs beyond one's immediate circles. As such, it can correlate with a desire for fame and was found in the Gauquelin studies to significantly occupy the **plus zones of famous actors and politicians** beyond the chance level. Adventurers and other people of action also were mentioned.[17]

These professions, the more traditional ones, in addition to the broadcast media and the advertising industry, entail a broader projection of one's presence, ideas or a desire to impact people. Jupiter in Level I also could be indicative of the person who is apt to attain success by moving away from the birth locale.

The job or the lifestyle must reflect appropriate outlets for Jupiterian drives, especially when the planet appears in the plus zones. These job-related duties could include any trait 9 occupational outlet discussed in Chapter 2. But the work must bring growth, recognition and advancement because dead-end jobs undermine aspirational needs.

In her comparative study of ten astrologers' keywords versus planetary plus zone positions, Françoise Gauquelin[18] remarks "that most textbooks do not provide a correct picture of Jupiter characteristics." After scanning seventy-one texts for Jupiter references, she concluded that many traditional keywords associated with a "badly" aspected Jupiter more accurately reflect Jovian traits while keywords for a well-aspected Jupiter are not supported by her findings. "The 'bad' keywords are then statistically good ones, and the 'good' keywords, are the statistically inconclusive ones."[19]

"In the Jupiter personality some characteristics seem always to be present: ambition, pride, gaiety, independence, wit and a kind of authority or presence."[20]

Obviously, these qualities are helpful for attracting advancement opportunities. Other traits the Gauquelins uncovered reveal characteristics traditionally attributed to the Sun or Mars: angry, argumentative, assured, caustic, conquering type, dominating, enterprising, impetuous, mocking, noisy, obstinate, pompous, powerful, pretentious, rash, self-confident, show off, sparkling and vain. This is not surprising. The Sun, Mars and Jupiter are fire planets and relate to psychological functions connected to the extroversion of the personality. While the Sun may symbolize a generalized aspect of selfhood, it functions **through** the more poignant energies represented by Mars and Jupiter which serve to drive one in the outer world. The fact that these three planets share many of the same traits can be attributed to the fire element also shared between them (see Chapter 8).

With Jupiter in Level I, or when trait 9 is otherwise strongly represented, the need to reach out, be known, important, rich or famous are essential vocational factors to consider. When the need to gain greater influence goes unrecognized, inappropriate job selection or all sorts of neurotic reactions, especially a high strung nervousness, can result. Again, this is the case whenever a personality need is highlighted in a chart, but is denied outward expression. The denial is an outgrowth of a limited self-image and fears of failure which can inhibit the function which Jupiter represents. That is why aspirational drives cannot operate optimally when the personality functions symbolized by the other vocationally-significant planets are not adequately developed. The likelihood of attaining eminent status in a field diminishes.

When Jupiter appears in or rules the sixth house (or in Virgo), any trait 9 need and job-related duty (see Chapter 2) can become pertinent to work routines and satisfaction, depending on the individual's interests. A 6/9 blend is represented (see Chapter 5). Space and freedom on the job, steady improvement, advancement and growing influence are needed. Growth comes from developing a needed skill, craft or talent based on important beliefs, theories or codified systems of thought, such as in the law, psychology or astrology. **In or ruling the tenth house (or in Capricorn),** the 9/10 blend emphasizes a need to develop the aspirational side of the personality and to broaden one's scope of influence. Additional schooling or training could be vital to obtaining interesting positions and it is possible to "grow" through the authoritative development of an expertise.

The least productive use of Level I Jupiter symbolism is to develop unrealistic expectations about self, abilities or what the job world has to offer (a propensity this planet shares with Neptune). This also can happen when Jupiter is involved in close aspects, especially to the Sun or Mars. Aspirations may need to be examined for their reality quotient. Some people can make themselves miserable when their aspiring needs are strong, but are unrealistic or undermined by a lack of effort and discipline. For others, it may be difficult to attain satisfaction from work if it is not considered important enough or does not provide sufficient influence or fame. If a sense of purpose is to be achieved, the view of life or of the self may have to change.

Jupiter as a singleton tends to represent a special interest in or need for trait 9 associated occupations or approaches to a career (see Chapter 2). Any special capabilities along these lines, however, are likely to manifest only when the other primary vocational functions are adequately shaped. **In the handle, leading or otherwise focalized position**, Jupiter also represents a Level I factor. It suggests that the drives symbolized by the pattern need to be channeled through trait 9 outlets or approaches. Similar needs will apply whenever any handle or leading planet appears in the ninth house or in Sagittarius, but to a greatly reduced degree.

Aesthetic or sensitive bowl drives, which often incline to self-containment, could (and need to) be more expansive when Jupiter leads the pattern. Creative, assisting or intellectual occupations also are possible with this combination, for example, writing (or any of the creative, performing arts) or psychology. With Jupiter leading a bundle structure, interesting work might surround a need to obtain advanced training or a college degree. Jupiter leading the more forceful locomotive pattern could indicate politics, advertising, astrology, the broadcast media or an influential executive position in a large corporation. With Jupiter as the handle of a bucket pattern, any occupation catering to an audience could prove rewarding, for example, an actor/actress or a worldwide lecturer.

Famous personalities with Jupiter Singleton: Vida Blue (north, bucket handle), Jean Cocteau (south), Tom McLoughlin (south, bucket handle), Pat Nixon (south, bucket handle), Jay North (west, bucket handle), Natalie Wood (north)

Jupiter Leading: Rossano Brazzi (bucket), LeRoy Gordon Cooper (bucket), Jimmy Hoffa (bowl), Paul Lynde (bucket), Dean Martin (bucket), Robert S. McNamara (bucket), Christopher Reeves (bowl, G-planet)

Jupiter Bucket Handle: Guy Ballard, Herman Hesse, Zubin Mehta, Vincent Price, Princess Anne, Phoebe Snow

Jupiter Focalized in a Seesaw: Henry Cabot Lodge

Jupiter G-Planet: Hans Christian Andersen, Paul Cezanne, Richard Chamberlain, Jacques Cousteau, Ram Dass, Phyllis Diller, Albert Einstein, Edna Ferber, Françoise Gauquelin, Pancho Gonzales, Vivien Leigh, Isabelle Pagan, Brooke Shields, Suzanne Somers

Saturn - Trait 10 (Level I)

The Saturnian personality function has never been very popular. The ancients labeled it the "greater malefic" and "bad" has been its middle name ever since. Only among more modern, psychologically-oriented astrologers has Saturn been viewed in a more positive light. Still, of all the planets examined by the Gauquelins, the traditional characteristics associated with this one never failed to "describe Saturn quite accurately..."[21]

When it appears as a G-planet, some of Saturn's more positive traits include calm, able to concentrate, detailed, discreet, laborious, methodical, modest, orderly, preserving, precise, reasoned, reserved, serious and unostentatious.[22]

As a personality function, Saturn symbolizes the need to grow into responsible adulthood and to maintain a tangible role within the collective. It is associated with a **need** to apply disciplined effort, to accept responsibility for one's decision-making actions and, as one of the vocationally significant planets, to develop the self as being competent to exercise authority. Is that so terrible?

Obviously the planet, along with other trait 10 factors, is integral to work. **The Gauquelins found Saturn appearing in the plus zones with greater than chance frequency for eminent scientists** – whose adequate performance relies on the characteristics Saturn symbolizes. Because such traits tend to hamper personality drives required for other occupations, the planet was found in plus zones at a significantly lower than chance frequency in the charts of creative writers and athletes.

Saturn usually is associated with technical or academic writing. However, do not assume Saturn in a plus zone alone or with other planets is inimical to creative expression for all individuals any more than it guarantees the birth of a scientist. It merely correlates with an introverted personality who **tends** to seek more serious, professional, detail-oriented or intellectual occupations. Or the person would tend to take a Saturnian **approach** to the occupation. The planet represents a **need** to apply oneself along diligent, responsible and realistic lines and to pull the self up through a career. Satisfaction is gained from work through this approach, while career obstacles arise when this approach is not taken.

AUTHORITY AND RESPONSIBILITY

The manner in which authority was exercised in the early home is worth examining when Saturn appears in Level I, is closely aspected or when trait 10 is otherwise accented. It tends to correlate with one or more of the following family experiences: academically-inclined parents; parents who are old, preoccupied, cold, distant or blame the world for setbacks they encountered; a smothering or overdirecting family atmosphere which inhibited the development of self-motivational drives; parental separations or separations from parents; an exposure to authority or criticism without a balance of love and affection; parents who were superdependable, conscientious, reliable, predictable – rock of Gibralter types; self-blocking parents, who retreated into illness, inadequacy or required parenting themselves.

While the experiences are many and varied, the key themes revolve around the handling of responsibility, authority and competence. Parents can set **positive** or **negative** examples of what **to** do or what **not** to do, although usually it will be some of both. As children, and later as adults, people can choose which example to follow and can make the same mistakes as their parents, do as well as their parents or surpass them.

The image of self as capable of exercising authority depends on how authority was delivered in childhood and how the individual responded to the situation. For some trait 10 people, early Saturnian experiences build self-reliance, profundity and a realistic desire to achieve along tangible lines (see Chapter 2). For others, similar experiences develop later into feelings of inadequacy or defeatist attitudes of worthlessness. They set low job ceilings for themselves. Still others pretend to be authorities. Saturnian types who do not work as hard as they could can be pipe dreamers and dilettantes of the worst variety.

The Saturn personality function keeps individuals on a realistic course and provides clues when work efforts may not be up to par. The obstacles traditionally associated with this symbolism are tests of abilities and the commitment to the chosen path. A struggle against them indicates exactly how much "on the line" people may be. When obstacles are successfully overcome, a stronger sense of competence is generated out of a firmer definition of one's abilities. A sense of "authority" develops because it has been earned. When obstacles cannot be surmounted, something can be learned, although the experience is usually less pleasant. "Success" and "failure" have something to teach because each helps to put the boundaries of self into a more realistic perspective. People who shirk effort and commitment to work, and who have Saturn in Level I, are attempting to evade a realistic view of their limitations; certain Jupiter and Neptune types can stand out and end up on a wild goose chase through the career world. (Refer to Chapter 2 for Saturn's satisfying vocational outlets and approaches.)

Without a developed work ethic, **Saturn in or ruling the sixth house (or in Virgo)** could spell unemployment difficulties due to superiors breathing down the neck all the time. A 6/10 blend is represented here (see Chapter 5) which, similar to

Mercury in the tenth house, can be interpreted as a need to develop gratifying skills or a technical capacity to become an authority at what one does for a living. Expertise and independent decision-making must be exercised on the job to experience it as fulfilling, but this is not likely to happen without discipline and hard work. The more interesting the work is, the less onerous the effort involved is likely to be. People with the 6/10 blend who find their work satisfying can be the best employees a boss could ever hope to have. Those who experience their work as meaningless, or who do not adequately develop their skills, potentially could develop health problems in an unconscious attempt to escape from a job that does not fulfill their needs.

In or ruling the tenth house (or in Capricorn), the 10/10 trait pair is highlighted (see Chapter 5). One needs to develop a sense of competence and to diligently apply oneself to become established. Depending on talents and innate abilities, this is likely to take time, so patience is required. Without these qualities, the individual is likely to experience career setbacks or boss-related difficulties. The vocational rug can be pulled out from under one when the aspirational reach exceeds the grasp of the effort quotient.

Saturn in Level I as a singleton also represents a need to pull the self up by the bootstraps, take career needs seriously and to dig in and work hard to develop one's skills or talents. It works best for those who have the other vocationally significant functions operating efficiently. Effort has the potential to result in earned and lasting distinction. When the need is not sufficiently responded to, career setbacks are likely. Much the same applies when Saturn leads in a chart pattern or represents the handle of a bucket structure. The vocational drives the pattern symbolizes must be worked at and developed to their best potentials. Otherwise, the trait 10 component can hamper the expression of these drives. To a reduced extent, similar situations apply whenever a handle or leading planet appears in the tenth house or in Capricorn.

In a bucket pattern, trait 5 self-expressive talents require focus and hard-earned development to experience a fulfilling career. One may have to work hard at being creative or to "make it" in the entertainment field, for example. Leading a locomotive, the capacity to drive unrelentingly toward tangible achievement and recognized authority exists. Scientifically-related fields could prove most rewarding. Leading the bundle pattern, the potential for hard mental or health care-related work exists, especially in occupations requiring efficiency, organization and great attention to detail.

Famous personalities with Saturn Singleton: Carol Burnett (south, bucket handle), LeRoy Gordon Cooper (north, bucket handle), Bob Crane (west, bucket handle)

Saturn Bucket Handle: Dr. Alexis Carrel, Van Cliburn, Clint Eastwood, Jim Jones, Morgana King, Leontyne Price, Marcel Proust (singleton south, G-planet), Bertrand Russell, David R. Scott

Saturn Leading: Guy Ballard (bucket), Hector Berlioz (bucket), John Cage (locomotive), Sir Alexander Fleming (bucket), Anatole France (bundle, singleton west, G-planet), Washington Irving (bucket), James Lovell (locomotive), Isabelle Pagan (locomotive)

Saturn Focalized in a Seesaw: Jean Francoise Millet

Saturn Focalized in a Splay: Paul Newman

Saturn G-Planet: Warren Beatty, Alexander Graham Bell, Otto Von Bismark, Ellen Burstyn, John Cage, Albert Camus, Phyllis Diller, Nina Foch, Zsa Zsa Gabor, J. Edgar Hoover, Caroline Kennedy, James Lovell, Walter Mondale, Pat Nixon, Brooke Shields, Lotte Von Strahl

Uranus - Trait 11 (Level I)

One of the outer, transpersonal planets, Uranus symbolizes an element in the psyche which seeks to break patterns that have become restrictive to personal growth. One difficulty with this planet is that its symbolized energies seem to originate from the environment, rather than from within oneself on an unconscious level. Circumstances **seemingly beyond control** can instigate sudden job or career changes. However, this disruption can work to the individual's advantage, provided one is realistically open to it.

Uranus represents an urge toward differentiation and originality, a need for excitement, expression without restraint, and independence from tradition.[23]

When this planet appears in Level I or makes close aspects

to the personal planets, an old occupation may be dropped in favor of a new, totally different and more stimulating one. Sometimes the needed change can appear in the form of a new dimension or approach to the current career and usually results from becoming aware of new self-expressive possibilities.

The odd thing about this change is that it might start from something seemingly "bad" happening, like getting fired. But the words "odd" or "ironic" have little place in the vocabulary of the metaphysically inclined. Situations develop as they do out of the needs and perspectives people possess (consciously or unconsciously).

When security-conscious traits are highlighted, such as 2 or 4, people may suppress Uranian urges and might not think of leaving a job unless forced to by "fate." Or perhaps the unconscious inner urge to make changes causes them to arrive consistently late to work or to be carelessly flip. Unaware of the intent of such behavior, control over it does not exist and the Uranian aspect of consciousness gets its way. The point is, these people attracted the situation to themselves. The more drastic and unpleasant the experience seems, the greater the likelihood that Uranian urges have been denied too long.

Once the individual is free of the job, however, room has been made for something new to take its place. It just takes time to discover what that might be. Without trust in a Higher Power, the experience can be shattering. But for anyone with Uranus in Level I, it is a good idea to be flexible about vocational changes because one could be ready for a more self-expressive occupation. Commitment, discipline, effort and the ability to establish oneself as competent must first exist before reaping the rewards of Uranian freedom, independence, innovation, or unconventionality. (Refer to Chapter 2 for rewarding Uranian vocational outlets and approaches.)

FREEDOM ISSUES

Many Uranian types are able to pursue a number of different vocations and usually require occupations that utilize a wide variety of self-expressive skills. A jack-of-all-trades, without a purposeful and stimulating interest, however, tends to scatter energies. Less constructively, the planet has been correlated with eccentricity, willfulness, rebellion, extremism, impulsive activity, obstinacy, impatience and a constant need for excitement and purposeless change.[24]

When these behaviors predominate, work stability can be in doubt and the resume can be dotted with one job after another. Quitting or getting fired, with an inability to graciously accept direction, are typical. More focused and disciplined Uranian types usually wish to master a particular subject and express themselves along intellectual, technical or authoritative lines. They can represent "shocking" agents for the change Uranus symbolizes – shattering patterns which have become constrictive to personal growth and perceptual outlooks.

The Gauquelins were unable to detect any significance or characteristic traits and occupations for Uranus. Although traditionally associated with scientific and technological endeavors, it was not relevant in the charts of the eminent scientists who were examined. The tilted planet is perhaps most significant to those involved in what could be described as "out-of-this-world" occupations, for example, space exploration, metaphysics or psychic investigation. Uranus also has been associated with the booming computer field and engineering, occupations which utilize highly intricate electronic equipment. Many Uranian types are attracted to work environments humming with electronic sounds, even if they do not have direct contact with the equipment. The television, film, record and radio industries use an entire barrage of electronic devices and also represent Uranian outlets.

Because most of the births examined for the Gauquelins' study took place between 1850 and 1910, electronically-related occupations could not play a major role, nor are all Uranian vocations considered viable outlets by the mainstream of society. Most of the charts this author possesses of astrological practitioners and serious students of the subject have Uranus in (or trait 11 associated with) one of the Level I chart positions, especially as the leading planet. All three of the outer planets can tie in to these vocational outlets (and other new age, metaphysical or "otherworldly" disciplines).

Inventiveness traditionally is considered a Uranian characteristic, along with an antitraditional approach. This planet might be significant to a backroom inventor or hobbyist, someone who likes to tinker around unfettered by structure or rules. Constructive Uranian types may be predominantly self-taught or may take a completely original point of departure on any subject that interests them. Some Uranians invent their own occupations, work unusual hours or work at out-of-the-ordinary jobs or places as a way to satisfy their urges. Others are more suited for independent fields such as sales, consulting, brokering or self-employment.

Uranus, Mars and freewheeling Jupiter all share a love of freedom and independence, although in different ways. In a comparative study analyzing Uranian keywords to planetary plus zone placements,[25] four out of nine sets of astrologers' keywords positively correlated with Jupiter in plus zones, a fifth correlated with Mars while the rest failed to show any correspondence to Uranus. However, Uranian "freedom" expresses along the mental plane (air) as opposed being action-oriented (fire) as are Mars and Jupiter. In this sense, Uranian types can be considered "broad-minded" because they are open to pursuing the new, the different or the avant garde. However, they are not necessarily broad-minded in all other regards. Many can be so thoroughly entrenched in their theories that they are closed off to new input due to the planet's fixed nature (see fixity in Chapter 8).

When the Uranian urge for freedom is carried to extremes, an unconscious fear of emotional closeness and commitment to anyone or anything can develop. This not only disrupts the ability to sustain relationships, but can disturb the vocational process. Without this sense of commitment to and stimulation from the occupation, the Uranian personality is likely to experience boredom as a major facet of the work life.

In or ruling the sixth house (or in Virgo), Uranus represents a 6/11 blend (see Chapter 5). The positive potential is to develop a capacity for highly technical or technological work. Other trait 11 outlets equally could be suitable (see Chapter 2). The Uranian need for group involvement or excitement and stimulation also is important to satisfying day-to-day job functioning. When trait 10 is responded to insufficiently, Uranus here can be indicative of the job-hopper or the person more suited for part-time employment.

The 10/11 blend exists when **Uranus is in or rules the tenth house (or in Capricorn).** It suggests potentials to develop proficiency in a trait 11 occupation as part of one's expression of authority; scientific, new age or metaphysical potentials are especially strong. While such skill development might not be easy, it would be rewarding because one could become a recognized authority in a field or become self-employed. Being friends with or an equal to the boss also can be important.

When the trait 10 component is inadequate or when one represses Uranian vocational needs, the boss could be erratic, or could be experienced as limiting or dictatorial. Job-hopping or getting fired could become a problem, due to inadequate skills and a failure to develop competence. The inability to accept direction or criticism could represent another deficiency. While the individual might justify such outcomes by not wishing to play by society's rules, fears of failure could be more to the point. The person may not wish to face the consequences (or the rewards) of putting oneself "on the line."

In Level I as a singleton, Uranus highlights trait 11 vocational needs and possibly an interest in or a special capacity for such employment outlets. For example, one could be mathematically inclined or a natural for computer programming or engineering. With Uranus **as a handle or leading planet,** the employment drives suggested by the chart pattern trait would have to incorporate Uranian outlets or needs to be a fulfilling experience. For example, colleague recognition might be important, or out of the ordinary work or the television industry could prove rewarding. It also is possible to apply oneself erratically (or independently) on the job. Similar possibilities exist, but to a diminished degree, when a handle or leading planet appears in the eleventh house or in Aquarius.

Famous personalities with Uranus Singleton: Robert Cummings (east), Herbert Von Karajan (east, bucket handle), John F. Kennedy (north, bucket handle), Benito Mussolini (east), Vance Packard (west), Peter Ustinov (west, leading/bowl)

Uranus Leading: James Arness (locomotive), Gustave Coubert (bowl), Honore Daumier (bundle), Adolph Eichmann (bowl), Keith Emerson (bowl), Uri Geller (bowl), Jimi Hendrix (bowl), Diane Keaton (locomotive), Caroline Kennedy (bowl), Pat Nixon (bucket), Suzanne Somers (bowl)

Uranus Bucket Handle: Johnny Carson, Jacques Cousteau, Alcide De Gasperi (singleton west/south), Phyllis Diller, Albert Einstein, Galileo (singleton north), Richard Gordon, Leo Guild, Fernand Leger, Henri Matisse

Uranus Near Angles: William Blake, Marlon Brando, William Jennings Bryan, Ellen Burstyn, Jack Kerouac, Vivien Leigh, Karl Marx (leading/bucket), Isabelle Pagan, Lotte Von Strahl

Neptune - Trait 12 - (Level I)

While Uranus may represent an aspect of personality seeking new freedom for self-expression, the Neptune function is associated with quite a contrasting urge – to experience freedom **from the ego self.**[26]

Orthodox psychology has yet to acknowledge the existence of this facet of personality (although transpersonal psychology does), most likely because it represents drives completely foreign to our competitive society. The urge Neptune symbolizes is to escape from the limitations of the material world and to experience another dimension of reality – a sense of oneness with the whole of life. This urge tends to be prominent when the planet appears in Level I or receives several close aspects. It represents a capacity to tap into a Higher Power (see Chapter 2), although it is difficult to properly interpret the longings with which Neptune coincides. Mostly they are misunderstood and often appear as confused feelings of guilt and sacrifice, anxiety and a general lack of clarity about identity and directions in life.

The planet can correlate with vague yearnings to participate in a greater whole as a significant contributor. The reality quotient and sense of commitment to this yen, however, are telltale. In our society such longings often translate into wanting to be part of the Pepsi generation: glamorous, influential, famous, etc. The "get rich quick" or fantasy approach to life can predominate in many cases. For others, religious or spiritual outlets appear to be rewarding, (similar in this regard to Jupiter), however they can be delusional or escapist in nature when Saturn themes are not developed. Such people could suffer more from a fear of competing in our rough and tumble society than from a desire to be free from the limitations of material existence!

FANTASY

Due to its propensity to fantasy, a Level I Neptune can indicate career problems when the individual is not realistically grounded. Delusions can surround the work effort, such as believing one is working harder or has more to offer than is truly the case. Work could appear to fulfill a godly mission to which all associated with it must be subjugated. One might "fizzle out" in one career after another because the needed sense of commitment is lacking. To be consistently productive, exceptionally gratifying occupations must be selected, ones in which realistic effort and beliefs play a major role. Without them, Neptune types have little to hang on to; they can become lost or attach themselves to the most prevailing influences. Much the same applies to an accent on trait 9; career directions can be unstable due to a lack of constructive ideology.

Living effectively in two worlds at once, the Saturn one and the Neptune one, takes an exceptionally developed consciousness. Many Saturnian types feel anxious over Neptune-related boundlessness, while some Neptunians experience anxiety when effort is required for the fulfillment of dreams. Sometimes pronounced Neptunians are drawn to the disciplines of science or math as a way to ground themselves through tangible, provable facts. However, trait 12's highest motivations stem from inspiration and the ability to move beyond Saturnian perceptual realities while utilizing them as a springboard. The career potential can be boundless in such cases and frequently is scholarly, visionary or artistic.

Traditionally, Neptune has been associated with the arts, aesthetic outlets, creativity, intuition, compassion, mysteries, film, photography, music, the intangible, imagination, idealism, sensitivities, receptivity, sympathy, higher spiritual or otherworldly qualities and interests. These outlets can be suitable when the planet appears in Level I, makes close aspects, or is in or rules the sixth or tenth houses (see Chapter 2). **The Gauquelin studies were unable to detect any significance or confirm characteristic traits and occupations for this planet.** However, because Neptune is a water planet, like the Moon, it is not surprising that eight out of nine astrologers' keywords for the planet positively correlated with the Moon in plus zones.[27]

These two functions share much in common on the personality level and occupationally. Suitable outlets for each have been discussed in Chapter 2.

In an unconstructive sense, Neptune symbolism can represent such undermining tendencies as a lack of ambition and evasion of responsibility; ego weakness, lack of confidence, pipe dreams, escapism, delusions, confusion, being easily imposed upon, deception and the con artist. When these approaches to work predominate, foggy or deluded career directions or an inability to sustain oneself in the job force are likely to result. One may be prompted to abandon the career world altogether or seek others to carry the load as workers type E do. A grounded self-image (trait 4), sustained, realistic effort and commitment (trait 10) are vitally important to an adequate expression of the needs and drives symbolized by a focus on Neptune or trait 12. In another sense, a highlighted Neptune can be a handicap in terms of selecting a career. So many possibilities seem available that it may be difficult to settle on one. Although significant beliefs and interests always are important in determining suitable career directions, they are especially important when trait 12 is pronounced.

In or ruling the sixth house (or in Virgo), Neptune correlates with a 6/12 blend (see Chapter 5). Positively, the symbolism suggests inspired trait 6 capacities, especially health or mental health care or any caring, assisting occupation that relies on the intuition. One also has the potential for inspirational creative works or to spread one's important ideas. One might possess finely tuned technical abilities. The possibilities are endless here (see Chapter 2) because Neptune represents boundless potentials.

When effort and discipline are not applied, job-hopping and any number of other delusions or escapist activities tend to surround the work (or nonwork) effort. Employers with Neptune here are well advised to thoroughly check the references of potential employees. Should an inordinate number prove disappointing, it could indicate that one's own work efforts are not up to par or one may be too inclined to believe that employees will be sacrificing because one **wishes** to believe so. One could also play savior to one's employees, or coworkers, or could attract victims or thieves.

Many of the same problems could apply when **Neptune appears in (Capricorn) or rules the tenth house.** The 10/12 trait pair (see Chapter 5) is in force here. Without discipline and effort to turn vocational dreams into a reality, people tend to fizzle out in one job after another. They could be deluded into believing that overnight success can be theirs, if only they could find that one magical career that is going to put them on top. But the 10/12 blend does not function that way and while inspirational potentials do exist with this placement, nothing is likely to come of them without hard work.

Those who believe in themselves and know they have something worthwhile to offer society take the time and the effort to develop competence at the occupations which inspire them. Their career potentials are boundless and could be related to science, the intuitive arts, spiritual pursuits or any trait 12 endeavor. They have the capacity to shed new light on the nature of reality and exhibit a passion for excellence, due to a need to "serve" in the highest sense of the term.

While **Neptune in Level I as a singleton** might represent someone with special interest in or capacities for trait 12 outlets (vocationally or avocationally), the delusional potentials are equally great when the trait 10 function is deficient. With Neptune **as a handle or leading planet** much the same applies. Vocational drives need to incorporate a trait 12 brand of sensitivity, realistic compassion or inspiration, or else they can become diluted through wishful thinking and lack of self-discipline. Without a sufficient self-worth profile, one also could be victimized in or outside of the work arena. Similar possibilities exist when any handle or leading planet appears in the twelfth house or in Pisces, only to a lesser extent.

Famous personalities with Neptune Singleton: Edmund G. Brown (north), Robert T. Cross (south, leading/bowl)

Neptune Bucket Handle: Robert Burton, Washington Irving, Maria La Laurie (singleton north, angular)

Neptune Focalized Seesaw: Andre Gide, Elbert Hubbard

Neptune Leading: Maurice Chevalier (bowl), Stephen Crane (locomotive), Claude Debussy (bowl), Guy de Maupassant (bowl), Edna Ferber (bowl), Paul Gauguin (bowl), Johann Von Goethe (locomotive), Rockwell Kent (bundle), Alan Leo, Le Petomane, George Patton (locomotive)

Neptune Near Angles: Lew Ayres, Honore De Balzac, David Bowie, Paul Cezanne, Phyllis Diller, Nina Foch, Jean Houston, Morgana King, Vivien Leigh, Pat Nixon, Princess Anne, Marcel Proust

References

1. Dean, Geoffrey, editor, *Recent Advances in Natal Astrology*, Western Australia: Analogic, 1977, p. 380
2. Dean, p. 385
3. Jones, Marc Edmund, *The Guide to Horoscope Interpretation*, Wheaton, Illinois: Theosophical Publishing House 1974, p. 76
4. Jones, p. 76
5. Gauquelin, Michel, *Your Personality and the Planets*, New York: Stein & Day, 1980, p. 83-84
6. Gauquelin, Françoise, *Psychology of the Planets*, San Diego: ACS Publications, Inc., 1982, p. 28
7. Gauquelin, Michel, *Your Personality and the Planets*, New York: Stein & Day, 1980, p. 135
8. Gauquelin, p. 134
9. Hyneck, J. Allen, Forward to *Cosmic Influences on Human Behavior*, New York: ASI, 1978, p. 13
10. Greene, Liz, *The Outer Planets and Their Cycles*, Reno, Nevada: CRCS Publications, 1983, p. 69
11. Gauquelin, Michel, *Your Personality and the Planets*, New York: Stein & Day, 1980, p. 111
12. Gauquelin, Françoise, *Psychology of the Planets*, San Diego: ACS Publications, Inc., 1982, p. 31
13. Dean, Geoffrey, editor, *Recent Advances in Natal Astrology*, Western Australia: Analogic, 1977, p. 84-88
14. Gauquelin, Françoise, *Psychology of the Planets*, San Diego: ACS Publications, Inc., 1982, p. 31
15. Arroyo, Stephen, *Astrology, Psychology and the Four Elements*, Reno, Nevada: CRCS Publications, 1978, p. 81
16. Gauquelin, Françoise, *Psychology of the Planets*, San Diego: ACS Publications, Inc., 1982, p. 31
17. Gauquelin, Michel, *Your Personality and the Planets*, New York: Stein & Day, 1980, p. 42
18. Gauquelin, Françoise, *Psychology of the Planets*, San Diego: ACS Publications, Inc., 1982, p. 61
19. Gauquelin, p. 62
20. Gauquelin, Michel, *Your Personality and the Planets*, New York: Stein & Day, 1980, p.32
21. Gauquelin, Françoise, *Psychology of the Planets*, San Diego: ACS Publications, Inc., 1982, p. 26

22. Gauquelin, Michel, *Your Personality and the Planets*, New York: Stein & Day, 1980, p. 57
23. Arroyo, Stephen, *Astrology, Psychology and the Four Elements*, Reno, Nevada: CRCS Publications, 1978 p. 81
24. Arroyo, p. 81
25. Gauquelin, Françoise, *Psychology of the Planets*, San Diego: ACS Publications, Inc., 1982, p. 20-21
26. Arroyo, Stephen, *Astrology, Psychology and the Four Elements*, Reno, Nevada: CRCS Publications, 1978 p. 81
27. Gauquelin, Françoise, *Psychology of the Planets*, San Diego: ACS Publications, Inc., 1982, p. 20-21

CHAPTER FIVE

THE ASPECTS OF PERSONALITY

Few areas of astrology are more complex than the relationship between aspects, personality and vocational aptitude. Using traditional orbs, as many as fifty or more aspects per chart can be generated. Customarily presented in cookbook fashion, the aspects often are conceived of as isolated tendencies, said to manifest positively under the soft, harmonious angles and negatively under the hard, inharmonious angles. Although evidence exists to prove that aspects function this way in synastry[1], little research exists to confirm these rules for natal or vocational astrology.

One study[2] investigated the connections between aspects, profession and personality factors. It involved nearly 12,000 charts, some 300,000 aspects and explored the occurrence of major aspects among groups of eminent professionals as compared to a control group. Out of approximately 270 tests, twenty-two were statistically significant. Although unreplicated, these findings support the traditional concept that aspects identify potential vocational capabilities. But are the traditional rules associated with aspect interpretation a reliable measure of these aptitudes?

Major and Minor Aspects

Natal aspects are classified as major or minor. Traditionally, the five major Ptolemaic aspects which are used in this text (five degree orb) are the conjunction, sextile, square, trine and opposition. They are said to have the greatest significance. The minor aspects used here (one degree orb) are the 22.5 degree aspect, the semisextile (30 degrees), the novile (40 degrees), the semisquare (45 degrees), the septile (51 degrees 43 minutes), the quintile (72 degrees), the sesquiquadrate (135 degrees), the biquintile (144 degrees) and the quincunx (150 degrees). Traditionally, the minor aspects are said to be weaker or less significant. However, given that fewer people are born under minor aspects, due to their reduced orbs, it is logical that these aspects would relate to something potentially unique about an individual.

This view is taken here. The traditional concept of stronger/weaker is better replaced by conceiving of **major aspects as signifying general attributes and prominent personality needs and drives. Minor aspects can be conceived of as potential aptitudes or more specific capabilities.** Because personality and vocational expression are interrelated, each aspect has important meanings.

Harmonious/Inharmonious Aspects

The distinction between major and minor aspects represents only one way to assess aspects for vocational purposes. Another traditional classification is by harmonious, or soft and ease-producing, versus inharmonious, or hard and stress-producing. Although the terminology is an improvement over the former good/bad or afflicted/unafflicted concept, this classification does not apply to vocational astrology in the manner commonly used.

The traditional viewpoint on harmonious aspects is that they:

> ...bring success, happiness and lasting accomplishment...[and that inharmonious aspects]...are innate limitations or inhibitions which present stress and difficulties. They do not always indicate a predisposition to failure, but they do indicate conflicts and struggles which need much constructive action before they

> can bring success, happiness and lasting accomplishment.
> In Vocational Astrology the harmonious aspects and some conjunction aspects represent the obvious trends of the horoscope which can bring success. It is true that a native of strong willpower, fixed determination, and perseverance may achieve success using the inharmonious aspects, but these bring much stress and slower progress. It is probably better to follow the natural flow of the horoscope by developing the harmonious aspects and the conjunctions. [3]

What underlies this viewpoint is a more fundamental outlook on life and work: the only good job is an easy job and the only good life is the easy life. It also assumes that harmonious aspects only function positively and that inharmonious aspects only function negatively. This is not true.

The positive qualities associated with harmonious aspects, and the innate limitations associated with inharmonious ones, stem from astrology's medieval past when serfs toiled endlessly while princes and kings kept their hands clean. Saturn's negative reputation came from the same source. Work and effort were equated with a lowly, unfortunate station and the equation mistakenly lingers for some contemporary practitioners. Other astrologers have alternative viewpoints:

> It stands to reason that, since to achieve anything notable is *ex hypothesi* difficult, the map of the man who does this must contain difficult elements; and as a rule we shall more often find in such cases Sun opposition Saturn, than Sun trine Jupiter...I have sometimes found that inharmonious contacts between certain planets are not noticeably worse, so far as success and true character go, than are the harmonious.[4]

Harmonious aspects do not always represent people's best career potentials, nor do inharmonious aspects always signify their worst. Different people respond differently to the same factors in their personalities and different people function through different work ethics. These factors are not specified in a chart. In general, planets linked by harmonious aspects indicate personality functions, urges and drives which **tend to** perform together relatively easily and reinforce each other. This is especially true of the trine aspect which represents an easy, flowing quality between the linked symbolism, as if a path of least resistance was established between them. Some individuals overdo the themes represented by trining planets, in which case trines could represent "negative" personality characteristics requiring correction! Sextiles represent more dynamic, often mentally enlivening, connections between personality functions. Both aspects indicate readily available character traits and vocational abilities. Contrary to tradition, however, there is no guarantee people automatically will respond constructively to them.

For example, consider Mars trine Jupiter versus Mars sextile Jupiter. The sense of identity and self-assertive drives can function well with the aspirational urges and belief in positive outcomes. Constructively demonstrated, these aspects can reflect dynamic, growth-oriented career potentials. A need to identify with far-reaching goals and to be recognized for important accomplishments exists. They indicate the possibility that when energies are constructively channeled, positive outcomes are plausible, not that "success" is automatic. The trine, however, is more inclined to excessiveness with a tendency to rely too much on luck or the easiest way out. The sextile aspect is less prone to this. It tends to highlight the mental/verbal/physical inclinations of the linked symbolism.

Inharmonious aspects are the most dynamic links in that they manifest on the personality and experiential level. They represent contradictory functions and needs which challenge each other for the upper hand. They are not easily expressed because they require a degree of conscious effort to moderate, blend or compromise the features they symbolize.

For example, consider Sun square Saturn (see trait pair 5/10 later in this chapter). The aspect indicates that a link exists between the desire to be a distinct human being capable of self-esteem and spontaneous self-expression and the need to buckle down, focus on tasks and work hard to achieve competence or distinction. A balance needs to be struck between these two.

Once individuals are aware of their inner conflicts, they have the power (consciousness) to moderate them at appropriate times. When such conscious reconciliation is achieved, stress is reduced. Sun square Saturn can be integrated by granting sufficient time for Sun-related needs and for Saturn-related needs. It is possible to combine authority (10) and self-expression (5) through a rewarding career as a hardworking professional or expert. Spontaneous self-expression (in the form of lecturing, teaching or performing) and the painstaking development of competence could play important roles. Ample relaxation time and vacations from work are refreshing (and necessary) ways to balance this aspect. One might grow to consider work (10) fun (5). Or one might take seriously (10) a career in any trait 5 occupation as a way to combine the symbolism.

To suggest that hard aspects always work out negatively or limit an individual's capacity to achieve is to take too simplistic a view of human behavior. Although career possibilities were quite limited centuries ago, when astrology's basic tenets were formulated, this is not true today. Our potentials are infinitely more vast, a reason why charts no longer specify success or failure. **Inharmonious aspects can indicate inner diversity as well as outer versatility, once they are reconciled**. Tension, stress and problems will continue to exist when a reconciliation is not achieved. One planet in the stress aspect tends to be carried to extremes, or is denied and repressed so that the other planet becomes extremist, or its symbolized disposition is projected onto others who are likely to exhibit it to excess.

The conjunction aspect expresses according to the nature of the planets involved. Planets that tend to "get along" are those whose natures are similar, for example, Moon/Venus and Sun/Mars/Jupiter. Mercury functions with the nine remaining planets according to their natures and the type of aspect formed. Saturn denotes a dampening of drives for purposes of focus and production, although the hard angles represent a more compelling need to limit the drives the other planets symbolize. Some people are more disposed to effort than others, although the harmonious or inharmonious nature of Saturn's aspects is not going to distinguish them automatically. Any close aspect to the outer planets can be uplifting, inspiring and creative or problematical, tense and difficult depending on the individual involved.

An ability to interrelate planetary symbolism is a must when it comes to analyzing aspects for vocational needs. Reading textbooks with an eye to how the author arrived at conclusions is more helpful than memorizing opinions about an aspect. *The Dynamics of Aspect Analysis*[5] is highly recommended for this exercise. A study of midpoints also is instructive and *Planets in Combination*[6] is worth reading.

Major Configurations

The traditional interpretation of major configurations denotes characteristics or aptitudes in their own right. **Grand trines** and **kites** (four planets linked by a series of sextiles) are patterns often thought to be beneficial, successful or creative in manifestation. However, they can indicate variable results, even negative ones.

The **stellium** configuration, four or more planets linked by conjunction, denotes a strong focus on the house(s) and sign(s) in which it is found. But there is nothing to guarantee how those issues will manifest or be resolved. Although the stellium can correlate with specializing in a certain occupation, it also could suggest potential talents or focused problem areas in life. Michael Meyer[7] offers constructive advice on major configurations:

> One should avoid overstressing the importance of these formations... The manner in which such patterns may manifest themselves, and to what extent, are very difficult to ascertain. Any formation may be indicative of a well-integrated, highly creative individual as well as a superficial, ego-centered personality with a sense of superiority over others.

Most important to consider when interpreting individual aspects and major configurations are the planets involved and the type of aspect which links them. However, another equally important factor for aspectual analysis is the degree of orb involved. This is the one variable most agreed upon as significant to aspect intensity, and it is the one variable which safely can be altered to simplify chart analysis.

Orbs

Use of orbs for natal astrology varies among practitioners. Most agree that smaller orbs, anywhere from one-half a degree to as much as three degrees of longitude, should be used for minor aspects. For major aspects, the permissible orb is greater (and less agreed upon): anywhere from less than five degrees to as much as fifteen or more depending on the aspect and planets involved. Agreement is universal that the closer any aspect is to partile the more significant it is likely to be.

Five degrees of orb for major aspects and one degree for minor aspects is suggested in this text. Ten degree orbs would produce about twice as many aspects per chart.

Many students and practitioners alike bristle over the idea of reduced orbs, as if asked to relinquish important factors in their personalities. However,

> Those who insist on large orbs should consider one point vital to all analyses, namely that a signal can only be significant if it rises above the noise. If the birth chart is considered as the signal, and the environment as the noise, it follows that accuracy is hardly possible unless the signals are adequately strong.[8]

The reduced orb represents the most effective means of simplifying astrological analysis by highlighting the important aspects for vocational consideration and disregarding what is less significant. (**The most significant aspects for vocational aptitude and expression are likely to be within one degree of longitude.**) This does not mean that larger orbs do not have a place in natal analysis. Research on parallels[10] suggests that while they have validity in progressions, their importance in natal work has been negated. They are not considered here.

Retrogradation

Retrogradation is a condition frequently thought to signify the debilitating, repressing or altering (often with negative consequences) of the outward expression of planetary symbolism. Statistical support for these attributes or the significance of retrograde planets, however, is not strong. The growing trend is to correlate retrograde motion as different from normal rather than being adverse in effect.[10] Because so many people are born when the planets Saturn through Pluto are retrograde, it is unlikely that these factors are significant to vocational aptitude. This does not mean that retrogradation is without significance.

The retrograde condition requires inner or self-motivation and correlates with a trait 12 theme as part of the planet's "cosmic state." Occupational outlets or approaches to the vocational possibilities suggested by the planet may be confused, deluded or inspired (trait 12). For example, a retrograde might manifest as being unrealistic about success in a related occupation and getting in over one's head. One could incorporate intuition, caring instincts or other trait 12 attributes into job-related duties, or take a committed or inspired approach to the career. Or, one may be unaware of the trait indicated by the retrograde planet as an important need, as if it was buried from consciousness.

How significant retrogradation is to vocational choice or aptitude would depend on how prominent a trait factor the retrograde planet or planets represent as well as how people individually respond. Because eminent personalities possess an inner motivation to succeed, the retrograde condition does not express as confused, deluded or blocked efforts. This is a good reason why research (which focuses on eminent people) has been unable to confirm traditional viewpoints on retrogradation.

Intercepted Houses

A similar trait 12 tinge can be associated with the outward expression of intercepted planets. People whose charts display a number of retrograde and/or intercepted planets may need a substantial amount of inner direction and self-motivation to express their unique potentials. This is true whenever trait 12 is highlighted in a chart.

Stations

Due to the fact that fewer people are born when planets make stations, this symbolism could represent individualized possibilities. Some evidence exists to support that a stationary planet can be quite significant to a chart analysis.[11] How or if this factor impacts vocational matters remains undetermined. More study is needed, although the trait associated with a stationary planet is considered here to be pertinent (or problematic) to vocational expression. It has been included in Level I of the analysis.

House Rulers

House rulers represent another dimension of the language of astrology. Tradition states that the planet ruling the sign on a house cusp affects the affairs of that house according to the planet's sign, house position and the aspects it receives.

The Church of Light[12] conducted an interesting study of Placidus house cusps. Using a minimum of one hundred cases for each event inspected, the study found that, without exception, a progressed major or minor aspect (orb one degree) to the ruler of the related house or houses existed at the time of the event. For obtaining or losing a job, a progressed aspect (100 charts, 100% of the time) was in effect to the rulers of the tenth and sixth houses. These are intriguing findings, but without control groups, and other test design problems, the results cannot be considered conclusive.

This is not to say that house rulers are without significance. They link activities between houses in much the same way aspects link planetary principles. However, the house ruler link is more subtle and suggests an appropriate avenue of expression or activity pertinent to the affairs of the house which the planet rules. Where the ruler of a house is located suggests a trait factor, activity or approach significant to the expression of the house it rules.

For example, in a chart where the ruler of the sixth house appears in the first, abbreviated in the astrological alphabet as 1/6, initiative and identity are connected to the work expression; the same applies when the ruler of the first house is located in the sixth. Whenever these traits combine it is important for individuals to work under their own direction and to experience their jobs as self-expressive because identity needs are tied to work. It also suggests that how these people fare in the job world will be contingent on the initiative and enterprise they exhibit. The delimiter of this initiative is defined by the nature of the planet which rules the first or sixth house. If this planet is Saturn, for example, it will be located in the sixth or first house. The combined symbolism is highly suggestive of a need to work hard. The initiative, enterprise and sense of identity (1) must encompass the pursuit and painstaking development of competence, authority or an expertise (10) at a purposeful skill, craft or talent (6).

Double-cusped houses also are linked as are the house affairs ruled by Gemini and Virgo or Taurus and Libra. How important these various house linkages will be to vocational analysis, when viewed in light of the trait pair they form, depends on whether the trait pair has surfaced in some other fashion.

An examination of trait pairs for vocational properties follows. **They do not reflect the full range of potential expressions of which these blends are capable.** On the trait grid portion of the needs analysis form, you circle the trait pairs appropriate to major aspects, using one color of ink to represent Level I. Minor aspects are indicative of more specific capabilities and also belong to Level I of the analysis. Use broken circles to denote them (using the same Level I colored ink). Keep this distinction in mind when completing the grid sheet on the form. Together with the prominent personality needs, discussed in the previous chapter, these general attributes (major aspects) and specific aptitudes (minor aspects) represent Level I of the vocational analysis and are most likely to shape vocational aptitude, choice and direction. Although all Level I chart factors are significant, any trait pair repeated from Level II or repeated three or more times from Level III will be significant.

For best results, the individual's interests, intelligence, education, age, effort quotient and work experience must be acknowledged. Despite indicated potentials, there is no way around one's personal reality and work background. The suggested vocational possibilities which follow should be considered in this light.

Trait Pairs

Attributes, aptitudes and specific vocational outlets for each trait pair are presented below. **The latter represent suggestions only intended to prompt individual formulation of additional lines of work which call upon the related capabilities**. Keep in mind that these definitions are most applicable when a particular trait pair appears in Level I (representing a close major or minor aspect) or when it is repeated in the analysis two or more times. Both constructive and nonconstructive applications of these combined traits also are provided.

Each trait pair also is categorized according to the following general classifications. Most jobs reflect a combination of two or more of these general aptitudes:

artistic: associated with the creative production/performance of form, beauty or design; the imaginative or performing arts.

practical: associated with everyday types of employment; job selection on the basis of financial return.

technical: associated with the trades and occupations requiring a degree of training, technical knowledge or manual skill.

intellectual: associated with the professions, sciences and occupations requiring more advanced training or a more authoritative application of technical knowledge, know-how and skill; can be in a position of authority and responsibility.

enterprising: associated with business management and occupations requiring initiative, risk-taking, competition, athletic ability or physical stamina; seeks advancement and leadership.

assisting: associated with sales, counseling, teaching and occupations serving/catering to the needs of others; works closely with others.

multicapable: refers to an ability for all or most of the above.

1/1: multicapable but predominately enterprising/ intellectual

- same as trait 1
- For details and suggested occupations, see trait 1 in Chapter 2, eastern hemisphere emphasis, Mars in Chapter 4, preponderance/diminished representation of cardinality/fire, New Moon phase, Aries rising.

1/2: predominantly practical, enterprising or artistic

Constructive applications:

- determined to further self, talents and to make one's own way in life through stable, practical career goals and drives
- ambitious but integrates risk-taking with financial security concerns
- hardworking when interests are sparked and takes action to establish financial security

- self-employment or artistic flair possible
- the appearance/presence affects the income and actively assists work

Nonconstructive applications:
- fails to develop rewarding talents or to make a self-sustaining income
- fails to fulfill identity needs (most likely due to a lackadaisical attitude or low self-worth)
- is unkempt (due to low self-worth) which undermines career opportunities
- overly relies on other people's resources until self-worth is achieved
- lazy and prefers not working

Possible vocations: performing artist, dancer, financial director, bank executive or teller, cashier, purchaser, model, art dealer, gift shop proprietor, furniture designer or builder, massage therapist, talented athlete, flower arranger, farm worker. (See Taurus rising for further details.)

1/3: multicapable
Constructive applications:
- busy, mentally alert, often physically on the go and outspoken
- an original thinker or develops a purposeful, skilled use for the hands or voice
- enjoys reading, learning, the dissemination/exchange of ideas or stimulating conversations
- a perpetual student
- requires space, freedom and seeks mental challenge
- uses telephone, reference materials or tools (instruments) as part of job
- sees or talks to customers, clients or patients on a daily basis
- may write, lecture, teach or travel

Nonconstructive applications:
- fails to develop mental/verbal skills, a purposeful use for manual dexterity, the speaking voice or to fulfill identity needs due to living in the head
- a chatterbox who lives on the surface of life and idles away time without purposeful activity
- difficulty sharing feelings due to fears of closeness or overdeveloped intellectual processes

- presents ideas too forcefully, at the expense of listening to others

Possible vocations: telephone/switchboard operator, receptionist, mechanic, tour guide, journalist, office worker, truck driver, dispatcher, any occupation requiring a skilled use of hands, machine operator, teacher, lecturer, ticket taker, sports commentator, linguist. (See Gemini rising for further details.)

1/4: multicapable

Constructive applications:

- experiences the environment in a personal, subjective manner but is aware that feelings and moods impact self-projection
- knows when to express and act on feeling states and when it is inappropriate to do so
- has separated the sense of identity from family influence
- actively seeks to secure a suitable home life, family or is actively nurturing to others without losing sight of one's own needs
- enhances the emotional nature, creativity or imagination
- private, although often ambitious, and establishes a business, professional practice or works out of the home

Nonconstructive applications:

- experiences difficulty balancing self-assertive drives with emotional security needs
- expresses emotional needs, one-upmanship or the need to win too forcefully, not forcefully enough, or at inappropriate times, thus undermining advancement opportunities
- often exposed to an overly passive role model and an overly excitable or angry role model, one of whom is unconsciously imitated
- is emotionally reactive, irritable, dominating, overly competitive, blunt, self-aggrandizing or shy, reserved, too soft-spoken and fearful of confrontations/competition until the emotional nature is balanced
- lacks separation between the sense of identity and family influence
- needs to develop the feeling nature or the creative imagination
- accomplishments in reverse proportion to self-aggrandizement

Possible vocations: business owner, real estate broker, worker for a family business, housekeeper, housewife, author, gastrointernologist, coach, activist, counselor, therapist. (See first quadrant focus, bowl pattern, Cancer rising for further details.)

1/5: multicapable, but predominantly artistic or enterprising
- characteristics manifest according to individual interests

Constructive applications:
- self-confident, cheery or humorous with strong needs for interesting, self-expressive work
- projects healthy self-esteem, thinks highly of own capabilities and desires recognition
- accomplishment-oriented, competitive, ambitious to succeed and certain of the ability to perform
- athletic, fun-loving, romantically inclined and integrates recreational activities (or hobbies) with enterprising work
- inspires confidence and often wins favors due to being reliable and hardworking
- a natural for business management, self-employment, risk-taking, creative flair or enterprise, extemporaneous self-expression or any work related to trait 5 or 1

Nonconstructive applications:
- lazy, self-indulgent "party" type who pursues fun more than career accomplishments
- fails to develop self-esteem, true self-confidence or the ability to lead and appears overly shy, self-conscious or fails to fulfill recognition needs
- inappropriate career directions, low achievement ceilings and lack of true self-confidence lead to boastful conceit, exaggeration of accomplishments and an excessive need to be special
- approval seeking until healthy self-confidence is gained
- is depressive or escapist when achievement, romantic or recognition needs are blocked

Possible vocations: business executive, athlete, sports car mechanic/driver, hobby shop owner, amusement park/carnival worker, product demonstrator, toy manufacturer, camp counselor, entertainer, lecturer, recreational director, gym or grammar school teacher. (See bucket pattern, Leo rising for further details.)

1/6: multicapable
Constructive applications:
- considers work and a rewarding skill, craft, talent or service important to self-expression (i.e., identifies with the job)
- works hard at jobs requiring initiative, exacting attention to detail, technical expertise or analytical skills
- leadership potential; works well without supervision
- self-employed or a committed employee who is organized, efficient, self-disciplined and diligent
- actively uncovers flaws to improve conditions
- ability for any trait 6 occupation or a service orientation to trait 1 outlets

Nonconstructive applications:
- fails to recognize the importance of rewarding work and skill development to self-expression
- feels inadequate, gets sick or emotionally fragile due to a lack of rewarding work
- does not pay proper attention to the appearance, health, hygiene or eating habits until skills are enhanced
- experiences extreme pressures to measure up which can result in too much criticism of self or others
- excessive workaholic tendencies keep one from having rewarding relationships

Possible vocations: health care practitioner, office worker, skilled mechanic/laborer, critic, lab technician, chef, repairer, sports analyst, self-employed. (See Mars in Virgo/sixth house, Virgo rising, bundle pattern for further details.)

1/7: multicapable
Constructive applications:
- balances the I-Thou principle and is outgoing, self-assertive, charming, ambitious and attracts assistance due to a considerate approach to others and recognition of their needs/abilities
- plays fair and works well in partnership or with a staff
- knows when to lead and when to take a second seat
- relies on interpersonal relating skills
- takes an enterprising approach to any trait 7 outlet or an aesthetic approach to any trait 1 endeavor
- deals with the public and readily attracts clients or customers

- people help to alter or enhance career directions or approaches

Nonconstructive applications:

- fails to achieve a proper balance between identity needs/self-assertion and the needs of others
- too passive, fearful of competition/confrontation and fails to assert enough of self in relationships (leading to resentment of partner)
- overly competitive, pushy, easily angered and dominating (leading to resentment from others)
- needs to develop mutuality and balanced interrelating skills before stable relationships and viable careers can be formed

Possible vocations: counselor, therapist, business partner, interviewer, administrative assistant, tennis player, automotive salesperson or dealer, diplomat, social director. (See Libra rising, nodes in Aries/Libra for further details.)

1/8: multicapable but predominantly enterprising

Constructive applications:

- through self-mastery develops a strong, stable sense of identity and purpose
- possesses pronounced physical/sexual drives and is highly competitive, strong-willed, intense or charismatic
- requires an absorbing or physically demanding occupation to which a dedicated commitment can be made
- capacity for any trait 1 or 8 occupation
- follows through on demanding tasks, gets to the bottom of things, researches and exhibits powerful concentration, persistence, a detail orientation or heavy labor
- works well under the own direction and can be a devoted employee
- desires recognition, prominence or influence; may be obsessed with accomplishing something of merit
- completely transforms the sense of identity and self-projection (masters emotional problems or self-indulgences)
- may use guns, instruments or tools or exercise "power" on the job
- influences the standards of practice of a given profession

Nonconstructive applications:

- fails to achieve a stable identity and is easily threatened due to fears of power and confrontation

- imitates early power figures and is wimpy or dictatorial, sarcastic, overly critical and opinionated with an obsessive need to control others
- abuses the rights of others
- manipulative tactics, power-playing, sexual intrigues or control issues undermine relationships or disrupt the career
- needs to develop healthy inner power, resourcefulness, stamina, self-mastery or give-and-take

Possible vocations: construction/demolition worker, driver of heavy equipment, business executive, politician, psychic, bodybuilder, exercise equipment dealer, powerful athlete, plumber, daredevil, healer, undercover agent, physician, dentist. (See locomotive pattern, Scorpio rising for further details.)

1/9: multicapable, predominantly enterprising but can be intellectual

Constructive applications:

- acknowledges needs to broaden the scope of influence
- highly self-confident, success-oriented, optimistic yet realistic about goals
- develops sense of self from pursuing an advanced education, philosophical understanding or any trait 9 endeavor
- conversant, adventurous, mentally or physically active, aspirational
- seeks wealth, knowledge, fame or influence
- successful at occupations related to traits 1 or 9
- takes risks, promotes self, appears lucky and may gain acclaim with little obvious effort due to positive self-confidence

Nonconstructive applications:

- unrealistic about life, one's capabilities or effort quotient by either over- or underestimating them
- gets in over the head hoping that luck will prevail
- fails to respond to realistic aspirational needs or to develop purpose in life (due to a diminished self-image)
- selects inappropriate careers (due to unrealistic self-appraisals) and needs to be more realistic and hardworking
- often gains weight when not fulfilling aspirational aims

Possible vocations: pioneering theorist, proselytizer, stunt car driver, gambler, wheeler-dealer, church worker, safari leader, athlete, travel agent, sportscaster, worker out of doors, publishing or advertising executive, promoter, fund-raiser. (See Sagittarius rising for further details.)

1/10: multicapable but predominantly enterprising/ intellectual
Constructive applications:
- committed to competence, authority and painstaking development of an expertise
- management potential with ability to work well under own supervision or to be self-employed
- serious about career matters, ambitious, realistic, goal-oriented, self-disciplined, responsible, hardworking with a determination to succeed which allows one to face obstacles, challenges and tests of authority
- restrains impetuosity and encourages effort
- approaches new activities with caution and/or diligence
- learns from superiors who often serve as mentors

Nonconstructive applications:
- fails to integrate risk-taking/needs to win with cautious planning and pragmatic viewpoints
- unrealistic goals, insufficient effort or lack of competency result in unconsciously attracting abusive superiors, accidents, disputes with authority figures or career setbacks
- fears responsibility and being put "on the line" which creates needs for close supervision, low achievement ceilings and unfulfilling careers
- job-hops due to a resentment of authority

Possible vocations: business executive, laborer, scientist, tool manufacturer, recognized authority/expert, demanding boss or professional. (See fourth quadrant focus, splash pattern, Mars in Capricorn/tenth house, Capricorn rising, Aries Midheaven for further details.)

1/11: multicapable, but predominately technical, intellectual or enterprising
Constructive applications:
- open to career changes and acknowledges stimulation needs on the job
- seeks excitement through constructive mental or physical channels, activities with friends or groups
- represents a company/group or prefers group participation to working independently

- cause- or client-oriented, individualistic, bright, authoritative, equalitarian, inventive, the "leader of the pack," resourceful, daring, initiating, shocking and original
- technical know-how, mathematical skills, or takes an antiestablishment approach to work
- needs to make a mark through a commitment to trait 11 occupations or activities
- bores easily and requires space, freedom and independent decision-making

Nonconstructive applications:
- fails to constructively channel excitement needs and is unable to make commitments
- demonstrates an excessive need for stimulation and change or completely fails to recognize such needs
- lands safe jobs due to unacknowledged stimulation needs or a failure to develop skills
- sudden changes in work circumstances are unconsciously attracted due to overblown or repressed stimulation needs
- too eccentric, too excitable, accident prone due to rashness
- gets fired or job-hops in search of excitement due to inability to accept direction
- lives in the head, appears cool, distant, authoritarian or overly detached from others

Possible vocations: construction/technical crew worker, consultant, scientist/inventor, theorist, fire fighter, association president, sales rep, computer operator or programmer, seminar/discussion leader, athletic club owner, electronics dealer, gadget manufacturer. (See Aquarius rising, splash pattern for further details.)

1/12: multicapable
Constructive applications:
- establishes a grounded, realistic sense of identity and purpose
- committed beliefs inspire action, courage, stamina and boundless hard work
- strongly self-motivated, self-assertive and needs to achieve through scholarly, creative or idealistic pursuits geared toward humanitarian service or enlightenment
- hidden feelings of inferiority may underlie achievement needs
- displays inner purpose, commitment and a sense of con-

tribution due to believing one is part of a larger plan
- takes risks, functions on elevated levels of consciousness or work ethics
- takes an enterprising approach to trait 12 occupations or an inspired approach to trait 1 activities
- often works alone and is independent of family influence
- pursues spiritual matters without losing the sense of identity

Nonconstructive applications:
- confused and in a fog over how to direct oneself, possibly due to operating under delusions
- fails to develop a solid sense of identity and body image which undermines ability to take constructive action
- unconquered feelings of inferiority lead to diminished achievement ceilings, a preference for not working or to escapist activities
- ego-denying spiritual pursuits further blur an already undefined identity
- may over- or underestimate the self and assume savior/victim/martyr roles in relationships due to identity delusions or early family problems

Possible vocations: swimmer, actor/artist, race car driver, inspired worker, nonworker, spiritual/metaphysical or intuitive leader, martial arts practitioner, health or mental health care practitioner, con artist, physicist, aerobics or yoga instructor. (See Pisces rising for further details.)

2/2: practical or artistic
- same as trait 2
- For details and possible occupations, see trait 2, Chapter 2, Venus in Chapter 4, preponderance/diminished representation of earth.

2/3: predominantly practical or artistic, but can be technical/intellectual

Constructive applications:
- values education, knowledge, artistry, objective reasoning, communicative or manual skills
- enjoys reading, studying, learning, verbal exchanges and makes productive use of facts or manual skills (due to interest in tangible results)
- appreciates beauty, creative mental or verbal ability and may

possess flair for art/design work
- has a pleasant voice, teaches or communication skills/ writing ability generate income

Nonconstructive applications:
- fails to value the mental/verbal functions, learning/education, aesthetic sense or productive use of the dexterous capacity
- overpreoccupation with financial matters inhibits career needs or changes
- refuses to develop talents and chooses practical, easy jobs (due to doubts surrounding the value of more rewarding capacities)

Possible vocations: calligrapher, sculptor, announcer, draftsperson, writer, fabric designer, art teacher, upholsterer, office worker, stock options trader, commercial designer, telephone salesperson. (See Crescent Moon phase.)

2/4: intellectual, assisting or artistic; can be practical
Constructive applications:
- healthy concern for financial security, artistic talents, counseling, healing or for building a prosperous business or profession
- values the heritage and the family may affect self-worth
- employed by the family, supports it or is supported by it in a way that enhances career opportunities or influences career directions
- is prepared for a fluctuating income which may be earned from or near the home
- gains emotional satisfaction from exercising gifts and talents

Nonconstructive applications:
- develops an excessive preoccupation with financial security which undermines pursuit of emotionally satisfying employment
- overly self-indulgent, lazy, a job-hopper or maintains work for its material advantages
- overly influenced by the family's values
- spends money for emotional gratification or overindulges in physical appetites rather than developing gifts and talents
- often searches for purpose not experienced in the early employment

Possible vocations: buyer, interior/furniture designer, domestic, investment counselor, house painter, scholar, real estate agent, author, banker, savings and loan officer.

2/5: predominantly practical or enterprising
Constructive applications:
- accomplishment-oriented and earns admiration for talents and integrity
- balances work and financial security concerns with fun, pleasure and relaxation
- values children, romance and self-expression
- takes calculated risks to further interests and can be a conscientious, cautious speculator
- derives income and self-worth from creative pursuits, hobbies, sports, speculative, recreational or entrepreneurial activities
- capacity for finance, accounting, figure work, freelance activities, extemporaneous expression, lecturing, teaching, acting or business management

Nonconstructive applications:
- fails to establish a confident self-worth profile and healthy sense of self-esteem or makes more out of the self than is warranted
- self-doubting, overly humble, self-effacing or conceited, pompous, boring and judgmental until realistic self-esteem is secured
- pursues a line of work because it is what one "should" be doing or prefers the easy job
- lazy, self-indulgent, pleasure-seeking with expensive tastes and expects someone else to be the provider
- wants to be admired for talents, income or possessions but is not motivated to earn them
- overly involved with prestige and money at the expense of developing self-expressive outlets

Possible vocations: commodity trader, toy or doll designer/ salesperson, freelancer, purchaser for children's store, a well-to-do person, flower arranger, business owner, accountant.

2/6: predominantly practical or technical but can be artistic/ assisting
Constructive applications:
- enjoys/values work and the daily expression of rewarding skills

- talent for a specialized or technical trait 6 line of work
- self-worth and income are connected to the work/service capacity, technical skill, health matters or the productivity of employees
- works closely with others, a partner, boss, special loved one, a trainer, secretary or editor
- knows when to spend money to enhance job prospects, for training or education, or for equipment, repairs, supplies and other work-related needs
- caters to people as part of job or works with things

Nonconstructive applications:

- fails to understand that self-worth is derived from gratifying work
- does not develop rewarding skills, due to self-doubts surrounding the ability to earn a living through them, and is slack on the job
- places too high a priority on the remunerative aspects of employment
- prefers not working rather than working at low-status jobs

Possible vocations: jewelry repair, self-employment, food caterer, physical or mental health care worker, cashier/teller, paste-up artist, supervisor, food service worker, employment counselor, clothing salesperson/designer, bookkeeper, editor, art critic, secretary, potter, trainer, dog groomer, carpenter. (See Venus in Virgo/sixth house for futher details.)

2/7: predominantly practical, artistic or assisting

Constructive applications:

- sociable, easygoing, considerate of others and values rewarding relationships
- enjoys the good life, but pulls own weight through productive teamwork/partnership
- needs intellectual, artistic or sensual expression and attracts clients or customers through charm, good looks or warmth
- income depends on balanced interpersonal relating skills, partnership, artistic flair or dealings with the public
- partnership often enhances income opportunities

Nonconstructive applications:

- fails to make one's own way in life and is overly dependent on others/partners to supply all resources or the sense of self-worth

- too nice, passive, complacent and lackadaisical or is selfish, cunning, self-indulgent, expects too much from others and is unwilling to carry own weight
- uses charm/good looks to gain unfair advantage
- judges others as better or worse than oneself or blames others when situations go amiss

Possible vocations: jeweler, clothing salesperson, actor, counselor, producer of functional yet artistic objects, social director, caterer, occupational therapist, investment advisor, assistant. (See seesaw pattern for further details.)

2/8: predominantly artistic or enterprising
Constructive applications:
- shares resources, power, sexual pleasures and masters appetites
- deeply committed to developing productive talents and significant employment
- works cooperatively with others and respects their opinions, values, rights and needs
- money, sex, influence or some form of power impacts self-worth
- could be artistic and possesses a magnetic, sexual quality or ability for corporate affairs
- sources of income, self-worth, the occupation or approaches to earning a living totally change
- intense about trait 2 occupations or takes a practical, money-making approach to trait 8 outlets

Nonconstructive applications:
- fails to develop stable self-worth or to master the self/appetites with respect to other's rights
- unable to share resources or power due to being possessive, willful and too demanding of support from others
- controlling partners or tumultuous business associations arise through failing to tap inner power
- sources of income can be wiped out
- difficulties in relationships or money-making activities due to a need to control and dominate others or from failing to stand up for one's rights
- sensual/sexual excesses interfere with productivity until self-mastery is achieved

Possible vocations: therapist, rare gun dealer, heavy machinery dealer, finance mogul, bank/trust department executive, wrestler, artist, medical supplies salesperson, occultist or dealer/producer of occult products. (See preponderance/diminished representation of fixity, nodes in Taurus/Scorpio, 7/8.)

2/9: artistic, intellectual or enterprising
Constructive applications:
- productive, realistic, achievement-oriented
- makes dreams a reality and expands the scope of influence through developing talents
- enhances self-worth or finances through travel, education or consciousness-raising subjects
- wants to be rich in a material sense or in metaphysical/philosophical/religious thought
- capable of large-scale endeavors which grow steadily
- learns to balance financial security needs with sense of adventure

Nonconstructive applications:
- fails to be realistic about self, talents, ability or earning power
- lazy, wasteful, negligent, pleasure-seeking and spends money irresponsibly
- fails to balance financial security needs with sense of adventure
- fears failure, travel or change
- financial security issues interfere with growth opportunities and may search for greater vocational expression in later years

Possible vocations: commodity trader, financial investor, social services worker, singer, actor, talented educator or pilot, advertising artist/designer, entrepreneur, art dealer, telecommunications salesperson, fund-raiser, importer/exporter of beautiful items.

2/10: practical, intellectual; can be artistic
Constructive applications:
- a responsible, serious, diligent hard worker who is reliable, thorough and gets the job done
- possesses management/organizational potential and a capacity for technical matters or details
- attracts the attention of superiors (due to talents and sound

work ethics)

- doubts surrounding self-worth or income-producing capacity spur achievement/financial advancement
- takes sensual needs or artistic expression seriously and balances sensual/artistic needs with practical realities and a sound work ethic
- recycles money into the career and applies creative or practical talents, steady effort, patience to gratifying or lucrative occupation
- develops a talent for a business or professional endeavor
- builds on experience and accumulates money, possessions or skills
- establishes a worthy, long-enduring reputation
- makes one's own way in life

Nonconstructive applications:

- fails to develop rewarding talents, self-worth or competence to perform difficult, demanding tasks— leading to financial setbacks, career changes, job-hopping, periods of unemployment or unfulfilling work
- laziness, doubts surrounding self-worth or income-producing capacity inhibit career drives and create low achievement ceilings
- self-worth or income suffers when competence is not achieved or when responsibility is not assumed
- blocks sensual or artistic expression due to self-doubts or an overdeveloped need to be practical
- overvalues sensual outlets at the expense of developing a sound work ethic
- experiences career frustrations, being taken advantage of or limited by the boss when an excessive need to be indispensable and to assume too much responsibility exists
- needs to be more realistic about the business world's "rules of the game" and what one has to offer

Possible vocations: government worker, art expert, architect, financial expert, sculptor, business services/supplier, seller of luxury items, worker in the food industry, dependable, productive employee, beautiful teacher/professor, expert in one's field. (See Venus in Capricorn/tenth house, Taurus Midheaven for further details.)

2/11: artistic, intellectual or practical

Constructive applications

- balances financial security concerns/practical necessities with change/innovation and stimulation
- loves freedom, independence, originality and the group process
- contributory and seeks to have influence through one's unique abilities
- capacity for technical endeavors, unusual, inventive perspectives or systems of thought
- sources of income suddenly change or sporadically generates funds from freelance, commission, consulting activities, avocations, part-time work or self-employment
- benefits and income result from referrals, friends, clients, an association with a group, club, organization, union, or a teamwork approach due to shared efforts and a sense of contribution
- sees clients or customers, has dealings with out-of-the-ordinary business associates or deals in an out-of-the-ordinary line of work
- foregoes financial security in favor of developing a stimulating line of work or suddenly leaves a practical job for more interesting pursuits

Nonconstructive applications:

- financial security concerns overshadow needs for stimulation and change or excessive needs for excitement, change and independence threatens a stable livelihood
- overly eccentric values or an antiestablishment approach leads to job-hopping
- spends money impulsively with insufficient funds for emergencies
- overly involved with the material side of life and maintains an unself-expressive job for its material rewards
- appears ultra conservative or ignores conventional values

Possible vocations: worker in the furniture industry, sales representative, coop farmer, video rental merchant, computer graphics artist, employee in radio/television industry, productive, talented consultant, producer or distributor of new age goods or services, computer operator or technician, cosmic scientist, cab driver.

2/12: artistic, intellectual or assisting

Constructive applications:

- inspired yet realistic ability to turn dreams and ideals into practical realities
- productively utilizes intuition, the creative imagination or caring instincts on the job
- sensitive, aesthetic, attractive, pleasant, imaginative, receptive to beauty with an ability for the ethereal, art, behind-the-scenes work, or for nonprofit, social service organizations
- derives income from and talent exists for trait 12 occupations or approaches
- intuitive about how and where to make money
- uncertainty over self-worth spurs ambitions
- possesses hidden or inspired talents/resources including silent backers
- digs deeply within to discover true talents or what has true value in life

Nonconstructive applications:

- fails to develop a solid, realistic self-worth profile or stable sense of values
- uncertainty over self-worth unconsciously limits income
- sources of income may be unstable, dry out, go bankrupt and require dependence for a time on unemployment compensation, welfare or charitable others (possibly due to waiting for the "perfect" job to come along)
- gets taken in by "get rich quick" schemes when realistic boundaries to self-worth are not achieved
- money slips through fingers due to carelessness or extravagance
- overly idealistic, lazy, irresponsible, unambitious, insecure or cunning and expects something for nothing
- experiences difficulty recognizing the boundary line between mine and yours
- needs to develop an expanded sense of values

Possible vocations: sensitive artist, poet, playwright, drug/alcohol clinic counselor, fabric designer, public aid worker, physician, decorator, glamorous salesperson, model, hospital worker, movie props manager, con artist, nonworker, film producer/backer. (See 7/12.)

3/3: multicapable but predominantly practical or intellectual
- same as trait 3
- For details and possible vocations, see trait 3 in Chapter 2, Mercury in Chapter 4, a preponderance/diminished representation of mutability or air.

3/4: artistic or intellectual, can be assisting
Constructive applications:
- integrates emotional sensitivities, intuition or caring instincts with objective reasoning and detached viewpoints (knows the proper time and place to assert one over the other)
- learning is emotionally gratifying and learns well by observation
- an intuitive thinker who is sensitive about ideas and enjoys being relied upon for one's insights
- a perceptive listener, teacher or lecturer who has a retentive memory and ability for conversation, the arts, counseling, assessing others and expressing feelings
- pursues intellectual or artistic endeavors or advanced degrees
- takes paperwork home

Nonconstructive applications:
- fails to balance reason and objectivity with feeling states so that emotions cloud reason or objective logic dominates emotions
- disinclined to study or learn (due to unconscious fears of intellectual inadequacy)
- nervous, hyper or a good rationalizer (due to mixing objectivity with too much subjectivity)
- a poor listener with difficulty expressing feelings, lives in the head and is impressionable, too subjective or exaggerates knowledge and self-importance
- know-it-all who is overly attached to ideas
- holds back information or hides insecurity behind incessant talking

Possible vocations: personnel office worker, bookkeeper, literary agent, therapist/counselor/advisor, dancer, author, playwright, public speaker, responsive teacher, warm receptionist, conducts in-home telephone sales.

3/5: artistic, intellectual or enterprising
Constructive applications:
- mentally alert, physically on the go, verbally expressive, career-conscious and goal-oriented
- approval over brainpower motivates creative or intellectual achievement
- a humorous or clearheaded speaker who loves learning
- ability for business negotiations, extemporaneous presentations or speculative ventures
- seeks variety, change and experiences sudden happy alterations in career circumstances
- often amused by intellectual games or conversations, creative hobbies/interests or by any trait 3-related activity

Nonconstructive applications:
- fails to (but needs to) develop confidence in mental/verbal faculties, evaluative judgments (possibly due to laziness or living in a of make-believe world of success)
- prefers the easy way out or could be an approval seeking know-it-all
- talks too much to prove intelligence (which hampers interviews)
- flimsy opinions replace mental achievement
- attempts to accomplish something beyond the capabilities
- absentminded, reluctant to talk or a gossiper

Possible vocations: product demonstrator, attorney, dramatic speaker, chess or game player/manufacturer, stock options trader, usher, top notch secretary, accountant, entertaining teacher/professor, account executive.

3/6: predominantly practical, technical or intellectual
Constructive applications:
- balances workaholic drives and pragmatic viewpoints with lightheartedness and casual conversations
- discriminating, uncovers and repairs flaws
- highly intelligent with fact retention and capacity for detail
- needs gratifying work where ideas and skills have practical, useful application
- early life criticisms or a perfectionist role model may have set an example to achieve academically or to perfect skills
- aptitude for health care or any occupation requiring a trained use of the hands, analytical capability, a detail-orientation,

efficiency with paperwork, figures, statistics or handicrafts
- a telephone or short trips may be indispensable to the job
- health issues, details or work occupy the mind
- holds down more than one job or pursues a variety of activities simultaneously

Nonconstructive applications:
- fails to integrate lighthearted, casualness with workaholic tendencies and an overly detailed, critical approach
- a pessimistic thinker who worries too much
- fails to develop rewarding work-related/communication skills and experiences unsatisfying employment
- early life criticism may have created doubts about intelligence or ability to measure up (and needs to be overcome)
- nervous, high strung, emotionally isolated and not always rational due to negative thinking or overstress
- lives in the head, ignores reality or growth potentials due to not developing skills or the discriminating faculties
- job-hops or is excessive about being useful
- overachieves on the job and is put upon by coworkers/clients/business associates/bosses until discrimination is developed and the rules of the working world are better understood

Possible vocations: precise lecturer, technical writer, critic, copy editor, customer service rep, accountant or bookkeeper, messenger service, scientist, highly efficient secretary, file clerk, skilled technician, analyst, health care worker, surgeon, dental hygienist, calligrapher. (See bundle pattern, Mercury in Virgo/sixth house.)

3/7: artistic, intellectual or assisting
Constructive applications
- on the go, extroverted, verbally/socially expressive, able to involve, listen to and enthuse others
- versatile, enjoys learning, attracts clients, customers or students due to a pleasant manner
- utilizes teamwork to complete projects
- good eye/ear for beauty or design, and attracts public attention or influences others
- a lively, pleasant conversationalist who enjoys social outlets on the job but can be persuasive and diplomatic in negotiations

- requires legal documents, contracts, agreements or a license as part of the occupation

Nonconstructive applications:

- keeps too many thoughts to the self (in an effort to keep the peace or to win approval) which hampers honest communication and true cooperation
- a con artist or uses false flattery
- all talk, in an effort to impress others, but little action taken on ideas
- excessive preoccupation with relationships interferes with productivity on the job

Possible vocations: provider of offices services, business broker/negotiator, office supplies salesperson, bus driver, public relations worker, interpreter, announcer, account executive, designer, agent, interviewer, persuasive speaker or teacher, sign painter, information booth attendant.

3/8: practical, technical or intellectual

Constructive applications:

- integrates objective logic with subjective feeling states
- concentrative, deep thinking, needs to be heard and involved, observant, able to get to the bottom of things, perceptive, analytical, critical, intensely opinionated, yet able to listen and keep secrets
- attracted to corporate or political affairs, the occult, psychology or explores (researches) interesting subjects
- may use intricate or dangerous equipment on the job
- factually conversant in any trait 8 endeavor or compulsively meticulous in any trait 3 outlet
- caustic, convincing or suggestive speech and balances skeptical intellect with objective research

Nonconstructive applications:

- fails to balance a skeptical intellect with objective reasoning which makes one suspicious, mentally on guard, and liable to dwell on the darker possibilities of life
- communication/rational mind was dominated in the early life by mind games which created severe doubts about the intellectual/perceptual capacity, the ability to trust what others say or to listen to others
- closed-mouthed, fears information will be used against one, or a vicious gossip desirous of hurting others

- develops convoluted notions of what others are thinking which wastes energy, creates unnecessary business losses or contractual problems
- denies reality or is a cunning, manipulative, ruthless business negotiator who abuses the rights of others
- prone to drastic verbal outbursts, overestimating the intelligence or concealing the thoughts
- power, sex or money overly preoccupies the mind

Possible vocations: editor, detective, medical librarian/transcriber, charismatic teacher/speaker, air traffic controller, researcher, psychologist, bank/office worker, mining technician, analyst, typesetter, office building maintenance worker, mover, forklift driver.

3/9: multicapable but predominately intellectual or enterprising

Constructive applications:

- balances fact and opinion, theory and reality, ponderous discussions with more lighthearted, casual conversations
- mentally/verbally/physically active
- enjoys reading, talking, studying, sports, travel, philosophical issues, psychology or other systems of thought
- knows one's facts and realistically acts on big dreams about fame, foreign places, spiritual or metaphysical issues or any trait 9 occupation able to "take one places" physically or aspirationally
- a good speaker or lecturer with a wealth of ideas, literary interests or good business judgment
- makes contacts with foreign or far-away places/persons
- optimism, positive thinking and grounded facts insure affairs develop as planned
- self-taught, a dabbler with many interests and capabilities

Nonconstructive applications:

- fails to broaden intellectual horizons or to realistically ground facts
- objectivity and reliability are deficient due to unrealistic thinking, carelessness, naiveté, nervousness, restlessness and impetuosity
- a pretentious know-it-all who confuses opinions with facts resulting in poor business judgment
- hyperactive, scattered, jumps to conclusions, absentminded,

not always truthful, inclined to wishful thinking and exaggeration

Possible vocations: teacher or professor, court reporter, pilot, magazine or book publisher or employee in the publishing industry, worker in advertising industry, broadcaster, long distance telephone operator, translator/linguist, foreign correspondent, flight attendant. (See nodes in Gemini/Sagittarius.)

3/10: multicapable but predominately practical, technical or intellectual

- siblings may influence career drives or choices

Constructive applications:

- develops the mental/verbal faculties or manual skills
- early life criticism, learning problems or fears of mental inadequacy spur scholastic achievement and tangible results
- a sibling serves as a mentor
- tempers rash thinking with practical goals and a concern for the reputation
- a serious, realistic, deep thinker capable of technical know-how, logical analysis, detailed mental work in isolation
- sounds intelligent, speaks with authority or takes a serious, committed approach to any trait 3 endeavor
- gains knowledge and techniques through hard-earned experience, practice and concentrated effort
- rises slowly but steadily in the career

Nonconstructive applications:

- fails to develop the mentality or manual skills (possibly due to not being listened to or taken seriously enough in childhood)
- a difficult early education, early life criticisms or learning problems prompt avoidance of occupations requiring mental discipline or evaluative judgment
- experiences difficulty in sharing innermost thoughts and is prone to grim outlooks, worry or overcompensation through know-it-all attitudes, incessant talking
- wants the most from the least effort and seeks the easy job
- ideas are criticized by self or others due to an inner critical attitude or not being as prepared as one should be

Possible vocations: researcher, laboratory worker, office manager, analyst, knowledgeable expert, lecturer, textbook author, executive secretary, editor, a serious teacher, letter carrier, dispatcher, scientist, attorney. (See Mercury in Capricorn/tenth house, Gemini Midheaven for further details.)

3/11: multicapable but predominantly technical or intellectual
Constructive applications
- a busy, on-the-go, inventive, stimulating thinker or speaker who enjoys client contact, students or customers and may speak in front of groups
- exercises the intelligence or masters a subject related to trait 11
- astute, intuitive, a quick learner who is outspoken and opinionated due to a wealth of facts and sound conceptual capacity
- a lively conversationalist sometimes given to sudden insights or psychic perceptions
- capacity for technical know-how, difficult foreign languages, science, engineering, math, physics or any cosmically-related endeavor (astrology)

Nonconstructive applications:
- fails to develop mentally stimulating interests or makes more out of the intelligence than is warranted
- spreads the self too thin with a multitude of activities going on at once
- thinks faster than the mouth can keep pace and leaves gaps in sentences or skips over facts
- a cranky, willful, blunt, nervous know-it-all who dominates conversations, cannot connect with feelings and jumps to hysterical conclusions
- prone to unstable viewpoints or moody, withdrawn behavior

Possible vocations: progressive teacher, word processor, camera crew member, union/association office worker, data processor, electrician, discussion group leader, lecturer, photocopy machine sales representative, electric typewriter repairer.

3/12: multicapable but predominately artistic or intellectual
- siblings can be sad, confused, sickly or inspired, brilliant

Constructive applications:
- integrates objective reasoning/logic with intuitive/creative approaches
- highly developed conceptualizing capacity, idealistic and

imaginative with ability for fantasy, visualization, intuitive logic
- creative with hands or voice and a natural at any trait 12 discipline
- inspires others, reads between the lines, profitably utilizes hunches in business
- double messages in childhood or difficulty over early learning spur intellectual achievement
- sounds scholarly, rational or practical but may not always know the origins of one's information (e.g., psychic)

Nonconstructive applications:
- fails to develop a capacity for concentration and to realistically ground thoughts/ideas in practical reality; needs to concentrate better to develop the intelligence
- exaggerates the intelligence or is overly secretive
- takes too long to explain ideas or gets lost in the middle of sentences
- blocks out the undesirable and lives in one's own world
- pretentious about knowledge, confuses fact with fantasy
- easily misunderstood through a lack of clarity or a failure to speak up
- contracts cause anxiety
- an undisciplined, naive, forgetful daydreamer with poor business judgment who tends to be easily duped or a successful liar, charlatan who dupes others

Possible occupations: back office worker, film deliverer or editor, calligrapher, magician, artist/dancer/singer, physical or mental health care practitioner, psychic, hospital information officer, careless or highly precise bookkeeper or teacher.

4/4: predominantly artistic or assisting though multicapable
- same as trait 4
- For details and possible vocations, see trait 4, Chapter 2, northern hemisphere emphasis, Moon in Chapter 4, preponderance/diminished representation of water, First Quarter Moon phase.

4/5: artistic, assisting or enterprising

Constructive applications:
- balances self-expressive activities with home/family needs
- develops healthy pride in self, abilities, accomplishments

and fulfills feeling needs through art, a secure home or loving family

- fun-loving, cheery, humorous, spontaneously supportive/ nurturing of others and thrives on close emotional ties
- creative flair, business leadership or counseling potential
- needs to be needed and seen as important, rich or as a professional
- security gained through trait 5 self-expressive activities including income-producing hobbies
- plays, presents or teaches to an audience
- needs warmth, affection, recognition, admiration, independence, acclaim
- self-reliant, a late bloomer, hardworking, stubbornly determined to succeed with ability to build a business or a professional career

Nonconstructive applications:

- fails to develop sense of adequacy and self-esteem due to dominating or smother-love parents who could not provide positive attention/nurturing, who expected too much or who tried to do too much for the child (thus interfering with one's self-expressive needs)
- under- or overestimates self-importance and has difficulty forming close emotional ties
- an uncommitted, irresponsible "party" type who is tied to the past with an inability to grow beyond it and continues to look for parenting far into adulthood
- maintains unfulfilling jobs rather than risking a change
- chooses jobs on the basis of family "shoulds" rather than for self-expressive needs
- is somber, childlike, self-effacing or pompous and overly concerned about appearances

Possible vocations: child care worker, caring, responsive, creative, fun-loving teacher or counselor, hobby or toy store proprietor, manager of a family business, child psychologist, camp counselor, author, job trainer, restauranteur, business executive, demonstrates products for the home, chef.

4/6: technical, artistic, assisting or intellectual

Constructive applications:

- combines compassion/nurturing with discriminating judgment so that deserving others benefit from support, assistance

- role models set examples of achievement and work ethics
- feels comforted when being needed, useful, productive and striving for perfection without going overboard
- considers work and a skill, craft, service or talent as vital to emotional stability
- takes a caring approach to trait 6 occupations, or handles trait 4 occupations with an eye for detail, efficiency or technical flair
- works at home or brings work home
- employed by the family, works for a family-owned business or predominantly works with women
- deals with the public or family/emotional issues at work
- a serious thinker, good advisor or critic, capable of exacting hard work
- needs to feel at home on the job and is easily upset when work routines go amiss
- pays special attention to matters of health and hygiene

Nonconstructive applications:

- fails to understand the importance of work to the sense of adequacy so that lack of rewarding work or coworkers becomes emotionally disturbing
- lacks discriminating judgment which undermines determining what is needed for work satisfaction
- overly self-critical or displaces fears of inadequacy onto others by being overly critical of them
- early family criticism or strict discipline undermined the self-image and confidence in the ability to perform
- sullen, complaining, depressive, prone to worry and anxiety
- experiences job changes, health problems or periods of unemployment (due to lack of fulfilling work)
- sense of inadequacy, guilt or too much of a need to be needed/useful leads to accepting lesser positions, overserving and being taken advantage of by others

Possible vocations: artistic designer, clerical worker, any form of repair work, social service worker, physical/mental health care worker, employment counselor, employee in food service or other domestic products and services, personnel advisor, home repairer or supplier of products for the home, building maintenance worker, family therapist, technical writer, homemaker, literary critic, skilled secretary, chef/cook, waiter, scientist. (See Moon in Virgo/sixth house for further details.)

4/7: artistic, assisting or intellectual
Constructive applications:
- balances emotional security needs with the needs of others
- intuitive/caring, a good listener and an excellent counselor
- artistically inclined and may attract public attention
- feels fulfilled when needed and assisting others
- emotionally rewarded from working with a partner or from close, loving relationships or marriage
- sees clients in the home or interacts with the public
- has a close-knit staff, patients, customers or students or works closely with others
- adjusts to the emotional needs of others without losing sight of one's own

Nonconstructive applications:
- expects emotional needs to be fulfilled by the partner while mutuality in fulfilling the needs of others does not exist
- gains weight due to overindulgences
- family influences the choice of mate or partnership
- abdicates emotional needs to maintain a partner which only guarantees that relationships will be unfulfilling
- relates to others on the basis of projected security needs or must be guided, assisted or supported by another

Possible vocations: real estate salesperson, interior designer, employment recruiter, artist, rental agent, customer service agent, public relations employee, author/poet, nurse, social worker, therapist. (See second quadrant focus for further details.)

4/8: artistic, assisting, enterprising or intellectual
Constructive applications:
- experiences deep sharing, trust and close, emotional bonds
- takes steps to enhance creativity, the sense of adequacy or to overcome emotional problems
- takes a committed approach to any trait 4 occupation and needs to be totally involved in the occupation, in assisting others or the boss
- exercises "power" or takes an assisting or creative approach to trait 8 outlets
- organized and efficient with capacity for healing, psychological or psychic insight
- a profound thinker able to endure pressure and stress due

to a determination to succeed
- willful nature and may work best under own direction

Nonconstructive applications:
- early parental manipulation, abuse or smother-love underlies feelings of inadequacy or self-doubts which lead to controlling the environment through various passive/aggressive tactics
- obsessed with security-oriented routines, experiences emotional compulsions and hides true feelings, thoughts
- unaccountable fears, resentments, covert competitive drives or suspiciousness interfere with the job, relationships or necessitate changes in employment
- may need psychotherapy before interesting work can be identified or before potentials can be realized
- overly influenced by the family or unproductively tied to it
- needs to be more accepting of self and others

Possible vocations: business administrator, psychologist, psychic, refurbisher of buildings, plumber, executive recruiter, owner of an adult bookstore, powerful author/artist, broker, intensive care nurse, pharmacist, politician, rehabilitation therapist, committed, hardworking employee.

4/9: artistic or intellectual

Constructive applications:
- emotional closeness and freedom needs are balanced
- constructively responds to aspirations by backing them up with effort
- seeks influence, fame, advancement or expanded knowledge, understanding
- trait 9 related occupations or approaches are emotionally gratifying (including travel) or growth is experienced through trait 4 areas (including assistance from the family)
- idealistic though often good at rationalizing behavior
- impressed with wealth
- moves from birth locale or establishes a religious/metaphysical/philosophical basis to life
- beliefs or higher education enhance sense of adequacy
- capacity for concepts, languages, foreign affairs or systems of thought (e.g., law)
- spots good opportunities and takes advantage of them
- establishes a successful business or professional practice

and makes a name for the self
- family often influences the beliefs and outlooks on life

Nonconstructive applications:
- fails to respond constructively to aspirational needs or needs for expanded knowledge/understanding
- aspirations are unrealistic given the amount of effort invested
- under- or overestimates the self
- seeks easy jobs with low achievement ceilings, remains closely tied to the family, fears travel or seeks occupations beyond one's competence level
- unable to balance needs for emotional closeness with freedom urges so that one need is excessive to the neglect of the other
- fearful, nervous, negligent, self-indulgent, wasteful, a pipe dreamer with overdeveloped needs to be important or rich, but hopes that luck, rather than effort, will pave the way to success

Possible vocations: teacher or professor, lecturer, preacher, metaphysician, employee in a charitable organization, real estate mogul/broker, actor, flight attendant, pilot, foreign correspondent, publisher, attorney, author.

4/10: multicapable but predominantly enterprising or intellectual

Constructive applications:
- integrates emotional closeness/caring with pragmatic/realistic viewpoints so that closeness is achieved and support is given to deserving others
- feels responsible for and supports the family
- seeks responsible positions and develops competence, authority which enhance the sense of adequacy
- practical, diligent, efficient with a scientific approach to any trait 4 occupation or a caring/nurturing approach to any trait 10 occupation
- insecurities or an unfortunate early life prompts achievement needs
- self-controlled, hardworking, ambitious, serious, a deep thinker, thorough, organized, conscientious with a sense of duty and integrity
- establishes a business or professional practice (self-em-

ployed) or finds work rewarding for its material advantages
- an excellent boss or employee who exercises authority and works under own direction

Nonconstructive applications:
- fails to develop the sense of adequacy, so does not devote effort to becoming competent at rewarding tasks
- self-restricting, self-conscious or self-effacing with a poor self-image so that fears of emotional closeness create periods of isolation
- one's repressed authority needs manifest through mean, cold, restricting superiors or work is experienced as boring drudgery
- responses to early life restrictions, too many early responsibilities, separation from the family or lack of nurture include selfishness, negative outlooks, low career ceilings, chronic, low-grade depressions, worry, fear of failure, alienation, hypersensitivity, fear of responsibility or job/career changes
- a bossy authoritarian, who is harsh and neglects one's own and others' emotional needs
- know-it-all attitudes and feeling that any means justifies the ends lead to misconduct, a failure to live up to responsibilities, and a damaged reputation

Possible vocations: business owner or administrator, a professional, hotel, motel or restaurant manager, head of a family business, competent housekeeper, builder or architect, professional advisor, recognized author, psychiatrist, intuitive boss or bossy authoritarian, therapist, scientific/technical writer. (See Moon in Capricorn/tenth house, Cancer Midheaven, nodes in Cancer/Capricorn.)

4/11: multicapable but predominantly artistic or intellectual
Constructive applications:
- integrates emotional security/needs for closeness with freedom urges/needs for excitement and fulfills both at the proper time
- colleague recognition is emotionally gratifying
- makes drastic changes to fulfill stimulation needs
- has close emotional ties to friends
- comes from an unusual or exciting family background
- inconsistent early nurturing leads to a determination to

succeed on one's own terms
- balances excitement, stimulation, independence with a cause-orientation or a sense of contribution to a greater whole
- takes a caring or creative approach to any trait 11 occupation, including seminars, conferences, meetings
- masters or takes a new age, technical, unusual or part-time approach to any trait 4 vocation and may establish a unique, out of the ordinary business or professional practice
- works with a crew or seeks membership in a special organization or club
- intuitive or artistic with ability for systems of thought, psychology, science, math, electronics or metaphysics
- insightful, somewhat excitable, ambitious, self-willed
- sudden career changes or successes arise from group affiliations, friends or acquaintances

Nonconstructive applications:
- fails to balance emotional security/needs for closeness with freedom urges/stimulation needs so that one set of needs overshadows the other
- repressed excitement/stimulation/change needs underlie sudden job changes or upsets, or attracts flakey, erratic, dictatorial superiors, coworkers or colleagues
- attracts unreliable, overly dependent bosses or clients when closeness and dependency issues are denied
- inconsistent early life nurturing or sudden family disruptions underlie later fears of closeness/dependency and excessive needs for excitement or change
- a stranger in the early home who may not always be grounded in practical reality
- prone to fanatical, self-deluded, irrational outbursts, self-aggrandizement or notions of being guided by godlike forces
- restless, stubborn and an incessant job-hopper when not stimulated or able to make independent decisions
- needs to break away from family influence to attain a sense of individuality

Possible vocations: insightful or inventive scientist, human rights advocate, new age business owner, intuitive or group therapist, technical consultant/advisor, writer, construction business owner/worker, unique artist.

4/12: assisting, artistic or intellectual

Constructive applications:

- functions on inspired levels and through realistic viewpoints
- ability for the arts, creative visualization, fantasy, any of the helping professions
- sickly or confused relative prompts early recognition of the value of compassion
- enjoys being needed, helpful and often is attracted to the sick, those needing assistance or to the glamour professions
- early feelings of inferiority prompt achievement needs and desire to attain inspired heights through commitment to a purposeful career
- highly intuitive, psychic, imaginative, impressionable, sympathetic and caring
- able to work alone or behind-the-scenes and needs a quiet place of retreat, or retreats to home
- ability for any occupation related to trait 4 or 12 especially with a social service or aesthetic orientation
- needs to feel part of a larger plan or organization

Nonconstructive applications:

- fails to develop the sense of personal adequacy, a realistic self-image and is unsure of what will bring emotional fulfillment
- expects too much from self or is overly dependent on and needs too much support from others
- unreliable, confused or sickly parents or other early family problems undermine emotional grounding, sense of adequacy, contact with reality and could lead to masochism or escapism
- absentminded, a liar, self-deluded and experiences confusion, loss of direction, a victim/savior/martyr complex, nebulous fears and anxieties, or an inability to withstand competitive challenges
- develops a grandiose self-image, is pretentious about knowledge and comes on strong to compensate for feelings of inadequacy or guilt
- taken advantage of by others due to savior/victim complex or is lazy, unstable and faultfinds to displace anxieties and fears of inferiority onto others

Possible vocations: social worker, physical or mental health care provider, artist, mystery, fantasy, science fiction or romance novelist, poet, academic, home health care nurse, priest/nun, psychic, physicist, interior designer, wine/food/liquor purveyor.

5/5: multicapable but predominantly enterprising
- same as trait 5
- For details and possible vocations, see trait 5, Chapter 2 and Sun in Chapter 4.

5/6: enterprising, artistic or intellectual
Constructive applications:
- balances work responsibilities with fun and recreational activities
- develops rewarding, self-expressive skills with a technical flair or service orientation
- hardworking, diligent with organizational skills, capacity for details and the analysis of facts, figures or people
- perfectionistic role model encourages achievement needs
- develops healthy self-esteem from self-employment, successful work or hard-earned recognition
- provides useful criticism and enjoys being indispensable on the job
- could work with a special loved one and needs to enjoy coworkers/staff
- plays or presents to an audience
- takes a technical, diligent and precise approach to any trait 5 area or an achievement-oriented, self-expressive approach to any trait 6 endeavor
- an excellent employee, business leader or homemaker willing to pour everything into the job provided the heart is in it and adequate appreciation is received
- easily finds good jobs due to confidence in skills and ability

Nonconstructive applications:
- lack of rewarding work and self-expressive skills or hobbies undermine health and psychological equilibrium
- selects jobs on the basis of "image" rather than on interests which leads to workaholism, stress, worry and a fear of not being able to measure up
- works too hard at the expense of health and relaxation
- experiences job drudgery, job changes or unemployment due to not working up to par

- early life criticisms create anxiety over the ability to perform and undermine skill development
- too self-critical or displaces fears of inadequacy onto others by being overly critical of them

Possible vocations: accountant, attorney, manufacturer or seller of children's clothes, creative advisor, camp counselor, office or business manager, health care specialist, cartoonist, teacher, gardener, skilled entertainer, supervisor or trainer, textbook author or editor, technical hobbyist or writer. (See Sun in Virgo/sixth house, Gibbous Moon phase for further details.)

5/7: artistic or assisting

Constructive applications:

- self-expressive, fun-loving, charming, enthusiastic, spontaneous with others and able to win them over
- works with a spouse or loved one, views others as contributing equals in the relationship or work effort
- loves teamwork, works closely with others, so work relationships are crucial to success, satisfaction, productivity and staying power
- able to attract clients, fun-loving partners and public attention due to graciousness and self-confidence
- seeks a staff or an assistant to enhance work opportunities or to make work more enjoyable

Nonconstructive applications:

- fails to see others as equals which leads to false flattery and using them to advance self interests
- fears others are better and criticizes in an effort to diminish them or follows their lead to the neglect of self-expression
- demands support or bends at the demand of others
- slack on the job and gets others to do the work or attempts to do everything for others to win their love or approval
- romantic involvements detract from work

Possible vocations: party or wedding planner, social/recreational director, seller of sporting goods or recreational equipment, child counselor, cheerful cashier or assistant, manager, window trimmer, toy store salesperson, school interviewer, artist, casting agent.

5/8: multicapable but predominantly enterprising or artistic
Constructive applications:
- masters intense self-expressive needs with respect to others' rights
- commitment to accomplish something important and special contributes to healthy self-esteem
- obsesses over creative projects and needs to throw self into deeply absorbing work
- undergoes a drastic transformation from the former self
- desires power, position, influence or wealth
- unlimited energy to work long and hard, to endure pressure and stress, but must be devoted to the work
- capacity for business management, corporate affairs, any trait 8 outlet or an intensely committed approach to trait 5 activities
- a self-reliant, deep, serious thinker who functions on principles and is magnetic, daring, risk-taking
- shares power and contributes to the benefit of a greater whole
- a natural leader who attracts the support of others or a demanding boss who is careful not to control the expression of others
- could be self-employed

Nonconstructive applications:
- lacks self-control so that compulsive, self-expressive drives overwhelm/dominate others
- needs to win at all costs which accounts for ruthless tactics and the abuse of others' rights
- fails to develop self-expressive needs and inner power; attracts power players or is passively aggressive and covertly controlling/obligating until fortitude/inner power are achieved
- overwhelming stage fright hampers ability to perform in front of an audience
- embroiled in office politics, romantic intrigues or convoluted perceptions of others which undermine self-esteem or ability to perform
- timid, fearful, wimpy, easily dominated, denies self-expressive needs and fears venturing out into life
- ruthless, manipulative, controlling, sneaky, needs to develop team spirit

Possible vocations: child/adolescent psychologist, bank or business executive, committed teacher, charismatic entertainer or lecturer, occult hobbyist, nightclub owner, welder, stunt person, investment wizard, recreational director, corporate climber, an employee or boss who is devoted to work.

5/9: artistic, enterprising or intellectual
Constructive applications:
- pursues realistic, heartfelt vocational dreams
- appears lucky, however, self-esteem, confidence, striving and cheerful, optimistic attitudes generate fortunate opportunities
- needs rewarding, interesting, self-expressive work that "takes one places"
- aspirational, idealistic, buoyant, confident with pronounced needs to be important, noticed, knowledgeable, famous or wealthy
- proclivity for adventure, calculated risks, fun-loving exaggeration or sports
- believes in far-out possibilities and grows through productive hobbies or other trait 5 or 9 pursuits
- advanced training or education enhances self-esteem/self-expression

Nonconstructive applications:
- fails to set realistic goals, has excessive need to be special/famous or does not respond to aspirational urges which robs youth and buoyancy
- self-satisfied, financially irresponsible, a good time Joe or a pipe dreamer who is poorly prepared, childish, nonachieving or depends too much on luck
- experiences vast disappointments due to unrealistic goals and reaching for more than is possible given the effort quotient or experiences difficulty in finding interesting work when aspirations are unacknowledged
- leaves jobs when dreams are impossible to fulfill or when insufficient acclaim/recognition is given

Possible vocations: outlandish entertainer, world-wide lecturer, gambler, cruise director, radio station manager, actor, astrologer, successful manager, fund-raiser, promoter, attorney, account executive, publisher of children's stories, import/export of luxury items/recreational goods, teaching manual writer, works out of doors, disc jockey.

5/10: multicapable but predominantly enterprising or artistic
Constructive applications:
- balances work/effort/duty with relaxation/recreation/fun
- acknowledges that creative talents or business ventures take time, patience and painstaking effort to develop
- achieves self-esteem through professionalism, authority, recognition, integrity and the ability to perform
- a responsible, career-conscious, unflamboyant individual who seeks authority, position, respect, admiration and learns to handle periods of blocked creativity or excessive hard work
- takes an intellectual, scientific or practical approach to trait 5 areas or a more outgoing, confident approach to trait 10 outlets
- turns a hobby into a career
- has a love affair with work, with a superior or participates in recreational activities with bosses
- hardworking, decisive, loyal, organized, dependable, executive with good business management/self-employment potential
- takes pride in hard-won accomplishments
- achieves quiet respectability, attracts public attention and a slow but steady rise through effort and commitment

Nonconstructive applications:
- is all work/no fun or lacks confidence to perform responsible tasks
- suffers from an over or under self-estimation, too many "shoulds," excessive image consciousness, fears of failure, inadequacy or unnecessary self-restrictions which lead to seeking nonself-expressive work, to establishing low achievement ceilings, or to periods of blocked activity
- fears spontaneity and performing in front of groups due to early life restrictions on self-expressive needs which must be overcome
- gives up too soon on difficult projects or becomes depressed when not in authority positions or pursuing creative endeavors
- stiff, inhibited and shy during interviews or comes on too strong
- authoritarian, selfish, cold, pretentious with excessive needs to prove importance, or too humble, self-effacing with inadequate career drives

Possible vocations: theatre manager, owner of an art gallery, theatrical/literary agent or critic, broker in stock options or commodities, skilled comedian, business administrator, executive or business owner, difficult boss, serious lecturer or teacher. (See Sun in Capricorn/tenth house, Leo Midheaven.)

5/11: intellectual, artistic or technical
Constructive applications:
- balances closeness and detachment, freedom urges, being special with an ability to recognize the specialness of others
- a true team player who is open to making career/job changes in search of healthy stimulation
- technical know-how, mastery contribute to healthy self-esteem
- speaks in front of groups and is technically proficient, exciting, fun, innovative with a flair for any trait 11 area or an original, avant garde approach to any trait 5 outlet
- pursues unusual hobbies, recreational activities, new age subjects or speculative ventures
- success-oriented with big dreams backed by effort
- needs to circulate on the job, socialize, become recognized or professional
- organizes, leads, manages or entertains groups (seminars, conferences)
- is bright, risk-taking, enjoys being friends with the boss or clients and playing a significant role in a larger structure or cause
- thrives on colleague recognition and friendship

Nonconstructive applications:
- fails to develop realistic self-esteem and a sense of specialness
- denies stimulation needs or is excessive about them
- unconsciously attracts unpleasant circumstances (e.g., being fired abruptly, the work place suddenly changes hands, business associates abruptly walk out) when needs for excitement/stimulation/change are repressed
- is excessively eccentric, rebellious or too detached from the needs of others (which creates unpleasant work circumstances)
- lacks a practical grasp of reality, gets in over the head or is

laissez faire and works as little as possible (including not working)
- acts the clown among coworkers and fails to get the job done
- reckless, foolhardy, needs discipline or a team spirit
- flaunts convention or is harsh, cold, too authoritarian
- the job or career may not fit the personality

Possible vocations: television or rock performer/manager, stock options trader, designer of electronic toys, recreational consultant, executive for an association or professional society, manager of a video arcade, exciting group discussion or conference leader, seminar coordinator, astrologer, computer game salesperson. (See nodes in Leo/Aquarius.)

5/12: artistic or intellectual
Constructive applications:
- turns big dreams into reality and contributes to the benefit of a greater whole
- spontaneous use of intuition or the creative imagination is part of work
- maintains committed beliefs and confidence in the goodness of life
- idealistic, ethical, caring, modest, wise, sympathetic, cheerful and practices what one preaches
- a visionary with purpose, inner confidence, self-esteem, otherworldly hobbies or interests which develop over time
- proclivity for the arts and other trait 12 outlets or an inspired, socially-conscious approach to trait 5 vocations
- able to enthuse, soothe or inspire others
- prefers solitude or the extremes of the limelight
- fears of inferiority or disorienting attention in early life prompt achievement needs
- attracted to acting, psychic, scientific, glamor or metaphysical fields, the sick, helpless, addicted or disturbed
- works in movie studios, other behind-the-scenes places, universities or nonprofit organizations where leadership and contribution can be realized

Nonconstructive applications:
- functions through an over or under self-estimation
- unrealistic beliefs, poor work ethic, pipe dreams or escapism undermine ability to turn visions into reality or to establish realistic goals

- lack of social consciousness hampers fulfillment of potentials
- longs for fame or wealth, but is unwilling to work for it
- prefers get rich quick schemes, tries to get others to carry the load or handle the less pleasant aspects of work
- hides behind a career or is pretentiously intellectual
- overly confident, unrealistic and lands jobs without ability to follow through (due to inadequate skills or a poor work ethic) or lacks confidence and feels weak against the odds
- lazy, frail, escapist, impressionable, self-deceived, self-pitying, confused over direction, purpose and the relationship to God
- a successful con artist, big bragger, poor employee or a dictatorial, pompous bore
- romantic, wishful thinking clouds realistic interactions with others
- falls under the influence of guru-types due to lack of self-confidence

Possible vocations: child care worker, theatre manager, writer/seller/designer of greeting cards, artist, toy designer, movie set designer, psychic entertainer, social worker, martial arts practitioner, photographer, psychologist, musician, actor, yoga instructor.

6/6: predominantly practical, intellectual or technical
- same as trait 6
- For details and possible vocations, see trait 6 in Chapter 2, Mercury in Chapter 4.

6/7: technical, artistic or assisting
Constructive applications:
- appreciates rewarding work and skill development (i.e., loves work)
- works closely with others on a one-to-one basis or through cooperative efforts and teamwork
- helpful, useful and serves others in a healthy sense
- versatile, diligent, technically proficient or artistically inclined; needs to work in attractive, pleasant surroundings
- works with a boss, the spouse or meets the spouse through work-related activities; caters to the needs of others on a daily basis

- a partner, close associates, a productive staff or an attractive, helpful assistant/employee aids work efforts
- deals with clients, students or customers, art or cash/ financial transactions as part of the job
- good looks or a pleasant demeanor enhance job prospects
- coworkers can be friends or lovers

Nonconstructive applications:

- an excessive need to be useful leads to overserving others, neglecting one's own needs and being taken advantage of or being overly critical, too demanding of others with a failure to show appreciation for their contributions
- fails to develop rewarding skills which leads to accepting lesser positions, boredom with work or slackness on the job
- failure to develop interpersonal relating skills undermines job advancement
- has difficulty accepting imperfection in others or mistakes them for servants and expects too much
- fails to carry one's fair share of the work load

Possible vocations: art dealer, recruiter, designer, salesperson, modeling agent or model, beauty supplies dealer, dental hygienist or assistant, actor/actress, secretary or receptionist, any work providing a one-to-one service, dietician, maker of handicrafts, cashier, word processor, carpenter, records-keeper, editor, analyst. (See 2/6.)

6/8: predominantly technical, intellectual or enterprising; can be assisting

Constructive applications:

- fascinated with the job, expertly hones skills and throws oneself into work with a total commitment to be of service
- shares power and decision-making on the job
- open to altering the approach to work or to making career/ job changes for more satisfying employment
- enjoys intense work environments and effectively deals with office politics
- the personality transforms due to skill development and a commitment to work
- demonstrates trait 8 needs or outlets on the job with an ability to work until exhausted and to exercise a form of power or insight
- precise, detail-minded, devoted, resourceful, hardworking or compulsive

- works without supervision, follows through on demanding tasks, and handles the less pleasant aspects of work or members of society
- capable of in-depth analysis, research, physical stamina or uses dangerous or intricate equipment

Nonconstructive applications:

- fails to recognize needs for deeply absorbing work or to display sufficient power on the job which leads to attracting mean, pushy bosses or power struggles with coworkers/ colleagues until sense of inner power is established
- fails to develop adequate skills or is obsessed by work to the detriment of health
- harshly critical, sarcastic, overdirecting and intrusive which eventually leads to the resentment of coworkers
- when inner power and resourcefulness are not exhibited, major crises in life surround work: unemployment, drastic health disorders, confrontations with authority figures or offensive office politics
- a difficult employee who professes to know best how to run things
- convoluted perceptions of others create unnecessary torment, job loss or difficulty in finding satisfying employment
- experiences long stretches of unemployment until inner power is established or toned down with respect to others' rights

Possible vocations: insurance adjustor, pest controller, scrap iron dealer, therapist, security guard, funeral director, physician/surgeon, construction/sewer worker, geologist, pipe fitter, metaphysician, police detective, stock broker, corporate employee, garbage collector, corporate analyst, comptroller, a powerfully involved, highly resourceful employee. (See 3/8.)

6/9: predominantly technical, intellectual or enterprising

Constructive applications:

- recognizes that trait 9 outlets are essential to rewarding job expression (i.e., seeks jobs that "take one places")
- understands that work and skills are important to fulfilling aspirational drives
- beliefs, concepts, theories or codified systems of thought play a major role on the job
- works in foreign parts, with foreigners or interesting others

who are helpful to advancement or expand horizons in other ways
- consciousness grows due to rewarding work and the attainment of goals
- capacity for abstract concepts, teaching, lecturing or organizing large scale projects
- an excellent employee or a good boss interested in the well-being of the staff

Nonconstructive applications:
- fails to respond to aspirational needs or aspirations are unrealistic compared to the effort quotient
- does not ground theories on sound facts and is unclear about one's true capabilities by over- or underestimating them
- careless, overlooks details or has big plans and dreams filled with sound and fury but signifying nothing
- lucky landing jobs, even with a poor work history, but may take on more than is realistic
- job-hops (due to a lack of satisfying work, skill development or advancement opportunity)
- nervous strain or health disorders arise from failing to respond to aspirational needs

Possible vocations: advisor/counselor, teacher, someone working out-of-doors, copywriter, flight attendant, pilot, bilingual secretary, attorney/judge, importer/exporter, aircraft or successful technician, college instructor, broadcast analyst, entrepreneur, horse trainer. (See 3/9.)

6/10: intellectual or technical
Constructive applications:
- exhibits a realistic, diligent commitment to perfect skills, develop competence and to do the best job possible
- readily assumes responsibility and ethically exercises or delegates authority
- highly concentrative and patient with capacity for analysis, flaw-finding and corrective action
- serious about work, technical proficiency, self-employment, authority and independent decision-making responsibilities
- specialized skills are on display for all to see
- a recognized professional who values intellectual/scientific achievement and pays the utmost attention to details, or a hardworking, trusted, responsible, organized and steady

employee able to interact with higher-ups and win their favor
- realistic about performance and understands/accepts the rules of the working world
- highly credentialed or seeks additional education, training, or promotion
- learns on one's own or as an apprentice

Nonconstructive applications:
- fails to work up to par, to take work, service, responsibilities and skill development seriously enough or takes work too seriously to the neglect of other personality needs
- a workaholic or never feels one is good enough or working hard enough
- over- or underestimates the intelligence or analytical capacity
- periods of unemployment, excessive worry, health disorders, job dissatisfaction, resentment of authority or difficulty getting ahead arise from incompetence, poor planning, short cuts, over self-estimation or failing to fulfill job responsibilities
- fails to understand the rules of the working world, lacks patience and may give up on a job too soon
- accepts unnecessarily low job ceilings, fears responsibility and prefers easy, routine work
- subject to controlling, dictatorial bosses and given limited or demeaning tasks to perform (when repressing a need to develop a critical, analytical or detailed approach to work)
- depressive or uses illness to escape from dull work routines

Possible vocations: highly competent employee, secretary or clerk, office manager, accountant, watch repairer, waiter or waitress, recognized authority, scrap iron dealer, self-employed professional, bureaucratic/government employee, health care professional, skilled crafts or tradesperson, scientist, statistician. (See Virgo Midheaven, 3/10.)

6/11: technical or intellectual

Constructive applications:
- balances diligence/practicality with originality, excitement and change
- makes job/career changes in search of healthy stimulation
- works part-time or makes contributions to a greater whole
- works with friends or turns coworkers into friends

- highly intelligent, innovative with capacity for quick or insightful analysis
- thrives on the recognition of peers/coworkers
- recognizes that trait 11 needs and outlets are essential to a rewarding job
- functions as part of a team, crew or is self-employed, an independent contractor, consultant or sales representative who makes brief contacts with clients or customers
- demonstrates a technical expertise for communications, electronics, health care, cosmic sciences, analysis, theoretical, unusual or new age subjects
- develops a sense of individuality at work or through productive skills
- works until exhausted (due to stimulation and interest in the job)

Nonconstructive applications:

- fails to recognize excitement, stimulation needs on the job or displays these needs too eccentrically/rebelliously
- unconsciously attracts/undergoes sudden job changes, gets fired, laid off unexpectedly or develops illnesses which quickly grow to unusual proportions and disrupt work (due to denied or excessive trait 11 needs)
- normal relations cannot be established with bosses or coworkers who are hyper, high-strung, disorganized, dictatorial, lackadaisical, insecure (or one can be such an employee) until originality/excitement needs are integrated with diligence/practicality

Possible vocations: midwife, industrial psychologist, works for a group practice or an association, sells/services/repairs or uses computers or other electronic equipment, worker in television industry, mathematician, video/camera equipment operator or seller, scientist, astrologer, cab driver, electrician, union worker. (See 3/11)

6/12: multicapable

- integrates reality and idealism, practicality and discrimination, compassion with caring, technical skills and intuition
- committed beliefs play strong roles at work
- assesses multifarious facts, learns new techniques with ease and is capable of the utmost in precision

- inspires coworkers/employees, is inspired by them or by work and needs to work with others who share similar ideals or work ethics
- highly intuitive and takes a serious, precise approach to any trait 12 field
- highly ethical, experiences a deep sense of service and commitment to perform to the best of the abilities
- often works behind-the-scenes, in institutions, back offices, movie sets, universities, hospitals or large organizations

Nonconstructive applications:

- fails to balance the divergent needs of this polarity
- overblows trait 6 needs into workaholism without a sense of purpose behind the service
- fears of inferiority obliterate compassion and understanding and lead to excessive criticism of others
- experiences mysterious problems with coworkers or employees who are careless, deceitful, lazy, thieving con artists (when one is out of touch with one's own idealistic side)
- may be unaware of how hard one works or a lazy, good-for-nothing who is deluded into believing one works harder than is the case
- can be totally unrealistic about capabilities when trait 12 is overblown
- cannot obtain satisfying employment (due to failing to develop skills)
- experiences emotional problems or illness to unconsciously escape from work
- the business/company collapses, the job phases out, periods of unemployment or job drifting result when one fails to recognize the importance of skill development, searches for the "perfect" job or fails to work up to ethical standards

Possible vocations: x-ray or lab technician, designer/artist, anesthesiologist, stop smoking counselor, metaphysician, liquor/wine sales, priest/nun, health foods, psychic, waiter/waitress, film editor, technical writer, window/dishwasher, social services, shoe salesperson, dietician, physician, nurse. (See nodes in Virgo/Pisces, 6/9.)

7/7: assisting, artistic or intellectual

- same as trait 7
- For details and possible vocations, see trait 7, Chapter 2,

western hemisphere emphasis, Venus in Chapter 4, Full Moon phase.

7/8: artistic, assisting or enterprising
Constructive applications:
- balances power, intensity with consideration for the rights of others
- is or has a dynamic, charismatic business partner, associate or undergoes a transformation of partnership/relationship needs
- performs any job requiring intense or powerful interaction with others
- needs physical contact and intensely close, committed relationships where efforts are equally shared
- drawn to financial, corporate or occult matters and may deal with the public
- uses the power of persuasion to change, influence or "read" others
- works closely with others and attracts their support
- flair for trait 8 occupations or approaches, or is intensely absorbed in trait 7 occupations
- attracts a dynamic business partner who changes the scope of the career

Nonconstructive applications:
- inner power and fortitude are not developed or power is used selfishly which interferes with the ability to participate in trusting, give-and-take relationships
- attempts to control others through overkilling kindness, obligation, guilt, sex, overgiving of material goods or sells out for material favors
- cooperation is a challenge due to being overtly/covertly dominating, jealous of others and their success, demanding of their support or sexual favors, or being passive, withdrawn, easily dominated and fearful of interaction
- encounters disturbing relationships and power struggles due to lack of honesty or fortitude
- an exploitative worker/boss or attracts such people until able to use own power wisely
- needs to eliminate tendencies to misperceive, control or obsess over others

Possible vocations: politician, artist, sex therapist, insurance salesperson, public aid worker, comptroller, market researcher, intensive care nurse, counselor, plastic surgeon, financial analyst, diplomat, lithographer, beautician, cosmetician, bank/corporate executive, dental assistant. (See 2/8.)

7/9: artistic, intellectual or enterprising
Constructive applications:
- balances needs for closeness with freedom urges so that relationships can be entered without fear of losing freedom or a sense of adventure
- benefits through purposeful belief system, higher education and through partnership or other trait 7 outlets
- trait 9 activities could involve the public
- loves adventure, theories, concepts, sports or religious pursuits
- travels, meets many people, teaches or lectures as part of the job
- talent for any field where friendly, refined, poised qualities count; is promoted due to them
- enjoys brushing shoulders with the rich, famous or influential and may be fortunate in dealings with them
- attracts a gifted agent or partner (sometimes foreign-born) who helps elevate the career
- travels with business associates, a partner or a spouse or meets the spouse while traveling

Nonconstructive applications:
- unrealistic about relationships and fears close ties due to feeling they will undermine freedom needs, or enters elitist relationships/partnerships to elevate the lifestyle or career
- lacks ambition, experiences difficulty establishing priorities or a constructive belief system, is self-indulgent, lazy, prone to weight gain, selfish, and expects too much support from others without reciprocating
- ranges in behavior from being nice and obliging to being critical, aloof and/or demanding
- tries to be all things to all people

Possible vocations: importer/exporter of fine or beautiful products, commercial artist, flight attendant, travel or literary agent, media worker, salesperson, actor, counselor, translator, playwright, preacher, lawyer, gambler, wedding or party planner.

7/10: multicapable
Constructive applications:
- develops interrelating skills and a sense of shared effort, fair play, duty and responsibility to others
- flair for business, science or government work and may attract public attention
- steady, practical, loyal, efficient, conservative, highly competent employee/partner or a charming superior able to provide purpose and structure for others
- works with the spouse, or other loved one, and needs fulfilling relationships as much as fulfilling work
- loves to exercise authority and can do so fairly due to patient consideration of others
- the career benefits from partnership or the assistance of others due to reciprocation
- appreciates competent work, professionalism, hard-earned achievements and recognition
- could fall in love with a superior or could be married to the career

Nonconstructive applications:
- does not develop interpersonal skills or competence
- fails to relate fairly and responsibly to others, which creates unnecessary career obstacles, or enters relationships solely for the prestige they offer
- fails to recognize one's authority needs, fears responsibility, creates unnecessarily low achievement ceilings which leads to attracting harsh, uncaring bosses who supervise one too closely
- seeks occupations solely for their material advantages
- a strict disciplinarian who alienates or exploits others, pays inadequately or uses socially unacceptable ways to earn a living
- a sad or isolated employee who experiences difficulty obtaining good jobs or meeting the bills due to failing to elevate skills and to acknowledge needs for distinction

Possible vocations: business manager, boutique or shop owner, bank executive, financial expert, job trainer, talented organizer or professional, upholsterer, highly skilled sales or craftsperson, therapist, artist, diplomat, business associate, professor. (See third quadrant focus, Venus in Capricorn/tenth house, Libra Midheaven 2/10, for further details.)

7/11: artistic, assisting or intellectual
Constructive applications:
- forms stimulating relationships due to integrating needs for closeness/intimacy with freedom/change urges
- innovative or part-time approach to trait 7 occupations or a flair for trait 11 occupations or approaches
- falls in love with a colleague, seeks colleague recognition, lovers become friends or friends become lovers
- wins public favor and attracts many clients, customers, patients or students due to sparkling charm, warm friendliness or unusual talents
- loves teamwork and is an enthusiastic, stimulating contributor to the group process
- is or has a brilliant or unusual business associate
- enjoys the out of the ordinary, self-employment or independent contracting, although benefits from the group, seminars, friends or from referrals
- needs stimulating coworkers/staff and often becomes friends with them or with clients
- forms business associations quickly which may or may not be long-lasting
- makes job changes in search of healthy stimulation

Nonconstructive applications:
- fails to balance closeness/intimacy needs with urges for freedom and change
- overly eccentric, antisocial or rebellious behavior coincides with fears of closeness and leads to abrupt conduct toward or from others
- others suddenly change their attitudes toward one
- business deals and partnerships break off suddenly due to taking relationships for granted or to not playing fair
- fails to fit in the group due to eccentricities or to not recognizing needs for healthy stimulation
- obstinate, demanding, walks off the job or has conflicts with coworkers/staff/superiors due to inability to make commitments to people or careers

Possible vocations: friendly, sparkling receptionist, provider of sales/service for electronic equipment, creator or seller of unusual gifts or high fashion merchandise, organizer of union or conference/seminar activities, worker for professional group practice or nonprofit association, purchaser of technical products, astrologer, television interviewer, new age or group therapist, inventive artist or salesperson, aerobics instructor. (See 2/11.)

7/12: artistic, assisting or intellectual
Constructive applications:
- takes an inspired or aesthetic approach to work and turns dreams or creative insights into reality
- proclivity for the arts, performing arts, sales, teaching, counseling, eastern religions or psychic matters
- compassionate, refined, quiet, idealistic, ethical with an intuitive, sympathetic understanding of others
- humanitarian, sincerely cares about the well-being of others, assists the handicapped or emotionally troubled
- possesses a refined, gentle touch with ability for handling small or fragile objects
- is or has hidden backers who provide inspiration or urge one on to success
- devoted to or uplifted by work, a business partner or the spouse

Nonconstructive applications:
- phony, unrefined, lazy, loud, fearful, insecure, unreliable, wants to be glamorous, rich and falls in with fads, deceptive business practices or associates through a need to get rich quick
- blind to what the partner needs or is doing
- easily duped by others due to a lack of clarity, projected idealism or one's savior/victim/martyr complex
- needs to be more realistic about relationships and one's value in them
- overserves and waits on others or deceives and cheats them
- a deceptive or deluded business partner or spouse who expects too much support from others, overestimates capabilities, exaggerates accomplishments and rationalizes failures by blaming others or "the system"
- clandestine relationships undermine the career or marriage

Possible vocations: musician, singer, actor, photographer, art teacher, spiritual advisor, yoga instructor, poet, novelist or playwright, fine artist, glass or jewelry dealer, candy maker, silent partner, worker in the food or liquor industries, intuitive interviewer/counselor, model, casting agent, interior decorator, hospital social worker, con artist. (See 2/12.)

8/8: predominantly enterprising or intellectual
- same as trait 8
- For details and possible vocations, see trait 8, Chapter 2, Pluto in Chapter 4.)

8/9: enterprising or intellectual
Constructive applications:
- seeks knowledge, insights about life which transform consciousness, rejuvenate one's being and are productively shared for the benefit of all
- idealistic, ambitious with grand, constructive aspirations
- desires and is realistic about power, influence, wealth or fame with an undying optimistic belief in self and capacity to succeed
- possesses psychological or psychic insight, strong sex drives, leadership potential and adamant viewpoints, especially about social or metaphysical issues
- takes calculated risks, or is interested in politics, corporate affairs, healing, the occult or mystical aspects of religion
- dynamic or intense in business dealings with capacity for large scale projects, broad social reforms; can influence public opinion
- benefits from a partner's resources or talents
- quickly rises through the ranks or appears to be an overnight success

Nonconstructive applications:
- fails to be realistic about power, its use and how it is tied to aspirational needs
- overly pronounced, uncontrolled sex drives with a might-makes-right attitude about sexual encounters
- seeks power by relating to influential others rather than developing one's own connection to power
- obnoxious, greedy, ruthless, excessively manipulative and controlling or excessively passive, insecure and fearful of confrontations (including sexual encounters)
- experiences legal or tax problems and generates powerful enemies until comfortable and effective with own idealism and power

Possible vocations: occult or sex magazine publisher, athlete, insurance salesperson, wheeler-dealer, high powered TV broadcaster or performer, pyramid company owner, promoter, healer, powerful attorney or judge, advertising executive, college professor, air traffic controller, market researcher. (See Disseminating Moon phase for further details.)

8/10: enterprising, practical or intellectual
Constructive applications:
- determined to become an authority or expert in a deeply moving, absorbing career
- works well under the own direction and can be a loyal, highly competent employee able to interact effectively with higher-ups and to delegate authority
- undergoes a transformation due to a fulfilling career or the career undergoes a transformation
- seeks intense experiences (even when this is unconscious) and is an ambitious, serious, painstakingly hard worker who makes an unrelenting commitment to elevate oneself through the career
- unusual capacity for discipline, details, organization, to endure stress, to face unpleasantness and to work alone
- an in-depth, highly precise expert who influences the direction of a profession
- takes sex, power and authority seriously and learns to utilize them fairly

Nonconstructive applications:
- fails to develop a sense of competence to perform difficult, responsible tasks which leads to low career ceilings and unacknowledged needs to be a person of distinction
- a ruthless, suspicious manipulator who misuses/abuses power, authority and responsibility and may experience a fall from grace before lessons are learned
- has convoluted perceptions of reality or of other people
- a hard, punitive taskmaster who is overly intense, mistrustful or is fearful, workaholic, security-conscious and isolationist
- experiences difficulty delegating authority or working under the supervision of another
- financial problems arise from ruinous associates, blocked corporate funds, mergers, unemployment (could lose everything) due to failing to live up to responsibilities

- experiences dark forebodings and tumultuous confrontations with intense, sexual, jealous bosses, associates, competitors or coworkers until one's own ambitions, competency, sexuality and desires for intense experience are constructively channeled

Possible vocations: highly competent researcher, professional or corporate employee/executive, business owner, president or tycoon, mining expert, bank administrator or worker, funeral director, hard laborer, cement finisher, urban planner, architect, services/drives heavy machinery, occult practitioner, explosives expert, government official, waste manager, junk dealer, buys, sells or rehabilitates businesses or buildings. (See Pluto in tenth, Scorpio Midheaven for further details.)

8/11: artistic, enterprising or intellectual
Constructive applications:
- balances security/determination to hang on with change/innovation so that both sets of needs are fulfilled
- seeks highly intense, stimulating experiences, committed causes, but balances them with objective reasoning, a humanitarian spirit and recognizes that one's actions impact a greater whole
- makes drastic changes or incorporates new approaches in search of healthy career excitement, stimulation
- displays unexpected talents when spirit of contribution exists and may suddenly gain power, influence or standing
- highly ambitious with incredible stamina and ability for large scale undertakings, to take charge over a large crew of people, to direct and to lead with decisiveness
- mesmerizes an audience through powerful public speaking capacity
- a natural with highly intricate electronic equipment, computers, corporate affairs or joint financial ventures and may possess psychic, musical or scientific research capability
- influences the direction of an organization/profession, reforms, reorganizes or renovates it
- takes risks, faces danger and makes an unrelenting commitment to a company, profession or cause
- has high-powered, brilliant, influential or talented business associates or friends

Nonconstructive applications:
- fails to balance trait 8 and 11 needs so that one need is overexpressed while the other is unconsciously attracted into one's life, often to negative extremes (until 8/11 are integrated and constructively expressed)
- fails to recognize how one's actions impact a greater whole
- harshly controlling, fanatical or authoritarian (when trait 8 is overexpressed at the expense of objective reasoning or humanitarianism)
- attracts powerful or jealous colleagues, incidences escalate to incredible proportions, corporate funds evaporate or partner's resources suddenly change (until inner power is attained)
- encounters subversive power struggles or is embroiled in businesses undergoing drastic changes or upheavals (whenever trait 11 is denied constructive expression)
- rebellious, fanatical, foolhardy, obsessive and has unstable career goals and drives

Possible vocations: corporate financial vice president, television producer, leader of new age reform, pioneering scientist, computer programer, designer or troubleshooter, industrial real estate developer, surgeon, inventor, high powered stockbroker, subversive activist, consulting technician, extraordinary psychic, executive director of an association.

8/12: artistic, assisting, enterprising or intellectual
Constructive applications:
- determined faith and committed beliefs in the goodness of life bring unexpected assistance due to positive outlooks and sense of contribution
- locates secret backers or business associates who contribute extraordinary ability to the career effort
- researches spiritual/religious matters, mysteries, hidden subjects or throws oneself into any deeply moving, inspirational occupation, not only for personal gain but for the benefit of a greater whole
- uncanny perceptual ability, can be highly intuitive or psychic and drawn to unusual subjects or occupations where science or assisting the underdog play a role
- eliminates fears of inferiority and attains the heights of achievement

- possesses fascinating allure, can mesmerize a group or confront the supernatural
- a natural at cosmic sciences with a capacity to work long and hard alone
- balances pronounced idealism with reality and needs a passionately romantic sex life

Nonconstructive applications:

- denies power/sexual needs: creates unconscious power struggles, unsavory sexual encounters (and other unpleasant ramifications) until inner power or a constructive ideology is established
- must learn to better align idealism and needs for perfection with what is realistically possible
- experiences unforeseen problems surrounding joint resources or corporate funds: resources may collapse at a moment's notice, business associates fail to do the job or resort to thievery (when one fails to integrate idealism and perfectionism with reality)
- prone to excessive sexual fantasies, slow dissipation or escapism
- unconscious compulsions and fears lead to lying and manipulation
- deluded about one's power or weakness
- loses power when not functioning through a spirit of contribution or to the best of one's capabilities
- can be fanatical, tortured and takes on more than the abilities warrant
- needs to undergo psychotherapy when idealism/power are not functionally developed
- suffers from sexual aberrations or is irresponsible about sex

Possible vocations: statistical researcher, intuitive business executive/tycoon, occult or psychic practitioner, politician, astronaut, psychic researcher, mystic, therapist, hospital financial administrator, institutional worker, oil rigger, mineralogist, film director/producer.

9/9: multicapable but predominantly enterprising or intellectual

- same as trait 9
- For details and possible vocations, see trait 9, Chapter 2, Jupiter in Chapter 4.

9/10: intellectual, enterprising or practical
Constructive applications:
- balances faith, optimism and the desire to expand horizons with a sense of reality, practicality and painstaking effort
- takes aspirations seriously and establishes realistic goals wherein authority, influence, leadership, achievement, status or wealth are sought
- higher education, beliefs, theories or philosophical concepts are significant to career advancement
- attracts opportunities, follows them up diligently and may achieve success in foreign parts
- travels as part of the job or prefers occupations which deal in absolutes
- hardworking, ethical, self-reliant, takes knowledge seriously and wins favor from higher-ups who are inspired by one's duty, honesty and ambitions
- obtains good jobs, exercises authority fairly and can be an inspiring boss
- establishes a sound, professional reputation or horizons quickly blossom once sincere career striving takes place

Nonconstructive applications:
- fails to integrate faith/optimism/risk-taking/expansiveness with practicality/realism/caution/hard work so that, until blended, one goes to extremes with either possibility
- a dictatorial know-it-all who exaggerates the position in life, has unrealistic goals or blocked aspirations, job-hops, prefers not to work, or takes the job course of least resistance (when trait 9 is overly expressed at the expense of trait 10)
- fears travel, continues to live with parents, is easily defeated, blocks aspirations, fails to achieve a sense of purpose or to obtain good jobs (when trait 10 is overly relied on at the expense of trait 9)
- fails to pursue an education or to develop a constructive belief system

Possible vocations: corporate climber, teacher, fund-raiser, bureaucrat, media expert, publisher, advertising agent, judge/attorney, college professor, traveling executive or worker in the travel business, corporate advisor, architect, wheeler-dealer, industrialist, importer/exporter, statistician. (See Jupiter in Capricorn/tenth house, Sagittarius Midheaven for further details.)

9/11: multicapable but predominantly intellectual or enterprising
Constructive applications:
- develops productive, stimulating interests and seeks knowledge or higher truths
- urgently needs to learn, to freely circulate, to disseminate important concepts or to meet unusual, exciting people
- establishes individual perspectives on religion or has unusual, adamant viewpoints
- thrives on exciting new adventures, stimulating work and peer recognition
- functions in or outside of the nine-to-five world
- takes an unusual, offbeat or new age approach to trait 9 occupations, or aspirations are fulfilled through teamwork, group activities, networking or other trait 11 outlets
- metaphysically inclined, cheerful, innovative, optimistic, farsighted, a quick learner, independent-minded, idealistic, hard-driven to succeed
- travels at the drop of a hat
- has good intuition, steadily increases the income and believes in positive outcomes
- popular, well-liked, ethical, able to work under stress and to organize others
- good with electronic equipment or consciousness-raising groups, ideas
- gets lucky breaks from friends or acquaintances which suddenly create a totally new, undreamed of career course

Nonconstructive applications:
- a blind optimist who fails to work up to par, counts too much on luck, and demonstrates excessive needs for stimulation, excitement, freedom
- nervous ailments arise when aspirations are denied or sudden, unfortunate alterations in the career take place when needs for change, stimulation or innovation are not acknowledged
- a lackadaisical job-hopper who loses touch with reality, exaggerates, takes on too much and crumbles over stress
- prefers not working over being tied down to a nine-to-five job
- stubborn, rebellious with authority and is deluded into believing in one's superiority
- inadequately formulated viewpoints or philosophies do not fit

into a workable structure

Possible vocations: television performer or business executive, electronics trade magazine publisher, radio announcer or DJ, publishing consultant, inventor/scientist, astronaut, test pilot, astrologer/metaphysician, part-time or unique attorney, conference organizer, explorer, new age publisher, speculating wheeler-dealer, promoter, worker out-of-doors or for charitable causes, construction engineer.

9/12: multicapable

Constructive applications:

- develops highly idealistic goals which are realistically backed by effort and service to a greater whole
- carries through on difficult, large scale projects due to committed beliefs
- a seeker of knowledge about one's field, higher truths or expanded consciousness
- a success-oriented, accomplishing dreamer or visionary who believes that nothing is impossible to achieve
- desires wealth, fame, achievement or gravitates to spiritual, new age, eastern philosophy or psychic matters
- intuitive, impressionable, can be highly creative and may possess scholastic or musical ability
- pursues advanced degrees or travels to exotic places
- lucky changes come from out of the blue due to spirit of contribution
- compassionate, humanitarian, outgoing or quiet and unassuming

Nonconstructive applications:

- unrealistic goals or insufficient effort fail to make dreams a reality
- waits for manna to fall or wastes time with escapist activities
- easily defeatist, experiences difficulty achieving a sense of purpose or suffers from feelings of inferiority when out of touch with aspirations, faith in a Higher Power or one's spiritual center
- a pipe dreamer who enjoys the glamorous "good life" but lacks drive to attain it and prefers that others pay the bills or do the work
- self-indulgent, disorganized, wasteful so that judgment is often distorted by wishful thinking about one's true capa-

bilities and future success
- hastily drops out of college or the working world
- self-righteous, arrogant, above it all, intolerant and critical of others even when living off of them (due to neglected aspirational efforts)
- a nonworking martyr with vague, unrealistic perceptions of reality

Possible vocations: hospital/social service, charitable work, actor, physician/nurse, photographer, artist, resort owner, science fiction/mystery writer, musician, mystic, speculator, statistician, artsy or glamor magazine publisher. (See splay pattern for further details.)

10/10: practical, technical or intellectual
- same as trait 10
- For details and possible vocations, see trait 10, Chapter 2, southern hemisphere emphasis, Saturn in Chapter 4, Last Quarter Moon phase, Capricorn Midheaven.

10/11: multicapable but predominantly technical or intellectual

Constructive applications:
- tempers stable, hard-driving, determined vocational goals/ drives with innovative approaches and an openness to change
- highly achievement-oriented or more practical and sedate
- contributes to the betterment of a group, company or profession
- works best under the own supervision, although can be friends with the boss, a good team worker or an important member of a crew
- conservative, sometimes artistic with ability to establish a business or professional practice
- takes an original, inventive or radical approach to the occupation and can endure hard, detailed work alone over extended periods
- successfully conducts several different projects at once or part-time
- teaches, lectures, writes as part of the job or works with friends
- changes career directions, suddenly rises to prominence or attracts the recognition of experts or colleagues

Nonconstructive applications:

- fails to develop the sense of competence or to balance trait 10 and 11 needs so that one is too heavily relied on at the expense of the other
- establishes low achievement ceilings, stays with boring, limited jobs, experiences incredible tensions at work (when trait 11 needs for stimulation remain unintegrated)
- trait 11 needs burst into consciousness as sudden, drastic employment changes
- attracts harsh, cold treatment from authority figures or resents and is rebellious about authority, "the establishment" or tradition (when trait 10 remains inadequately developed)
- suddenly falls from grace due to unrealistic self-appraisals, insufficient effort, abusing one's authority or failing to live up to responsibilities

Possible vocations: worker in television industry, union or association president/executive/worker, astrologer, pioneering scientist, orchestra conductor, inventor or mathematician, computer expert, manager of group practice, business consultant, construction worker, meeting/conference organizer, technical writer. (See splash pattern, Uranus in Capricorn/tenth house, Aquarius Midheaven for further details.)

10/12: artistic, intellectual or assisting
Constructive applications:

- integrates realism, practicality, effort and achievement with ideals, dreams, visions and alternative perceptions on the nature of reality
- tempers stable, practical, hard-driving, disciplined career drives with intuitive approaches and/or compassion so that one is compassionate and realistic, exhibits disciplined effort and intuitive approaches
- an accomplishing dreamer who is highly intelligent, perceptive, ambitious, serious, contributory and functions from inner convictions
- a proclivity for any of the helping professions, science, the arts or the glamor industry
- experiences positive career changes due to working to the highest capacity and sharing insights or knowledge
- develops an unusual or modest reputation or image

- capacity for hard, painstaking work in isolation, for the utmost in precision and a detail orientation
- overcomes insecurities and seeks to perfect abilities
- works toward inspired goals and turns dreams into reality

Nonconstructive applications:

- fails to develop competence or to adequately integrate trait 10 and 12 vocational needs so that one is too heavily relied on at the expense of the other
- suffers from vague anxieties, defensiveness, fears of inadequacy, isolation, workaholism or overly rational, harsh or critical attitudes toward others (when uncomfortable with idealism or other trait 12 needs)
- a pipe dreamer when the effort quotient and sense of competency/reality are deficient
- the job or business collapses (possibly due to poor or unethical work efforts)
- fears of worthlessness prevent one from participating in the career world to the best of one's abilities
- meek, passive and fearful of persecution or is involved in scandals, illicit activities (until comfortable with one's own idealism)
- seeks a meal ticket or an easy job rather than working too hard (due to fears of failure)
- escapist, unrealistic, mixes fact with fantasy, exaggerates the accomplishments and the capabilities (until effort and competence are displayed)
- hides vulnerabilities behind a career or a phony image

Possible vocations: skilled musician, scholar, film director/producer, fish store proprietor, art critic or expert, hospital worker/administrator, scientist, intuitive professional, martial arts expert, spiritual leader, photographer, priest, theatre or arts manager, metaphysician, fashion expert, bartender. (See Neptune in Capricorn/tenth house, Pisces Midheaven for further details.)

11/11: predominantly intellectual or technical

- same as trait 11
- For details and possible vocations, see trait 11 in Chapter 2, Uranus in Chapter 4.

11/12: artistic, assisting or intellectual

Constructive applications:

- balances objective reasoning/intellectual detachment with intuition/compassionate caring
- seeks higher truths (enlightenment) and unravels mysteries about spiritual/philosophical/religious issues or those related to one's occupation
- needs inspiring work to which a devoted commitment can be made to uplift others or to uplift one's profession
- an uncanny perceptual or conceptual sense, inspires others, seeks to shed new light on the workings of the world or one's profession
- possibly artistic with a capacity for science, mathematics or technology
- ability for occupations requiring technical know-how, mental mastery of a subject or activity coupled with an intuitive or caring approach to others
- experiences sudden flashes of insight or logical deduction
- highly idealistic with an elevated team spirit and pronounced needs to be of service, to participate in worthy causes/groups and to make a contribution to society
- a visionary who breaks with convention and accomplishes the extraordinary
- spiritual or psychic inclinations, religious or metaphysical concerns, sometimes desires fame or wealth
- attracts the support of others due to sincerity and high idealism/ethics
- has enlightening, uplifting friends, colleagues, artistic associates
- able to make a long enduring commitment to a company, group, cause or profession

Nonconstructive applications:

- fails to be realistic or discriminating about others which, at extremes, can correlate with emotional disturbances or the pursuit of fanatical goals
- fails to balance objective reasoning/intellectual detachment with intuition/compassionate understanding so that one is overly relied on at the expense of the other
- maintains a cool distance from others to the extreme of being coldly detached from their feelings (when trait 11 is overblown)

- experiences difficulty achieving a sense of purpose from life due to a nonparticipatory, noncontributory stance
- troubled over the sudden intrusion of psychic content or unable to deal effectively with sadness and emotional losses due to being overly rational
- can be excessively eccentric when behind the scenes
- displays unstable, unrealistic goals and believes that what one wants to be true is true, (when trait 12 is overblown)
- associates create anxiety when one is overly impressionable; needs to be more discriminating about who deserves support and who does not
- totally absorbed in society's fads and values to the neglect of higher understanding and a broadened awareness of life

Possible vocations: film director, performer or producer, physician, nurse, counselor, therapist, political or television commentator, psychic researcher, video tape sales representative, unusual/inventive artist, proficient computer programer, new age activist, author, at the top of one's profession. (See Balsamic Moon phase for further details.)

12/12: predominantly intellectual, artistic or assisting
- same as trait 12
- For details and possible vocations, see trait 12, Chapter 2, Neptune in Chapter 4.

References

1. Dean, Geoffrey, editor, *Recent Advances in Natal Astrology*, Western Australia: Analogic, 1977, p. 323
2. Dean, p. 313-5
3. Ann, Sue, *Vocational Astrology: Personality and Potential*, Tempe, Arizona: American Federation of Astrologers, (no date), p. 63-64
4. Carter, C.E.O., *The Astrological Aspects*, England: Fowler, 1975, p. 12
5. Tierney, Bil, *The Dynamics of Aspect Analysis*, Reno, Nevada: CRCS Publications, 1984
6. Burmyn, Lynne, *Planets in Combination*, San Diego, California: ACS Publications, Inc., 1987
7. Meyer, Michael, *A Handbook for the Humanistic Astrologer*, New York: Anchor, 1974, p. 189

8. Dean, Geoffrey, editor, *Recent Advances in Natal Astrology*, Western Australia: Analogic, 1977, p. 347
9. Dean, p. 430
10. Dean, p. 434-441
11. Dean, p. 443
12. Doane, Doris Chase, *Astrology: 30 Years Research*, Tempe, Arizona: American Federation of Astrologers, 1979, p. 62-3.

CHAPTER SIX

DEVELOPING A PURPOSEFUL IDENTITY

An inaccurate self-image often underlies inappropriate career functioning and choices. However, people without an identity hardly can be expected to pull one out of a hat. What can be done to overcome this deficiency?

The answer lies in the symbolism surrounding the Ascendant and the Midheaven (also called the "angles" of the chart). These angles coincide with attitudes and approaches which can generate a more realistic, purposeful identity and lead to a more self-reflective occupational expression. Each angle, and the planets which naturally rule them, represents vital interconnected processes of personality formation and productive functioning in the outer world. The Moon's nodes pinpoint a developmental tension which also needs to be resolved before a sense of wholeness can be achieved.

Ascendant - Trait 1 (Level II)

Arroyo's[1] definition of the Ascendant is a good one.

> It reveals what sort of approach to outer life one would prefer to take in order to feel free and unencumbered by other concerns,

> but there are often other factors in the chart which can inhibit such an intensely personalized approach (especially close aspects to the Ascendant). One can say, however, that the element of the Ascendant represents a type of self-projection that is physically energizing and which has a strong impact on one's self-confidence and sense of individual freedom and uniqueness.

This definition can be condensed to mean that **the rising sign represents what one needs to pursue for the sake of ego formation and identity awareness.**

One way selfhood is experienced is to pursue activities which allow one to see oneself in action – to learn-by-doing and freely acting on the environment. All trait 1 chart features are associated with this aspect of identity formation on which the ego is built. The Ascendant, especially, its ruler and any first house planets represent a **process** of establishing a basic sense of identity. This identity is connected to an interior level of being (linked to the Moon, the unconscious self-image and the IC) which directly impacts the exterior expression of self and the ability to grow into responsible adulthood (symbolized by Saturn and the Midheaven). Through freely acting on the world, basic qualities about self are made conscious and are experienced as being under one's control. Confidence then is gained to direct oneself and to pursue activities through which the identity can be expressed.

Some individuals come from upbringings which fostered their self-projection and helped to create the sense of individual freedom and uniqueness of which Arroyo writes. For them, the rising sign, and an identity, are developed more readily so that later, the ability to identify appropriate careers takes place more easily. For others, ego formation and self-expression may have been held up. Early attempts to express natural inclinations may have been hampered.

When this is the case, uncertainty over how to present the self can result. Some individuals restrict self-projection and the Ascendant portion of the ego formation process. Little that feels real and natural about their personalities can be developed and projected outwardly (leading to neuroses). The entire learning-by-doing process and the later ability to generate an expanded sense of individual competence, linked to the Midheaven, become disrupted. Deprived of an ability to know and act on who they are, it is no wonder some people remain in the dark about purposeful careers. Until contact with identity (1) is secured, the ability to maintain a viable occupation (10) will remain disturbed.

For this reason, when bearings in life are lost, fostering the constructive attributes symbolized by the ascending sign, its ruler, and any first house planets can assist ego formation and self-expression. **The Ascendant ruler,** by house and sign, represents an area of life, and an important psychological function (refer to it in Chapter 4), crucial to self-expression. Its aspects suggest additional factors impacting ego/identity formation.

Midheaven - Trait 10 (Level II)

Tradition has always made a strict distinction between the Ascendant and the Midheaven. The former has been said to concern "personality" while the latter has been described as manifesting occupationally, through the "calling," reputation or attainments in life. However, according to Dean[2], the Gauquelin findings, the vocational research conducted by the Church of Light and by H.B. Von Klocker, "do not support such a distinction." Other research by Charles Jayne and Ronald Davison also suggests the Ascendant and Midheaven "are less different than supposed."[3] Why might this be the case?

The Ascendant and Midheaven symbolize different, albeit interconnected, **processes** involving identity/ego formation and an ability to function productively in the outer world. While these angles may be easy to separate in theory, this may not be the case in the reality of astrological practice.

As discussed, the Ascendant represents a learning-by-doing approach which allows a person to gain a sense of self-direction. The MC relates to identity formation by taking the Ascendant process one step further. It does not represent the vocation as such, but only an important factor about **competence** which, in turn, affects occupational choices and performance.

This facet of identity formation occurs when an individual seeks to become a contributing member of a larger social structure. A fuller experience of selfhood is gained from learning what **tangibly** can be accomplished and by recognizing one's "authority" (competency) to assume an expanded vocational role. Some people develop stronger connections to this aspect of selfhood than others.

When the sense of self as competent is diminished, striving beyond immediate employment needs does not take place and the identity formation process, linked to the Midheaven, can become thwarted. People need to express themselves on their own terms (Ascendant) and to sense themselves as a functioning part of a greater whole (Midheaven), whether a company, community, profession or society at large. All first and tenth house indications **need** to be consciously developed to grow into oneself and to sense this self as a productive member of society. People suffering from career-related problems suffer from a lack of this need fulfillment. They are "alienated" from the career world because they are alienated from themselves and their true vocational needs. **An unhappy job life is a signal that identity needs are not being met or, perhaps, those needs are out of line with the personal reality and effort quotient**.

The Ascendant and MC symbolize what **needs** to be expressed to demonstrate a productive identity in the vocational world. They are **interconnected processes**, a possible reason why researchers have found them to be less different than traditionally suggested. The house and sign location of the **MC ruler** suggest areas and important psychological functions crucial to ego formation and the development of competence.

In general, when **fire signs** rise or culminate it becomes important to develop basic trait 1 characteristics and occupational approaches, including initiative, leadership, stamina, enterprise and the courage to fight for one's place. When **earth signs** are associated with these sensitive points, the symbolism suggests that tangible rewards and a practical, determined achievement orientation must figure into vocational expression. With the element of **air** rising or culminating, mental and communication faculties, in addition to the sense of objectivity and interrelating capabilities, are highlighted for development. The **water** signs suggest a need to enhance one's sensitivities, imagination, emotional foundations or caring instincts in order to develop the personality and vocational expression.

The following suggests pertinent identity needs, problems and a few antidotes for each trait when associated primarily with the Ascendant or the Midheaven and, secondarily, their rulers by house and sign. **These discussions also apply to the**

corresponding planets when they appear in the first or tenth house. Always refer to Chapter 2 for a complete analysis of the characteristics and vocational outlets or approaches appropriate to each trait. Also refer to the appropriate trait pair discussions in Chapter 5.

Trait 1

Aries on the Ascendant (1/1) or the MC (1/10); rulers of the first in the tenth or in Capricorn; trait 1 associated with the sign or house of Ascendant or MC rulers; ruler of first or tenth in the first house or in Aries.

With Aries, constructive trait 1 characteristics or vocational approaches are symbolized as paths to identity formation and a viable goal orientation. It is a calling to develop a strong sense of identity, purpose and self-assertive drives by demonstrating initiative, self-reliance, striving, leadership, competence or an expertise so career achievements can help define important qualities of selfhood. Aries without a rewarding goal thrashes about like a fish out of water.

When this trait is developed, individuals believe in themselves, their capabilities and their rights to express themselves as leaders. They are accomplishment-oriented and take the initiative to enhance their talents. In a diligent, single-minded fashion, they work to hone skills, become professionals, build businesses, or become key leaders in one, and attempt to reach the forefront or break new ground through their pioneering efforts. Self-expression, recognition and to be number one often serve as prodding motivations. Their keys to success include an ability to integrate initiative and risk-taking with caution, determination, patience, hard work and firm, constructive goals.

They identify with self-promoting or idealistic careers and thrive on action, independence and facing new challenges, ever mindful of a need to stay one step ahead of competitors. Some are intense, self-absorbed, dynamic, decisive and ready to throw down the gauntlet to anyone. Others, while decisive and self-determining, do not project themselves with the same degree of power. Still, each possesses magic and sparkle when striving to attain worthwhile goals. They develop a greater sense of themselves out of their efforts, achievements and recognition received.

Not all individuals are able to constructively project this trait. Some fail to recognize their trait 1 needs because they believe they could never attain important goals. They lack confidence in the ability to direct their own actions. The early life probably was filled with too many pressures, strains or angry displays which cramped the learning-by-doing process. As adults, these individuals experience difficulty achieving a sense of individuality and competence. Some job-hop or isolate themselves as a way to gain control over their lives. With Libra on the Descendant or IC, however, this response is not likely to prove fulfilling. They tend to attract excessively dominating bosses, brazen coworkers, colleagues or career setbacks until the trait 1 side of their personalities has been properly integrated. Until then, energies dam up and become overly focalized on non-trait 1 areas of life, which foster a whole range of mental aberrations. Sometimes these involve spiritual delusions, persecution complexes or delusions of grandeur, a need for glamour, wealth or ease.

Rather than exerting effort to attain rewarding goals, such people may prefer to wait for a "big break," expect others to carry the load or hope to find the "savior" who will pull them out of their dreary mess. Life is expected to adhere to teenager idealism. Individuals may dodge responsibility or are easily defeated when confronted with challenges. Others boast, bluff or swagger without tangible achievements to show for it, and are quick to blame others or "the system" for their troubles. Without a purposeful goal and some recognition, they can become complainers and malcontents.

The antidote to this dilemma is to establish a more realistic self-concept and proper self-assertive drives. (This may require therapy.) Repressed vocational desires to be at the forefront of a job or career must be recognized. They represent the crux of vocational dissatisfaction. Developing trait 1 characteristics or vocational approaches can be helpful to identity formation (see Chapter 2). But there must be a willingness to take risks, seek challenges, **work hard**, face competitors and accept responsibility. People can learn as much from "failures" as from their achievements.

Aries rising : Ada Byron (♂♈ 1st), Charles Gordon (♂♉ 2nd), Sandy Koufax (♂♒ 12th), Marcel Proust (♂♎ 6th), Helen

Reddy (♂♈ 12th), Barbra Streisand (♂♊ 3rd ☍ MC)

Aries MC : Jack Anderson (♂♑ 7th ☍ MC), Jack Nicholson (♂♐ 5th), Sam Peckinpah (♂♉ 11th), Fritz Perls (♂♌ 1st ☌ Asc.), George Sanders (♂♋ 12th), Eric Satie (♂♈ ☌ MC), Phoebe Snow (♂♎ 4th ☍ MC)

Trait 2

Taurus on the Ascendant (1/2) or the MC (2/10); trait 2 associated with the sign or house of Ascendant or MC ruler; rulers of first or tenth in the second house or in Taurus; ruler of the second in the tenth or first or in Capricorn or Aries.

With Taurus, constructive trait 2 characteristics or vocational approaches are highlighted. For many people, developing interests or creative talents can be a path to identity formation and to enhancement of the self-worth profile. For others, incorporating down-to-earth, practical or more determined approaches into their work may be more to the point. It can be tempting to take the easy way out. Balancing ease, comfort and financial security concerns with rewarding pursuits can be a major challenge of this symbolism. Self-doubts must be conquered.

When responsive to trait 2, people doggedly work to build vocations of a highly rewarding nature. They refine themselves through aesthetic pursuits or by accumulating knowledge about their fields of interest. Because physical appearance and personal appeal often can be important to vocational success, many enhance their looks, "style," wardrobes or patterns of speech and communication skills. They sufficiently value professionalism and their ability to make their own way to be more than willing to put themselves "on the line" and go the distance. They seek to excel and very often provide tangible evidence of their capabilities through a business, an award, book, painting, song, movie, something which can be pointed to or held in the hand.

When such qualities are not developed, some distortion of the value system can take place. Because the person tends to doubt the ability to succeed, the job world often gets viewed as a place to rent one's body for the mandatory forty hours a week. Lethargy, complacency or self-indulgences surface, obscure aspirational needs and undermine motivation to elevate skills.

"Safe" jobs, offering ease and financial security but without personal growth, can be preferred. However, the less significance a money-making occupation generates, the less stable the sense of identity and self-worth are likely to become. People eventually grow out-of-tune with themselves. Some do not sufficiently exert themselves in the job world or rely on other people for financial sustenance. Living off of or using others allows these trait 2 types to avoid facing the rigors of the working world or testing the value of their own capabilities.

People with this symbolism who grow dissatisfied with "safe" jobs, or purely lucrative ones, recognize that something is missing in life. While early circumstances may have required financially secure work, later on the lack of occupational substance can create emotional discomfort. They cast about for a more rewarding vocational expression. Depending on age, education and skill level, it is not always possible to move into a new line of work. However, individuals can still develop a greater sense of purpose from aesthetic avocational pursuits (see Chapter 2).

Taurus rising : Pancho Gonzales (♀♉ 12th), Vivien Leigh (♀♎ 6th), Herman Melville (♀♋ 3rd), O'Henry (♀♌ 4th), Percy Bysshe Shelley (♀♌ 5th), Suzanne Somers (♀♐ 7th), Nikola Tesla (♀♋ 3rd ☍ MC)

Taurus MC : Muhammad Ali (♀♒℞ 7th ☍ Asc.), Chris Chubbuck (♀♍ 2nd), Nina Foch (♀♊ 11th), Michel Gauquelin (♀♐ 5th), Karl Kraft (♀♋ 11th), Alan Leo (♀♋℞ 11th), Henry Matisse (♀♒ 7th ☍ Asc.)

Trait 3:

Gemini on the Ascendant (1/3) or the MC (3/10); trait 3 associated with the sign or house of the Ascendant or MC ruler; rulers of first or tenth in the third house or in Gemini; ruler of the third in the tenth or first or in Capricorn or Aries

With Gemini, constructive trait 3 characteristics or vocational approaches are highlighted. Depending on individual inclinations, these might include the pursuit of an education or the development of other mental/verbal processes, such as wit, logic, objectivity, use of the speaking voice, communicative skills or manual dexterity (see Chapter 2). However, integrating thought and communication with the feeling nature may be necessary to fully develop the quality of life and the vocational expression.

People who express this trait constructively often want to be known for what they know, say or otherwise communicate. The accumulation of facts, the dispersal of information or a skilled use of the hands play vital roles at work or else a youthful air and buoyant attitude may be more likely to get the job done. These people require space and freedom and express best when busily engaged in work that permits them variety, freedom, new places or faces and verbal exchanges. Some acquire advanced degrees or include academic outlets, such as writing, teaching or lecturing in their careers.

Individuals who do not relate well to their emotional needs often surround themselves with a wall of "air" which is difficult to penetrate. They can appear self-absorbed, distracted and tend to be more comfortable in work environments where emotional demands are minimized. Some are insulated behind their knowledge and as long as the occupation offers academic outlets, a minimum of job dissatisfaction is likely to be experienced. For others, a barrage of endless chatter and excuses wall them in. Because their minds are constantly buzzing, they believe they are actually "doing" something when, in reality, they may be only spinning their wheels. Still others withdraw into a disinterested coldness. Living exclusively in the head, and not reaching out to others, is the cause of their boredom and discontent, not only with the job world, but with life in general.

The solution is to understand that the identity can only be reflected through what tangibly is accomplished, not through what one "thinks" one can accomplish. Ideas need to be grounded in practical reality. Growth in consciousness also can come about once individuals become aware that they fear dependency needs and emotional issues. It frequently stems from early family dynamics and the modes of communication that existed then. Feeling needs may have been superseded by rewards for intellectual attainments or a chatty liveliness. Role models, unable to thoroughly relate to their own emotional needs, could have been deficient in dealing with the emotional needs of their offspring. On occasion, the career shifts to more rewarding directions as one begins to tune in on emotional levels.

Relationships to siblings, cousins or other third house personalities are also worth exploring. They may have influenced identity formation and sometimes the vocational choice. This does not always have to be negatively, because sibling rivalry also can have positive ramifications. Early competition can be helpful to self-assertion and getting points of view across, even if it means shouting them over the family dinner table. However, everything depends on where these individuals experienced themselves within the family structure. Just as easily, they could have been overwhelmed by a more dynamic or authoritative sibling who seemed to receive a greater portion of parental attention. Such early family dynamics can be important to understand and overcome when trait 3 symbolism is involved with the Ascendant or Midheaven, or when Mercury occupies Level I.

Gemini rising : Phyllis Diller (☿♋ 3rd), Rockwell Kent (☿♋℞ ☌ 2nd cusp), Michael Love (☿♒ 9th), Robin Moore (☿♏ 6th), Sir Lawrence Olivier (☿♉ 12th), Burt Reynolds (☿♒℞ 9th ☌ MC)

Gemini MC : Warren Beatty (☿♈ 7th), George Bush (☿♉ 9th ☌ MC), Albert Camus (☿♐ 3rd), Zsa Zsa Gabor (☿♓ 6th), Jean Houston (☿♈ 8th), Morgana King (☿♉ 9th ☌ MC), Brooke Shields (☿♉ 9th)

Trait 4

Cancer on the Ascendant (1/4) or the MC (4/10); trait 4 associated with the house or sign of the Ascendant or MC ruler; rulers of the first or tenth in the fourth house or in Cancer; ruler of the fourth in the first or tenth or in Aries or Capricorn.

With Cancer, the need to develop trait 4 characteristics or vocational approaches becomes evident (see Chapter 2). The early upbringing and its influence on the sense of identity or achievement ceiling must be considered. Typically the family was experienced as less than supportive, although this is not always the case. Still, the symbolism suggests that steps must be taken to acknowledge, explore and develop the sensitivities or creative outlets which the upbringing **may** have neglected.

Disturbed family relations are not uncommon here. One parent could have been overreactive, touchy or not always rational, while the other parent was passive and fearful. Sometimes separations from the family occurred and a parent left the home or the child was sent away. Comfortably growing into a sense of adequacy, belonging and emotional security can be delayed for some. Other individuals must establish an identity independent of the family's influence or approval. The career may be used to nurture the sense of adequacy that was not achieved in the early life. Every ounce of their being can be poured into ambitiously attaining positions of respect or acknowledged authority. Some individuals need to create families of their own, in addition to a career, to better express their feeling needs.

When independent emotional grounding has been achieved, people may adopt parental values or approaches to the occupation. Some may follow in the vocational footsteps of a parent, work with family members or for the family's business. If they do, however, it will be on the basis of their own individual needs, style or authority completely apart from familial control. Others choose self-employment or occupations which call upon their assisting natures, intuition or other trait 4 qualities. Sometimes the imagination is developed and creative outlets are featured in their work, especially writing, acting, public speaking or design.

When emotional grounding apart from parental influence has not been successfully established, people tend to remain tightly bound to family strings They might select inappropriate careers due to parental prodding or continue living with a parent far into adulthood, content to have routine, secure jobs and never trying their vocational wings. An inability to develop a solid sense of adequacy, security and a positive self-image undermines their vocational expressions.

Others are nervous and shy. Unable to inspire the confidence of employers, they may experience a number of career setbacks. Often they are relegated to unsatisfying job slots with minimal authority and responsibility. They may suppress their own feelings and bottle them up or explode like champagne corks from all the internal pressure that builds up over the years. Some fail to take responsibility for their lives and blame their parents without recognizing the roles played by their own insecurities and choices. They can retreat into self-absorbed, private worlds and unconsciously seek parenting from others. Growth takes place once these individuals realize that defensiveness and emotional insecurity are infecting their self-image and undermining a more aspirational vocational expression. The antidote is to squarely face the past, one's faulty self-concepts and to develop one's inner, feeling nature.

Cancer rising : Ram Dass (☽♐ 5th), Rob Hand (☽♏ 5th), Isabelle Pagan (☽♋ 12th), Sam Peckinpah (☽♒ 8th), Franz Peter Schubert (☽♓ 10th), Phoebe Snow (☽♌ 2nd), John Travolta (☽♍ 2nd ♂ 3rd cusp)

Cancer MC : Arthur Ashe (☽♎ 12th), Lew Ayres (☽♓ 6th), Jimmy Carter (☽♏ 1st), Alice Cooper (☽♐ 3rd ☍ MC), Wendell Phillips (☽♋ 9th), Sidney Poitier (☽♎ 1st), Natalie Wood (☽♉ 7th)

Trait 5

Leo on the Ascendant (1/5) or the MC (5/10); trait 5 associated with the house or the sign of the Ascendant or MC rulers; rulers of the first or tenth in the fifth house or in Leo; ruler of the fifth in first or tenth or in Aries or Capricorn.

Leo symbolizes a calling to adopt trait 5 characteristics or vocational approaches as a path to identity formation (see Chapter 2). Realistic self-confidence, self-esteem and an ability to perform well in a job are emphasized.

When such qualities surface, people recognize their needs to have exceptionally self-expressive occupations. Because their work is fun, they willingly strive to get ahead through their creative talents, a technical expertise, speculative interests or business management potentials. Vocations offering outlets for extemporaneous expression, such as teaching, acting, public relations or any job that caters to an audience, can be especially rewarding. Self-reliance allows many to profitably pursue self-employment or to accept managerial positions with independent decision-making responsibilities. They excel by putting quality effort into tasks and earning the limelight.

Due to their easygoing confidence and cheerful manner, they are quick to catch the eye of a prospective employer and easily win over others during the interviewing process. They often rise in the ranks more rapidly than most. Without adequate skills, however, they can get out on a limb when more is expected of them than they feel capable of doing. Still, if their hearts are in the endeavor, they are willing to try just in case they can make a success of it, knowing that hard work pays off.

When self-esteem and self-confidence have not been developed properly, the roots may lie in an inability to achieve a feeling of being "special" as a distinct human being. Parental figures could have falsely praised their child's inadequate performances or denied their child sufficient praise and attention. Different responses are likely to result. Some people are self-conscious, self-effacing or approval-seeking and place too little credence in their capabilities. Occupations nonreflective of self-expressive needs are likely to be selected and low ceilings can be placed on career attainments.

Other people hide their fears of inadequacy behind bravado or haughty self-importance even when worthwhile accomplishments do not exist to back up the display. They are infected with a strong image-consciousness, so that boasting can be used to cover insecurity and a weak sense of selfhood. The belief in the "big break" prompts many to hold on to a dream too long and not take the necessary steps toward establishing a viable career. Because the sense of specialness can be distorted, many fail to push themselves on the job and would rather be "discovered," win a sweepstakes, or get by the easy way. Unrealistic, "high school" idealism may lead them to jump from one whimsical goal or romantic involvement to another in search of a needed sense of specialness. Some believe life is "against them" and refuse to accept responsibility for the choices they have made.

When an over- or underestimation of self exists, developing realistic self-love can be a path not only to a more purposeful identity, but also to a more satisfying life and career. Should shyness be a problem, one might profitably take acting lessons or work with children. Tempering the need for approval is likely to develop self-expression more fully, as can pursuing creative hobbies for fun.

Others with this symbolism have to face their limitations and accept themselves as they are, not as whom they think they should be. Once constructive self-confidence has been gained, a whole new view of self, life and the working world takes place.

Close romantic attachments also can be formed more readily, something which is vital to trait 5 fulfillment.

Leo rising : Muhammad Ali (☉♑ 6th), Chris Chubbuck (☉♍ 1st ☌ 2nd cusp), Nina Foch (☉♉ 9th ☌ MC), Michel Gauquelin (☉♏ 4th), Alan Leo (☉♌ 12th), Fritz Perls (☉♋ 12th), Charles Steinmetz (☉♈ 10th ☌ MC)

Leo MC : Ellen Burstyn, (☉♐ 2nd), Johnny Carson (☉ ♎ 12th ☌ Asc.), Clint Eastwood (☉♊ 7th), Sigmund Freud (☉♉ 7th), Diane Keaton (☉♑ 2nd), Louis Pasteur (☉♑ 3rd), Princess Anne (☉♌ 10th)

Trait 6
Virgo on the Ascendant (1/6) or the MC (6/10); trait 6 associated with the sign or house of the Ascendant or MC ruler; rulers of the first or tenth in the sixth house or in Virgo; ruler of the sixth in the first or tenth or in Aries or Capricorn.

With Virgo, trait 6 characteristics or vocational approaches are pertinent to identity formation and a proper goal orientation (see Chapter 2). It is important to perfect a rewarding skill, craft or talent and use it efficiently in the service of others. Because the earth element is involved, tangible rewards and practical achievements also must figure into vocational fulfillment.

Those who express this trait best recognize the importance of work in their lives and how it is tied to their sense of identity and purpose. They tend to be serious, somewhat reserved personalities who work hard, pay their "dues" and earn respect often in an overseeing or technically advisory capacity. They keep track of even the smallest details, apply themselves in a diligent, organized manner and can make themselves indispensable to the efficient operation of any company, office or department. Many view their work or craft as an art form, even if it is not in the standard sense of the term. The most progressive learn to approach others in a balanced, give-and-take manner because they realize that fulfilling interpersonal relationships are as important as fulfilling work.

When such qualities are not developed, the motivation to elevate skills is not likely to exist. A "bill paying" job, with little or no independent decision-making responsibilities, can be selected. Because the sense of identity is intimately connected to work, unsatisfying employment can lead to emotional fragility or illness. A conflict between a need to make a contribution on or through the job, and the reality of an unsatisfying work life can diminish the work ethic, damage the self-image and undermine self-esteem. The problem may manifest as a slovenly or unkempt appearance, alienation, poor health and eating habits, a withdrawn or nervous demeanor, acting "crazy" or making too many fault-finding judgments of others.

Growth takes place once individuals understand that a lack of satisfying work and accomplishment are the roots of their problems. Developing skills to enhance the self-image is one antidote. A willingness to work hard and to accept increased responsibilities are others.

The early home life, however, may need to be examined. Parental nit-picking about how they should act, what they should wear, say or even do for a living could have made growing into an adequate sense of identity difficult. Individuals may have had to perform constantly and justify their every move, almost as if they had to pay for parental inadequacies. Some individuals were so thoroughly prohibited from developing a sense of adequacy and competency that they refused to enter the job world, or they leave it due to the stress of having to perform.

More basic than a lack of satisfying work may be the need to develop healthy self-love and a sense of personal adequacy, the lack of which prompts people to disregard the importance of health, hygiene or proper food intake. Rewarding skills may not have been developed or, when they have been, individuals may not find contentment from them. In such cases, more extensive measures, such as psychotherapy, may be required to allow a freer vocational expression.

Virgo rising : Warren Beatty (☿♈ 7th), Albert Camus (☿♐ 3rd), Zsa Zsa Gabor (☿♓ 6th), Jean Houston (☿♈ 8th), Morgana King (☿♉ 9th ☌ MC), Brooke Shields (☿♉ 9th), Oscar Wilde (☿♏ 3rd)

Virgo MC : Marlon Brando (☿♈ 5th), Edna Ferber (☿♍ 10th ☌ MC), Benito Mussolini (☿♌ 9th), Jack Nicklaus (☿♑ 2nd), Friedrich Nietzsche (☿♎ 10th), Elvis Presley (☿♑ 2nd), Rafael (☿♈ 5th ☌ 6th)

Trait 7

Libra on the Ascendant (1/7) or the MC(7/10); trait 7 associated with the house or sign of the Ascendant or MC rulers; rulers of the first or tenth in the seventh or in Libra; ruler of the seventh in the first or tenth or in Aries or Capricorn.

With Libra, constructive trait 7 characteristics or vocational approaches are paths to identity formation (see Chapter 2). Because growth occurs through rewarding relationships, balanced interpersonal relating skills are requisite to vocational satisfaction and advancement.

When this trait is developed properly, people have a way with others through charm, diplomacy, tact and a gentle, yet firm, persuasiveness that gains their cooperation. They recognize others' needs and rights and incorporate them into their game plan. Some work with a spouse, profit by partnership or rely on teamwork, such as hiring a staff or freelancers to enhance their careers. Others may be in the public eye or exhibit artistic flair, competition or one-to-one interaction on another level, such as through sales, counseling, recruiting and having or being an agent or representative.

When trait 7 is unproductively developed, different expressions are possible, although each stems from the same source. Objectivity, associated with the air element, and a balanced sense of give-and-take, associated with Libra, can be totally missing and must be developed. Interaction with others may be avoided on the job or outside of it, but this is as conducive to identity formation and getting ahead in the job world as living in a closet. A fear of sharing self underlies the problem, possibly due to an early exposure to family disputes, separation or overdirecting parental influences. Learning to relate to others or understanding the value of mutual give-and-take may have been distorted.

For other individuals, similar early life experiences lead to overvaluing others at the expense of the self. Unproductive relationships are maintained which do not permit proper self-expression because individuals acquiesce to demands to keep the peace at all costs. Others, wittingly or unwittingly, enter relationships for status, financial support or to achieve a sense of identity they otherwise lack. Because they seek to establish an identity through the other person, as opposed to developing a better grasp of themselves **through** the interrelating process, they often blame partners for unfulfilling relationships. They fail to realize that unintegrated aspects of self cannot be successfully lived through others.

Still another type takes charge **over** others, never permitting them to express their needs or identities within the relationship. They can become exceptionally competitive, manipulating or paranoid personalities who, instead of using charm and cooperation, use overt or covert force. They may be blind to the needs or value of others and use power selfishly for their own advantage.

When trait 7 is improperly expressed, career difficulties stem from an inability to functionally relate to others or a failure to recognize the important role others play in the career, although career troubles could result from a diminished work ethic. One could be lazy, passive and unconsciously expect others to carry the load. Steps have to be taken to overcome these blind spots, develop trust and learn to relate to others as equals. Once individuals become convinced that how they relate, fail to relate and how hard they work, have a bearing on job satisfaction and success, they are motivated to alter unproductive behavior.

Libra rising : Max Baer (♀♒ 4th ☍ MC), Ellen Burstyn (♀♏ 1st), Jimmy Carter (♀♌ 10th), Jacques Cousteau (♀♉ 8th), Princess Anne (♀♋ 9th), Natalie Wood (♀♍ 11th)

Libra MC : Alan Alda (♀♐ 12th ☌ Asc.), Steve Allen (♀♐ 12th ☌ Asc.), Fred Astaire (♀♈ 4th), Ingrid Bergman (♀♎ 9th), Jimmy Hendrix (♀♐ 12th), Jim Jones (♀♈ 3rd ☍ MC), Caroline Kennedy (♀♑ 1st)

Trait 8

Scorpio on the Ascendant (1/8) or the MC (8/10); trait 8 associated with the sign or house of the Ascendant or MC rulers; rulers of the first or tenth in the eighth or Scorpio; ruler of the eighth in the first or tenth or in Aries or Capricorn

With Scorpio, constructive trait 8 characteristics or vocational approaches are highlighted as paths to self-discovery. Some form of power, influence or inner conviction must be demonstrated through the occupation (see Chapter 2). Because the water element is involved, the inner nature may have to be developed in some cases, mostly the sense of inner power, personal charisma, self-reliance, stamina, mastery of the appetites or resourcefulness, before an appropriate vocational expression can be achieved.

An early exposure to overt or covert parental control or domination may underlie this need. Some individuals learn from role models how **not** to act while others adopt the parental behavior. Personal effectiveness and relationships may be undermined by the various control tactics discussed in Chapter 2. A lack of trust and feeling disconnected from their inner selves often results. Many may need to alter, or deepen, their perceptions of life and master debilitating self-doubts as antidotes to this problem. Psychotherapy, occult investigation or other forms of self-development can be used. Not only the identity but career directions can change totally once the transformation process has been initiated.

Other people are not so troubled by similar early life experiences, but become obsessive about their careers and determined to succeed. They throw themselves into an occupation early in life where they seek "power," influence, insight or renown. Situations that test their inner strength or require them to confront challenges to their authority often arise. Many become "crusaders," and attempt to influence the standards of practice in their fields. They often are magnetically attractive, intense or sexual and are drawn into highly competitive occupations, or highly charged work environments. They need careers which completely absorb them and to which they can make a lifelong commitment. Honest give-and-take relationships with underlying emotional or sexual exchanges are important; these people need deep sharing, intense involvement and a powerfully absorbing career.

When emotional development does not take place, individuals fail to tap inner power and easily succumb to fears, suspicions or self-doubts which undermine self-expression and appropriate career directions. Some isolate themselves, or drop out of the working world, to gain control over their lives. They can appear darkly forbidding, unapproachable or overly competitive and ready to pounce at the slightest (often imagined) provocation. They can be compulsively involved with others to control and exploit them for their talents, money or sexuality. When career activities do not bend to their will, they are convinced that some outside force is obstructing them.

Other individuals are self-repressed, fearful and quick to back down from even a hint of a confrontation – the classic wimp syndrome. They attract dominating, if not abusive, superiors, colleagues or coworkers until inner power is owned back and integrated. Some leave themselves open to sexual exploitation or other forms of abuse – the classic masochist. It is difficult to comprehend that a series of unhealthy relationships or sexual involvements can ever lead to anything worthwhile. However, such circumstances can make people aware of a need to undergo a transformation. They must acknowledge how they are held back and create unnecessary problems for themselves by denying their own power. Excessive manipulative tactics or their unapproachable demeanor also may be involved. Psychotherapy can free them for more healthy self-expression and a strong, resourceful, yet balanced emotional nature.

Scorpio rising : Johnny Carson (♂♎ 12th/♇♋ 9th), Edna Ferber (♂♋ 8th/♇♊ 8th), Diane Keaton (♂♋℞ 9th/♇♌ 9th), Jack Nicklaus (♂♈ 5th/♇♌ 9th), Maurice Ravel (♂♐ 2nd/♇♉ 7th), Johnny Weismuller (♂♇♊ 7th)

Scorpio MC : Sean Connery (♂♊ 6th/♇♋ 7th), Roberta Cowell (♂♍℞ 8th/♇♋ 7th), Paul Newman (♂♈ 3rd/♇♋ 6th ☍ Asc.), Pat Nixon (♂♇♊ 5th), Leontyne Price (♂♉ 3rd ☍ MC/♇♋ 6th), Michael Tilson Thomas (♂♐ 11th/♇♌℞ 7th), Lotte Von Strahl (♂♐ 11th/♇♊℞ 5th)

Trait 9

Sagittarius on the Ascendant (1/9) or the MC (9/10); trait 9 associated with the sign or house of the Ascendant or MC rulers; rulers of the first or tenth in the ninth house or in Sagittarius; ruler of the ninth in the first or tenth or in Aries or Capricorn

With Sagittarius, trait 9 characteristics or vocational approaches are suggested as paths to self-discovery. It especially is a calling to broaden horizons, the scope of influence or knowledge and understanding through a number of possible channels. Because the fire element is involved, recognition, initiative, leadership, independence and achievement also must figure into vocational expression.

When these qualities are constructively expressed, aspirations, ideologies or ideals often are taken seriously. These people reach out for life, sometimes by moving away from the birth locale. They develop strong convictions about the goals or lifestyle they aspire to attain. Not easily defeated, they often are cheerful, humorous or optimistic while being equally hardworking. Occupations which offer independence, exposure or advancement opportunities are a must, although other needs exist depending on individual interests and capabilities (see Chapter 2).

Some individuals best achieve their goals by obtaining an advanced education or by teaching; others by developing a philosophical/religious perspective on life and by preaching. An old way of life may be dropped to espouse certain doctrines or alternative lifestyles. Any trait 9 endeavor can enhance the sense of identity and goal directions.

Problems develop for those who do not attempt to broaden their horizons or scope of understanding. A fear of failure and a poor self-image cause many to block their own aspirations. Life can seem hollow and purposeless without a heartfelt goal to which to aspire. Low grade, chronic depressions, nervous ailments or other disturbances are common results when their aspirational needs are not adequately realized.

Others overestimate themselves and are unrealistic about life, their capabilities and the role effort or responsibility plays in the attainment of any goal. They talk about the future, as if the talk will make their dreams materialize. A false expectation about a "big break," coupled with an unrealistic self-image, often keep such people in a vocational dream beyond its time or prevent them from committing themselves to a line of work. The grass appears greener elsewhere and they may prefer living off others until the next ideal vista beckons.

Of all personalities, those with trait 9 highlighted and inappropriately expressed can be the most resistant to altering their approach to the vocational world. Those with an underinflated self-image can be just as deeply rooted as those suffering from the opposite problem. Each fails to see the self in a realistic light. Only when steps are taken to recognize and confront the dilemma can the situation change. Pursuing trait 9 related activities, such as travel, a college education, religious, metaphysical or philosophical instruction or any activity that broadens consciousness in a positive manner, can be helpful to forming a proper identity.

Sagittarius rising : Fred Astaire (♃♏℞ 11th), Ingrid Bergman (♃♊ 6th ☍ MC), Marlon Brando (♃♐ 1st), John Glenn (♃♍ 9th ☌ MC), Richard F. Gordon (♃♊℞ 6th), Jimi Hendrix (♃♋℞ 7th), Caroline Kennedy (♃♎ 10th)

Sagittarius MC : Garth Allen (♃♑℞ 11th), Carol Burnett (♃♍℞ 6th), David Carradine (♃♑ 10th), Dorothy Hamill (♃♍ 7th), James Hoffa (♃♑ 10th), Karl Marx (♃♑℞ 11th), Rollo May (♃♍℞ 7th)

Trait 10

Capricorn on the Ascendant (1/10) or the MC (10/10); trait 10 associated with the sign or house of the Ascendant or MC rulers; ruler of the first or tenth in the tenth house or in Capricorn

With Capricorn, trait 10 characteristics or vocational approaches are highlighted as paths to self-discovery (see Chapter 2). This especially includes a capacity for commitment and painstaking hard work. Developing competence, professionalism or authority through persistent, disciplined effort and tangible achievement are essential to the sense of identity and purposeful goals. Because the earth element is involved, tangible rewards and practicalities are important to career selection.

When trait 10 is developed, people identify with their careers and usually want to make names for themselves as authorities or experts. They work to hone their skills and are naturally self-disciplined— or readily become so when interests are sparked. They patiently review situations before making moves, knowing that a great deal is at stake. They see persistent effort as the soundest way to achieve lasting status and view career challenges as tests of their capabilities. Instead of grumbling, they turn lemons into lemonade.

Status conscious, they often seek prestigious occupations, sometimes academic in nature, where they can excel or be in charge. Some build their own businesses or revered professional reputations and usually need something concrete to show for their efforts—be it a book, a sizable income or ten blocks of skyscrapers. Progressive types eventually influence their professions by leaving behind important theories or discoveries.

When trait 10 is not functionally developed, different responses are possible. Though ambitious to achieve status and respect, aspirations could be unrealistic, or the discipline to realize them may be lacking. Others avoid the rigors of a career and gain their coveted status by marrying someone who already possesses it.

Such people can be childishly poor planners, quick to act on rash, emotional decisions, and always expect luck to see them through. Some rest on past laurels or try to make more than is warranted out of their accomplishments. The worst turn into selfish users who feel any means justify their ends. Eventually, however, they are abandoned by supporters and may suffer damaged reputations or unnecessary losses as a result.

Other individuals, blind to their needs to be taken seriously, may fail to apply sufficient effort toward developing competence or avoid responsibilities by living the life of a perennial student or casual job drifter. Perhaps they fantasize about having important jobs, but are easily defeated and settle for less strenuous occupations which do not fulfill their prestige needs. Fear of failure and a diminished self-image are the roots of this situation. Until they realize how their self-restricting attitudes, or disinclination to work, are responsible for their problems, they are likely to remain depressive sad sacks who find work boring. Effort, responsibility, commitment and competence are the most important features of their self-discovery paths. Dodging hard work and responsibility, or abusing authority or social responsibilities, are the surest routes to an unfulfilling or disrupted vocation.

Capricorn rising : Alan Alda (♄♓ 2nd), Sean Connery (♄♑℞ 12th ☌ 1st), Jim Jones (♄♑℞ 1st), Ted Kennedy (♄♋ 1st), Michael Tilson Thomas (♄♋℞ 6th), Arturo Toscanini (♄♏℞ 10th), Lotte Von Strahl (♄♏ 9th ☌ MC)

Capricorn MC : Ada Byron (♄♒ 11th), Liza Minnelli (♄♋℞ 3rd ☍ MC), Percy Bysshe Shelly (♄♉ 1st ☌ Asc.), Suzanne

Somers (♄♌ 4th), Barbra Streisand (♄♉ 2nd), Nikola Telsa (♄♋ 3rd)

Trait 11

Aquarius on the Ascendant (1/11) or the MC (10/11); trait 11 associated with the sign or house of the Ascendant or MC; ruler of the first or tenth in the eleventh house or in Aquarius; ruler of the eleventh in the first or tenth houses or in Aries or Capricorn

With Aquarius, constructive trait 11 characteristics or vocational approaches are suggested as paths to self-discovery (see Chapter 2). It is especially important to develop an expanded awareness by recognizing that one's actions impact a greater whole. The person is sucked into a larger game plan, frequently only experiencing a vague sense of "mission." How this feeling is interpreted depends on how stable one can be over the long haul. This sense of mission reflects a need to contribute to something greater than the self. Understanding what it means "to be a star among the brotherhood of stars" while maintaining one's individuality is not easy. It is, however, a basic need related to trait 11.

When this trait is developed, people often seek to align themselves with a larger group, company, professional association, cause or community where individualized contributions are pooled for effective results. These individuals prefer a boss who pitches in, or with whom they can be friends, rather than the warlord type who directs from an armchair. They thrive on recognition from colleagues and peers. A cause orientation, or sense of teamwork, contribution and belonging, is significant to their vocational fulfillment. (See Chapter 2 for other trait 11 needs.) Some people develop interest in the arts or writing and often display unique talents which are "shocking" or somewhat ahead of their time. The most progressive delve into life's mysteries along the planes of consciousness or the physical universe. They learn to deal effectively with the nonrational elements of existence without losing their balance. They make contributions to society designed to enhance an understanding of the human condition. While they often may or may not join actual groups, they experience a sense of belonging to a greater whole on the basis of the contributions they make.

Other individuals are not so fortunate or well balanced. Some suffered from so many early life limitations that growing into a comfortable sense of identity was hampered. Feelings of persecution, inadequacy and an inability to relate effectively to others usually underlie later career disturbances. Because they did not achieve a sense of belonging to their own families, they experience difficulty fitting in on a greater scale. Many complain about, but maintain boring jobs rather than risk more self-expressive directions. How little they know themselves. Stimulating interests or activities involving friends, clubs or hobbies can be helpful in such cases and supply the kind of exhilaration which is lacking from the job.

When carried to an extreme, the lack of belonging results in reclusiveness. Hampered from an ability to participate in the beauty of close, mutual give-and-take relationships (shown by the air element), these people can become hypercritical of others and prefer to work alone. They turn into isolated eccentrics or drifting "rebels without a cause" (or without much income either). Others suffering from the same lack of interrelating capability may join groups or causes. However, they often try to take over, as if the group existed solely for their benefit. They do not recognize how their actions stifle others and they are left in the lurch due to their delusions of superiority and to abusing their authority. (Aquarius is co-ruled by Saturn.) They are blind to their own dictatorial qualities and self-interest. As the *I Ching* instructs, "To rule truly is to serve," and for trait 11, to live truly is to feel a sense of belonging to something greater than oneself.

Aquarius rising : John Dean (♄♈℞ 2nd/♅♉℞ 3rd), Edgar Degas (♄♎ 8th/♅♒℞ 1st), F. Scott Fitzgerald (♄♅♏ 9th ☌ MC), James Hoffa (♄♉ 3rd/♅♒ 12th), Pat Nixon (♄♉ 3/♅♒ 1st ☌ Asc.), Leontyne Price (♄♐ 10th/♅♓ 2nd), Pierre Renoir (♄♑ 11th/♅♓ 1st)

Aquarius MC : Francoise Gauquelin (♄♐℞ 7th/♅♈ 11th), Johannes Kepler (♄♏ 6th/♅♑ 8th), Vivien Leigh (♄♊℞ 2nd/♅♒ 9th ☌ MC), O'Henry (♄♍ 5th/♅♊ 2nd), Sir Lawrence Olivier (♄♓ 11th/♅♑℞ 8th), Vance Packard (♄♊ 1st/♅♒℞ 9th ☌ MC), George Bernard Shaw (♄♋ 2nd/♅♉ 12th)

Trait 12

Pisces on the Ascendant or the MC; trait 12 associated with the sign or house of the Ascendant or MC rulers; ruler of the first or tenth in the twelfth house or in Pisces; ruler of the twelfth in the first or tenth or in Aries or Capricorn

With Pisces, constructive trait 12 characteristics or vocational approaches are highlighted as paths to self-discovery (see Chapter 2). Because the water element is involved, the inner nature, beliefs and emotional sensitivities may need to be developed. This could include the imagination, assisting nature, aesthetic qualities, intuition, visionary or scholarly capabilities.

Initially, this is not an easy symbolism to live with. It is like trying to perceive an identity through a fog. That is why the emotional nature is likely to require conscious development. Without it, bearings can be lost. Transpersonal issues undermine identity formation by generating anxieties or yearnings of an ill-defined nature. Ultimately, trait 12 highlights a calling to understand, on a deep inner level, how human beings are linked to one another and to the universe.

Not all people are driven to fulfill this trait along such metaphysical lines. Some adhere to the commercialized values of our day, including the desire for wealth, fame, beauty and success. For others, the oneness of life is experienced through Art, a religious experience, intellectual or scientific exploration, introspection, eastern religions, meditation or "otherworldly" interests. They are different routes to the same goal.

When trait 12 characteristics are developed, a peaceful self-acceptance and an honest self-belief take hold, along with the capacity to endure the vicissitudes of life in a realistic fashion. Such a response stems from understanding the ultimate goodness of life, and an ability exists to accept one's own and other people's foibles. A sense of purpose begins to emerge, possibly stemming from an inspired source, which gives life new meaning and shapes vocational directions. A sense of belonging to a greater scheme of things exists along with an improved awareness of what contributions can be made.

Some people painstakingly develop skills and talents to fulfill their sense of purpose. They turn dreams and ideals into practical, tangible realities through persistent effort. Sharing their visions and thoughts about life or their professions may become important, so writing, lecturing and other forms of communication can play important career roles. They often rely on intuition, scholarly knowledge or creativity as part of their work and may pursue a number of simultaneous activities as different sources of income. The most progressive learn to live effectively in two worlds—the Saturnian and the Neptunian. They find purpose in knowing they participate in a greater plan without falling into a trap common to this symbolism: godlike notions of superiority. They tend to be cheerful, unassuming and may soar to the top of their vocations.

When trait 12 is inadequately developed, an unclear self-image, anxieties, lack of purpose and feelings of inferiority interfere with progress in life. Drugs or other forms of escapism may be used to blot out these feelings, with some people wallowing in them daily as if wearing a "kick me" sign. The proper balance of self-assertion and self-sacrifice can be confused, a problem which finds its source in the early life. There may have been an unreliable, sickly or disturbed relative with whom normal, healthy rapport could not be established. One's own development and emotional needs may have been neglected or abused.

Due to the uncertain self-image, "safe" or menial occupations can be selected. Some people drift from job to job because they fear commitment and do not apply themselves. They may dream of becoming famous, glamorous or rich, but again, do not exert the necessary effort. Others invent identities or join a group and form their identities around its codes and standards. Such ploys only insure difficulty in facing the real self. Ungrounded trait 12 people can become so disoriented from overexposure to psychic or spiritual pursuits that realistic footing in the vocational world easily is lost. Such quests and interests can become excuses for not working (or doing anything of a practical nature).

Emerging from the fog can take some people longer than others. Career changes and the elimination of bad relationships are not uncommon once the identity begins to unfold on new levels. The process usually is stimulated by new insights and perceptions about the self gained through introspection, study, psychotherapy, relationships, a purposeful belief system or any number of other trait 12 outlets. Learning to face fears of the unknown, overcoming feelings of inferiority and giving shape to a previously undefined identity can open the door to a new and stable vocational expression.

Pisces rising : James Arness (♃♏℞ 8th/♆♌ 6th), Carol Burnett (♃♆♍℞ 6th), David Carradine (♃♑ 10th/♆♍ 7th ☍ Asc.), R.D. Laing (♃♓ 12th ☌Asc./ ♆♌ 6th) Zubin Mehta (♃♐℞ 10th/♆♍℞ 7th), Walter Mondale (♃♓ 1st/♆♌℞ 6th ☍ Asc.), Robert Redford (♃♐ 9th/♆♍ 6th)

Pisces MC : Ram Dass (♃♋ 12th ☌ Asc./♆♍℞ 3rd), Albert Einstein (♃♒ 9th/♆♉ 11th), Rob Hand (♃♋℞ 1st/♆♎ 4th), Ryan O'Neal (♃♉ 11th/♆♍℞4th ☍ MC), Isabelle Pagan (♃♓ 9th/♆♈℞ 10th), George Patton ♃♍ 4th/♆♉℞ 12th), Franz Schubert (♃♓ 10th/♆♏ 5th)

The Nodes

The Ascendant and Midheaven are not the only paths to a more conscious and purposeful identity. The Moon's nodes also symbolize personality factors which can bring a growth in consciousness. The axis they form represents a developmental tension and, like any opposition aspect, both sides require expression at the proper time and place. A delicate balance needs to be struck between these two points which suggests that opposite, though complementary, natures in the personality must be reconciled before consciousness can develop. The balancing act between them produces the tension and possibility of growth, not that one end of the axis is more growth-oriented than the other. People able to strike this balance know how to temper these sides of their natures and are aware of the proper circumstances in which to express one end over the other.

ARIES/LIBRA - FIRST HOUSE/SEVENTH HOUSE - TRAITS 1 and 7

Here, developmental tension surrounds the I-thou principle. One must integrate self-expression, dynamic leadership, enterprise and a need to win with a developed interrelating capacity, concern for others and a sense of fair play. Balance is achieved when individuals know the proper time to take action and assert themselves and when to stop, look and listen to the needs of others. It represents an "I'm OK, You're OK" stance. Growth is sparked through one's own initiative, although partners or important others can inspire a new cycle of development and outlook on life.

Growth is disturbed when the trait 1 node is underdeveloped. Partnership can be sought for status, financial support or to provide a sense of identity that one does not possess otherwise. Lack of identity formation undermines an independent achievement orientation to life. This often leads to becoming overly dependent on others, or the partner, and failing to develop one's own identity and self-assertive drives.

However, when the trait 1 node is overblown, excessively self-assertive behavior can have equally negative ramifications. It represents an "I'm OK" stance but "You're not nearly as important." Dictatorial qualities, a lack of cooperation or self-control, unfairness, "winning" at all costs, and "I always come first" surface and thoroughly disrupt the vocation by creating resentment and enemies. Integration of this nodal polarity is achieved when assertion and compromise are balanced, when the needs of the self are balanced with the needs of others.

North node in Aries or the first house: Fred Astaire (1st house ♐), Ingrid Bergman (1st house ♑), Sean Connery (♈ 3rd house), Ram Dass (♈ 10th house), Jim Jones (♈ 3rd house), Pat Nixon (♈ 2nd house), Fritz Perls (♈ 10th house)

North node in Libra or the seventh house : Steve Allen (♎ 9th house), James Arness (7th house ♍), Larry Csonka (7th house ♊), Rennie Davis (♎ 5th house), Richard De Mont (7th house ♐), John Dillinger (♎ 3rd house), Jack Nicklaus (♎ 11th house)

TAURUS/SCORPIO - SECOND HOUSE/EIGHTH HOUSE - TRAITS 2 and 8

Here, the I-Thou principle must be achieved to a greater, more in-depth degree. One must plunge into life and experience deep sharing and involvement on all levels of being. Personal assets including talents must be developed, but the very soul also must be offered up and shared without any strings attached. For this to take place, a developed self-worth profile and an ability to provide for the self materially must exist. They are the wellsprings from which inner power, deep commitment and the ability to give and receive can be tapped. Individuals cannot share love, pleasure, power or assets, the major issues related to this polarity, when these qualities are not already owned.

These nodes are balanced when an ability exists to make one's own way in life coupled with a willingness to accept assistance from others when needed; when one can give **and** receive pleasure and share on a equal basis control and decision-making responsibilities within relationships. Such a balance also requires knowing when self-indulgences are "OK" and when appetites must be postponed until work is satisfactorily completed.

Growth is halted until an honest sense of self-appreciation and inner power are achieved. Without these, talents and other personal resources are unlikely to be developed to the degree implied by this polarity. Individuals must purge themselves of self-deprecating attitudes because they are likely to attract others who are more than willing to teach them how little they value themselves. It is no wonder that they are likely to experience a dearth of beauty, love, money, comfort or pleasure in their lives until this lesson is learned. In such instances, the node related to trait 2 has not been developed and the denial capacity signified by the other node maintains the upper hand. People may feel they are undeserving of the good things in life and control issues (discussed in Chapter 2) are likely to abound when proper self-love does not exist.

Those who rely too much on the trait 2 node attempt to live on the surface of life. They are likely to be stodgy, self-indulgent, overly materialistic and make rather boring company because they are completely wrapped up in their own needs. Important others can be treated more like possessions than loved ones until a willingness exists to be open to the depths of what life has to offer.

North node in Taurus or in the second house: Muhammad Ali (2nd house ♍), Jacques Cousteau (♉ 8th house), Clint Eastwood (♉ 6th house), Morgana King (♉ 9th house), Suzanne Somers (2nd house ♊), Lotte Von Strahl (2nd house ♓), Natalie Wood (2nd house ♏)

North node in Scorpio or in the eighth house: Max Baer (8th house ♊), Phyllis Diller (8th house ♑), Uri Geller (8th house

♊), Jimi Hendrix (8th house ♌), Jean Houston (♏ 3rd house), Diane Keaton (8th house ♊), Caroline Kennedy (♏ 11th house), Burt Reynolds (8th house ♑)

GEMINI/SAGITTARIUS - THIRD HOUSE/NINTH HOUSE - TRAITS 3 and 9

When either node is associated with these traits, it is a calling to develop the mental faculties, manual dexterity, the speaking voice or to enhance the communication skills through a formal or self-education. One must also respond to realistic aspirational urges and, in many cases, disseminate important ideas by seeking public exposure. These nodes could be the mark of the perpetual student, teacher, traveler or searcher, one whose mind is always eager to take in new knowledge.

Without purposeful study and a perspective on what all that information might mean, however, this polarity also could represent the casual job-drifter whose feet rarely touch ground long enough to make sense out of anything. A balance must be achieved between learning for its own sake and the need to heighten consciousness through knowledge and understanding. Curiosity must be reconciled with a sense of purpose and long-term goals or beliefs. Balance is indicated through the capacity to know when lighthearted, casual and detached exchanges with others are appropriate and when conversation needs more intense, meaning-oriented discourses.

Growth is disrupted when one fails to pursue interests, to develop the mental/verbal/dextrous capacity or to put life into a purposeful perspective. Perhaps early disappointments about religious instruction or education were experienced or role models exhibited a dearth of interest in such matters. Such individuals may float uncommitted through life or fail to accept anything other than minimal job responsibilities. Unrealistic expectations about the role luck plays in the job world often lead to dreams of fame or wealth without the effort to make them a reality. Integration of the 3/9 polarity takes place when new ideas are explored, and action is taken to make one's dreams come true.

North node in Gemini or in the third house: Jack Anderson (3rd house ♍), Ada Byron (3rd house ♊), Michel Gauquelin (♊ 10th house), Jean Houston (3rd house ♏), Jim

Jones (3rd house ♈), Isabelle Pagan (3rd house ♍), Suzanne Somers (♊ 2nd house)

North Node in Sagittarius or in the ninth house: Fred Astaire (♐ 1st house), Marlon Brando (9th house ♍), David Carradine (♐ 10th house), Johnny Carson (9th house ♌), Dorothy Hamill (9th house ♐), Brooke Shields (9th house ♊), Phoebe Snow (9th house ♈)

CANCER/CAPRICORN - FOURTH HOUSE/TENTH HOUSE - TRAITS 4 and 10

With these nodes, the calling is to develop the sense of personal adequacy and competency to carry through on important vocational responsibilities. Developmental tension surrounds reconciling pragmatic, realistic viewpoints with a sensitive, caring and compassionate nature. Growth is enhanced through integrating authority, responsibility and a drive for achievement with emotional sensitivities and an acknowledgment of one's healthy dependency needs. Breaking away from family expectations and establishing a career based on individual values apart from it is usually required. Discipline, hard work and striving for competence and respect are helpful to the process. One might also seek to enhance creativity, intuitive capabilities or the caring instincts, build step-by-step a business, trade or profession, assume responsible or prominent positions, have a family or become an acknowledged expert. Parents, employers and other revered personalities are highlighted as mentors, even if it is on the basis of the negative examples they set.

Growth is disturbed by an inability to recognize oneself as a person capable of exercising authority. A diminished self-image usually lies at the root of the problem so that effort to develop competency may never be expended. Individuals may be tempted to get-by on the job. A lack of self-discipline often creates a need for close supervision. Because the node related to trait 10 has not been adequately responded to, the situation is not likely to be a comfortable one. Individuals can be too easily influenced, overly sympathetic, sentimental, dependent or need to be needed too much. They are unable to determine when caring compassion versus a firm and unyielding stance are likely to be more effective.

When the node related to trait 4 has not been adequately

developed, a failure to exercise authority in a caring, sensitive way can bring harsh career setbacks. People can be too cold, authoritarian, punitive or dictatorial, or too hardworking and try to do everything, the latter at the expense of their emotional needs. Integration of the 4/10 nodal polarity is shown when realism and compassion, practicality and empathy exist.

North node in Cancer or in the fourth house: Chris Chubbuck (♋ 12 house), Adolph Eichmann (4th house ♌), Keith Emerson (♋ 12th house), Manuel De Falla (4th house ♓), Gustave Flaubert (4th house ♒), Marc Edmund Jones (♋ 9th house), Leontyne Price (♋ 5th house)

North node in Capricorn or in the tenth house: Ingrid Bergman (♑ 1st house), Ram Dass (10th house ♈), Phyllis Diller (♑ 8th house), Edna Ferber (10th house ♍), Michel Gauquelin (10th house ♊), Fritz Perls (10th house ♈)

LEO/AQUARIUS - FIFTH HOUSE/ELEVENTH HOUSE - TRAITS 5 and 11

Here, developmental tension surrounds the need for romantically close, emotional ties which must be balanced with freedom and friendship outlets. Intense involvements must be reconciled with detached viewpoints. There also must be an ability to sense one's "specialness" and to acknowledge the specialness in others through an objective, egalitarian consciousness. Personality growth is stimulated through a determination to succeed at self-expressive, off-the-cuff, technically-related, creative or fun-filled vocational activities balanced with an understanding of how they impact and are able to serve a greater whole. Although it is important to develop self-esteem and confidence in one's capabilities, the sense of contribution, or a cause-orientation, should be equally strong. One must also enjoy and be stimulated by work and coworkers, and believe one has something significant to contribute to the work process. Developing recreational activities, hobbies or intellectual pursuits into income-producing endeavors worthy of acclaim can be helpful to the process, as can work involving children, teens or groups of people. Acquaintances, clients, friends, children or lovers can spark new cycles of development and outlooks on life.

Growth is disrupted by overly confident, egocentric attitudes and the expectation of acclaim without having to earn it.

In such instances, the node related to trait 5 has been overly developed. Exaggerated accomplishments, self-importance, excessive pride, chronic complaining or narcissism can be problems. Or, growth can be hampered by failing to develop self-esteem and confidence in one's ability to perform. A get-by approach to work is likely to be established. A continual search for pleasure, fun or glamour and the easy way out lead to floating through life. A failure to overcome a painful, neglected childhood often lies at the root of the problem.

When trait 11 is improperly relied upon, rebellion, excessive eccentricity or an unwillingness to form close, emotional ties can result to the extreme of exhibiting a callous detachment from others. Integration of the 5/11 nodal polarity is demonstrated when people can respond to both their heads and their hearts; when intensity and pride are balanced with objectivity, logic and humanitarian principles.

North node in Leo or in the fifth house: Arthur Ashe (♌ 11th house), Ellen Burstyn (5th house ♓), Johnny Carson (♌ 9th house), Rob Hand (♌ 3rd house), Jimi Hendrix (♌ 8th house), Leontyne Price (5th house ♋), Princess Anne (5th house ♓), Helen Reddy (5th house ♍)

North Node in Aquarius or in the eleventh house: John Glenn (11th house ♎), Dustin Hoffman (11th house ♐), Caroline Kennedy (11th house ♏), Edward Lalo (♒ 8th house), Vivien Leigh (11th house ♓), Alan Leo (♒ 6th house), Liberace (11th house ♐), Carl Sandburg (♒ 5th house)

VIRGO/PISCES - SIXTH HOUSE/TWELFTH HOUSE - TRAITS 6 and 12

When either node is associated with these traits, it is a calling to integrate dreams, visions and ideals with discriminating, analytical viewpoints and hard work. This is not easy. Personality growth is enhanced through recognizing the importance of work and the development of finely tuned skills. However, practicality, an exacting nature and critical attention to detail also must be integrated with inspired, uplifting beliefs, the caring instincts, intuition or the creative imagination. Striving to attain honors and recognition in a craft, skill, service or profession is beneficial to the process. Sensitivity, open-mindedness, compassion, understanding and a willingness to serve without abdicating important personality needs also are vital to developmental growth.

Growth is disturbed by failing to recognize the importance of skill development, or the enhancement of the critical judgment, to one's emotional equilibrium and sense of well-being. A deeply-ingrained sense of inadequacy may hamper identity formation or the determination of appropriate career goals. In such instances, the node related to trait 6 has not been adequately developed and some people may be here to learn how to work and to be more disciplined and exacting. With trait 12 overly expressed, they are free to dance in the light and to escape through their illusions. Some choose the path of the goody-two-shoes or the bad apple. Others can end up being the victim on the lookout for a savior or the savior looking for victims. Without an ability to discriminate between who needs love or support and who does not, both types can end up being taken for a ride. Others, while capable of skill development and exacting hard work, may not understand people's motives and the reasons for their presence in their lives. They can choose unrewarding jobs unrelated to true identity needs which only make them feel deprived or used. Periods of confusion and disorientation often result, which may not be overcome until energy is directed to elevating skills or the discriminating faculties.

At the other extreme are people who believe they are or should be "perfect." Compassionately accepting the imperfections in others can be beyond them until the trait 12 node has been developed. Individuals can be workaholic and must attend to every little detail, feeling only they can do it right, but they may lack a true sense of purpose from their work. They can be hounded by needing to measure up which sometimes can be turned on self or displaced on others. Such people can be too hard on themselves, and end up feeling insecure, or other people can be made to feel they must measure up. The constructive trait 6 ability to uncover flaws and improve conditions becomes distorted into critical nit-picking to displace hidden fears of inadequacy onto others. For growth to proceed, faith in the goodness of life must be tapped and a renewed sense of self-acceptance must be achieved.

North node in Virgo or in the sixth house: Muhammad Ali (♍ 2nd house), Jack Anderson (♍ 3rd house), Marlon Brando (♍ 9th house), Clint Eastwood (6th house ♉), Edna Ferber (♍ 10th house), Isabelle Pagan (♍ 3rd house), Helen Reddy (♍ 5th house), Barbra Streisand (6th house ♍)

North node in Pisces or in the twelfth house: Carol Burnett (12th house ♓), Ellen Burstyn (♓ 5th house), Chris Chubbuck (12th house ♋), Vivien Leigh (♓ 11th house), Tyrone Power (♓ 5th house), Franz Schubert (12th house ♋), Lotte Von Strahl (♓ 2nd house)

References

1. Arroyo, Stephen, *Astrology, Psychology and the Four Elements* , Reno, Nevada: CRCS Publications, 1975, p. 138-9
2. Dean, Geoffrey, editor, *Recent Advances in Natal Astrology*, Western Australia: Analogic, 1977, p. 375
3. Dean., p. 376

CHAPTER SEVEN

CONSCIOUSNESS AND THE JOB IN LIFE

When a real sense of self is dim or nonexistent, people can be blinded to their proper places within the cosmos. The Sun/Moon phase can be helpful in deciding this issue. It suggests a vocational approach or career contributions which can create more purposeful participation in the working world. Dane Rudhyar was the first to classify personality according to the cyclical relationship between the Sun and Moon at birth. He called it the lunation birthday.[1]

> What we discover when we use the lunation birthday **as a foundation** is above all the manner in which a person meets the challenge of relationships, and uses his life force and his consciousness in order to work out in actual everyday practice **the basic purpose of his life** as a concrete human personality.

Rudhyar tends to be mystical and borders on being mystifying at times, especially if one has difficulty keeping pace with his long sentences. He proposes that all people are born in response to a particular planetary need, almost as if to suggest there is a "job" to perform in life. Purpose can be found in fulfilling the duties, obligations and responsibilities that the job entails. The author also recommends Marc Robertson's description of the phases of the Moon because it is easy to digest.[2] The joint efforts of Busteed, Tiffany and Wergin[3] have produced a stunning volume on Moon phases based, in large part, on William Butler Yeats' *A Vision*.

The phases outline eight different ways of being in the world. It is the evolutionary process all human beings go through to develop a more consciously understood perspective on their roles within the cosmic order. Career-troubled people usually lack awareness of their potentials or the perspectives they should develop to bring purpose and fulfillment into their lives. Living in tune with the birth phase is essential to a balanced way of life, and a fulfilling career, because it represents a form of psychological grounding in the world in which one lives.

The phases begin at the conjunction of the Moon with the Sun and move through the complete cycle to New Moon again. The **waxing phases** refer to the period when the Moon grows in light until the Full Moon is reached. At that time, from our vantage point on Earth, the disk of the Moon appears to be roughly the same size as the Sun. After Full Moon, the **waning phases** commence as the Moon eventually loses light to the sliver point and vanishes into darkness at the conjunction with the Sun again.

Light, in a metaphysical sense, symbolizes consciousness. During the waxing phases, developing consciousness is the primary objective. The emphasis is on the "I" portion of the "I-Thou" principle. Subjective self-focus and instinctive activity are the factors that must be set into motion. The individual discovers self by defining the boundaries of one's capabilities. Self-awareness and a sense of purpose develop from confronting the values and traditions handed down by the family or heritage (New-Crescent). Old, lifeless issues must be cleared away so that a suitable new foundation can be built to sustain a more "real" and substantial personality (First Quarter-Gibbous). By the end of the Gibbous phase, if work on self has been completed satisfactorily, the person should be sufficiently grounded to take on the increasing social obligations signified by the waning phases.

During the waning phases, self-focus is meant to decline. One must learn to function with and through others; the "Thou" portion of the I-Thou principle becomes increasingly focal to a purposeful career and way of life. The intent of the waning phases is to reach an objective view of self, and the purpose for one's life. This comes about from relating important qualities of self to the not-self (Full), to broader reaches of society (Disseminating-Last Quarter) or to humanity at large (Balsamic). One's obligations to others and the broader social structure mount as the Moon loses light. The needs of society, or the closer community (or profession), must be consciously incorporated into the vocational game plan. One is not here exclusively to satisfy personal goals and needs.

All human beings must go through each stage of this symbolic process to attain a state of higher, or objective, consciousness. **The phase at birth highlights a segment of this process which is most important to an individual's growth in this lifetime.** But everyone must begin by developing their **true** potentials and using those potentials to the best of their capability. The universe is not necessarily seeking contributions of grandiose proportions, merely those of an individual, heartfelt nature.

The Sun/Moon phase is not an indication of one's development, or level of consciousness, along the evolutionary path. These factors cannot be known from the horoscope. It would be a grave mistake to label an individual an old or young "soul" according to Moon phase. The trait or trait pair assigned to it only suggests the types of work people can do to fulfill their "job in life" and to experience rewarding vocational roles within the cosmic order. Famous examples are provided to show how their vocations and contributions reflect their soli-lunar phases.

New Phase - Trait 1 - Level II

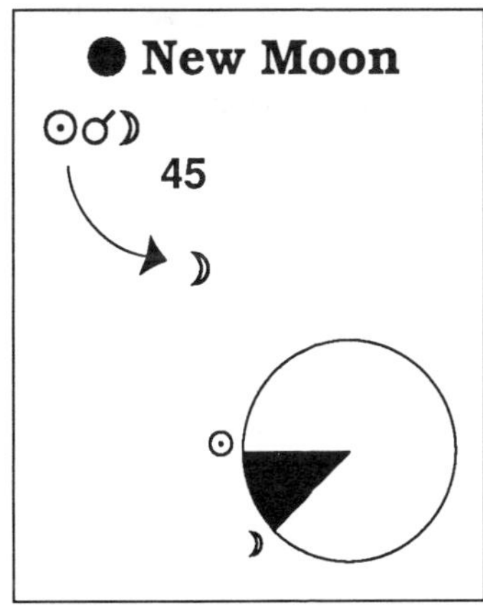

The New Phase begins at the conjunction of the lights and lasts until the Moon has moved forty-five degrees ahead of the Sun counter clockwise. The phase symbolizes a new cycle of experience, a fresh start, or the fresh upstart. An inner vision of individual accomplishment is meant to be tapped. When a chart contains other important trait 1 factors, vocational fulfillment is likely to surround trait 1 occupations or approaches.

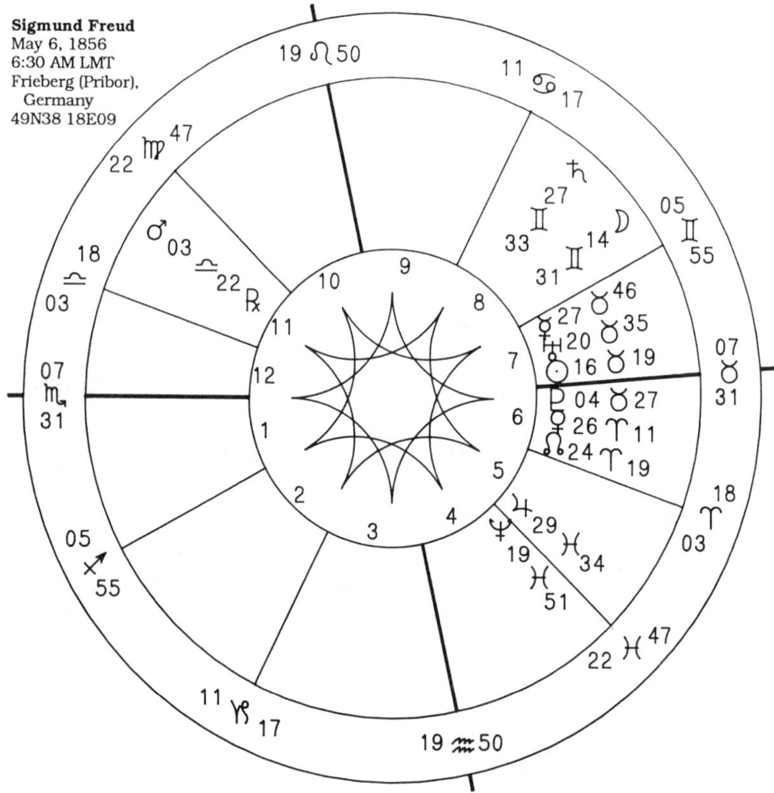

Sigmund Freud is an excellent example of New Moon achievement possibilities. Mars, significant to physicians, is a Level I singleton east and the handle of a bucket pattern. Pluto, which rules the Ascendant, is located three degrees away from the Descendant. Pluto signals deep emotional probing, healing and an intense or revolutionary approach to the field of interest. Without doubt, Freud fulfilled his prominent vocational needs, but also his New Moon job by pioneering psychoanalysis.

Under this phase, the "job" in life is to discover identity boundaries by striving to attain an inner vision of individual achievement. Initially, new phasers do not possess a firm sense of themselves; their accomplishments provide definition. A totally open-minded, independent, self-determined approach to work is requisite. Overdirecting instructions from a boss, for example, would interfere with the learning-by-doing process. Joy comes from making something happen that is completely self-originated because selfhood is discovered through what can be accomplished. A risk-taking nature and a daring attitude are meant to be called into action, without necessarily considering how these might affect others. Such considerations belong to later Moon phases and may detract from the New Moon purpose. Although some new phasers create resentment by inadvertently overstepping boundaries, their "job" is to break new ground, not to be another "yes" person.

When inner needs are met, and especially when the fire traits are represented, New Moon types are eager to confront challenges and competitors. They do not need a stockpile of credentials behind them before taking on tasks, only the confidence that they can do the job. They believe in themselves and their right to push forward on self-established terms. Fearless or foolhardy, they can be quick to risk a new approach, a new career direction, to try out new techniques or to take on the odds. The vocation demonstrates action, excitement, banter, growth, advancement, recognition and competition— typical trait 1 approaches. Any work that requires a major thrust of mental or physical energy, initiative, leadership or a totally self-involving approach can be suitable (see Chapter 2).

Striving to attain the inner vision is essential to a purposeful way of life. However, defining the vision within realistic boundaries— without limiting the pioneering spirit— can pose problems. Some New Moon types require grounding through the influence of a working mate or close, trusted colleagues. It is too easy to rush off into impractical directions, especially when traits 1, 9 or 12 are otherwise emphasized. A strong right arm, secretary, editor or trainer could fill this role and help keep rash decision-making from ruining things.

Developing a realistic self-concept is a key to success here because true accomplishments can be at the opposite end of the spectrum from what some new phasers believe they can accomplish. The extremes of under- or overrating the self can surface. Because a functional display of trait 1 rests on the sense of adequacy associated with trait 4, a realistic self-image must exist. A sensible boundary must be drawn between the inner vision and the available capabilities. The vision, coupled with needing to be on top and win, could outweigh the effort required to reach the goals. Although a developed Saturn function is always vocationally important, under this phase trait 10 is critical to achievement potentials. When adequately displayed, the fulfillment of one's job in life is enhanced. When trait 10 is inadequately responded to, the spirit of New Phase achievement can be hampered and the job in life can remain unfulfilled. How can potentials be discovered if one does not push, strive, take risks or realistically place oneself "on the line"? Disciplined, sustained effort is key to New Phase success or whenever trait 1 is highlighted. For many new phasers, the lesson can only be learned through a trial-and-error bout with the working world.

Another vital mechanism behind the New Phase process is bragging. It represents a form of self-motivation and self-expression. All the fire traits experience a need to brag. New phasers can and must be good at it to visualize their goals or to establish conditions through which they are required to achieve. However, without a true sense of adequacy, self-discipline, stick-to-itiveness and tangible achievement, bragging is nothing more than vocal fantasizing. And it is not uncommon for unrealistic New Moon types to fantasize aloud about accomplishing a grand scheme, even though it is way beyond their prior accomplishments. They fail to see themselves in a realistic light and often resist the notion that they might not be able to accomplish what they fantasize. Still, as immature as this naive self-aggrandizement might be, it is more true to the New Moon spirit than people who fail to tap their trait 1 needs.

When low career ceilings are established, and striving or bragging is not exhibited, it is a clue that **something is wrong.** The individual is out of sync with self and lacks a connection to the inner vision that so motivates others born under this phase. When this response is made, the early life probably was troubled by harsh or overdirecting parental instruction which inhibited the free development of self-assertive drives. The identity later becomes entangled in other people's expectations and the individual may not learn how to be self-directing until later in life. Boring job ruts result when the New Phase challenge to dare and risk goes unrecognized.

The new phaser requires an abundance of stimulating mental or physical activity. It is inappropriate, not to mention emotionally draining, to sit chained to a desk all day doing dull, routine work. At best, vague discontent results, while at worst, denied trait 1 needs cause one to get fired, to experience crises at work or to attract superaggressive coworkers and superiors.

How can one possibly do a job well that is so contrary to the inner nature? Any New Moon person who consistently loses or leaves jobs is being provided with a clue that something is wrong. Work-related difficulties may stem from a limited or grandiose self-image. Either way, the spirit of the New Phase is debilitated and the psyche is up in arms about it. To experience contentment from the job, trait 1 outlets or approaches must be realistically incorporated.

Famous personalities with New Moons: Muhammad Ali, Carol Burnett, Sean Connery, Sigmund Freud, John Wayne Gacey, Michel Gauquelin, Elton John, Diane Keaton, Princess Anne, Brooke Shields, Phoebe Snow

Crescent Phase - Trait Pair 2/3 - Level II

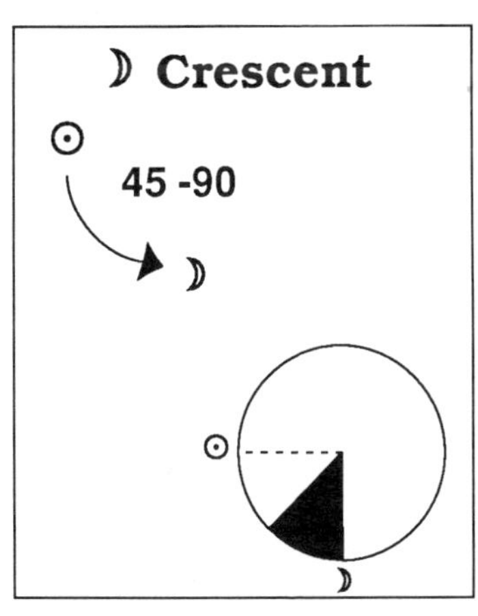

The Crescent phase begins when the Moon has passed forty-five degrees ahead of the Sun and remains until the ninety degree, first quarter square aspect has been reached. It represents a transitional phase in the development of consciousness requiring one to separate the values implanted by the family and heritage from one's own individualized needs. For growth to take place, every human being must discover the distinction between the two.

Edna Ferber, playwright, novelist and Pulitzer Prize winner, was born under this phase (trait pair 2/3) with both the Moon (trait 4) and Jupiter (trait 9) in primary plus zones. Neptune (trait 12) is within two degrees of the Descendant and leads in a bowl structure (trait 4). Notice how her occupation sustained a combined expression of these traits.

The Crescent type is implanted with the inner vision of the New Phase spirit. The "job" is to tap it, bring it out and sustain it in the world. Fulfilling this job is easier for those who come from upbringings which actively valued aesthetic appreciation,

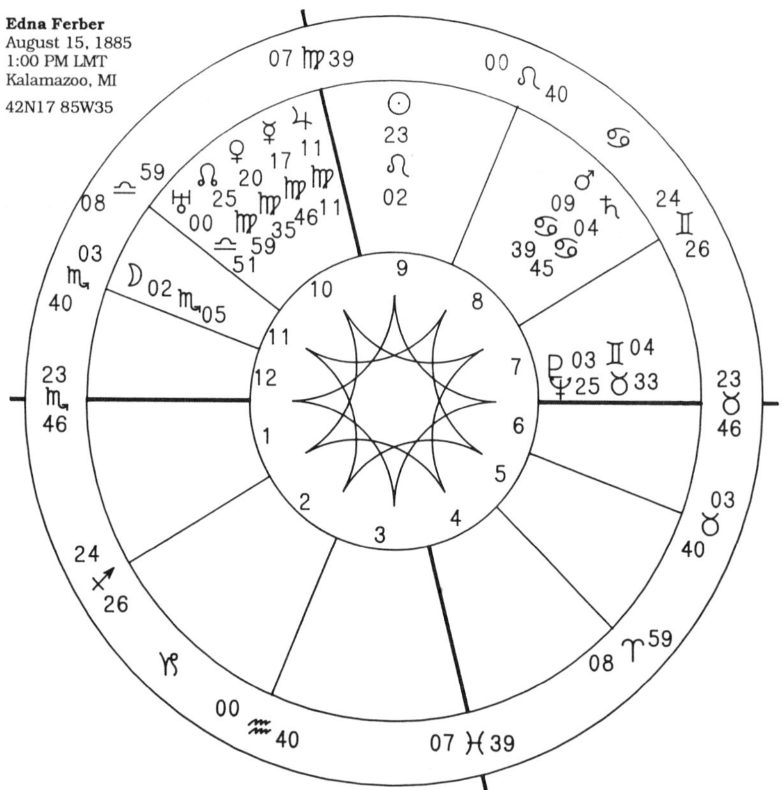

intellectual development or a combination of the two. However, other Crescents can experience roadblocks. The new approach to life may be quite different from what they were raised to believe was important. It can take them longer to find satisfying careers, but it is their job to tap this inner vision despite opposition or apparent disinterest from other people.

Crescent phasers are highly susceptible to the values or foibles of their family backgrounds. In many instances, early difficulties existed for or between the parents, frequently about finances and earning power. Separations from the parents also could have occurred literally, such as through death, divorce, or figuratively, through temperamental differences, drinking problems or an overbearing manner. Or, a role model may have been experienced as weak, withdrawn or ineffectual. Still, many crescent phasers remain bound to family values and perspectives.

Struggling with parental expectations is the major source of stress Crescent types tend to face and must overcome. Stress is lower for those whose true, inner values match those espoused by the family or who find their "calling" early and make a break with the past. For others, the desire to live up to spoken or unspoken familial expectation often conflicts with a need to create their own unique lifestyles. For example, a debutante who was groomed to marry into more wealth, but would prefer to groom horses for a racetrack, might have been born under this phase. Some people try to live both lives, the one they want and the one parents expect of them. However, this is like trying to be two different people while attempting to make sure they never meet.

FAMILY EXPECTATIONS

When unhappy employment is experienced, it frequently can be traced to this problem (although a diminished work ethic could be at fault). The job, career or even the lifestyle may exist as an unconscious attempt to please parents or is selected due to a fear of being someone other than who the family expects. Before anything can unfold in life, especially a fulfilling career, this Crescent type may have to separate from the family's identity and stamp of approval. A new lease on life begins when this step is taken.

The relationship to siblings, if existing, also must be thoroughly examined. Sibling rivalry and attempts to win parental love often can play major roles in familial stress patterns and may influence careers directions. This can have positive or negative ramifications. Any emphasis on trait 3 in the chart can signal a need to examine sibling relationships. However, under the Crescent phase, Cain and Abel may to be played out as part of this need to discriminate selfhood from family values.

Some Crescent types shy away from an occupation because it is the domain of a successful brother or sister with whom they do not wish to compete. Others more or less follow in the vocational footsteps of a sibling, sometimes in an unconscious attempt to win parental love, when a different occupational pursuit may be more true to individualized liking.

Still other Crescent types evade artistic or otherwise interesting occupations, sensing they could not be successful at them. This also can be true whenever trait 2 (or 7) or the 2/3 blend is repeated sufficiently in the chart. The crescent family experience tends to play a major role behind such career evasions. Parental role models may have taken a get-by approach to work or placed an inordinate value on the practical, remunerative aspects of employment (or a combination of the two). It can be difficult to tap the inner vision until a break with the family's values takes place.

Many Crescents have a flair for the arts, design, writing, or communication, but choose more stable, conventional or "practical" work to insure a steady paycheck. The family might have dissuaded them from acting or painting, for example, because such occupations were considered "frivolous" with little guarantee of success. Crescents often come from early homes where financial needs outweighed most others. They were drummed in from day one, while praise and support for other, less practical talents could not fill a thimble. However, talents or interests eventually may need to be incorporated into the vocation or avocation to fulfill one's job in life.

Financial and familial considerations are not the only factors responsible for influencing career choices under this phase. Whenever trait 2 is highlighted in a chart, doubts surrounding the worth and value of talents and abilities also can exist and must be overcome. When an independent sense of self-worth is not achieved, low job ceilings can be established or the wrong occupation can be entered. Such Crescent types could plod along on a vocational course similar to that of the parents and later wonder why they are so unhappy with their work. That is why an independent evaluation of one's worth and one's values is so important under this phase. Without it, the "job" in life may go unfulfilled.

Once the identity has been separated from familial expectations, striving takes place and Crescents begin to take fresh approaches to work and life. Often they undergo a complete change in career or add a totally new facet to the current occupational expression. Suitable careers for this phase are described in Chapter 2, traits 2 and 3. (Also see trait pair 2/3 in Chapter 5.)

Famous personalities with Crescent Moons: Lew Ayres, Johnny Carson, Chris Chubbuck, Jacques Cousteau, Clint Eastwood, Edna Ferber, Caroline Kennedy, Vivien Leigh, Helen Reddy, Ronald Reagan

First Quarter Phase - Trait 4 - Level II

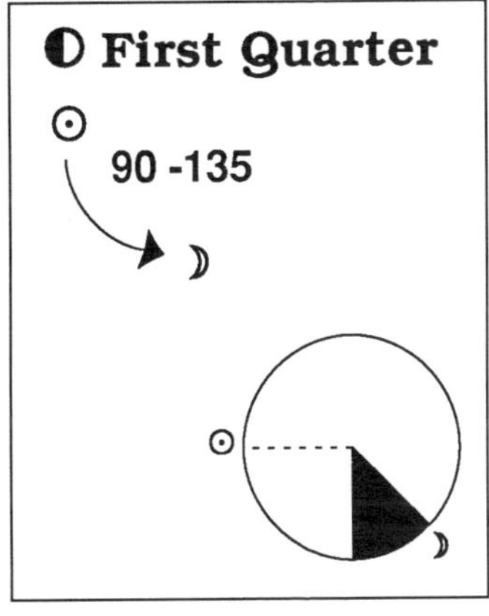

This phase begins at the lower square of the Sun and Moon and lasts until the Moon has moved 135 degrees ahead of Sol. Here, Crescent struggles over family expectations now develop into "crisis" proportions. Under the First Quarter phase, definite steps must be taken to overcome any debilitating ties to early life programming and parental values. The situation no longer can be avoided if growth in consciousness is likely to proceed.

World renowned conductor Zubin Mehta was born under this phase. He began studying piano and violin at age 7 under the direction of his conductor father. It is not uncommon for trait 4 types to vocationally follow in the footsteps of a parent. However, such career choices are only likely to be successful when they reflect personal needs, values and interests independent from parental control.

The "job" under this phase is to build new emotional structures and perspectives based solely on a personal frame of reference. Freed from family strings, individuals can define themselves by intimate values and needs and share with the world the best they have to offer. It is a challenging process and, as painful as it might become for some, it is not without purpose. The inner vision of the New Moon spirit, which struggled to break ground under the Crescent phase, must now develop strong, unwavering roots to grow to greater heights. Without a firm inner foundation and true emotional grounding, whatever has been "planted" cannot blossom.

Due to its association with trait 4, personal adequacy, family matters and the ability to withstand the demands of responsible adulthood are issues which must be faced. Some First Quarter types are willfully determined to push to the forefront of a career and strive for recognition. Some yearn for greatness and the heights of achievement frequently, but not always, surrounding trait 4 approaches or endeavors. Parent-

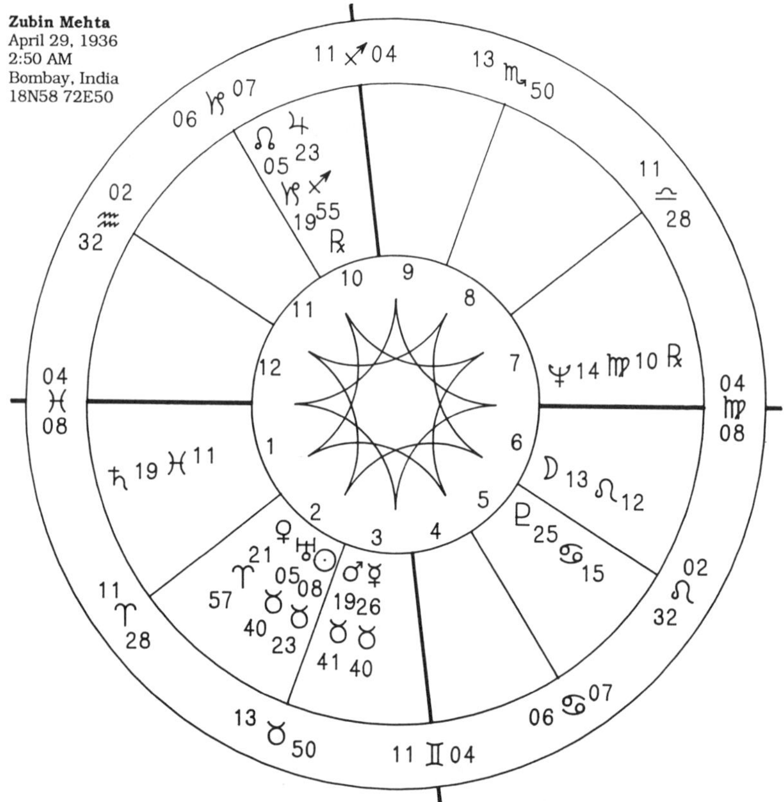

hood also can be a worthy "calling" for many First Quarter people (or anyone with trait 4 highlighted). In this day and age, however, once children become reasonably self-sufficient, women may find it advisable to aim their sights at an expanded career role. Trait 4, however, is a water-related chart factor, and water can move along with the flow, nurture and sustain an achievement drive or wash it completely away.

The First Quarter phase crisis relates to a deep, inward and usually unconscious need to completely change the orientation to life. People must refrain from seeking support or validation from others and develop a more independent, self-sufficient stance. Crises tend to arise when this challenge to maturation is not squarely faced. The family, the past, the partner or "others" can be blamed for problems when the fault lies in unacknowledged fears of standing on their own two feet. A fear of failure prevents many from trying vocational wings. Issues related to the early home life and heritage, where we all have our "roots," must be considered whenever trait 4 is accented in the chart. Some families provide fertile soil for future growth.

For many First Quarter types, however, a positive early life experience can turn into a vocational handicap. They may not consider a path which significantly differs from their parents'. Life seemed to work out so well for them that First Quarter types may wonder why they should try a different route. Many prefer to marry young and frequently recreate the traditions and values by which they were raised. A great deal of role-playing tends to go on in such marriages. One partner often acts as the guiding "parent" while the other plays the role of the needy "child." It represents a symbiotic tie which serves to provide direction for each. The "parent" gains a sense of authority through directing the "child," while the "child" is taken care of and does not have to fend for the self.

This desire for security, continuity and support can undermine personal growth by preventing anything revitalizing from entering the life. This is not the best approach to a First Quarter Moon or to trait 4; a parent merely may be exchanged for a spouse. True inner foundations are unlikely to be tapped and the partner is often unconsciously looked to for support, validation or direction. But what if something happens to the mate or the marriage? Under the First Quarter phase, a "crisis" can erupt whenever independent validation has not taken place. When such marriages break up, identity problems often break loose. Many First Quarter types (or others with a trait 4 emphasis) need to be their own mothers and fathers, to support and direct themselves rather than expecting this to come from others.

When early home experiences were less than supportive, different responses are likely. People may have difficulty developing close relationships, especially when trait 11 also is emphasized in the chart. In many such cases, the career can take the place of a family or other important relationships. Another response is to become extremely dependent on others, even when one is unaware of it. However, it is not always easy to find people who will put up with childish demands for attention and constant nurturing. Marriages are unlikely to withstand the strain, and business crises can result, because individuals are out of phase with inner needs for independent grounding.

Do not get the impression that everyone born under this phase experiences a life of disruptive crises. When healthy emotional self-validation is established, crises are like obstacles to be overcome, even though they may pop up with some frequency. But this has more to do with the energetic nature of the First Quarter personality rather than a cosmic need to reorient one's response to life. However, those who fail to recognize how they are intended to fit into the universal plan do experience crisis. For most, the confrontation with a completely new mode of existence, which is what the crisis signifies, can be the best thing to ever happen. The more severe it appears to be, the greater the chance that independent validation has been overlooked and the opportunity is being provided to set one on the right path. Suitable job outlets/approaches for this phase are listed under trait 4 in Chapter 2.

Famous personalities with First Quarter Moons: James Arness, Arthur Ashe, Ellen Burstyn, Albert Camus, Morgana King, Zubin Mehta, Herman Melville, Jack Nicklaus, Leontyne Price, Nelson Rockefeller, Barbra Streisand

Gibbous Phase - Trait Pair 5/6 - Level II

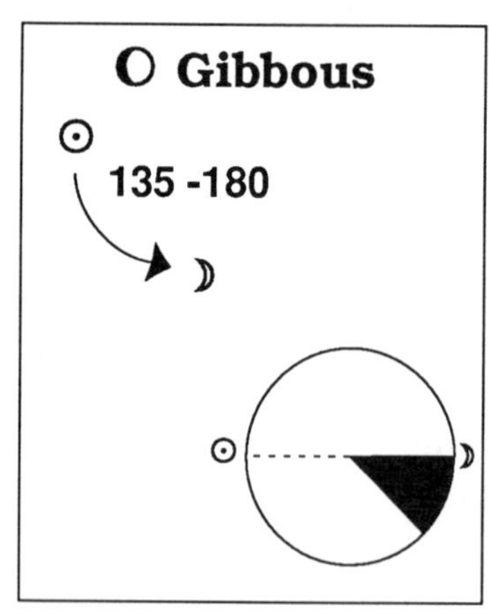

The Gibbous phase begins when the Moon is 135 degrees ahead of the Sun, moving in a counter clockwise direction, and remains until the Full Moon is reached. R.D. Laing, described by Lois Rodden as analyist, philosopher, writer and counter-culture cult figure, was born under this phase (trait pair 5/6). He also possesses the seesaw chart pattern (traits 2 and 7) significant not only of the interrelating process, but of artistic expression as well. Jupiter (trait 9) and the Moon (trait 4) are located in the rising plus zone with Uranus (trait 11) angular conjunct the Ascendant. Notice how his vocational expression combines not only traits 4, 7, 9 and 11, but also encompasses trait pair 5/6. (See Chapter 5 for a discussion of this trait pair.)

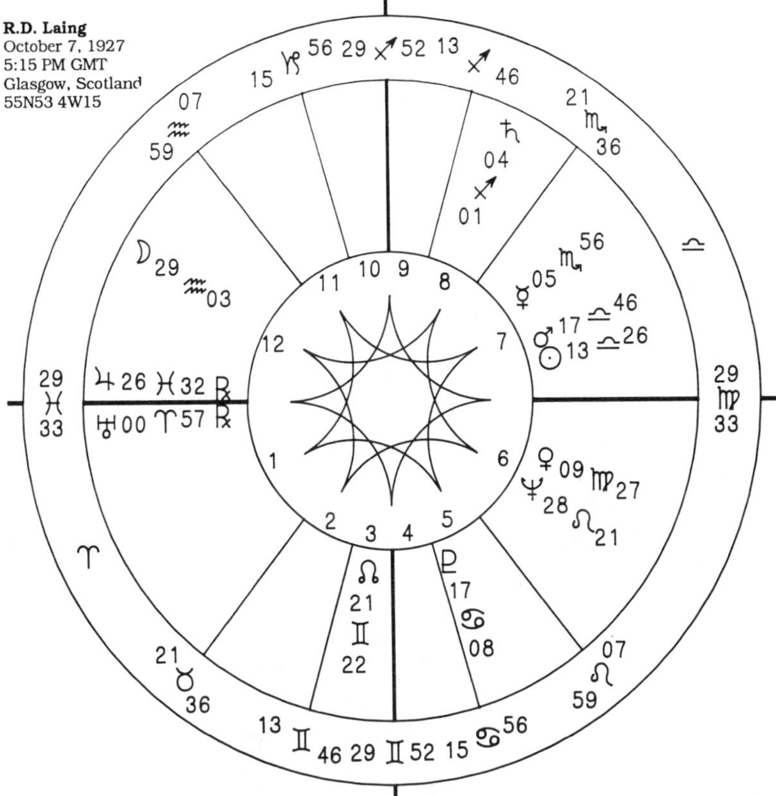

The Gibbous phase represents another transitional stage in the development of consciousness. One "job" in life is to eliminate feelings of inadequacy or debilitating ties to family expectations which interfere with productive relationships and mature functioning in the outer world. Self-analysis or self-perfecting can and should take place to refine the personality, make it more "real" and true to self. "Work," both on oneself and in the career world, is important to the Gibbous segment of the evolutionary process.

The phase correlates with a combination of traits 5 and 6 (see Chapter 2). Developing skills or the mental faculties (6) and confidence in an ability to perform (5) are requisite. A fruitful connection to selfhood is not readily achieved when important, self-expressive skills are not developed. A negative self-image tends to take hold which undermines formation of the close emotional ties equally necessary to satisfaction under this phase. Worker D's, without significant outside activities and relationships, and many E types born under this phase may experience emotional problems. In extreme cases, paranoia, living in a fantasy world or nervous breakdowns occur due to a lack of rewarding work, hobbies and relationships.

This stems from a lack of awareness of a deep, creative urge within the Gibbous personality— an inner need (the "job" in life) to perform a special, useful service or skill. This unique career contribution or avocation, however, must be intimately personal and can be tapped only when a valid connection to the inner self exists. Career-troubled Gibbous people must make a sincere effort to delve within for this connection. When this creative urge is denied, or is befuddled by family issues, trouble begins to brew. In some instances, the desire to be "special" can outweigh the effort or talent it takes to become special, so that "get-rich-quick" schemes can be preferred. But the hard-earned development of a special craft or service is vitally important to Gibbous types. Without it, individuals can slip further and further back emotionally, a process which usually begins by limiting contact with others or by withdrawing from the work force. Failure to work on the inner world or in the outer world, however, only exacerbates the problem.

Because this phase encompasses trait 5 issues, Gibbous types who develop their skills but fail to contact the "self" may experience disappointments in their love lives. Relationships do not seem to "work" for very long. Other skilled gibbous types may pursue inappropriate careers— those prompted more by a need to be "somebody" than due to true vocational needs. The prestige of work can supercede expressing oneself in a rewarding fashion. When frustration, stress or conflict represent a continual dynamic on the job, it may be a signal that something is faulty with the vocational choice or approach to the career.

Because trait 6 is also at issue here, measuring up to perfectionistic role models can play a part in vocational dissatisfaction or stress. Before consciousness can grow, career choices must be examined for their relationship to true vocational needs. One may or may not go into a line of work to win parental approval. Or, one might be undermined at work due to early life criticism. Such criticism, which often stems from an unconscious parental need to project inadequacies onto a child, must be thoroughly reviewed so that any lingering ill effects can be eliminated.

When the Gibbous phase challenge is met, work on self, or therapeutic assistance from others if needed, can result in tapping creative resources. Something of value in the service of individuals, the company or humanity can be produced. It is essential to enjoy one's work, to express oneself through it, to like the people with whom one works or to work with a special loved one. It is also important to feel indispensable on the job or to feel one's service, skill or business performs a useful, helpful or creative function. The need to be needed and useful also could be fulfilled through parenthood. When personally significant and useful capabilities are not developed, and when an appropriate sense of adequacy has not been achieved, aims of the entire waxing Moon process become defeated. Work on self may need to be done before appropriate functioning in the career world is likely to take place.

Gibbous types who overcome neurotic needs or tendencies (this is not to imply all Gibbous Moon people are neurotic) and who develop a solid occupational expression tend to live happier, more fulfilled lives. They identify with their work and the contributions they make vocationally (or avocationally).

Romantic love, in the Leo sense, also represents an important facet to Gibbous fulfillment. Some Gibbous types, however, pour too much energy into their work at the expense of love/art outlets. Workaholics who drive themselves on the job may do so in an unconscious effort to make sure nothing is left over to devote to personal relationships. There can be a fear of true emotional closeness and an inability to withstand the insecurities that arise whenever one is in "love." But, Gibbous Moon types are here to learn to balance love and work, and to realize that each contributes to a fuller, happier life.

Famous personalities with Gibbous Moons: Ingrid Bergman, Lord Byron, Prince Charles, Françoise Gauquelin, George Gershwin, Heinrich Himmler, R.D. Laing, Nathan Leopold, Walter Mondale, Louis Pasteur, George Sanders, Lotte Von Strahl

Full Phase - Trait 7 - Level II

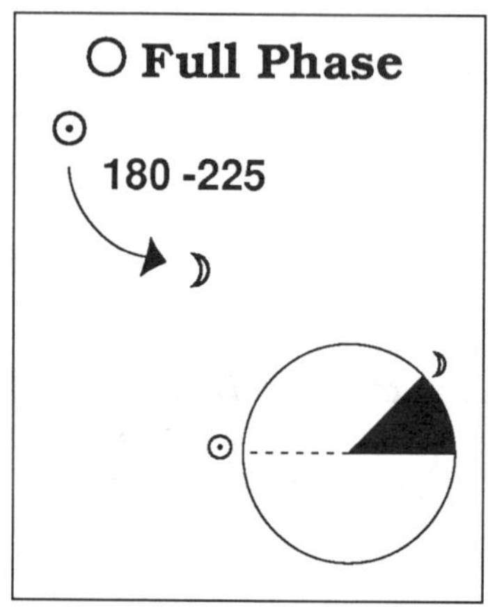

The Full phase begins when the Moon is 180 degrees from the Sun and remains until it is 225 degrees ahead, moving in a counter clockwise direction. The symbolism suggests a new vista has been reached and the "I-Thou" principle, with a growing emphasis on "Thou," is in effect. The inner vision of individual accomplishment, symbolized by the new phase, which is rendered substantive through the remaining waxing phases, must now incorporate other people's inner visions. In this phase, one must take a more objective, considered and considerate approach to others. Successful functioning in life and in a career depends on a developed and grounded personality. One's "job" is to share this developed self, and one's ideals, with others in a balanced, purposeful and committed fashion.

Through the interrelating process, a new level of consciousness is meant to be achieved. One must gain a greater understanding of self through close interaction with the not-self. Learning to balance the needs and perspectives of others with one's own is a challenge to all of human existence. However, facing this challenge is imperative for those born under the Full phase. Growth and vocational purpose are dependent on productive interrelating skills. This can be true whenever trait 7 is accented in the chart, and it is contingent on the adequate formation of traits 1 and 4. One cannot functionally relate to others when the sense of identity (trait 1) and personal adequacy (trait 4) are faulty.

The need under this phase is to work with others, in a partnership arrangement, in a group setting, through teamwork or through one-to-one interaction (see Chapter 2). Artistic pursuits represent still another suitable outlet. How one relates to and feels about others in the work environment tends to play a major role in job satisfaction and successful functioning.

Working by oneself, unless it involves an absorbing creative endeavor or the interrelating process, is not appropriate for Full phasers.

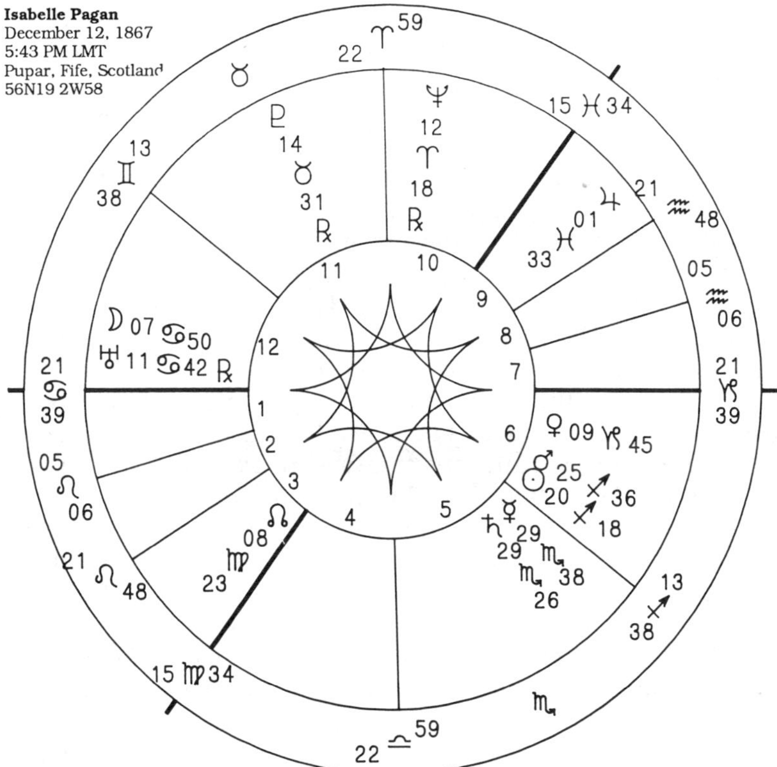

Astrologer and author Isabelle Pagan was born under this trait 7 phase, a trait repeated through her seesaw chart pattern. Venus is also significantly located in the sixth house, less than twelve degrees away from the Descendant. The Moon conjunct Uranus rises past the Ascendant in a plus zone while Jupiter culminates just past the Midheaven. Her occupational choice encompassed the diversity of her personality needs and talents: assisting, intuitive nature, capacity for writing and public speaking (trait 4), an interrelating capability (trait 7), notoriety, a need to understand life and to disseminate ideas (trait 9), technical know-how, the mastery of stimulating subject matter (astrology) and group participation (fulfilled through the Theosophical Society) [trait 11].

Part of the Full phase consciousness is a nascent attunement to idealism. This is not to suggest that only Full phasers are capable of devoting themselves to significant ideals. Traits 9, 11 or 12 also can represent career expression through important ideals (causes), just as authors or artists (traits 4 or 7) often conceive of and share visionary perspectives through their imaginations. However, under the Full phase, purpose in life, and in a job, surrounds a need to seek, experience and express a personal ideal. This can be a significant love relationship (committed attachment), partnership or the interrelating process where the two form something greater than their individual parts. Provided self-analysis and self-refining have been adequately conducted, symbolized by the Gibbous Moon process, Full phasers can demonstrate through a career the significance of life on an intimate level.

When self-refining has not taken place, interrelating skills and the ability to understand others' needs can be hampered. Self-centeredness can consume the personality and create difficulties. Alienation from bosses or coworkers, flare ups, arguments or more quiet separations become standard situations in the love and work life until social skills and a thoughtful, considerate approach to others improve. The problem can lie in failing to develop traits 1 and 4 and an under- or overdeveloped self-assertiveness tends to result. Some Full phasers appear peculiar, harsh or shy and lose promotions due to presenting themselves too forcefully or not forcefully enough.

The interrelating difficulty often stems from an early exposure to parental disputes, separation and/or unreal habits of relating (see Chapter 2). In such cases, the ability to form balanced, give-and-take relationships in which the identity of one is balanced with the needs and identity of the other, was not adequately learned in the early life and has to be developed later. In other cases, similar parental influences stimulate resentment which can result in viewing the everyday expectations of working with others as an infringement on individual freedom. Some people imitate the early controlling influences and never permit others to fully express themselves. Too much may be demanded without proper give-and-take becoming part of the exchange and stronger people may be avoided because they are unlikely to put up with one-way relationships of this nature.

Fears of closeness can develop with these less than positive responses, leading some individuals to mistakenly believe that no relationship is the best relationship to have. They often prefer working alone. For others, relationships can be entered, but only with people unwilling to commit to true closeness. Unless steps are taken to alter these perspectives, the purpose of the Full Moon phase cannot be fulfilled. Dodging close relationships becomes an act of running away from one's self and it is unlikely to help one fulfill the job in life.

The option here is to retrace the Gibbous process and undergo honest self-examination or therapeutic intervention to eliminate the problem. An entirely new self-concept can be achieved, one capable of experiencing productive give-and-take in relationships. Developing consciousness of self leads to an appreciation and heightened consciousness of others which significantly contributes to the value of life.

Famous personalities with Full Moons: David Bowie, Nina Foch, Andre Gide, Johann Von Goethe, Merv Griffin, Isabelle Pagan, Giacamo Puccini, Camille Saint-Saens, Percy Shelley, Richard Speck

Disseminating Phase - Trait Pair 8/9 - Level II

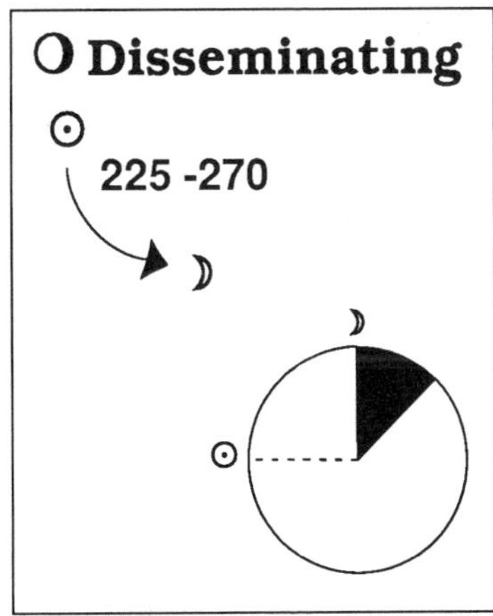

The Disseminating phase begins when the Moon has traveled 225 degrees ahead of the Sun and lasts until the upper, last quarter square aspect (270 degrees) has been attained. In this phase, relating to others takes on broader connotations. One is urged to reach out to experience and impact more of life. The idealism associated with the Full Moon phase is intended to encompass expanded reaches of society. Aspirations (trait 9) become integral to a growth in consciousness and vocational fulfillment. While close, personal relationships can be purposeful to existence, they are no longer intended to consume a singular focus. Under the Disseminating phase, the "job" in life is to project out into extended spheres of social interaction whatever is perceived to have individual merit, and not necessarily to be tied down to only one significant relationship.

It is also important under this phase to heighten the emotional or intellectual perceptions, to expand the scope of influence through them and to be known beyond one's immediate milieu. Disseminating types must make connections to the many, not the few, because deep down they have something of committed value to share with the world. This "something" must be sought out and usually rests on a belief system, a theoretical or philosophical approach to life, which in-phase personalities work hard to develop. They wish to make the world a better place by their standards of improvement. Knowledge (9) indeed is power (8). They are among the world's teachers and preachers, even if they do not enter those professions, and they wish to share their ideas (hopefully without jamming them down other people's throats).

This need, however, may not register in consciousness without an experience of personal torment, possibly brought on by a career failure, a disastrous relationship or a series of unfulfilling ones. But such are among the painful circumstances they (as well as others) may need to force them to examine inner needs. Because the waning cycle is involved, this belief or cause should encompass not only personal goals, but the perceived needs of a greater whole (perhaps even society).

Albert Einstein was born under this phase (8/9) with Jupiter (9) in the culminating plus zone and Uranus (11), located in the third house, as the handle of a bucket pattern (5). Notice the important repetition of trait 9. Although it is not possible to know from his chart alone, his self-expression was on the genius level. His interest in math and physics, coupled with his drive to know more and share that knowledge, motivated him to found the theory of relativity by the age of twenty-six, fulfill his job in life, and later win the Nobel Prize.

Under the Disseminating phase, work-related skills must be developed to fulfill the job. Crusaders, above all, must possess a realistic self-image and a constructive, determined goal orientation. Lack of emotional stability and an unrealistic

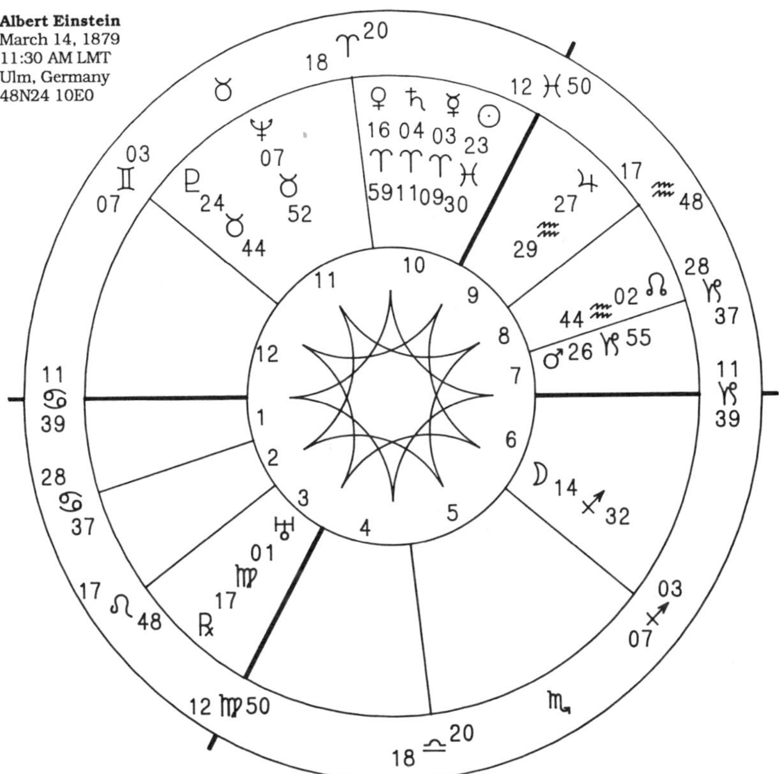

approach to life do not eliminate the Disseminating need, but such factors obviously can interfere with successfully carrying out the job in life. Aspirations need to be realistically grounded and the psychological state has to be in good working order. Everything is called to task and when traits 1, 4, 7 and 10 are not functionally developed, Disseminating types may not be up to the challenge. The more people attempt to reach out and influence society, especially through deeply committed beliefs, the more important the solidarity of the inner self becomes. Consequently, therapeutic assistance for any dysfunction is wisely sought.

Happily employed Disseminators select occupations that thoroughly capture their interests, and cater to their significant beliefs, needs for expanded influence, leadership, knowledge or renown (trait 9, see Chapter 2). Almost any occupation can bring fame or influence, provided the effort quotient is sound and talents warrant public attention. For some Disseminators, influence can manifest as building up a huge business or taking on a public office. Power, death, sex, metaphysical matters or money are equally moving concerns and sources of fascination. Many disseminators like to brush shoulders with powerful or wealthy people, sometimes in the hope that their influence will rub off. In some instances, marriage to an influential person can become a goal in itself. For other Disseminators, the philosophical, knowledge or theory-orientation of this trait pair takes precedence, as it did for Einstein. (See Chapter 5.) Dead-end jobs that do not provide advancement opportunity, influence, power, or significant beliefs undermine aspirational needs.

The urge to become a "legend" also can emerge for those born under this phase (or who otherwise have an emphasis on trait pair 8/9). Sometimes a superiority complex can develop as an outward defense against not being "important" enough. Others do not respond to their aspirational needs, believing they have nothing to offer the career world. Neither response is likely to generate a rewarding way of life. For a few, struggles also take place between needs for space and freedom (9) and needs for intensely involving or disruptive encounters with others (8), even though this might not be consciously recognized. These Disseminators can experience difficulty maintaining relationships, especially with people who do not offer challenge.

When one fails to tap aspirations, or to seek knowledge or influence, it is as undermining to emotional grounding as taking to drugs or drink. The personality is out of sync with self. An inaccurate self-image and an undeveloped belief system are usually at the root of the problem. In such cases, boring, routine jobs which have nothing to do with the beliefs, aspirations or "job" in life, tend to be wrongfully selected. As discussed in Chapter 2 on trait 9, denied aspirations can lead to psychosomatic problems and cause people to use up every sick day permitted or to job-hop.

Rather than searching within for a link to self, some Disseminators focus on locating the perfect lover or soul mate, as if such a person holds the key to that link. They do not realize the meaning of their lives lies within themselves. Others develop pie-in-the-sky goal expectations and invent all sorts of excuses to hide their career frustrations, with "spiritual" beliefs heading the list. Although such pursuits can be productive for Disseminators who have a mature and developed ego structure, others must be careful that the philosophy is not simply a cover up for a fear of failure. Fears could underlie their resistance to realistically establish themselves in fitting career roles.

Who can tell another person what to believe or what is important to pursue in life? It is personal and is recognized from life's experiences or through a purposeful, though at times turbulent, soul searching process. To grow in consciousness and to attain a sense of fulfillment from work, Disseminators need a realistic connection to the inner self, and they need to believe in something strongly enough to be committed to sharing it with others. Whatever is unreal is without substance or endurance. Career-troubled Disseminators, or those who have the related traits emphasized in their charts, must understand their inner needs for a constructive belief system and a realistic approach to life. They possess something of value they inwardly, though not necessarily consciously, need to share.

Famous personalities with Disseminating Moons: Eddie Albert, Ram Dass, John Dean, Albert Einstein, Zsa Zsa Gabor, Dorothy Hamill, Jimi Hendrix, Jean Houston, Alan Leo, Burt Reynolds, Suzanne Somers, Noel Tyl

Last Quarter Phase - Trait 10 - Level II

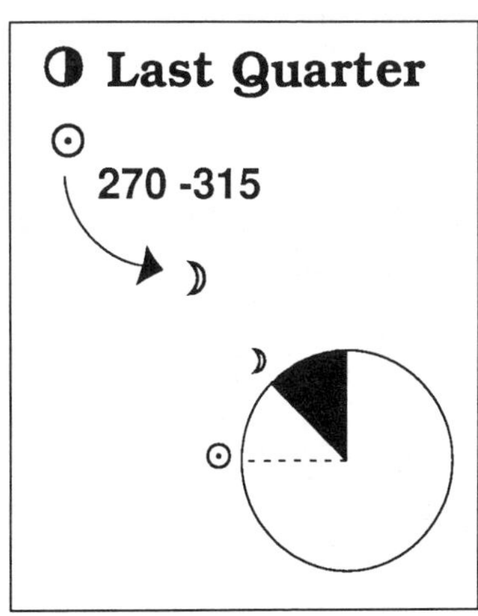

This phase begins at the upper square of the Sun and Moon and remains until the Moon has moved to a semisquare aspect between the lights (315 degrees). As the waning phases proceed, consciousness must develop further beyond a personal orientation to include broader spheres of social interaction. By the time the Last Quarter phase is reached, the Disseminating need to influence others or society becomes a more pressing imperative. Increased obligations come with expanded involvement and additional responsibilities must be fulfilled. The person should come to realize that there is a greater whole to which one is accountable. A socially conscious perspective, which began under the Full Moon and developed under the Disseminating phase, has become an absolute necessity.

The Last Quarter "job" is to consciously perform a vocation or avocation that contributes to a greater whole, be it a company, community, profession or society. The development of an authoritative skill, craft or talent is essential to fulfilling this job. The Last Quarter Moon correlates with Saturn and all other trait 10 chart factors. Sustained effort, the ability to accept responsibility and to earn a place in society are called to task under this phase and there is no way of avoiding it.

When in-phase, Last Quarter people want to rise in life, and many do pull themselves up by the bootstraps through sheer effort and persistence. As part of their socially conscious nature, they adhere to staunch codes of ethics as they work to enhance their competence and authority. Some come from humble or difficult early home lives and the individual response to these early life beginnings sets the stage for what unfolds in life. Many pursue a career which, at a superficial glance, appears far removed from what the family expected them to do. Ties to the past often can be irrevocably broken. Due to family conflicts or differences between parental temperaments, a number of Last Quarter types become overly self-sufficient. Every ounce of energy can be poured into the career or avocational interests.

British critic, novelist and playwright George Bernard Shaw was born under the Last Quarter phase and exemplifies many of its highest potentials. The Moon (4) occupies the rising plus zone while both the Sun in Leo (5) and Venus (2 and 7) anticulminate in a secondary zone. Mars (1) in the sixth house represents the hard working handle of a bucket pattern (5). The dynamically self-expressive, creative and artistic needs of this personality should be clear. Shaw, who advocated a socialist philosophy, expertly honed his abilities and made contributions to society (Last Quarter) which later won him the Nobel Prize for literature. Regardless of one's feelings about socialism, the man fulfilled his job in life by offering the world something

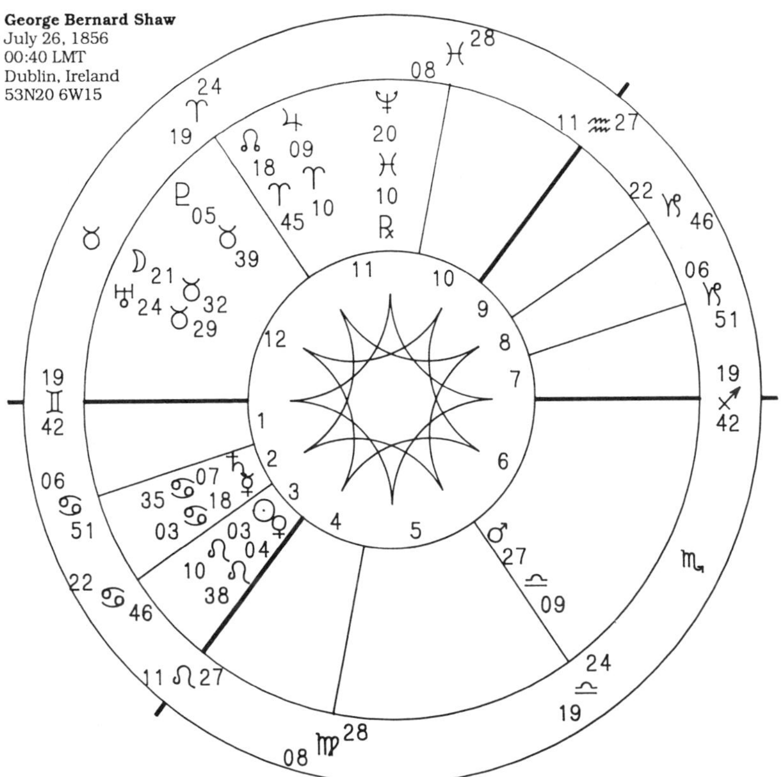

which he believed in his heart to be of significant value. The cosmos asks nothing more or less from other Last Quarter types.

The urge to make a mark in life represents a hard-earned flowering of the inner vision symbolized by the New Moon phase. Because this vision springs from the inner self (perhaps as Rudhyar suggests, in response to a cosmic need), it portrays something which is uniquely personal and of universal consequence. It is imperative for Last Quarter types to have rewarding, self-expressive careers, not merely jobs, and to work hard. Perhaps this need developed from a healthy response to an early home situation in which they were dismissed as incapable of achieving anything outstanding or the parents were ignorant of social consciousness beyond simply earning a living. The desire to become a professional, the boss, an expert, an enduring authority or a person of distinction worthy of public attention can result (see Chapter 2). Others respond differently and are infatuated with becoming "somebody." Prestige, money, power or associating with influential people can become more important than developing competence at tasks.

Under this phase, nurturing attention must be given to the foundations beneath the public facade. Emotional security, home and family matters must provide sound support for any career climb. Purpose must be found not only in making a name for oneself, but in believing that the vocation (or avocation) is making a useful contribution. For this reason, some Last Quarters can grow dissatisfied with one career direction and seek another able to provide enhanced authority or influence. Sometimes this can be accomplished by adding a new dimension to the current vocation or by taking a different approach to it.

To be fulfilling, the occupation must permit one to exercise authority or to be left in charge at times, for example, when the boss is away. Working closely under the supervision of another might prove difficult when independent decision-making is disallowed. A commitment to serve or to assist others must be included. Any range of job can be suitable, from the conventional, the scientific to the aesthetic, provided this service orientation exists.

Last Quarter types who dodge responsibility or fail to develop their competency are likely to experience career setbacks or other unpleasant manifestations associated with trait 10. Loneliness could result from isolationist tendencies. Some take short cuts or turn to crime, the fast buck or various forms of usury rather than make constructive social contributions. When purely personal ends are sought, however, problems can result. People can be on top of the heap and plummet when insufficient attention is given to how their activities impact others, or when personal needs are neglected in favor of getting ahead. A more mature, responsible and committed approach to life is required and the cosmic order is completely disinterested in excuses for selfish, irresponsible behavior.

Some Last Quarter types measure their occupational achievements against society's popular values. They convince themselves that they should participate in a grandiose endeavor and fail to find purpose in occupations of lesser magnitude. A realistic self-concept is vital under this phase, however, because the desire to be "somebody" can be strong. Certain individuals do not recognize their limitations and develop grandiose expectations. They seek "impossible dream" occupations. Although such dreams have been known to come true, they require commitment, time and enduring effort before they materialize.

Other Last Quarter people live in a self-conscious fish bowl, hamstrung by a limited self-concept. A fear of failure or worthlessness can swell to such proportions that competently establishing themselves in a career can be negated. When the self-concept is undermined in this manner, it tends to limit the energy available to develop competence. At rock bottom, a lack of effort and an unrealistic or limited self-image are responsible for most career difficulties. However, these factors most apply to Last Quarter individuals and others with highlighted trait 10.

Famous personalities with Last Quarter Moons: Kareem Abdul-Jabbar, David Carradine, Larry Flynt, Hermann Goering, Victor Hugo, Mick Jagger, Carl Jung, Evel Knievel, Mario Lanza, Fritz Perls, George Bernard Shaw, Natalie Wood

Balsamic Phase - Trait Pair 11/12 - Level II

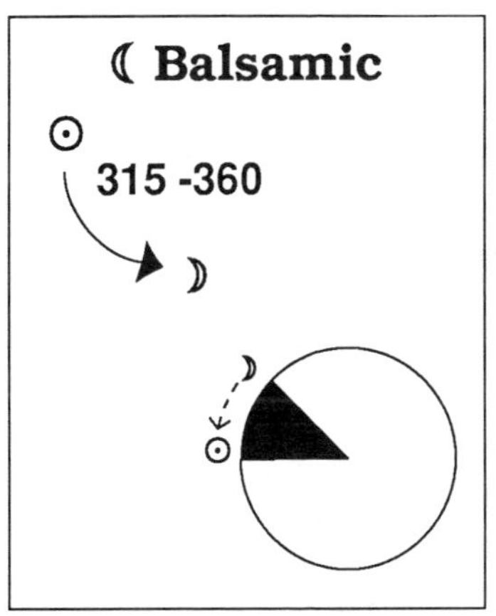

As the Last Quarter closes and the Balsamic phase begins, one is exposed to a form of consciousness little understood in the everyday world. Without realizing it, the Balsamic type must function through a collective spirit of vast, often ill-defined, proportions. The "job" in life is to be totally committed to developing an aspect of self, not merely for profit or recognition, but as an ambassador working through a humanitarian concern. Something new is meant to be brought out through the individual, be it an invention, art form or a new perspective on the profession. The difficulty associated with this phase is to strive and develop this "something" with a minimal concern for the prestige that might result. Egocentric aims and trait 12 rarely mix with positive consequences.

This is a difficult perspective to comprehend, especially since society's motto could be "What's in it for me?" The Balsamic phase runs counter to this line of thinking and urges group consciousness on an intangible "spirit" or soul level. To add to the confusion, Balsamics frequently enter the world with diffused identities and often are overly sensitized to the conditions surrounding the early home environment. This can be true whenever trait 12 is emphasized in a chart. It is initially difficult to separate self from the not-self and to develop a solid, realistic sense of identity.

Much of the out-of-this-world sense of self can be traced to the early home and the individual's response to it. Nothing was as it appeared to be and proper emotional grounding may have been difficult for some to achieve. One or both parents may have been unusual, sickly or not like other parents. They could have been eminently successful, avant garde, emotionally unbalanced, or pursued strange lifestyles or out of the ordinary interests. Nurturing was unavailable and inconsistent, or sudden, mysterious disruptions undermined the family structure. Some Balsamics felt alien within the family circle, as if a mistake had occurred and they had been dropped off on the wrong planet. For many, this feeling can be carried on throughout a lifetime, usually with only a subliminal awareness of it, so that achieving a sense of belonging and solidarity can be difficult. The vocation often serves as a vehicle to attain a stronger definition of self.

Some Balsamics felt vaguely responsible for alleviating the family's problems. These types respond more to the watery, trait 12 side of this phase (see Chapter 2 for suitable vocational outlets or approaches). However, without a proper balance of objectivity, symbolized by airy trait 11, the extremes of a doormat/victim complex or savior of the world can take hold. Others, unable to deal with sad family circumstances, deny their existence, and wish to get as far away as possible. They favor the trait 11 side of the phase (see Chapter 2). However, without a proper infusion of compassion and understanding, aloof intellectualizing or a coldly critical attitude toward others often emerges. While these people might think they have escaped the past, denied emotional roots come back to plague them as sudden, mysterious career or relationship upheavals, until compassion is established.

Both responses to Balsamic consciousness can be alleviated through self-understanding or insightful therapeutic intervention, although typically the latter personality is most resistant. But there is always method to the seeming madness of the cosmos, even though it is not always easy to fathom. As discussed under the Disseminating phase, emotional pain and loss are among the circumstances that drive people to look within for answers. Through the process, the real self just might make an appearance. Why most people do not learn equally well through experiences of joy is a shame, but without the lows, the heights may not be known.

More than anything, Balsamics are haunted by an inner calling to do or achieve "something" in life and these vague longings nag them until confronted. The tricky part is properly interpreting the longings. Some Balsamics mistakenly sense them as a mysterious calling to fame or a TV lifestyle of being rich and glamorous. For others, a vague sense of self coupled with an equally vague sense of "destiny" is intolerable. Rather than tapping the inner self, they force the issue and assume a "somebody" role to play in life. Such Balsamics can become doctors, lawyers or metaphysical gurus more from a need to have an identifiable occupational role than from love of the work. A messiah complex can develop as a defense against groundlessness. A realistic self-image and a commitment to persistent, responsible effort are essential under this phase. It is a mistake to assume the call to destiny manifests of its own accord; digging must be done and accomplishments quarried much like heavy rocks from a deep canyon.

When the longings of the inner self are denied expression and people do not live up to the responsibilities of the Balsamic "job," eventually the rug gets pulled out. The universe does not support the career or the false identity. Individuals may be left angry, frustrated and confused over why life is not working out as planned. The plans, however, could have been all wrong from the beginning and the approach to the career could be faulty because contact with the real self has not been made. Aspirations may need to be reviewed for their reality quotient. More likely than not, such individuals have grown too involved with the worldly aspects of achievement or have failed to exert sufficient effort. They flounder, fail and become lost at sea.

Those true to the inner calling know no limits to vocational accomplishments. They are frequently surprised by the heights they attain since, initially in life, they battled with feelings of inadequacy. Those who emerge intact from the ordeal display inventiveness, originality, creativity and commitment to perfecting their skills. Because they wish to contribute to a greater whole, these Balsamics frequently participate in organizations or groups where shared ideals or individualized efforts are pooled to enhance the standards of a profession.

These in-phase types grow to be inner-directed often with a unique facility for their work. Though group-conscious, in spirit or action, most tend to be individualistic and refreshingly open to new experiences or people. Interest in mastering the profession often develops, not only to see what can be accomplished, but to bring this believed-in "something" into existence for the benefit of the greater whole. Maintaining humility under this phase, however, is a key to self-mastery. All kinds of delusions can invade consciousness once resourceful capabilities begin to be tapped.

The most suitable occupations for Balsamics are based on the beliefs, theories or perspectives that eventually become important to them. (Refer to Chapter 2 for more inclusive discussions on traits 11 and 12 and to Chapter 5 for this trait pair.) Inspiration, a cause, highly developed skills, creativity, the caring instincts or intuition must be visible on the job. A sacrifice of time and energy in the service of others may need to become part of the vocational expression; however, time also must be set aside to work or be alone. Ego drives and even relationships may have to take a second seat to the work performed.

Balsamics who "manufacture" identities tend to experience a difficult life. Longings and yearnings never go away and "something" is experienced as missing. Outlandish notions of superiority can interfere with proper functioning (also possible whenever traits 11 and 12 are highlighted in the chart). The world gets viewed as if through the wrong end of a telescope and at the worst, the pipe dreamer, ne'er-do-well or paranoid isolationist can result.

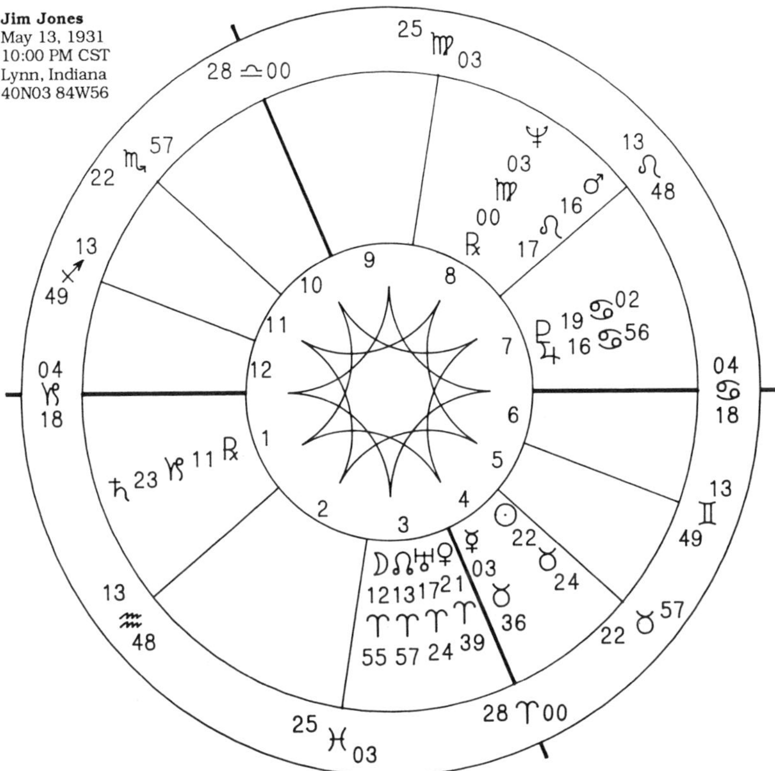

Jim Jones, the leader of The People's Temple who was responsible for the mass suicide of his congregation, was born under the Balsamic phase (11/12). He is a fitting example of its unpleasant possibilities. Venus (2 and 7) anticulminates in a secondary zone and represents, among other possibilities, an ability to handle people effectively. The combined Venusian qualities and Balsamic symbolism suggest the potential for an uncanny perceptual sense of others. Saturn (10) in the first house represents the handle of a dynamic bucket pattern (5) and suggests one who needs to lead and aggressively conduct vocational matters in a mature, responsible and realistic fashion. When all of this symbolism is considered in light of the consciousness intended to evolve under this phase, the potential for a heightened responsibility to others can be discerned. For a time Jones was able to effectively carry this load and was undoubtedly of benefit to many people early in his career.

However, his troubled personality could not adequately manage Balsamic longings and once he identified with God, he got carried away.

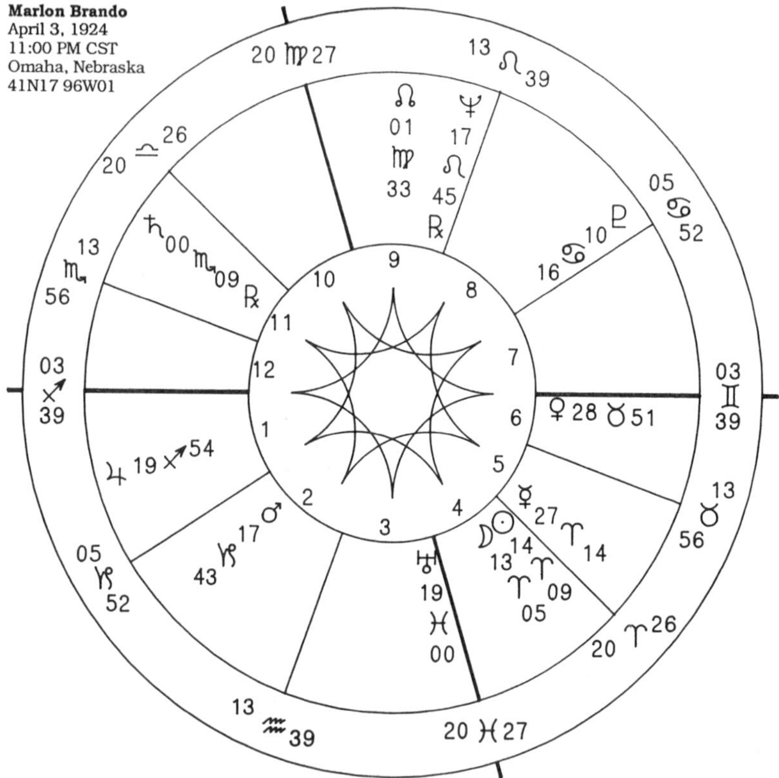

Oscar winner Marlon Brando also was born under this phase, with Venus in the secondary zone under the Descendant. He has been able to channel his talents along more creative, productive lines. Trait 11 is pronounced in his chart and is repeated through his splash pattern and angular Uranus located in the third house side of the IC. The plight of the American Indian aroused him and he used his influence to draw public attention to this cause.

Whenever a brick wall or vocational purposelessness is encountered, Balsamics must think carefully about what it all might mean. Perhaps one is on a wrong path or is not working up to true potentials; one may be living a false life or looking at the world through a false perspective. A complete review of who one is may have to be made to establish appropriate career directions. A longing for greatness, fame, the glamorous limelight or victim/savior complexes frequently are responsible for steering these types off course.

Famous personalities with Balsamic Moons: Steve Allen, Jack Anderson, Marlon Brando, Phyllis Diller, Anatole France, Uri Geller, Robert Hand, Jim Jones, Immanuel Kant, Pat Nixon, Vincent Price

References

1. Rudhyar, Dane, *The Lunation Cycle*, Berkeley, California: Shambhala Publications, 1975, p. 48
2. Robertson, Marc, *Not a Sign in the Sky But a Living Person*, Seattle, WA: Astrology Center of the Northwest, 1975
3. Busteed, Marilyn et all, *Phases of the Moon*, Berkeley, California: Shambhala Publications, 1974
4. Rudhyar, Dane, *The Lunation Cycle*, Berkeley, California: Shambhala Publications 1975, p. 54

CHAPTER EIGHT

THE SIGNS OF CONSCIOUSNESS

The Moon phases portray an evolutionary process which requires maturation beyond childhood dilemmas and egocentric motivation. Because human beings possess different **types of consciousness**, or ways of perceiving and ordering reality, the ancient mariners of astrology devised the **elements and the qualities**. Their distribution in a chart reveals additional conditions surrounding consciousness and rewarding vocational direction.

A distinction must be made between the terms "consciousness." and "personality". Consciousness represents a capacity to be aware of oneself as a thinking, feeling being, to know what one is doing at any given moment, and why, as well as to be aware of what is happening around one. It is the human capability to perceive and order one's inner and outer realities. Different people possess different degrees of consciousness about their own behavior and existences. Some people can be highly objective (or conscious) about what they are doing and why, while others are less aware or even out of touch with who they are, why they do what they do or how their behavior impacts others. People also perceive life in different ways. Some people order their sense of life around tangible, provable realities (an earth-type consciousness). Others perceive reality through their feeling states (water consciousness) and react accordingly. Still others view life in terms of how they can act upon it (fire consciousness), while other types assess reality through ideas and concepts (air).

Personality, as defined here, refers to habitual patterns and qualities of behavior demonstrated by an individual's **physical**, emotional and mental activities. A person can possess a certain way of acting on reality (personality) which also reflects the degree of consciousness from which that person functions. For example, an individual might be an assertive personality and function through a high, mid-level or low level of consciousness about the use and impact of those self-assertive drives.

The qualities and elements traditionally are said to denote certain characteristics when found in a condition loosely termed a "lack of" or a "preponderance." Many astrologers consider two to three planets appearing in signs of the same quality or element to be a sufficient representation of that factor, fewer than two is said to constitute a lack of that factor, while five to six or more is said to signify a preponderance.

The term "lack," however, may be a misnomer because in some minds it implies not merely a shortage or deficiency (terms which are judgmental), but often the absence of something which, in the language of astrology, is not possible. Because planets and houses also correspond to various elements and qualities, (i.e., Mars is a cardinal fire planet; the first house is a cardinal fire house), it is illogical to say a chart lacks a type of consciousness (based on signs) if the corresponding planets or houses are highlighted or if the corresponding planet makes close aspects.

For example, few practitioners would dispute that the Moon or Neptune is a "water" planet. Suppose water signs are unoccupied in a chart, but the Moon or Neptune appears in Level I. Water-related occupations (trait 4) are likely to be rewarding, given the presence of other Level I factors, because the person possesses strong water-type needs, drives and attitudes. **Level I chart positions, especially the G-planets, always take precedence over the "lack" of a quality or element when this factor is defined by sign only.** (A demonstration will follow.) Every sign also appears somewhere in a chart, even if that sign is not tenanted by planets. For example, earth signs on the cusps of earth houses denote an earthy consciousness about those areas of life. How can one "lack" something if it is present somewhere?

This concept of a "lack" may not be fair for other reasons. One concerns the entire judgmental nature associated with such terms as weakness, lack, deficiency, shortage, etc. Astrologers often are enamored of black-and-white concepts, but consciousness is not the most well-charted terrain. So who honestly can say that one type of perspective on reality is needed more than another or, **especially**, specify how much is needed? People merely possess different ways of perceiving, ordering and acting on life. Additionally, it is **very** common to find charts in which less than two planets appear in signs of the same element. Out of the 487 personal charts used for this text, 465 demonstrate less than two planets in signs of the same element! There is a reason for this.

If one considers there are only ten planets, and only four elements, two-and-a-half planets per element can be considered the "average." This is stated simplistically because the author is not statistically conversant. Due to the duration of the Neptune and Pluto orbits, their length of stay in particular signs probably influences the situation above and beyond simply stating that 2.5 is the "average." At certain periods in time, some charts are likely to demonstrate greater or lesser incidence of preponderance or lack by sign. However, if the average is so close to a "lack," then lack of an element by sign becomes the norm. It is normal to be deficient in at least one type of consciousness, if only sign placements are considered. The picture significantly alters for preponderances. From the identical sampling of charts, 89 demonstrate more than five planets in signs of the same element which reduce to 36 charts when six or more planets are considered.

Because signs also consist of three different qualities, three planets in signs of the same quality is the average. For this reason it is less common, though by no means rare, to find charts "lacking" a quality. Again, out of the 487 charts used, 121 demonstrate lack of a quality by sign. Because there are three qualities, as opposed to four elements, the incidence of a preponderance by quality escalates. From the sample, 147 charts show more than five planets appearing in signs of the same quality.

Because planets, houses and signs consist of elements and qualities, all of these chart factors should be assessed to arrive at realistic perspectives on element and quality distribution. Using Bob Dylan's chart, here is a demonstration that visually assesses what planets interrelate with which elements and qualities.

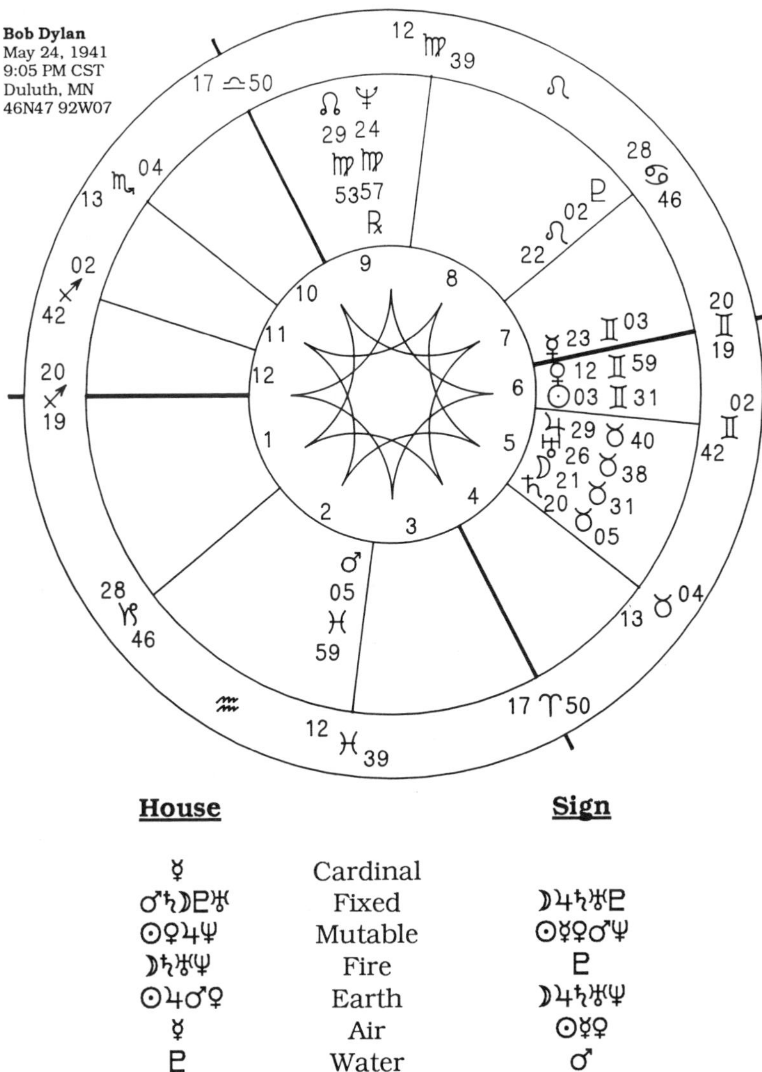

House		Sign
☿	Cardinal	
♂♄☽♇♅	Fixed	☽♃♄♅♇
☉♀♃♆	Mutable	☉☿♀♂♆
☽♄♅♆	Fire	♇
☉♃♂♀	Earth	☽♃♄♅♆
☿	Air	☉☿♀
♇	Water	♂

If only sign placements are considered, Dylan would be considered preponderantly earth-bound. Notice too that Saturn in Taurus leads (Level I) in a bucket pattern and closely conjuncts the Moon in Taurus – additional factors which support an earth predominance. However, earth as a preponderant element is not traditionally known for imaginative insight and vision (see earth later in this chapter), although Dylan is known for this. Called the "Robert Burns of the '60's pop revolution," this singer/songwriter deluged the music scene with poetic songs of protest.

But earth has been assigned to trait 2 in this book. Although this trait can correspond to individuals who select jobs for their ease or remunerative qualities, it also is significant of those whose occupations need to reflect personal values and rewarding talents. Venus (2 and 7) sets just under the Descendant in a secondary plus zone and is significant of writers and performing artists. Additionally, other factors in Dylan's chart counter a traditional interpretation for an overload of earth. Among these are the Balsamic Moon phase (11/12), a trait pair repeated in the close trine between Uranus and Neptune, the close square between Mercury and Neptune (3/12), a trait pair repeated through Pisces on the third house cusp, and the fact that aspirational Jupiter, revolutionary Uranus and visionary Neptune mingle with the earth element portion of the above schema. Considering all these factors, Dylan's chart is not as earth-bound as the sign placements alone might suggest.

Notice the complete lack of cardinality in his chart, if only the signs are considered. No cardinal sign is tenented and only Mercury appears in a cardinal house. But Dylan could hardly be accused of lacking initiative or other cardinal traits. This is because Mars (1) represents the bucket (5) handle in Level I of his chart and closely squares the Sun (5). Sagittarius also rises (1/9). Lack of cardinality is easily offset by such factors, when only sign placements are noted. Besides, lack of cardinality only indicates that fixity and/or mutability are going to predominate. Both are strongly represented in Dylan's chart and life.

When assessing the thrust of a chart in this manner, it is most important to determine what quality or element predominates, especially if any obvious emphasis is involved. Vocational satisfaction is likely to surround its related trait or trait pair. For the career-troubled personality, however, preponderant or diminished features may be a clue that the symbolized approaches and perspectives must be developed or more adequately integrated into the vocational expression.

The Qualities

CARDINAL - TRAIT 1 (LEVEL II)

Arroyo[1] writes the cardinal signs "correlate with the principle of action in a definite direction." In essence, then, cardinality can be considered a trait 1 related factor, given that its nature is similar to the Mars personality function. This is not to suggest that the elements do not modify the nature of cardinality. Among them, fire is the most similar to the cardinal quality and, for this reason, Aries (Mars' ruling sign) represents the epitome of cardinality: direct, self-initiating and self-assertive. Any emphasis on this sign (planet or trait) suggests an urgent need to express the self, to lead and do or, in another vein, a need to develop the sense of selfhood and identity.

Water is the least compatible with cardinality. Water's nature is to move along with the flow, take the course of least resistance, and not be pushed. Consequently, the water in Cancer (or the Moon) can **seem** to "wash away" or undermine cardinal urges, especially in the vocational world. **But this lack of drive results when individuals fail to develop a sense of personal adequacy (4)**. While some people with an emphasis on this sign, related house or planet may prefer to hide in a shell, once personal adequacy is achieved, cardinal motivations and ambitions emerge, along with a desire to expand career horizons (see First Quarter Moon in Chapter 7).

Cardinal Predominance

A definite cardinal emphasis, when adequately channeled, could represent a heightened success drive urging one to make a statement in life at all costs. There could be pronounced needs to be a leader, at the forefront of one's occupation. The work environment would have to be exceptionally fast-paced and the job would need outlets for short-term goals, projects or deadlines requiring immediate bursts of mental or physical energy. The ability to handle crisis situations as they arose also could be enhanced. This can be a plus in the business world, although any job requiring trait 1 characteristics or approaches could be appropriate (see Chapter 2).

However, an emphasis on cardinality does not always exhibit as a stick of dynamite. In some cases, nervousness or hyperactivity is pronounced, a reason why the vocation must keep the person active and involved. When these factors are not adequately channeled, the individual could go overboard, be too hasty, rash and leap first without thinking. Ill-considered career decisions can be made, frequently based on a "high school" idealism. Such outcomes would depend on how the stabilizing features in the chart, especially Saturn and the earth element and houses, were being expressed.

The work history is bound to tell the story. An emphasis on cardinality tends to correlate with periodic life crises. This especially is the case when emphasized trait 1 needs are denied appropriate expression– and that includes sexual needs. The career could be moving along when something flares up like a bonfire to change the situation. When Aries predominates, the change can be consciously self-initiated. When self-assertive drives are dammed up, however, an unexpected problem in the personal life or an accident, not only a desire for new adventure, could be responsible for the change. When Cancer, Libra or Capricorn predominate, conscious intention is less likely to underlie such flare-ups. Because the cardinal motivation seeks outlets, even amid the more security-oriented water and earth elements, crises often arise due to a failure to take action or an attempt to live with an unpleasant status quo. Such people often view others, not their own blocked motivations, as responsible for the situation. In the case of Libra, unconscious expectations of, or unrealistic demands on, others can lead to dissension or crises.

An emphasis on cardinality works best when it is directed through strong vocational interests. This can help keep individuals on track. Achievement, recognition and other trait 1 needs or outlets are a must. Otherwise, energy tends to dam up, reach an overload point and require a crisis to correct the imbalance.

Diminished Cardinality

According to Carter[2], lack of cardinality equates with "lack of initiative and lethargy." However, this statement cannot be taken at face value. Too many factors in a chart overshadow a decreased cardinal representation by sign. Among these are Mars as a G-planet, Mars or Saturn in a cardinal house (especially the first or tenth), cardinal houses occupied, close Mars aspects, a New Moon, an emphasis on fire or a number of other cardinal-related traits (especially trait 1). Only when such factors fall completely into the background of a chart does a diminution of cardinality suggest that motivation may be lacking to advance through a career because little desire for recognition, leadership or achievement through one's own efforts may exist. More important than the lack of cardinality, however, is that another quality is likely to be pronounced and, therefore, is more important vocationally.

Here are famous people whose charts show less than two planets in cardinal signs. Their occupational achievements do not reflect traditional interpretations for a "lack" of cardinality because cardinal traits are otherwise represented in their horoscopes (although only the obvious ones are listed here).

Muhammad Ali (see chart page 105): Mars as a G-planet, Venus in the seventh house opposite the Ascendant, three other planets occupy the tenth house, including a G-planet Saturn, New Moon; relatively balanced among qualities although mutability predominates.

Nicolaus Copernicus: Mars as a G-planet (located eleven degrees from the Descendant into the sixth house), fire planets dispersed among the four cardinal houses, including Saturn in the tenth; mutability predominates.

Robert De Niro: Moon, Saturn and Venus as G-planets, Mars closely aspecting the MC, fire planets Sun and Jupiter in fire signs, one cardinal house occupied, Full Moon; mutability predominates.

Bob Dylan (see chart page 319): Mercury in cardinal seventh house opposed the Ascendant, four planets in fire houses, one planet in a fire sign, Sun closely squares Mars, bucket (fire) pattern; mutability predominates.

Leontyne Price: Mars as G-planet, Saturn as tenth house

G-planet, six other planets dispersed among remaining cardinal houses, including Sun and Jupiter in the first, First Quarter Moon; cardinality actually predominates.

Barbra Streisand (see chart page 127): Mars and Venus as G-planets, Sun and Mercury in the first house, First Quarter Moon; fixity predominates.

Cardinal predominance: Steve Allen, Jack Anderson, Ingrid Bergman, Marlon Brando, Albert Camus, Johnny Carson, Sean Connery, Ram Dass, Clint Eastwood, Jim Jones, Suzanne Somers

FIXED - TRAIT PAIR 2/8 - LEVEL II

The fixed quality symbolizes a stabilizing factor which functions to sustain efforts in the working world. Perhaps the concept of "containment" is most descriptive because fixity holds back the urges of the elements for purposes of development and tangible production. In the process, a motivational tension is created.

Of all the elements, earth is the most comfortably contained and Taurus (trait 2) represents the epitome of the fixed nature: tenacious and enduring, yet easygoing. Any emphasis on this element, sign or trait suggests a need to secure tangible assets or less tangible factors such as self-worth and talents. One or both underlie the fixed motivation, the reason trait 2 has been assigned to this quality.

Fixity, however, poses difficulty for the remaining elements. Each is resistant to containment because control is required to hold back their urges. Decidedly fixed personalities are usually self-contained, determined of purpose and willfully desirous of making life bend to their rules. Many have staunch opinions and believe their values, concepts or causes are the only "right" ones. When ego drives are motivated by such strict principles, power and control issues become their kissing cousins. For this reason, trait 8 also has been assigned to fixity. Control, sex appeal, money, power or intense encounters with powerful personalities often have roles to play at work for those preponderating in this quality.

Water can respond to containment, as shown in the enduring stamina and reliability of Scorpio. However, without fresh input, even water that is contained too long can stagnate. Hence Scorpio's water needs to purge and eliminate old, outworn ego concepts to make room for something new to be contained. Because fixity urges containment, while water can endure it for only so long, an emphasis on trait 8 in a chart can correspond to deep-seated, turbulent undertows in the personality. The needs of the fixed nature battle it out with water urges.

Air is the least responsive to containment. Although Aquarius symbolizes fixed air, its very keywords— freedom-loving, sudden changes, sudden upsets, etc.— seem to belie the traditional concepts associated with this quality. But just as the atmosphere surrounding Earth moves and seems "free," it is nonetheless "contained." Trait 11 types often seek groups in which to freely circulate and, no matter how vast the group, it still represents a definable, containing structure. Trait 11 keywords describe the tensions that result when a conscious appreciation of life (air) resists containment. It is what happens to a rubber band when stretched too far; it "suddenly" snaps.

Fixed air (Aquarius) symbolizes a need related to rational consciousness. To develop the "mind" (air), stabilization (resistance to change or new input) is required to "fix" attention on an idea long enough to thoroughly develop its potentials. Without some resistance to new input, as symbolized by fixity, concepts cannot be grasped beyond a basic factual level. But the rational intellect requires fresh input on occasion from new ideas and new methods. Without new "air," it too will stagnate. A proper balance needs to be maintained between the divergent urges of fixity and air, otherwise, like a pressure cooker, something is likely to change suddenly. The air urge motivates a decision to "suddenly" drop the subject matter, to make room for something new and stimulating to be contained, or the fixed component closes off new input, in this instance through an overattachment to one's point of view.

The situation is reminiscent of Harry Truman's comment about people who consider themselves to be "experts:" they are afraid to learn anything new for fear of no longer being expert. And while determination of purpose and enduring self-will (fixity) are vital to the mastery of complicated subject matter, or to produce anything of a lasting nature, the dark side of fixity can be blind, overbearing ego attachments which stubbornly maintain opinionated outlooks.

All the fixed signs share such die-hard ego attachments and the selfish, opinionated, dark potential of fixity. Leo is no exception. Fire is an element equally resistant to containment. It burns up or uses itself up, and, of all the elements, it needs the containment principle of fixity. The fire-breathing, heat- and light-giving Sun is nature's grandest display of fixed fire, and all of life hinges on the consistency of this force. Without humankind's ability to harness, control and fix fire for purposes of warmth, cooking and light, the power of life would still be in the hands of the gods.

Leo symbolizes that dynamic energy and the expression of identity (fire) must be contained long enough so that something can be made to prosper. While pure fire may thrive on change, in its fixed form fire needs to be focused, concentrated and have limits set on its drives. However, because fire can burn only so long, it must have new input in the form of new activities which can capture and hold the attention. For this reason, trait 5 people do not thrive on drastic changes as much as on new input through progress and a steady growth of influence. It is like throwing new logs into a fire. Just as fire burns up, trait 5 types seek promotion, advancement and excitement, and will bring new things into the vocation to further it, rather than seek a completely new line of work. However, when the "heart" is no longer involved in the job, the fire component of this trait prompts changes so that something new can be contained and just as eagerly burned.

Air and fire people need the freedom to choose and, unlike earth and water types, will opt for a vocational change, provided it is when, where and how it suits their interests. They dislike change when it is forced on them from the outside. However, because air and fire are freedom-oriented, such people are likely to accept forced changes in their careers or to do something when vocations get dull. But trait 5 individuals also can resist change due to stubborn pride, image concerns, financial reasons or out of sheer laziness. Similarly, certain trait 11 types can persist in boring job routines when their air needs for new input are repressed.

Fixed Predominance

The more fixity is pronounced, the greater the potential to be thorough and persistent over the long haul. Predominately fixed types often are strongly determined to succeed. Because convictions run high, a commitment to a vocation can be made at a young age. They potentially are well-suited for projects or occupations which take a long time to mature or require them to endure pressure. They tend to stay on track with heels dug in. This has pluses and minuses. On the plus side, especially when a planet like Mars or Jupiter appears in the Level I, go-getting career drives potentially can be backed up by the persistence and follow-through of fixity. On the minus side, strongly fixed types can hang on to certain job ruts long beyond the misery point and still resist making changes or bringing in new input, for example, in the form of returning to school. This is most obvious through earth and water which favor financial security and/or resist vocational changes due to doubts surrounding talents, worth and the ability to succeed.

Control issues often emerge in the employment picture and frequently represent factors dating back to early childhood. Perhaps too many controls were experienced and these individuals learned ways to block out disturbing interferences. Or, perhaps parents were so lacking in control that such children came to overvalue this factor in life. This habit of perceiving and relating to others can be difficult to break and can make predominantly fixed people appear somewhat inscrutable. Some shield themselves with a dark mysteriousness, often with strong sexual overtones. Others use a light, airy or jovial exterior to keep people at arm's length (see Chapter 2, trait 8 for the discussion on control tactics). What appears to be willful determination or a stubborn nature in many cases may be a need to maintain control and to protect themselves from what they perceive to be the harassment of outside influences or others' attempts to control, use or manipulate them.

As a consequence, a confrontation with perceived or imaged limits underlies a predominantly fixed nature. Much of their purposeful determination stems from this. Frequently power struggles or clashes of will take place on an overt or a covert level. Fixed individuals are naturally territorial and are easily angered over interference with their methods. As bosses they can experience difficulty delegating authority, often insisting on doing it their way. As employees, they can be hardworking and determined or willful depending on whether or not they respect the boss's decisions.

Although the containment of fixity can be a source of security, it also can lead to **complacency**. Change takes energy and some fixed types can drain themselves in their attempts to ward off imagined influences. While earth may appear to function adequately in such a static state, the other elements do not. It eventually leads to stagnation or the tension grows to the point that the psyche forces unwanted changes. This is most obvious in the case of trait 11, when air needs for new stimulation no longer can be contained.

Mostly fixed personalities need to know when to set limits on their tendency to set limits because they can set themselves up to be boxed in vocationally in the later years. This is especially true of Scorpio and Taurus, although it can apply to Leo and Aquarius when fire and air needs go unrecognized. It is difficult to counsel them out of unrewarding job ruts or to elevate their skills. They may procrastinate and wait for some outside force, like a tide moving out, to pull them along in a new direction. Some unconsciously wait around to get fired. It is a way to avoid taking responsibility for their lives, just in case the change does not lead to improved conditions or asks more of them than they care to give. But life is a process of change and offers no guarantees— something many fixed types prefer not to be the case.

Diminished Fixity

Carter[3] has written that a lack of fixity correlates with an "absence of principle, ballast and consistency," but this is hardly the rule. Saturn and the earth houses and signs also symbolize stabilizing, grounding factors in a chart. Pluto or Saturn in a plus zone, or in close, major aspects to the personal planets, easily offsets a lack of fixity by sign. Even if these factors fall into the background of a chart, it still means that cardinality or mutability predominates. These factors are much more significant of vocational needs than a diminution of fixity. The charts of the following famous people demonstrate less than two planets in fixed signs, but they do not exhibit any of the characteristics Carter suggests— because fixed traits otherwise exist in their charts.

Jack Anderson: Pluto leads a locomotive pattern, conjuncts the Ascendant and is closely squared by Saturn which is opposed to the MC, two fixed houses occupied; cardinality predominates.

Lew Ayres: Saturn as G-planet opposite the Ascendant in a secondary zone, all earth houses occupied including Mars in Scorpio in the second, Sun within six minutes of opposing the MC.

Sean Connery: Saturn as G-planet conjunct the Ascendant, four planets in fixed houses; earth predominates; cardinality predominates.

Charles Laughton: five planets in fixed houses.

D.H. Lawrence: Saturn opposes MC and squares the Ascendant, three planets in fixed houses, four planets in earth signs.

Walter Mondale: Saturn and Venus as G-planets, two earth houses occupied, Sun conjunct Mercury in eleventh house closely opposing Pluto in fifth house.

Fixed Predominance: Ellen Burstyn, Uri Geller, H.R. Haldemann, Jean Houston, Diane Keaton, John F. Kennedy, Alan Leo, Pat Nixon, Ringo Starr, Barbra Streisand, Arturo Toscanini

MUTABLE - TRAIT PAIR 3/6 - LEVEL II

Traditionally, mutability has been associated with impartial mental attitudes and such traits as versatility, changeable behavior, flexibility, adaptability and cleverness. It is innately attuned to life's changing panorama and functions through logic, reason and a certain idealism.

Mutability learns by observing other people, talking to them or reading about their lives. It is what Maritha Pottenger refers to as "vicarious" experiencing rather than participating in the thick of things. It is something like being a reporter on interview through life. When this quality is emphasized in the overall chart analysis, and stabilizing symbols are diminished, flying above the crowd might be preferred to participating in the real world (which does not measure up to a theoretical standard). A strong representation of earth could balance this out and potentially direct mutable urges along more productive lines.

Mutability correlates with an ability to step back and gain a perspective on things, especially on one's own behavior and how that impacts others. Synthesizing facts is essential to its *modus operandi*. Due to the emphasis on vicarious experience, space and freedom to circulate is another characteristic need. Commitment to one occupation, without a sufficient degree of lively input, is difficult when mutable circulating urges gear up. When grounding features of a chart fall into the background, nervousness, lack of perseverance, scattered drives, being too easily swayed, undependability or a reluctance to assume responsibility may emerge. These characteristics are not likely to be pluses in the working world.

Of all the elements, air thrives on the circulating mode. This is why Gemini (trait 3), Mercury's ruling sign, represents the epitome of mutability: mental, verbal and curious. Any emphasis on this sign, trait or element in a chart suggests needs for stimulating mental or verbal input/output and diverse social contacts. Being alone with one's thoughts is not always comforting. Restlessness is also a keynote due to eagerness for stimulation through the new, the different or the controversial. A preponderance of this quality is the most significant to consider vocationally. It correlates with an active mentality or a great deal of nervous mental energy which needs outlets on the job through trait 3 or 6 activities (see Chapter 2). When these needs are not vocationally satisfied, career changes readily ensue due to the air motivation to seek lively stimulation. For some individuals this can degenerate into job-hopping, although the behavior is often rationalized as their need to taste and experience life.

Earth's nature requires tangible production which, when combined with this quality, stabilizes circulating urges for the purpose of developing the rational intellect or skills. As a consequence, Virgo (Mercury's other ruling sign) is likely to demonstrate stability on the job more than the other mutable signs whose elements respond more freely to mutable circulation. In the process of blending with this element, however, irritation is created. Mutable urges are motivated to escape from the confines of earth. As if chaffed or gnawed at by something, the situation often surfaces in the mind as worry or pessimism or is displaced onto others in the form of criticism.

Fire is responsive to circulation, though not always productively. Its nature is to consume and burn up whatever lies in its path. When combined with mutability, fire's restless urgency to travel on and burn new ground peaks as Sagittarius (Mercury's sign of detriment). The mind takes on wings and can aspire to more knowledge or other forms of exposure, through travel, fame or telecommunications. But aspirations become flights of fancy when they are not grounded in reality. Unrealistic career goals and idealism keep such people on the run.

To an equal extent this is problematic for water, the nature of which is to flow and take the course of least resistance. Although responsive to circulating, mutability is not necessarily water's most productive mode. Water needs containment and motivated direction. Without such factors in the chart, Pisces (Mercury's other detriment sign) is free to dance in the light. It is mentally active and appreciates life through the feelings, a combination which sometimes resists logic and reason. Idealized subjective feeling states can take one even higher above the crowd, but could also leave one less attuned to harsher or more practical realities.

For this reason Pisces can represent motivations to soar intellectually or to take incredible, fantastic journeys. Without sufficient effort to ground them in reality, this can degenerate into know-it-all attitudes, escapism and pipe dreams. Great achievements, works of art or stimulating concepts can be inspired or are never produced due to a failure to develop true competence.

Mutable Predominance

All of the elements are enlivened mentally or verbally through blending with mutability. However, to be consistently productive, they require the containment of fixity in the chart. Otherwise, it is as if a little train is speeding around in people's heads, urging them to move on and making it difficult to relax. This characteristic is more obvious in people who do not express themselves through their occupations. Satisfying work (or hobbies) can smooth over many of the lesser ramifications of predominating mutability.

Pronounced mutable types seek fulfillment through being busily occupied during the the working day. Those with a developed sense of competence often seek authoritative, academic or intellectual expression through their vocations. Other mutable types take work less seriously, but need to express thoughts and judgments as part of the daily routine. Nervous disorders tend to arise when such outlets are denied vocational or avocational expression. Mental ability probably was not recognized or guided in the early home and may not have been fostered. Doubt surrounding the ability to succeed in occupations calling for judgment or brain power can exist. Such individuals can fail to recognize what line of work would be appropriate and end up searching for a "perfect" career. Due to a reluctance to accept responsibility, some do not "grow up" and can remain childlike.

Hustle-bustle, beehive environments are especially suitable for predominately mutable types, preferably with hordes of people coming and going. Freedom to circulate, to be on the go, to move about, from place to place, activity to activity or from person to person, also is needed. The more mentally engaging the activity or social contacts in the environment, the more it soothes the nerves. Sitting around with nothing to do for long stretches only leaves time for the restless mind to invent problems.

Diminished Mutability

Mutability is the most easily overshadowed of the qualities. Too many chart features exist which mitigate a lack of this quality by sign, such as Jupiter, Mercury or Neptune in Level I, or a focus on the mutable houses, the air houses or an emphasis on air. It is very difficult not to register mutability somewhere in a horoscope.

In the charts of the following famous people less than two planets appear in mutable signs, but they cannot be seen to lack mental acuity or verbal activity. The predominating quality is relied on more heavily.

Mahatma Gandhi: Mercury rises; three planets occupy mutable houses; mutable signs on mutable houses.

H.R. Haldemann: predominates in fixity; mutable angles in tight square; Mercury ruling Ascendant tightly aspects Saturn, Uranus and Neptune.

Jim Jones (see chart on page 313): Mercury in fourth house opposed to the MC and tightly trining the Ascendant and Neptune, third house heavily occupied, mutable signs on mutable houses; cardinality predominates.

Bobby Stone: mutable signs on third and ninth houses;

Mercury conjunct Jupiter sextiles the MC; air and cardinality predominate.

Mutable Predominance: Muhammad Ali, Fred Astaire, Alice Cooper, Nicolaus Copernicus, Robert De Niro, Dorothy Hamill, Jimi Hendrix, Helen Reddy, Brooke Shields

The Elements

FIRE - TRAIT 1 (LEVEL II)
The fire element can be linked with internal buoyancy, self-confidence, initiative, enthusiasm, energetic or physical action, idealism, courage, enterprise, recognition needs, risk taking, independent decision-making, learning by doing, self-assertion or leadership. Although each fire sign projects these attitudes more or less according to their qualities, for vocational purposes, fire can be abbreviated into a trait 1 attitudinal approach or need.

The Sun, Mars and Jupiter, and the first, fifth and ninth houses in the chart, also share "fire" characteristics. A "lack" of fire (by sign) easily can be offset when these planets appear in Level I, when they (or other planets) appear in the fire houses or if they are in close, major aspects to the personal planets. An emphasis on cardinality also can mitigate a "lack" of fire by sign. Additionally, Saturn in a fire sign or house can imply the suppression of fire-related characteristics, often giving the impression the element is diminished. However, it is only inhibited for lesson-teaching purposes and its vocational fulfillment can be as significant as if the fire element predominated. Also, the Sun or Moon in a fire sign can be suggestive of a fiery nature even when not backed up by other symbolism. Consequently, judgments regarding the strength or lack of fire-related needs in a chart must include all of these factors.

Diminished Fire

When the element or trait is diminished in the overall chart analysis, it may suggest that trait 1 occupations or approaches are not natural to the individual. The motivation to achieve recognition may not exist to a sufficient degree, unless trait 8 or 10 makes a strong appearance in the horoscope. Depending on which elements predominate, people may function better in other outlets which do not require the on-site, aggressive thrust or self-promotion of fire. However, if the job life is troubled, diminished fire could be a clue that this person must develop trait 1 attitudes and personality characteristics to experience a more rewarding career.

This might appear to be illogical. Why should people wish to develop characteristics that may not be natural to them? But people do not live in a vacuum. We are surrounded by a culture which values enterprise, achievement and most characteristics associated with trait 1. Those with diminished fire, or people not in touch with the fiery side of their dispositions, can feel they are out in left field. Because it is desirable for most human beings to feel they belong, societal values can be important to attaining a sense of satisfaction from life. Consequently, it is not advisable to counsel those with diminished fire **away from** jobs which require trait 1 drives. They merely have to be informed about their need to enhance those characteristics.

Work can be an excellent place to develop the self along trait 1 lines. For the person with diminished fire, a lack of self-belief is frequently behind a failure to push forward vocationally.

The lack of internal confidence, which springs from an innate love of and belief in self, tends to be missing. It can account for low job ceilings or a failure to recognize suitable career directions. The person must be willing to make an investment in self, and encouragement is needed through tangible achievement or from others. Feeling good about the accomplishments and the vocation is vital to vitalizing them.

Fire Predominance

When fire preponderates in the charts of the career-troubled, it could be a signal to more realistically integrate these needs and drives into the vocation. They could be overblown and undermine successful career functioning due to being overvalued. Acting too confidently or boastfully with an excessive need to achieve, people can attempt to go too far too fast and become discouraged when dreams fail to materialize quickly. Perhaps short cuts were taken and a minor oversight turned into a giant mishap. Predominantly fire types are self-absorbed and dream about the heights of fame. Some realistically act on their dreams and tend to be accomplishment-oriented and constantly busy with work or hobbies. Others only talk about their dreams and, without achievement and recognition, grow downcast, become reclusive or appear hypernervous and high-strung. Emotional stability can be in doubt because they fail to view themselves and their goals realistically.

This need for achievement, recognition or fame often stems from the response to the early family atmosphere or, perhaps, to one family member who tended to be achievement-oriented or achievement-depressed. In many instances, the father was absorbed in his work and did not pay sufficient attention to the predominantly fire child. Perhaps the individual was never given credit to achieve anything of merit and, consequently, was relegated to the sidelines. This especially can be the case for females with an overload of fire in the chart. (Not just the family, but our entire cultural conditioning encourages women to block their fire sides and project them on to men. Society also encourages men to block their water sides— and project them onto women.) Career achievements can be an effort to make up for this early lack of recognition or they can be dismissed by the individual because achievement was not supported in the early life.

In other cases, the reverse was at play and too much may have been expected of the person too early in life. Early failures to live up to familial expectation can create a hyperreaction when it comes to achieving later in life. Recognition can become an overly valued career need or a fear of failing can keep people from striving to get ahead.

This is the major problem with which a preponderance of fire tends to correlate. The need to achieve and gain recognition can be paramount. Without realistic striving toward a purposeful goal, and a degree of achievement along the way, a sad sack disposition or a fantasy life may occur. People invent imaginary identities or a barrage of talk about future activities and the "big break." In some cases, the fantasy self-image can take over and undermine an ability to see the self realistically. Others with fire predominating are more capable of channeling their drives. They are, or develop into being, self-motivated, idealistic or entrepreneurial types who demonstrate tremendous dedication to their vocations.

In the charts of the following notables, less than two planets appear in fire signs, but because fire traits are otherwise represented, they cannot be seen to "lack" this element or an achievement orientation to life.

Muhammad Ali (see chart page 105): Mars in plus zone, earth predominates.

Sean Connery: Mars and Jupiter oppose the Ascendant; earth and cardinality predominate.

Jacques Cousteau: Jupiter in plus zone, Sun in ninth, Moon in Leo, Pluto in ninth conjunct the Midheaven; mutability predominates.

Edna Ferber (see chart page 288): Jupiter in plus zone; Sun in Leo in ninth house tightly squares the Ascendant; Mars tightly sextiles Jupiter and the Midheaven; water and cardinality predominate.

Zsa Zsa Gabor: Sun, Mars, Uranus in fifth house; fixity predominates.

Vivien Leigh: Jupiter in plus zone; Mars tightly sextiles the Ascendant; Sun tightly sextiles Jupiter; earth and cardinality predominate.

Brooke Shields: Mars and Jupiter in plus zones, Sun tightly conjuncts Jupiter, mutability predominates.

Fire Predominance: Steve Allen, Marlon Brando, Ram Dass, Uri Geller, Dorothy Hamill, Heinrich Himmler, Jean Houston, Jim Jones, Alan Leo, Barbra Streisand

EARTH - TRAIT 2 - LEVEL II

A predominating or diminished representation of earth can be condensed into trait 2 characteristics and vocational needs. Saturn, Venus and the second, sixth and tenth houses also share "earth" characteristics, needs and activities. A lack of earth (by sign only) can be offset by a prominently placed or aspected Saturn, planets appearing in earth houses or fixity highlighted in the chart. Additionally, the Sun or Moon in an earth sign can suggest an earthy nature even when no other planets appear in earth signs or houses. Consequently, judgments regarding the strength or lack of earth in the chart should encompass all of these factors.

Traditionally, the earth element has been associated with practicality, stability, determination of purpose, common sense, conservative or sober attitudes and a methodical, sustaining or preserving nature which is geared to tangible production or achievement. Less positively, it is said to manifest in the form of rigidity, a stubborn conservatism, routinized approaches, overly security conscious, materialistically motivated, too matter-of-fact or closed off to alternative perspectives on reality. In general, a predominate or diminished representation of earth is a clue that the career-troubled individual may need to incorporate constructive earth characteristics into the vocation or to deal more realistically with earth's lesser manifestations to achieve a sense of fulfillment.

Diminished Earth

When earth is diminished in charts, it is often indicative of people who can be a bit lost in the vocational world, although this is not always the case. Some latch onto an interest early in life and make a career out of it. To stick with a job, however, it must be highly rewarding.

Fulfillment for some trait 2 personalities can rotate around a secure, if not substantial, income while for others, only occupations incorporating rewarding talents are suitable (see Chapter 2). Sometimes financial security will be the predominant factor behind occupational choice. However, the safe, secure job can be selected due to doubts surrounding the worth and value of other, more engaging talents. For this reason, it can take some people lacking earth longer to find satisfying work, often because they are torn between a need for a secure income and an occupation able to incorporate talents or interests.

When work is experienced as rewarding, those with diminished earth can pursue it with a purposeful vengeance, idealistic commitment and an unwavering determination to succeed. They often possess unique talents or insights. Boundary lines between what is possible or impossible to achieve tend to fade from consciousness and occupations frequently take on inspired trait 12 overtones. When emotional fulfillment is not experienced, low earthers tend to "fizzle out" in that career or change jobs frequently. It is inadvisable for them to leave one job without having secured another or to stay out of the work force too long. They can experience difficulty in motivating themselves to return. When trait 12 also is strong in the chart, job-hopping is common because they are off in vague pursuit of their vocational dreams, only stopping to work now and then to help make ends meet. When traits indicative of independence and freedom are meagerly responded to, people may be tempted to live off others.

Many low in earth experience a "stranger in a strange land" syndrome, especially about belonging in their families. Low earth may correspond to physical neglect or lack of affection in infancy and childhood. If this is true, it could account for the divergent responses people with diminished earth demonstrate. Lack of early physical attention for some may stimulate later needs to accumulate possessions, money or to experience a great deal of physical/sexual contact, while the same experiences for other people may lead to disinterest in such situations. The chart, however, cannot "reveal" which response is likely to be made.

Financial and other practical issues also may have been highlighted in the early home. A good deal of money may have been available at one time, or the parents experienced financial difficulty. Either way, money and material things tended to be an often discussed concern within the family atmosphere. This prompts some individuals to make money, while others take money matters for granted and devote themselves to their interests. Some get along with a meager income while others panic over the prospect and desperately cling to "safe" jobs, no matter how unsatisfying they may be.

Earth Predominance

Out of the 487 personal charts used for this book, only nine show five or more planets in earth signs. This small number makes sense, given that most **predominantly earth** types, by standard textbook description, are unlikely to consider astrology as a viable source of information. However, the few examples at hand seem to share this divergent manifestation between a need for a financially secure occupation versus an otherwise personally rewarding one. Not all people with a preponderance of earth respond identically.

The traditional descriptions for an overload of earth suggest that such people often lack imagination, vision or are overly concerned with material matters. While this description may be true in some cases, just as it can apply to many low in earth, it is not apparent in others, as the list of famous personalities who share the preponderance attests. Besides, people can change over time. Greene[4] has this to say about earth:

> This element has been the unfortunate victim of a body of popular opinion which suggests that matter, or the materialistic view of life, is in contradiction to, or exclusive of, spirit or the spiritualistic view of life...

She goes on to write, however, that:

> ...The entire esoteric concept of initiation is connected with Capricorn specifically and the earth signs in general because the initiate has not earned his initiation until he is able to apply the higher consciousness he has discovered to the body and the environment in which he functions as a personality. Only when the physical world is made a fitting garment or symbol of the inner spirit is his task complete.

Whether a diminishment or a preponderance of earth exists in the chart, issues related to self-worth, the management of money, time, other resources and/or talents tend to stand out and impact vocational need fulfillment. Some people place an emphasis on the remunerative aspects of work, while others emphasize the expression of their talents.

In the charts of the following famous people, less than two planets appear in earth signs. While some (not all) can be seen to lack conservatism, they could not be accused of lacking determination of purpose or tangible achievement.

Jack Anderson: exceedingly high in cardinality, diminished earth with only Mars in Capricorn and Neptune in the second house; however, Saturn tightly squares Pluto leading a locomotive pattern conjunct the Ascendant.

Albert Camus: Saturn in plus zone, all earth houses strongly occupied; cardinality predominates.

Phyllis Diller: Saturn in plus zone, second and tenth houses occupied, cardinality predominates.

Uri Geller: Saturn in plus zone conjuncts Pluto in tenth house, second house occupied, Ascendant ruler Venus in tight conjunctions with Moon and Jupiter; fire predominates.

Dorothy Hamill: Saturn in plus zone, three planets in sixth house; mutability and fire predominate.

Vivien Leigh: although Jupiter in Capricorn represents the only earth sign occupied, four planets occupy earth houses and Venus tightly trines Saturn, making earth her predominating element.

Leontyne Price: Saturn in tenth house plus zone, second and sixth houses also occupied; cardinality and fire predominate.

Earth Predominance: Muhammad Ali, Greg Allman, Carol Burnett, Glen Cambell, Chris Chubbuck, Sean Connery, Alexandre Dumas, Bob Dylan, Morgana King, Vivien Leigh

AIR - TRAIT 3 - LEVEL II

For vocational analysis purposes, a preponderance or diminished representation of air can be abbreviated into trait 3 characteristics and needs. Mercury, Venus, Uranus and the third, seventh and eleventh houses, also share "air" characteristics, needs and activities. When these planets are prominently placed or aspected or, when houses 3, 7 and 11 are occupied, the balance of air can be strongly affected. Additionally, the Sun or Moon in an air sign can suggest an airy nature, especially if in an air house, while Saturn in an air house, sign or in tight aspect to Mercury can suggest an inhibited or disciplined promotion of air-related approaches and drives. Mutability predominating also can offset a lack of air by sign. Consequently, judgments about the strength of air in a chart must include a consideration of all these factors.

Air traditionally has been associated with thought and logic, gregariousness, objectivity, intellectual expression, an alert mind, a desire to learn and exchange ideas, detachment, refinement, inventiveness, working with ideas, sociability, theory orientation or abstract points of view. Less positively, it is said to manifest as superficial, imitative, nervous, scattered, aloof, cold, restless, living in the head, gossipy and having theoretical considerations without practical application. Preponderant or diminished air in a chart may be a clue that the career-troubled individual needs to incorporate more constructive air characteristics into the vocation or more realistically deal with its lesser manifestations.

Of the four elements, air is the least predictable about its vocational expression. Famous personalities with either imbalance tend to express through their vocations trait 3 related **needs** which are by no means always "intellectual" (see Chapter 2). Some occupations require a developed capacity to think, access facts and make independent evaluations, while others do not. The amount of air in the chart cannot discern which general vocational direction will be selected or may be suitable. It all depends on the person's interest in developing the rational intellect.

Greene[5] has this to say:

> If we consider that the airy signs are connected with the enormous potential of the human mind in its creative aspect, a rather sad fact presents itself: the great majority of people are not able to utilize the potential of this element for they have not yet developed the capacity to think. A person can be born with a natal chart which shows a predominance of planets in air, but this does not necessitate his being able to express these planets in a manner which partakes of the divine nature of the creative mind. What we consider ideas are frequently opinions, and these are not the same thing; this is particularly true of ideas which become ideologies. The faculty of detachment is not often to be met; instead, we may perceive a coldness which is the result of fear, rather than true detachment, or a rigid control of the feeling nature which is based on a terror of its potency.

Air Predominance

When a chart demonstrates a preponderance of air, it does not necessarily mean individuals are likely to be overly intelligent or necessarily care about such matters. Trait 3 can swing in a number of different directions. A predominance of air basically suggests personalities who rely more heavily on an air type of consciousness to perceive reality. The ability to soar above the crowd and gain a perspective on life often is enhanced. To say that their perceptions are always accurate, however, is another story which the chart does not reveal. They could just as easily operate through the less constructive characteristics of air.

How the other elements and qualities are represented also has a bearing on the matter. A strong representation of earth, for example, suggests a potential for writing or obtaining an education when air predominates. Ideas can be put to work in practical ways. When earth appears diminished and air is highlighted, the potential to be dissociated from the physical body or the environment escalates. A diminished representation of water, coupled with a preponderance of air might highlight a strange, avant garde or estranged upbringing. A strong water presence might suggest creative use of the imagination, due to an ability to combine logic with feelings, or frustration from attempting to assess reality through such divergent types of consciousness. Because fire and air like to be up and about, this combination suggests lively, aspiring people who need to be on the go. However, without sufficient grounding, the situation could degenerate into all talk and no action when it comes to the fulfillment of dreams.

With trait 3, everything is up in the air and potentially possible, given the range of human intellect and the functions this trait symbolizes. Career-troubled individuals with an emphasis on air feel "different" and often find it difficult to relate to their own or to anyone else's feelings. Many can hold themselves at a distance behind an impenetrable wall of chatter or withdrawn silence. However, too much isolation or a failure to truly reach out to others may lead to living in the head and a loss of objectivity. The situation often can be traced to something dry or repressive about the upbringing or the parental relations. Especially when water is diminished in a chart, a predominance of air can suggest initial difficulty assessing feelings and emotions.

Diminished Air

Tradition has implied that people lacking air tend to lack reasoning power or an articulate way of expressing themselves. However, different people respond differently to trait 3 issues. Some rise to the challenge of consciousness that a preponderance or diminished representation of this element symbolizes while others do not. These different responses probably can be traced to the early home environment and the value placed on intellectual accomplishment, or independent decision-making, and how seriously one's communications were listened to in childhood.

When a child's vocal expressions are glossed over as unimportant, some individuals later develop a **need** to learn and express thoughts and judgments, verbally or on paper, to make up for this early form of neglect. Other people may shy away from occupations encompassing judgments or disciplined study. They may conceive of themselves as lacking sufficient brain power or believe their ideas are not worth the bother to express. Such individuals tend to prefer intellectually "lighter" occupations, ones which depend more on routine verbal communication, use of phone, etc., (see Chapter 2), than those expressive of too much individual thought.

In households where intellectual accomplishment was prized, again divergent responses can be in evidence. One individual may grow to value such expressions vocationally while another may fear and avoid them. Either imbalance can be the mark of the shallow dilettante, the original thinker or the lighter personality who needs fairly routine verbal exchanges or activities during the course of the day. What can be apparent, however, is the **need** for the occupation to incorporate some type of trait 3 outlet. Which outlet wholly depends on the individual and the level of interest shown in developing the mental faculties.

In the charts of the following famous people less than two planets appear in air signs. Many favor intellectual pursuits, while others express trait 3 in different ways, such as through use of the speaking voice or the wit.

Marlon Brando (see chart page 314): relatively low air, Uranus conjunct IC. Saturn in the eleventh house; cardinality and fire predominate.

Carol Burnett (see chart page 138): Mercury, ruler of third house, in Aries and Uranus in Aries in the first house– all of which suggest a tie between the expression of identity and trait 3, Saturn in Aquarius conjunct the twelfth house cusp is a singleton and handle of a bucket pattern.

Albert Einstein (see chart page 303): four planets in air houses with Uranus as bucket handle in the third house, Mercury in Aries conjuncts Saturn in the tenth house linking identity, trait 3 and career; strong representation of mutability.

Michel Gauquelin: Mercury conjunct the IC in exact quincunx to Uranus.

Jean Houston: (see chart page 116): Mercury in Aries rules both first and tenth houses and makes an exact conjunction with Saturn, thereby tying together the expression of identity with trait 3 and the vocation; fire predominates.

Jim Jones (see chart page 313): five planets in air houses, Mercury conjuncts the IC.

Isabelle Pagan (see chart page 299): Mercury exactly conjuncts Saturn; predominates in mutability and water.

Air Predominance: James Arness, Jack Benny, Ingrid Bergman, Phyllis Diller, T.S. Eliot, Lillian Gish, Thomas Huxley, Marconi, Pat Nixon, Bertrand Russell, Suzanne Somers.

WATER - TRAIT 4 - LEVEL II

For vocational analysis, an imbalance of water at either end of the scale can be abbreviated into a sensitive and vulnerable trait 4 characteristic or need. Such imbalances tend to suggest something focal about the sense of personal adequacy and relationship to the feelings.

Keep in mind that the Moon, Neptune, Pluto and the fourth, eighth and twelfth houses in the chart also share "water" characteristics. Water expression can be affected when these planets are represented in Level I, closely aspected or when these houses are occupied, especially by personal planets. Additionally, Saturn in a water sign or house can inhibit water needs and drives while the Sun and, especially, the Moon in a water sign or house can be highly suggestive of a watery nature. Judgments regarding the strength of water in a chart must include these factors.

Traditionally, the water element has been associated with the emotional, feeling, deeper psychic or imaginative realms of existence. It is said to have such characteristics as receptivity, sensitivity, compassion, self-protectiveness, intuition, vulnerability, imagination, psychic ability, impressionability, maternalism/paternalism, reserve, understanding, shyness, sympathy and the ability to enter others' feelings. Negatively, water may manifest as fear, general insecurities, overly self-protective attitudes, hypersensitivity, excessive emotionalism, escapism and being easily influenced by others (the latter due to an unclear self image). In general, a preponderant or diminished representation of water may be a clue that **the career-troubled individual** needs to vocationally develop or more realistically integrate positive water characteristics, needs or approaches to achieve a sense of fulfillment.

Diminished Water

Many people with a diminished representation of this element tend to experience unpleasant, disrupted or emotionally void early home lives, especially when air-related traits are the most pronounced in the chart. Comfortable relations with one or both of the parents could have been disturbed or loss was experienced through the death of a parent, a divorce or through pronounced personality differences. Sometimes parents could have been so highly emotionally reactive that it was difficult to understand and assimilate their behavior, while at other times they were more aloof, distant or seemingly "rational." Or, one parent may have been excessively emotional, while the other one was overly detached. These contradictory displays of feeling states often result in confusion over how to express feelings or what value should be placed on them.

Some people grow to mistrust their own feelings and intuitive judgments, or feel uneasy when acknowledging them, and prefer more logical, abstract ways of dealing with emotions. Some block any awareness of their fears or insecurities. It all depends on how painful the early life was and how individuals respond to the situation. When denial takes place, diminished water personalities can appear cold, aloof and have trouble dealing with their own as well as other people's feelings. Others lacking the water attunement respond differently, and search for love, feelings or develop their intuitive or imaginative abilities.

Water Predominance

Human beings can make different responses when confronted with early life emotional disturbances. A similar divergency can be seen in people whose charts contain stressed lunar factors, including an "excess" of water. Lundsted writes that individuals with a preponderance of this element can appear hard or cold because there is a wall of protection around them.

> There may be a fear of emotional involvements because they question whether or not they can survive the ordeal if their relationships don't work out. They may be methodical in their everyday activities because they don't want the Water to flow all over the place! On an inner level, they are tremendously sensitive, often very psychic and interested in some form of spiritual development or the occult[6].

What is at issue when either imbalance exists is the management of feelings, emotions, sensitivities, insecurities or "pain," whether that pain is experienced on the emotional or physical level. Different people respond differently and while some may choose to have a head-on confrontation with their "pain," others head off in the opposite direction. They deny their own inner fears. A preponderance or diminution of this element does not specify which response will be made. The vocational choice or approach is often revealing of how imbalanced water people elect to cope with these sensitive issues in their lives.

Some individuals confront emotional experiences through the back door and assume a maternal/paternal vocational role as a way to experience nurturing through another's reception of it. This is most often true when air or fire is emphasized. In such cases, occupations dealing with other people's feelings or providing them assistance, as in the helping, health or metaphysical professions, can be selected. Dealing with the emotions or needs of others can help people better cope with their own. Others express their feelings through creative, imaginative outlets vocationally or avocationally. Still others may seek comfort **from** emotional issues through occupations involving a strict intellectual discipline or physical activity.

For either imbalance, exceptionally strong or weak career drives can exist. Some want to make a mark in life at all costs, while others take a career course of least resistance. They maintain such jobs for financial security or out of fear of making a change. In the former instance, a career as a talented professional or business owner may be nurtured diligently as a way to establish adequacy and emotional grounding. In the latter instance, failure to achieve a solid sense of adequacy can lead to selecting the safer occupation, or it can pose difficulty in adequately sustaining oneself in the job force.

Less than two planets appear in water signs in the charts of the following famous personalities, but all do not lack water in the traditional sense; water traits are otherwise represented. Those who are decidedly diminished in this element rely on other types of consciousness through which to perceive and order reality.

Muhammad Ali (see chart page 105): Moon appears in secondary plus zone and makes a number of close aspects including a tight square to the MC; earth predominates.

Fred Astaire (see chart page 106): Moon appears in secondary plus zone, four planets in water houses, Pluto tightly opposes the Ascendant.

Max Baer: four planets in water houses, tight opposition between the Moon and Neptune make water his second-most emphasized element; air predominates.

David Bowie: Neptune rises conjunct the Ascendant, Sun and Mars in fourth house, tight conjunction between the Moon and Pluto, air least represented; earth predominates.

Carol Burnett (see chart page 138): relatively diminished water, Moon and Pluto form close sextile; earth predominates.

Albert Einstein (see chart page 303): slightly lower in air than in water; earth predominates.

Evel Kneivel: three planets in water houses, Moon and Pluto oppose the Ascendant, Mars conjuncts Neptune, air predominates and water is more represented than earth.

Barbra Streisand (see chart page 127): Venus in Pisces in twelfth house as G-planet, hemispheric singleton, and leads in bowl pattern; northern hemisphere emphasis; First Quarter Moon—all point to trait 4 representation.

Water Predominance: Garth Allen, Benvento Cellini, Honore Daumier, Edna Ferber, Zsa Zsa Gabor, Galileo, Michel Gauquelin, Victor Hugo, Rockwell Kent, Mario Lanza, Isabelle Pagan, Helen Reddy, O.J. Simpson

References

1. Arroyo, Stephen, *Astrology, Psychology and the Four Elements*, Reno, Nevada: CRCS Publications, 1978, p. 74
2. Carter, Charles E.O., *The Principles of Astrology*, Wheaton, Illinois: Theosophical Publishing House, 1963, p. 62
3. Carter, p. 62
4. Greene, Liz, *Saturn: A New Look at an Old Devil*, New York: Samuel Weiser, Inc., 1977, p. 34-5
5. Greene, p. 54
6. Lundsted, Betty, *Astrological Insights into Personality*, San Diego, California: ACS Publications, Inc., 1980, p. 57

Epilogue

Monday morning I woke up, put my feet on the floor and realized I was going to spend the day in prison. My public relations career, once rewarding, had become meaningless. The reason why completely escaped me. After all, I was "successful," a yuppy's dream come true. The year before I had been promoted to a job I thought was five years down the road. So why the empty feeling? Didn't I always want to be a business executive? (The fact I refused to carry a briefcase should have been a clue!)

Then astrology bounded into my life and public relations quickly became history. My family thought I had gone off my rocker. I gave up a Gold Coast apartment for cheaper accommodations until I could earn a decent living doing charts. Astrology gave my life new purpose...and now you know why I wrote *Planets in Work*.

Clients soon proved that this story is hardly unique, so I wanted to share their experiences. Some people needed only a little encouragement to open them up to new horizons. Others wanted a form of magic I could not supply: the assurance of success with minimal effort. That's why I included their stories. Choices in life are always up to individuals, not the "stars" or the astrologers who speak for them.

I have designed *Planets in Work* to help people make better vocational choices. Astro Computing Services has been invaluable in this endeavor. Thanks to Rique Pottenger and his programming expertise, we created a report which works out the vocational needs analysis I devised herein. It computes the important traits/pairs and refers you to the appropriate pages in the book. Adept practitioners can use the needs analysis form in the appendix or develop their own system for spotting prominent traits.

Astrology has been a tool for self-knowledge for me and, I hope, *Planets in Work* will be beneficial for you or your clients. May you satisfy your needs and fulfill your career potentials!

Best celestial wishes,

Jamie Binder

Appendix

Vocational Needs Analysis Form

This form can be used with the text. It will help identify important vocational needs, aptitudes and suitable career directions as well as factors pertinent to employment-related difficulties.

Level I = traits related to G-planets, leading, handle, focalized and other planets within six degrees of the angles; stationary planets; singletons by hemisphere; pairs related to major (orb five degrees) and minor (orb one degree) aspects.

Level II = traits or trait pairs associated with the Sun/Moon phase, Ascendant, Midheaven, their rulers by house position; the Sun, Moon, Mars, Saturn and the Ascendant/Midheaven rulers each by house and sign; the trait or trait pairs associated with a diminished representation or a predominance of a quality or element (only when an obvious imbalance registers).

Level III = traits or trait pairs associated with hemisphere emphasis, quadrant focus, chart pattern, the remaining planets by house and sign, the signs on the remaining house cusps, double cusped houses, houses ruled by Taurus and Libra, houses ruled by Gemini and Virgo, each node by house and sign; the remaining house rulers by house only.

TRAITS AND
TRAIT PAIRS:

1	2	3	4	5	6	7	8	9	10	11	12
1/1	1/2	1/3	1/4	1/5	1/6	1/7	1/8	1/9	1/10	1/11	1/12
	2/2	2/3	2/4	2/5	2/6	2/7	2/8	2/9	2/10	2/11	2/12
		3/3	3/4	3/5	3/6	3/7	3/8	3/9	3/10	3/11	3/12
			4/4	4/5	4/6	4/7	4/8	4/9	4/10	4/11	4/12
				5/5	5/6	5/7	5/8	5/9	5/10	5/11	5/12
					6/6	6/7	6/8	6/9	6/10	6/11	6/12
						7/7	7/8	7/9	7/10	7/11	7/12
							8/8	8/9	8/10	8/11	8/12
								9/9	9/10	9/11	9/12
									10/10	10/11	10/12
										11/11	11/12
											12/12

On the trait grid sheet, using one color of ink, circle the traits appropriate to Level I of the analysis. (Note the sample demonstration on page 38 in Chapter 2.) The greater the number of Level I traits that exist, the more the occupation must be able to sustain a wide variety of self-expressive skills. Using the same colored ink, circle the appropriate trait pairs of planets making aspects in light of the astrological alphabet (i.e., Moon square Midheaven = 4/10), noting only whether the aspect is major or minor and disregarding for the moment the distinction of harmonious or inharmonious. That can be considered later.

(Minor aspects can be noted as broken circles.) Although all Level I chart factors are significant to vocational needs and expression, the most significant will be circled two or, especially, more times.

Using a different color, go back over the trait pairs and circle those appropriate to Level II. Using a third color, or a pencil, circle trait pairs or traits associated with Level III. Look for the most emphasized trait pairs, especially between Levels I and II. These are highly significant of vocational needs and expression. Disregard trait pairs in Level II unless they are repeated twice or repeat a trait or trait pair from Level I or III. Level III traits or pairs may be disregarded except when repeated three times or repeating a trait or trait pair from Level I or II.

G-Planets—Primary Plus Zones

Trait ____ is significant to a rewarding occupational expression.
Trait ____ is equally significant.
Trait ____

G-Planets—Secondary Plus Zones

Trait ____, while still significant, is somewhat less so (except Mars).
Trait ____
Trait ____

Other Planets within Six Degrees of the Angles

Trait ____ is pertinent to a rewarding vocational expression.
Trait ____
Trait ____

Singleton

Trait ____ is pertinent to vocational expression.

Leading Planet

Trait ____ represents drives related to a rewarding vocational expression.

Handle Planet

Trait ____ represents drives related to a satisfying vocational expression.

Focalized Planet

Trait ____ represents drives related to a satisfying vocational expression.

Stationary Planets

Trait ____ may play a significant or problematical role in vocational expression.

Sun/Moon Phase
Trait or trait pair ____ is significant of the "job" in life.
Predominate Quality (by house & sign placements)
Trait(s) or trait pair ____ may need to be more adequately integrated into the personality, or is relied on as part of the vocational expression.
Diminished Quality (by house & sign placements)
Trait(s) or trait pair ____ may need to be developed in the personality, or is relied on as part of the vocational expression.
Trait(s) ____
Preponderant Element (by house & sign placements)
Trait ____ may need to be more adequately integrated into the personality, or is relied on as part of the vocational expression.
Diminished Element (by house & sign placements)
Trait ____ may need to be developed in the personality, or is relied on as part of the vocational expression.
Hemisphere Emphasis
Trait ____ is fundamental to a rewarding occupational expression. Failure to adequately develop or express this trait points to a flaw which underlies vocational difficulties or dissatisfaction.
Quadrant Focus
Trait pair ____ represents a dimension of experience important to rewarding occupational expression. Failure to adequately develop or express this pair could cause basic job- or career-related difficulties.
Chart Pattern
Trait(s)___ represents how overall drives can be applied for the most rewarding vocational results.
Sun – These trait pairs must be expressed through the occupation to experience it as fulfilling:
Trait pair __/5_ (Sun sign)
Trait pair __/5_ (Sun house)
Trait pair ____ (house & sign) Trait ____ (a conjuncting planet) also impacts vocational need fulfillment.
Trait ____ (Leo ruled house[s]) is a sphere of experience important to self-expressive needs.
Moon – These trait pairs must be expressed through the occupation because it signifies what is needed for emotional fulfillment:
Trait pair _4/__ (Moon sign)

Trait pair _4/__ (Moon house)
Trait pair ____ (house & sign) Trait ____ (a conjuncting planet) also impacts vocational need fulfillment.
Trait ____ (Cancer ruled house[s]) is important to emotional fulfillment.
Mars – These trait pairs are important to occupational expression because they signify how/where vocational drives specifically need to be directed:
Trait pair _1/__ (Mars sign)
Trait pair _1/__ (Mars house)
Trait pair ____ (house & sign) Trait ____ (a conjuncting planet) needs to be combined with self-assertive drives.
Trait ____ (Aries ruled house[s]) is a sphere of experience important to identity awareness and also suggests where action needs to be taken.
Saturn – These trait pairs represent how/where effort needs to be applied to develop a sense of competency and authority:
Trait pair __/10 (Saturn sign)
Trait pair __/10 (Saturn house)
Trait pair ____ (house & sign) Trait ____ (a conjuncting planet) is pertinent to this process.
Trait ____ (Capricorn ruled house[s]) is important to vocational expression and suggests where/how effort needs to be applied to develop competency or authority.
Jupiter – These trait pairs suggest how or where to reach out for expanded understanding or influence:
Trait pair __/9_ (Jupiter sign)
Trait pair __/9_(Jupiter house)
Trait pair ____ (house & sign) Trait ____ (a conjuncting planet) needs to be incorporated into the reaching out process.
Trait ____ (Sagittarius ruled house[s]) is pertinent to the reaching out process.
Ascendant
Trait pair 1/___ represents approaches and characteristics which need to be pursued for the sake of identity awareness. The same applies to any planets appearing in the first house, trait ____, trait ____.
Trait pair ____ (house & sign of Ascendant ruler) suggests avenues through which identity awareness can take place.
Trait ____ (a conjuncting planet) needs to be incorporated into self-assertive drives.

Midheaven

Trait pair ___/10 represents qualities which need to be developed and made part of the goal orientation. The same applies to any planets appearing in the tenth house, trait ____, trait ____.
Trait pair ____ (house & sign of Midheaven ruler) suggests how/where authority/competency can be developed or expressed.
Trait ____ (a conjuncting planet) is important to the development of authority/competency.

Retrograde and Intercepted Planets

Trait ____ may be delayed in terms of fully expressing itself occupationally, but can express in a highly original or inspired manner.
Trait ____
Trait ____

North Node

Trait pair ____ (house & sign) needs to be balanced and synthesized with the South Node.

South Node

Trait pair ____ (house & sign)

Sixth House – These trait pairs need to be expressed as part of daily job functioning:
Trait pair ___/6 (sign on cusp)
Trait pair ____ (sign & house of ruler) also needs to be expressed as part of daily job functioning.
Trait pair ___/6 (intercepted sign) also needs to be expressed as part of daily job functioning.
Trait pair ____ (house & sign of ruler) also needs to be expressed as part of daily job functioning.
Trait ____ is a sixth house planet, a function of personality pertinent to daily job functioning.
Trait ____ is a sixth house planet.
Trait ____ (Virgo ruled house[s]) represents a sphere of experience pertinent to daily job functioning which needs to be approached with diligence and care.

Bibliography

Arroyo, Stephen. *Astrology, Psychology and the Four Elements.* Reno, Nevada: CRCS Publications, 1978

Burmyn, Lynne. *Planets in Combination.* San Diego, California: ACS Publications, Inc., 1987

Busteed, Marilyn et al. *Phases of the Moon.* Berkeley, California: Shambhala Publications, 1974

Carter, Charles E. O. *The Principles of Astrology.* Wheaton, Illinois: Theosophical Publishing House, 1963

Carter, Charles E. O. *The Astrological Aspects.* England: Fowler, 1975

Dean, Geoffrey, editor. *Recent Advances in Natal Astrology.* Western Australia: Analogic, 1977

Dobyns, Zipporah. *The Astrologer's Casebook.* Los Angeles, California: TIA Publications, 1973

Doane, Doris Chase. *Astrology: 30 Years Research.* Tempe, Arizona: American Federation of Astrologers, 1979

Gauquelin, Francoise. *Psychology of the Planets.* San Diego, California: ACS Publications, Inc., 1982

Gauquelin, Michel. *Your Personality and the Planets.* New York: Stein and Day, 1980

Gauquelin, Michel. *Cosmic Influences on Human Behavior.* New York: ASI, 1978

Greene, Liz. *The Outer Planets and Their Cycles.* Reno, Nevada: CRCS Publications, 1983

Greene, Liz. Saturn: *A New Look at an Old Devil.* New York: Samuel Weiser, Inc., 1977

Jones, Marc Edmund. *The Guide to Horoscope Interpretation.* Wheaton, Illinois: Theosophical Publishing House, 1974

Lundsted, Betty. *Astrological Insights into Personality.* San Diego, California: ACS Publications, Inc., 1980

Meyer, Michael. *A Handbook for the Humanistic Astrologer.* New York: Anchor, 1974

Robertson, Marc. *Not a Sign in the Sky But a Living Person.* Seattle, WA: Astrology Center of the Northwest, 1975

Rodden, Lois M. *The American Book of Charts.* San Diego, California: ACS Publications, Inc., 1980

Rudhyar, Dane. *The Lunation Cycle.* Berkeley, California: Shambhala Publications, 1975

Tierney, Bil. *The Dynamics of Aspect Analysis.* Reno, Nevada: CRCS Publications, 1984

Von Klocker, H. B. *Astrology and Vocational Aptitude.* Tempe, Arizona: American Federation of Astrologers, 1974

Index

Boldface indicates major discussion of a topic.

A

Abdul-Jabbar, Kareem 309
absentminded 198, 201, 212
absorbing work (needs) 100, 215, 222, 263
abuses (others) 185, 201, 215
academic **77**, 254, 266, 331
acclaim 185, 205, 216, 277
  (See also fame)
accomplish, accomplishment-oriented 11, 58, 74, 86, 119,172, 182, 190, 198, 215, 248, 250, 254, 335
accomplishments 204, 217, 283-285, 311-312
  (exaggerates) 182, 231, 242, 267, 278, 286
  (lack of) 258, 260
accomplishing dreamer **85**, 102, 118-119, 239, 241
accountant, accounting 67, 190
achieve, achievement 46, 59, 75, 79, 119, 173, 182, 194, 206, 229, 235, 237, 239, 241, 250, 259, 265, 276, 284, 286, 291-292, 312, 322-323, 331, 334-335
  (needs) **43**, 140, 187, 212-213, 219
  (-oriented) 44-45, 59, 96, 193, 213, 240, 249, 273, 335-336
  (tangible) **77-78**, 112, 156-157, 251, 266, 286, 334, 337
acting, actor/actress 9, 75, 123, 128, 132, 151, 154, 190, 219, 256-258
adequacy (sense of) 54, 56, 86, 91-94, 96, 98, 100, 112-113, 139-140, 142, 149, 205-210, 212, 256, 260, 276, 285-286, 291, 297-298, 321, 344, 346
admiration (seeks) 205, 217
adulthood (responsible) **77**, **247**, 291
advanced degrees, See education
advancement 48, 58, 67, 75, 96, 112, 151-153, 179, 181, 194, 208, 221, 223, 237, 261, 265, 285, 304, 326
adventure, adventurers, adventurous **74-75**, 151, 185, 193, 216, 228, 238
advertising 49, 55, 149, 151, 154
advisory capacity **62**, 259
aesthetic (abilities, needs) **47-49**, 64-65, 85, 113, 127, 133, 153, 164, 196, 212, 231, 252-253, 270, 287, 308
agent 67, 99, 228, 261
aggression, aggressive 108, 112, 129
agriculture 48, 50
ailments 61, 76, 238, 265
  (See also health disorders, illness, sick)
air (element), See trait 3
  (signs on ASC/MC) 249
Albert, Eddie 305
Alda, Alan 135, 262, 267
Ali, Muhammad 97, 103, 105 (chart), 117, **125-126**, 131, 147, 253, 274, 280, 287, 323, 333, 336, 340, 346
alienated, alienation **26**, **249**, 260, 300
Allen, Garth 121, 266, 347
Allen, Steve 97, 101, 117, 150, 262, 273, 315, 324, 336
Allman, Greg 340
alone (works) 67, 69, 188, 202, 212, 233, 236, 240, 242, 269, 301, 312
aloof 82, 228, 310, 340
ambition, ambitious 56, 98, 140, 152, 179, 181-183, 186, 196, 209, 211, 232-234, 237, 241, 267, 321
  (lacks) 99, 164, 228
American Book of Charts 43
amusements, See recreation
analysis (aptitude for) 61, 202, 222-223, 225
  (of facts, figures, people) 138, 145, 213
analytical, analyzing 62, 109, 137, 183, 198, 200, 224, 278
Andersen, Hans Christian 154
Anderson, Jack 96, 100, 117, 150, 252, 275, 280, 315, 324, 328, 339
angles (the) **246**, **248**
Ann, Sue 244
anticulminating **124**, 306, 313
  (See also plus zones)
anxieties, anxiety 141, 163, 204, 206, 212, 214, 242, 244, 270-271
appearance (physical) 67, 180, 183, 252, 260
appreciation (needs) 58, 213
apprentice 224
approval, approval-seeking 17, 59, 182, 198, 258
aptitude for (vocational) 26-29, **123-128**, 169, 172, 175-176, **178-179**
  (artistic, creative occupations) 55, 65, 125, 127, 132, **179**, 182, 188-193, 195-199, 203-205, 207-208, 210, 212, 214-219, 226-228, 230-231, 234-235, 241, 243-244, 346
  (See also art, creative, performing arts, talent)
  (assisting occupations) 125, 127, **179**, 189-191, 196-197, 199, 204-205, 207, 212, 214, 221, 226-227, 230-231, 235, 241, 243-244
  (See also counseling)
  (enterprising occupations) **179**, 182, 184-186, 190, 192-193, 198, 201, 204, 207, 209, 213, 215-217, 221-222, 227-228, 232-238
  (handling people) 66
  (intellectual occupations) **179**, 185-186, 188-189, 193, 195-203, 205, 207-210, 212, 216,

aptitude (intellectual occupations) (cont.). 219-224, 226, 228, 230-238, 240-244
(practical occupations) **179**, 188, 190-191, 193, 195, 197-198, 200, 202-203, 220, 233, 237, 240
(technical occupations) **179**, 186, 188, 190, 198, 200, 202, 205, 218, 220-224, 240, 242
(See also technical)
Aquarius, See trait 11
argumentative, argumentativeness 44, 152
Aries, See trait 1
Arness, James 93, 98, 117, 162, 272-273, 294, 344
arrogance, arrogant 59, 240
Arroyo, Stephen 148, 167-168, 246-247, 280, 321, 347
art, the arts 47-48, 64, 127, **132-133**, 164, 166, **179**, 188-189, 196-197, 205, 212, 219, 221, 231, 241, 268, 270, 290, 309, 331
(See also performing arts)
artist, artistic 48, 50, 55, 58, 85, 101, 107, 123, 132-133, 164, 180, 189, 191-192, 194, 197, 207, 211, 220, 240, 243, 261, 289, 294, 298, 300, 306
Ascendant 32, 37, 123, **246-249**, 272, 299
(ruler) 37, **247-249**, 284
Ashe, Arthur 97, 112, 131, 256, 278, 294
aspects 37, **169-175**, 177
(afflicted/unafflicted [good/bad]) 170
(harmonious) **169-173**
(inharmonious) **169-173**
(major) 37, **169-174**, 178
conjunction 33, 37, 119, 121, 170, **173-174**, 283
sextile 37, 170, **172**
square 33, 37, 170, **172-173**, 287, 291, 301, 305
trine 37, **170-172**
opposition 37, 106, **170-171**, 272, 298
(minor) 37, **170-174**, 178
22.5 degrees 37, 170
semisextile 37, 170
novile 37, 170
semisquare 37, 170, 283, 287, 305
septile 37, 170
quintile 37, 170
sesquiquadrate 37, 170, 291, 294, 298, 301
biquintile 37, 170
quincunx 37, 170
(Ptolemaic) 170
(traditional interpretations for) **169-171**
aspiration, aspirations **6-7**, 17, **21**, **29**, **78-79**, 117, 208, 216, 237-238, 265, 267, 301, 303-304, 311, 331
(blocked, denied) 76, 237-239
aspirational (drives, needs) 5, 52, **74-75**, 86, 88, 91, 97-98, 151-153, 172, 185, 201, 209, 216, 222-223, 232, 240, 252, 265, 275, 304
assertiveness (blocked) 33, **129**
(training) 46, 116
assets 324
assistant 67, 214, 221, 256
assisting (occupations, qualities) 110, 153, 165, **179**, 270, 346
assisting, assists (others) 35, 54, 111, 141, 207, 299, 308
associates 199, 218, 221, 227-228, 230-231, 233-236, 243-244
associations (professional) 80, 119, 268
Astaire, Fred 96, 100, **106-108 (chart)**, 262, 266, 273, 276, 333, 347
astrological alphabet **32-34**, 36, 42, 177
astrologer 29, 31, 34-35, 110, 121, 160, 171, 299, 317
astrology 11, 26, **31-35**, **41-42**, 60, 66-67, 81, 151, 153-154, 169, 203, 248, 299
(as symbolic language) 31, **33-35**, 177, 317
(natal) 174-175
(vocational) 26, **29**, 31, 169-171
athlete, athletic 123, 129, 155, 179, 182
attached, attachment (to work place) **55**, 141
(See also belonging, closeness)
attention (needs) 113, 144
audience (job caters to, needs to have an) **58**, 104, 113, 146, 154, 205, 213, 215, 234, 257
author, See writer
authoritarian 210, 217, 219, 235, 277
authority (needs, seeks positions of) 24, 33, 62, **77-79**, **83**, 86, 96, 120, 137, 141-142, 145-146, 150, 152, 157-158, 161-162, 172, 177, 179, 186, 209, 217, 237, 256, 263, 266, 276, 306-308
(See also distinction, expertise)
(abuses) 241, 267, 269
(delegates) 223, 233, 327
(exercises) 155, 210, 229, 237, 277
(figures) 70, 130, 186, 222, 241
(freedom from) 17
(resents) 101, 186, 224, 241
(sense of) **156**, **248**, 293
avant garde 83, 102, 110, 161, 218, 310, 342
avocation, avocational (interests, pursuits) 11, **15-16**, 22, 26, 56, 126, 129, 133, 166, 195, 253, 290, 296-297, 306, 308, 332, 346
Ayres, Lew 166, 257, 290, 329

B
backers 231, 235
Baer, Max 262, 274, 347
Ballard, Guy 154, 158
Balsamic Moon phase 87, 244, 283, **309-315**, 320
Balzac, Honore De 139, 166
Baudelaire, Charles 142
Beatty, Warren 96, 101, **117-119 (chart)**, 158, 255, 260
beautiful objects (work involves) 47, 107, 132
beautifying 47, 50
beauty **131-132**, **179**, 188, 196, 199, 270, 274
behind-the-scenes (works) 196, 212, 219, 226, 244
Belafonte, Harry 119, 143
Belgium Committee for the Scientific Study of Paranormal Phenomena **124**
belief system, beliefs **74-75**, 85, 112, 117, 151, 153, 164-165, 187, 208-209, 219, 222, 225, 228, 235-237, 239, 265, 270-271, 275, 278, 302-305, 312
(lacks a) 118, 164, 304
belief in self 85, 87, 94, 102, 232, 270, 334
Bell, Alexander Graham 139, 142-143, 158
belonging (sense of) **55**, 139, 256, 268-270, 310, 334, 338
(See also attachment, closeness)
Benny, Jack 344
Bergman, Ingrid 96, 101, 108, 135, 262, 266, 273, 277, 297, 324, 344
Berlioz, Hector 150, 158
Berrigan, Philip 150
"big break" (the) 76, 251, 258, 265, 335
Bismark, Otto Von 135, 158
Black, Hugo 147
Blake, William 143, 162
Blue, Vida 154
books, reference materials (uses) **52**, 180
boredom, boring (job, work) 21, **23**, 72, 83, 109, 116, 161, 210, 221, 241, 254, 267, 269, 286, 304, 326-327
bores (easily) **51**, 120, 187
boss, bosses 46, 58-59, 61, 73, 116, 157, 162, 165, 194, 199, 210-211, 215, 217, 222-225, 227, 229, 234, 237, 251, 256, 276, 284, 300, 306, 308, 327
(assists, works closely with) 141, 191, 207, 220
(equal to, friends with) 162, 218, 240, 268
(need to be one's own) 3, 81, 113, 142
(See also authority [freedom from], self-employed, superiors)
Bowie, David 166, 301, 347
bowl pattern, See trait 4
bragger, bragging 8, 147, 220, **286**
Brando, Marlon 93, 100, 121, 135, 162, 260, 266, 276, 280, **314-315 (chart)**, 324, 336, 343
Brandt, Willy 147, 150
Brazzi, Rossano 154
broadcast (industry/ media), broadcasting 75, 81, 151, 154
Brown, Edmund G. 150, 166
Bruce, Lenny 131, 139, 147
Bryan, William Jennings 131, 163
bucket pattern, See trait 5
bundle pattern, See traits 3 and 6
Burmyn, Lynne 244
Burnett, Carol 93, 98, 114, **138-139 (chart)**, 158, 266, 272, 280, 287, 340, 343, 347
Burstyn, Ellen 95, 98, 158, 163, 262, 278, 280, 294, 329
Burton, Robert 166
Bush, George 255
business 32, 48, 113, 125, 194, 217, 321
(administration) 134, 146, 190, 229
(builds, establishes a) 55, 78, 205, 208-209, 240, 250, 267, 276
(management) 57-58, 145, 179, 182, 186, 193, 215, 217, 257
(negotiations) 198-199, 201
(partner), See partner
Busteed, Marilyn 281, 315
busy (needs to be) **51**, 180, 331, 335
Byron, Ada 134, 251, 267, 275
Byron, Lord 297

C
Cage, John 139, 158
calligraphy 22-23, **52-53**
Cambell, Glen 340
Camus, Albert 93, 98, 108, 150, 158, 255, 260, 294, 324, 339
Cancer, See trait 4
Capricorn, See trait 10
cardinality, See trait 1
career (the) 33, 79, 306, 310
(See also achievement, employment, job, vocational)
(analysis) **34-35**
(changes), See change
(-conscious) 198, 217
(counseling) 4, 14-15, **29**
(difficulties, obstacles, problems, setbacks), See troubled job life
(dissatisfaction), See unfulfilling
(purposeful) 212, 248, 282
(satisfaction), See fulfillment
(-troubled people) **7-8**, 90, 282, 296, 305, 320, 334, 337, 340, 342, 344
caring (approach, instincts) **54-55**, 85, **87**, **139**, 176, 196-197, 206-207, 209, 211-212, 219, 225, 243, 249, 276-278, 312
(occupations) 165
Carnegie, Andrew 8
Carradine, David 139, 266, 272, 276, 309
Carrel, Dr. Alexis 158

Carson, Johnny 95, 98, **114 (chart)**, 131, 139, 147, 150, 162, 264, 276, 278, 290, 324
Carson, Rachel 8
Carter, Billy 139
Carter, Jimmy 150, 257, 262
Carter, Charles E. O. 33, 89, 244, 323, 328, 347
cash (handles) **48**, 107, 221
Casteneda, Carlos 25
causes, cause-orientation **80**, **103**, 119, 187, 211, 218, 234, 243, 268-269, 277, 300, 302, 312, 314
caution, cautious 69, 186, 250
ceilings (achievement, career, job) 56, **79**, **97**, 100, **110**, **130**, 139, 142, 148, 156, 182, 186, 188, 194, 209-210, 217, 224, 229, 233, 241, 255, 258, 286, 290, 334
Cellini, Benvenuto 139, 347
Cezanne, Paul 131, 135, 154, 166
challenges (faces) 44, 186 250
Chamerlain, Richard 154
Chambers, Joe 142-143
change, changes (career, job) **48**, **82-83**, 121, 148, 158, 186-187, 195, 198, 206, 208, 211, 213, 218, 221, 224-225, 230, 234, 236, 238, 240-241, 308, 326, 328, 330, 337
(fears) 193, 211, 238, 346
(needs) 211, 230, 234
charisma, charismatic 116, 150, 184, 263
charismatic personality (needs to develop a more) **70**
charitable (organizations) **81-82**
charm, charming 65, 107, **132**, 183, 191-192, 214, 230, 260, 262
chart (patterns) 36-37, 90-91, **103-121**
(synthesis) **31-32**, 41-42
Cher **103-105 (chart)**, 114, 135, 138-139, 143
Chevalier, Maurice 166
children (works with) 57-58, 113, 146, 189, 258, 277
childhood, See early home life
Chubbuck, Chris 95, 98, 109, 143, 150, 253, 277, 280, 290, 340
Church of Light **177**, **248**
circulate (on the job) 218, 238, 332
Clemenceau, Georges 134
cleverness 329
Cliburn, Van 158
clients (works with) 61, **81-82**, 109, 134, 180, 183, 195, 199, 203, 207, 211, 214, 218, 221, 225, 230, 277
Clift, Montgomery 150
close (emotional bonds, ties) 205, 207, 210, 278
closeness **55**, 119, 208-211, 218, 228, 230
(See also attachment, belonging)
(fears) 14, **82**, 161, 180, 210-211, 228, 230
clubs 15, 80, 120, 211, 269
Cocteau, Jean 134, 154
colleagues 82, 211, 222, 230, 235, 243, 251, 264, 285
(recognition) 80, **82**, 110, 120, 162, 210, 218, 230, 240, 268
college, See education
comedienne 139
commission **45**, 195
commitment 8, **10**, 17-19, **68-69**, 81, 86-87, 115, 119, 121, 149, 156, 159, 161, 163-165, 184, 187, 212, 215, 217, 221, 223, 226, 230, 233, 243, 263, 266-267, 271, 274, 309, 312, 327, 330, 337
committed 112, 176, 192, 202, 207, 234, 302, 308-309
common sense 336
communication, communicative skills **50-51**, 108, 135, 137, 188-189, 199-200, 225, 249, 252-253, 271, 275, 290, 343
compassion, compassionate 164, 166, 205, 212, 225-226, 231, 239, 241, 243, 276-278, 310-311, 344
competence, competency, competent 17, **21**, 25, 33, 41, **77-78**, 86-87, 91, **96**, 104, 119-121, 137, 142, 155-157, 159, 166, 172-173, 177, 186, 194, 209-210, 223, 229, 233-234, 242, 247-251, 260, 266-267, 276, 306, 308-309, 331
(fails to develop, lacks) **162**, 186, 233, 241, 308, 331
competition, competitive 17, **43-44**, 55, 110, 128, 131, 179, 181-182, 184, 208, 212, 261-263, 285
(fears) 163, 184
competitors 70, 234, 250, 285
compulsions, compulsive 208, 215, 221, 236
computer (field, programming) 81, 160, 162, 234
con artist 86, 165, 200, 220, 226
conferences (work involves) 110, 211, 218
confidence, confident 94, **144-146**, 206, 213, 216-217, 219-220, 247, 277-278, 285, 295
(lacks) 165, 217, 220, 251, 334
(See also self-confidence)
confused, confusion 165, 175-176, 212, 220, 279, 311
Connery, Sean 101, 264, 267, 273, 287, 324, 329, 336, 340
consciousness **35**, 118, 148, 159, 164, 193, 220, 223, 232, 239, 241, 254, 266, 268, 272, 275, 277, 283, 287, 291, 295, 301, 305, 309, 311, 313, 318, 325, 339, 341
(level of) **10**, 44, 188, 283, 298, 317

C (cont.)
consciousness (cont.)
(-raising) 193, 238
consciousness (different types of) **316-317**, 342, 346
construction (work) 45, 69
consultant, consulting **80-81**, 119, 121, 161, 195, 225
"containment" **324-327**, 331
contentment 20, 60, 147
contractor (independent) 225, 230
contracts (job requires) 200, 204, 215, 219, 224, 240, 268, 306, 312
contribution, contributor, contributory 77, 80, **82**, 102-103, 119, 163, 187, 195, 211, 219, 230, 234-236, 239, 241, 243, 248, 277
control (issues, tactics) 69, **72**, 149, 185, 263, 274, 324, **327**
controls (others) **71-72**, 185, 192, 215, 227, 264
controlling 215, 232, 235
controversial 330
conventional (jobs) **52**, **136**, 179, 308
convictions 241, 263, 265
convoluted (perceptions of others) **70**, 215, 222, 233
Cooper, Alice 257, 333
Cooper, Leroy Gordon 154, 158
cooperation 64, **261-262**, 273
Copernicus, Nicolaus 323, 333
corporate (affairs, world) 69-70, 116, 149, 192, 200, 215, 227, 232, 234
(funds) 233, 235-236
"cosmic clock" **31**
cosmic state (of a planet) **129**, 139, 175
cosmic sciences 225, 236
Coubert, Gustave 147, 162
counseling, counselor 66-67, 99, 121, 127, 179, 189, 192, 197, 205, 207, 231, 261
(requires) 113, 116, 140
courage 43, 128, 187, 249, 333
course of least resistance (job, career) **321**, 331, 346
Cousteau, Jacques 97, 101, 114, 154, 162, 262, 274, 290, 336
Cowell, Roberta 264
coworkers 46, 58-59, 70, 73, 82, 130, 165, 199, 206, 211, 213, 219, 221-222, 224-226, 230, 234, 251, 264, 277, 286, 300
craft (work as a) 61, 130, 137, 141, 145, 153, 177, 183, 206, 278, 296, 306
(See also technical)
crafts 48, 62, 199
Crane, Bob 158
Crane, Stephen 166
creative, creativity 49, **55**, 58, 60, 107, 110, 113, 132, 140, 142, 153, 164, 174, 181-182, 187-188, 190, 194, 198, 203-205, 207, 211, 217, 239, 255-257, 271, 276-277, 297, 299, 306, 312
(See also aptitude for [artistic occupations], art, performing arts)
Crescent Moon phase 189, 282, **287-291**
crew (works with a) 211, 225, 234, 240
crime, criminals 25, 145, 308
(See also thieves)
crises, "crisis" (handles) 46, 286, **292-294**, 321
critic 206, 306
critical, criticism **62**, 155, 162, 183, 185, 198-199, 202, 206, 213-214, 221-222, 224, 226, 228, 240, 242, 278-279, 310, 330
Cross, Robert T. 166
"crusaders" **263**, 302
Csonka, Larry 273
culminating (plus zone) **123-124**, 148
Cummings, Robert 162
customer service 66
customers (has) 61, **81-82**, 109, 134, 180, 183, 195, 203, 207, 211, 225, 230

D
"Dan" **5**, 7, 23, 46, 76
danger (faces) 69, 234
dare, daring 44-45, 69, 98, 187, 215, 285-286
Dass, Ram 95, 103, 121, 135, 150, 154, 257, 272-273, 277, 305, 324, 336
Daumier, Honore 162, 347
Da Vinci, Leonardo 131
Davis, Rennie 131, 273
Davison, Ronald 248
dead-end (job) 151, 304
deadlines (works on) **44**, 321
Dean, John 135, 269, 305
Dean, Geoffrey 89, 123, 167, 244-245, 248, 280
Debussy, Claude 166
deception, deceptive 165, 231
decisive 217, 250
"deep involvement" (in a job) 68
"deep sharing" 263, 273
"deeply moving" (career) 233
De Falla, Manuel 277
defeated (easily), defeatist 113, 156, 237, 239, 267
defensiveness 242, 256
Degas, Edgar 143, 269
De Gasperi, Alcide 162
delusions, deluded 163, **165-166**, 175-176, 188, 226, 251, 269, 312
De Maupassant, Guy 16
De Mont, Richard 131, 147, 273
De Niro, Robert 143, 323, 333
Denver, John 121
dependency (issues, needs) **56**, **72**, 94, 99, 211, 254, 276
dependent (on others) 212, 293
depressed, depression, depressive **76**, **79**, 182, 210, 217, 224, 265
Descendant 123, 251, 299, 314, 320
design (ability for, occupations) **48**, **179**, 189, 199, 256, 290

"destiny" 311
detached, detachment 82, 218, 243, 340-341, 345
details (aptitude, capacity for) **61-63**, 78, 109, 134, 137-138, 154-155, 158, 183-184, 193, 198, 202, 206, 213, 221, 223-224, 233, 242, 259, 278
determination, determined 33, 48, 69, 94, 129, 205, 234, 250, 324-327, 336
devoted, devotion (to work) 87, 184, 215, 221
dexterity **51-52**, 180, 202, 254, 275
(See also hands, use of)
"Diane" **18-19 (chart)**, 49
dictatorial 95, 185, 211, 237, 269, 273, 277
dilettante **86**, 102, 156, 343
diligence, diligent (approach) **61-62**, **77**, 96, 139, 155, 183, 186, 193, 209, 213, 220, 224-225, 250, 259
Dillinger, John 273
Diller, Phyllis 95, 98, 134, 154, 158, 162, 166, 255, 274, 277, 315, 339, 344
diplomacy, diplomat, diplomatic **64-65**, 108, 132, 134, 199, 261
direction, directions (career) **4**, **13**, 26, **29-30**, **144**, 163, 165, 184, 212, 220, 289
(See also vocational direction)
(works under own) **69**, 177, 184, 208, 210, 233
discipline, disciplined 14, 41, 77, **79**, 81, 91, 97, 103, 157, 159, 183, 186, 233, 241, 276, 279
(lacks) 153, 165-166, 204, 219
discriminating, discrimination 198-199, 205, 225, 278
(fails to be) 243-244, 279
disorganized 239
Disseminating Moon phase 283, **301-306**, 311
distinction (needs, seeks positions of) **77-78**, 86, 96, 146, 172, 307
(See also authority, prestige)
(fails to recognize needs for) **97**, 229, 233
diurnal motion 110
diversity (needs) **51**, 173, 299
Doane, Doris Chase 245
Dobyns, Zipporah **32**, 89
doctor, See physician
domestic **56**, 140
dominates, dominating, domination **71-72**, 184, 215, 227, 263
Dore, Paul Gustave 134
Downs, Hugh 147
dreams (vocational) **4-5**, **7-8**, 17, 78, 85, 87, 103, 119, 164-165, 193, 196, 201, 216, 218-219, 223, 231, 239, 241-242, 258, 265, 270, 275, 278, 334-335, 338, 342
"dreamy" (occupations) **140-141**
drifter, drifting (job) 267, 271, 275
(See also job hops)
driving (job entails) **51**, 109, 136
Dumas, Alexander 150, 340
duty 209, 217, 229, 237
Dylan, Bob 131, **319-320 (chart)**, 323, 340
dynamic, dynamism **44-45**, 125, 129, 133, 172, 232, 250
Dynamics of Aspect Analysis 173

E

early (learning) 204
(home life) **11**, **52**, 55-56, 62, 71-72, 82-83, 87, 93, 99, 144, 148, 155, 200, 209-210, 219, 251, 254, 260-261, 263, 269, 278, 286, 293, 300, 306, 310, 327, 332, 335, 338, 342, 345
(life criticisms, programming, restrictions) 202, 214, 217, 291, 297
earth (element), See trait 2 (signs on ASC/MC) 249
ease-producing aspects, See aspects, harmonious
eastern hemisphere emphasis, See trait 1
eastern philosophies 239
(See also religion)
Eastwood, Clint 96, 101, 158, 274, 280, 290, 324
easy (job, work) **48-49**, 78, 133, 202, 209, 224, 242, 253, 278
eccentrics, eccentricity 159, 187, 195, 218, 225, 230, 244, 269, 278
"Ed" **21-23 (chart)**, 53, 83
editor 67, 99, 133, 191, 285
education 21, 23, **29**, **51-52**, 60, 75, 78, 151, 154 178, 185, 188, 193, 197, 208, 216, 224, 228, 237, 239, 253, 266, 275, 341
efficiency, efficient 109, 158, 183, 206-207, 209, 229
effort **4-5**, **7-8**, **10**, 13-14, 17-18, 29, 33, 76-79, 81, 86-87, 91, 96, 100, 102-103, 118, 125, 130, 142, 146, 155-157, 159, 164-165, 171-173, 186, 194, 202, 208-210, 217-218, 237, 238, 241-242, 257, 265-267, 271, 275, 285-286, 296, 306, 309
(lack of, insufficient) **10**, 23, 59, 96-97, 134, 153, 156, 165, 186, 239, 241, 309, 312, 331
effort quotient **8**, **59**, 118, 157, 178, 185, 216, 223, 242, 249, 303
ego **8**, **44**, 61, 128-129, 147-148, 165, 174, 247, 312, 324-325
(-denying) 35, 188
(formation), See identity formation
egocentric 277, 310, 316
Eickmann, Adolph 162, 277
Einstein, Albert 8, 97, 103, 114, 143, 154, 162, 272, **302-305 (chart)**, 343, 347

E (cont.)
electronics **80-82**, 211, 225
elements (the) 37, **316-321**, **333-347**
(diminished representation) 37, **321**
("lack of" [by sign only]) **317-318**
(preponderance) 37, **317-321**
Eliot, T. S. 344
Emerson, Keith 162, 277
"eminent" professionals 34, **123**, **125**, 129, 143, 152, 169, 176
emotional 254, 317, 335, 344-346
(discomfort, disturbances, problems) **82**, **148**, 150, 207, 226, 243, 253, 260
(foundation, grounding) 249, 291
(probing) **69**, 150, 284
(security) 141, 181, 207, 210-211, 256, 308
(sensitivities, See sensitive)
employee, employees 130, 165, 183, 191, 210, 213, 220-226, 229, 233, 327
employment (satisfying), See fulfillment
(unsatisfying), See unfulfilling
employers, See boss, superior
engineering **81**, 160, 162, 203
entertainment (field), entertains **58**, 114, 138, 218
enterprise, enterprising **43-44**, 91, **94**, 152, 177, 182-183, 249, 272, 333-334
entrepreneurial **44**, **60**, 190, 335
equipment (uses dangerous, electronic or intricate) 160, 200, 222, 234, 238
escapism, escapist **86**, **163**, 165, 182, 188, 212, 219-220, 236, 239, 242, 271, 331, 344
ethical, ethics 226, 231, 237-238, 243, 306
evolutionary (path, process) **282-283**, 295, 316
example-setters **58**
excitement (needs) 80, **82**, **84**, 120-121, 158-159, 161, 186-187, 195, 210-211, 218, 224-225, 234, 238, 285, 326
executive (drives, positions) **44**, 83, **94**, **104-105**, 113, 123, 129, 154, 217
(account) 58
exhausted (works until) 221, 225
expert, experts 119, 172, 233, 240, 266, 276, 307, **325**
expertise **77-78**, 121, 153, 157, 177, 183, 186, 250
exposure (needs) 265, 275, 331
extemporaneous (impromptu, spontaneous) **58**, 112, 114, 172, 182, 190, 198, 257, 277
extraordinary (achievement) **6-7**
extroversion, extroverted 112, 125, 151-152, 199

F
fact retention, See memory
facts, factual knowledge (job relies on) **50**, **52**, 135-137, 164, 188, 201, 203, 225, 254, 341
(See also knowledge)
(confused with fantasy) 204, 242
"failures" **251**, 302
(See also fears failure)
fair play 183, **229-230**, 272
faith 235, 237, 239
false role playing **108**
fame, famous **17**, **19**, **59-60**, **74**, **117-118**, 147, 151-153, 163, 185, 201, 208, 216, 220, 228, 232, 239, 243, 270-271, 275, 299, 303, 311, 315, 331, 334-335
(See also exposure, important, "somebody", special)
family 15, 181, 282, 287, 289-290, 308, 335
(atmosphere) **52**, **55**, 72, 141, 155, 335, 338
(background) **55**, **59**, 93, 110, 139, 142, 210, 288, 293
(disruptions, problems, separations) 107, 210-212, 256, 261, 306, 310
(expectations) **17**, 276, 289-291, 295, 335
(influence) **13**, **54-56**, 93, 99, 181, 188-189, 207-209, 211, 256, 261
(members [works with]) **55**, 256
(needs a) 204-205, 256, 276
(-owned business [works for]) **55**, 189, 206, 256
(tied to the) 209, 256
(See also parental)
fanatical 211, 235-236, 243
fantasy, fantasies, fantasize **4-5**, **7**, 23, 86-87, 118, 163, 204, 212, 286, 335
fascination (with work) 68, 304
fate **159**
father (experience of, relationship to) **59**, **144-146**, 335
father image **144**
fault-finding 212, 260
fearful 215, 227, 231-233, 256, 264
fears 70, 208, 212, 215, 236, 263, 292, 344-346
(closeness) **82**, 297, 301
(failure) **7-8**, 10, 14, 78, 81, 97, 102, 112, 142, 146, 152, 156, 162, 173, 193, 210, 217, 242, 265, 267, 292, 305, 309, 335
feelings 197, 200, 342, 344-346
(See also sensitivities)
Ferber, Edna 97, 112, 154, 166, 260, 264, 277, 280, **287-288 (chart)**, 290, 336, 347
Fermi, Enrico 147

fiction, See writing, creative
figure (work) **51**, 199
film 128, 160, 164
finance, finances **47-48**, 190, 193
financial (considerations) 290, 326, 338
(problems) 233
(security) 1, **48-49**, **132**, **179**, 189-191, 193-195, 227, 252, 327, 337, 346
(ventures [joint]) 234
fire (element), See trait 1
(fighting) 45
(-related planets) 125
(signs on ASC/MC) 249
fired (getting) 83, 159-160, 162, 187, 218, 225, 286, 328
first quadrant focus 36, **98**, 182
First Quarter Moon phase, See trait 4
Fitzgerald, F. Scott 143, 269
fixity 161, 320, **324-329**
(diminished representation) 193, **328-329**
(preponderance) 193, 324, **326-329**, 336
"fizzle out" (on a career, job) 119, 164-165, 337
Flaubert, Gustave 277
Fleming, Sir Alexander 143, 158
Flynt, Larry 309
focalized planet **106**, 117
Foch, Nina 97, 103, 121, 147, 158, 166, 253, 301
Fonda, Peter 147
food service 136
foolhardy 235, 285
foreign affairs 208
foreign cultures, places (job entails) **74**, 151, 201, 222, 237
foreigners (works with) 222, 228
fortitude **58**, 70, 73, 85, 150, 215, 227
Foster, Stephen 150
fourth quadrant focus **102-103**, 130, 186
France, Anatole 109, 158, 315
freedom (needs) **75**, **81**, **109**, 159, 161, 163, 180, 187, 195, 209-211, 218, 228, 230, 238, 247, 254, 304, 326, 338
freelance **45**, 190, 195, 261
Freud, Sigmund 131, **284 (chart)**, 287
friends, friendship **83**, 186, 210-211, 218, 230, 234, 238, 243, 269, 277
(works with) 224, 240
fulfillment (career, employment, job, vocational, work) **4**, **13**, **28-30**, 58, 67, 70, 82, 91, 93-96, 99-101, 103-104, 122, 141, 145, 150, 206, 214, 221-222, 225-226, 233, 259, 261-262, 268, 283, 298, 301, 305-307, 320, 331, 337, 339, 344
(emotional) 110, 212
Full Moon phase, See trait 7
fun **13-14**, **57-60**, 112, 173, 190, 213, 217-218, 257-258, 277-278
(-loving) 182, 204, 214, 216

G

Gabor, Zsa Zsa 93, 100, 108, 150, 158, 255, 260, 305, 336, 347
Gacey, John Wayne 287
Galileo 147, 162, 347
Gandhi, Mahatma 332
gaps (in chart patterns) **105**, **110**, **114-115**
Gauguin, Paul 166
Gauquelin, Francoise 95, 108, 122, **143**, **152**, 154, 167-168, 269, 297
Gauquelin, Michel **28**, 30, 93, 100, 119, **122-123**, **129**, **132**, 139, 167-168, 253, 275, 277, 287, 343, 347
Gauquelin (findings, research, studies) 6-7, 28, 34, 91, **122-125**, **129**, **135-136**, **140**, **143**, **148**, **151-152**, **154-155**, **160**, **164**, 248
Gauquelin planets, See G-planets
Geller, Uri 95, 98, 112, 162, 274, 315, 329, 336, 339
Gemini, See trait 3
genius 85
Gershwin, George 297
"get-by" (approach, work) 2, 23, **61**, 86, **93**, **98**, **107**, 109, 120, 132-133, 258, 276, 278, 290
"get-rich-quick" 145, 163, 196, 220, 231, 296
"getting ahead" 101, 308
gets in (over the head) 88, 185, 218
Gibbous Moon phase 61, 145, 214, 282, **294-298**, 300-301
Gide, Andre 108, 166, 301
Gish, Lillian 344
give-and-take 72, 95, 101, 149, 185, 261, 263, 269, 300-301
glamorous, glamour 118, 163, 212, 219, 231, 239, 241, 251, 271, 278, 311
Gleason, Jackie 119
Glenn, John 266, 278
goal-oriented 129, 140, 186, 198, 250, 259
goals **4**, 67, **94**, **97**, 179, 185, 216, 219, 223, 235, 237, 239-240, 242, 250, 258, 265-266, 275, 279, 285, 335
(short-term [needs]) **44**, **321**
God 87, 220, 314
Goering, Hermann 309
Goethe, Johann Von 166, 301
"Golden Rule" (the) **100**
Gonzales, Pancho 103, 154, 253
good looks **65**, 107, 134, 191-192, 221
Gordon, Charles 139, 251
Gordon, Richard F. 162, 266
government (work) 66, 229
G-planets **36**, 45, **122**, **125**, **129**, 154, 317
(See also vocationally significant functions)
grand trine 115, 117, **174**
greatness (desires) **291**, **315**

G (cont.)
Greene, Liz 140, 167, **339**, **341**, 347
Griffin, Merv 301
group (activities, participation, process) 61, **80**, 119, 161, 186, 195, 211, 230, 238, 240, 243, 269, 299, 310, 312, 325
(practice) 53, **67**, 75, 81
growth (in life) 199, 261, 273-274, 275-279, 287, 293, 298
(job, career) 151-152, 285
Guild, Leo 162
guns (uses) **45**, 184, 192
guru 220, 311

H
Haggard, Merle 135
Haldemann, H. R. 329, 332
Hamill, Dorothy 96, 100, 266, 276, 305, 333, 336, 339
Hamilton, Sir William Rowan 147, 150
Hand, Rob 100, **129**, 257, 272, 278, 315
handicapped (people) **137**, 231
handicrafts, See crafts
handle planets 36, **105**, 112, 122, 126, 128
in Aries or first house **129**
in Taurus or second house **133**
in Gemini or third house **138**
in Cancer or fourth house **142**
in Leo or fifth house **146**
in Virgo or sixth house **138**
in Libra or seventh house **133**
in Scorpio or eighth house **150**
in Sagittarius or ninth house **153**
in Capricorn or tenth house **157**
in Aquarius or eleventh house **162**
in Pisces or twelfth house **166**
hands (skilled use of) **50**, **52**, 62, 109, 180, 198, 204, 254
(See also dexterity)
hard (angles/aspects), See aspects, inharmonious
(works) 104, 137, 177, 213, 215, 236, 251, 259-260
(See also effort, hardworking)
hard work, worker, hardworking 41, 146, 157, 166, 179, 182, 185-187, 206, 209, 213, 217, 221, 223, 233, 237, 242, 250, 258, 265-266, 276-279, 327
(See also effort)
healing 141, 150, 189, 207, 232, 284
health (care professions) 56, 62, 137, 158, 165, 191, 198, 225, 346
(disorders, matters, problems) 61, 76, 157, 183, 199, 206, 213, 222-224, 260
(See also ailments, illness, sick)
helpful (needs to be) 212, 220, 297
helping (professions) 55, 212, 241, 346
hemisphere emphasis 37, **90-97**, 103
Hemingway, Ernest 112, 150
Hendrix, Jimi 103, 112, 162, 262, 266, 275, 278, 305, 333
heritage, See family background
Hesse, Hermann 131, 154
hidden (aspects of life) **68-69**
Higher Power **87**, 119, 159, 163
Himmler, Heinrich 150, 297, 336
hindsight technique **126**
hobbies, hobbyist **4**, 15, 53, **57**, **60**, 83, 113, 160, 182, 190, 198, 205, 213, 216-219, 258, 269, 277, 296, 331, 335
Hoffa, James 154, 266, 269
Hoffman, Dustin 96, 101, 278
home **54**, 206, 308
(See also family)
(works from) **55**, 110, 141, 181, 189, 206
homemaker 213
honesty 227, 237
Hoover, J. Edgar 158
horizons (broaden, expand) **74-75**, 151, 237, 264-265
hospitals (works in) 226
(See also nurse, physician, etc.)
house (angular) 6
(cusp) 37, 177
(rulers) 34, 37, **177-178**
(systems) 31
Houseman, Alfred E. 143
houses **34**, **317**
first 32, 60, 177, 247-250, 313, 317, 323, 333
second 32, 336
third 32, 255, 302, 314, 340
fourth 32, 140, 344
fifth 33, 114, 333
sixth 33, 92, 177, 299, 306, 336
seventh 33, 340
eighth 33, 344
ninth 33, 75, 333
tenth 33, 140, 177, 249-250, 323, 336
eleventh 33, 340
twelfth 33-35, 123, 125-126, 344
(air) 332, 340
(cadent) **6-7**, **124**
(cardinal) 317, 320, 323
(double cusped) 37, 178
(earth) **336**
(fire) **333**
(mutable) 332
Houston, Jean 96, 101, **115-117 (chart)**, 131, 166, 255, 260, 275, 305, 329, 336, 343
Hubbard, Elbert 166
hubris 44

Hugo, Victor 100, 309, 347
humanitarian 80, **82**, 119, 187, 231, 234-235, 239, 278, 309
humor, humorous 58, 146, 182, 198, 205, 265
Huxley, Thomas 344
hygiene 183, 206, 260
Hyneck, J. Allen 135, 167
hyper 109, 136
hyperactivity 322
hypersensitivity 344

I

IC (nadir) **247**, 251, 314
I Ching 269
I-Thou (principle) 183, **272-273**, 282, 298
idealism, idealistic, ideals **85**, 164, 187, 196, 203, 208, 216, 219, 225-226, 231-232, 236, 238-239, 241-243, 250, 258, 265, 270, 278, **298**, **300-301**, 312, 322, 329, 331, 333
identity 20, 23, 43, **45**, **56**, **75**, **91**, **93-94**, **98**, **108**, **125**, 172, 180-181, 184, 187, **247-248**, 250, 253-255, 259-261, 263, 265-266, 269, 272-273, 279, 284, 286, 290, 293, 298, 310, 321, 326
(crisis) 20
(developing a purposeful) **246-272**
(formation) **45**, **247-252**, 255, 257, 259, 261, 270, 279
(lack, loss of) 66, **107**, **163**, 246, 273, 311
ideology, See beliefs
illicit (activities) 86, 242
illness 26, **61**, 99, **145**, 156, 224-226, 260
(See also health disorders, sick)
illusion **86**, 279
image, image conscious **59**, 213, 217, **258**, 326
imagination, imaginative 35, **54-56**, 85, **87**, 110, **139**, **141**, **164**, 196, 204, 212, 219, **249**, **256**, **270**, 278, 300, 338, 342, 344-346
immersion (in the occupation) **69**, 150
important (needs to be) 205, 209, 216
(See also fame, "somebody", special)
impressionable 212, 220, 239, 244, **344**
impulsive, impulsive activity **44**, **159**
inadequacy (fears, sense of) **59**, **62**, **70**, 94, 111, 113, 156, 197, 202, 206, 208, 212, 214, 217, 242, 258, 269, 279, 295, 312
in charge 115, 308
income 45, 48, 189, 191-192, 194-196, 238, 337
(See also financial)
independence, independent 14, 43, 45-46, 81, 115, 119-120, 152, 158-159, 161-162, 195, 205, 211, 250, 265, 284, 292, 338
(decision-making) 58, 69, 75, 101, 155, 157, 187, 211, 223, 257, 259, 308, 333, 342
independent-minded 115, 238
indispensable (needs to be) **62-63**, **145**, 194, 213, 259, 297
individuality 211, 225
indulgences **48**
(See also self-indulgent)
inferiority (fears of) **71**, 187-188, 212, 219, 226, 235, 239, **271-272**
influence, influential (to have or be) **17**, **29**, **74-75**, 112, 133, **151-153**, 184-185, 193, 195, 208, 215, 228, 232, 234, 237, 263-264, 302-304, 308, 326
(See also prestige)
(the masses, society) 69, 147, **149**, 303, 305
(standards of an occupation/profession) **149-150**, 184, 233-234, 263
information (disperses, exchanges) 50, **52**, **136**, 254, 340
initiative **43-45**, **91**, **93-94**, 128, 131, 177, 179, 183, 249-250, 265, 273, 285, 333
inner (directed, direction) 86, **93**, 176, 312
(security), See adequacy
(vision) 86, **283-288**, 290-291, 298, 307
innovation, innovative **81**, **159**, 195, 218, 225, 230, 234, 238, 240
insecure, insecurities 209, 232, 242, 257-258, 279, 344-346
inspiration, inspirational **6-7**, **10**, 23, **29**, 164, 166, 231, 235, 312
inspired **5**, 35, **85**, 165, 175-176, 196, 212, 219, 231, 270, 278
inspires (others) 204, 219, 243
inspiring (work) 226, 243
instruments (uses) 45, 180, 184
intangible rewards **17-20**, 23
integrity 209, 217
intellect, intellectual **51-56**, 60, 82, **87**, 119, 135, 141-142, 153, 155, 160, 180, 191, 197, 200-201, 217, 220, 243, 254, 270, 277, 288, 302, **325**, 330-331, **340-341**, 346
intellectual (achievement) 198, 204, 223, 342-343
intelligence, intelligent **135**, **178**, 198, 201-204, 224-225, 241, **341**
intelligence quotient (IQ) **35**, **51**, **135**
intense 184, 192, 215, 227, 232-233, 234, 250, 263, 284
(interaction with others) **68-69**, **304**, 324
interception (houses/planets) 37, **176**
interdependent personality functions, See personality functions
interest, interests **4-5**, **7-8**, **10-14**, 17, **26**, **29**, 48, 52, 100, 113, 119, 126, 128, 132, 146, 165,

I (cont.)
interest, (interests) (cont.) 178-179, 201, 203, 213, 238, 252, 269, 275, 290, 303, 337
(lack of) **23**, **26**, 94, 118
interesting (work) **14**, **19**, 112, 157, 216
interpersonal, interrelating (capacity, process, skills) **64-67**, 83, 91-92, **95**, 101, 107-108, **131**, 134, 149, 183-184, 191, 221, 229, 249, 259, 261-262, 269, 272, 294, 298-300
interviewers, interviewing, interviews (job) 65, 67, 116, 132, 198, 217, 257
introspection 56, 270-271
introverted **155**
intuition, intuitive 35, **54-55**, **85**, 110, 141, 164-165, 176, 196-197, 203-204, 207, 211-212, 219, 225-226, 231, 235, 238-239, 241, 243-243, 256, 270-271, 276, 278, 299, 312, 344-345
invent (one's occupation) **161**
invention, inventive, inventiveness, inventor **81**, 102, 110, **160**, 187, 203, 240, 309, 312, 340
irresponsible 196, 205, 216, **308**
Irving, Washington 158, 166
isolation, isolationist 210, 233, 242, **308**, 312

J
"Jack" **16-17 (chart)**, 56, 83
jack-of-all-trades 159
Jagger, Mick 109, 131, 309
"Jane" **14-15**
Jayne, Charles 248
jealous 227, 235
"Jean" **4-5**, 7, 146
"job" (in life) **281-315**
job (See also career, employment, vocational, work)
(changes), See change
(dissatisfaction), See unfulfilling
(hopper, hopping, hops) 8, 14, **52**, **86-87**, 102, **118**, 134, 136, 161-162, 165, 186-187, 194-195, 199, 211, 223, 237-238, 251, 267, 304, 330, 338
(loss of a) **2**, **20**, 26, **29**, **177**, 222
(obtaining a) **177**, 213, 229, 237
(performance) **2**, **130**
(quiting a) 145, 160, 216
(satisfaction), See fulfillment
(trainer) 58
jokester, joking 72, 135
John, Elton 121, 287
"Jon" **66-67 (chart)**
Jones, Jim 93, 98, 143, 158, 262, 267, 273, 276, **313-315 (chart)**, 324, 332,
336, 344
Jones, Marc Edmund **103**, **111**, 121, **126**, **128**, 167, 277
Jones, Tom 109
journalist, See writer
judgment (relies on) 21, **51-52**, **135**, 198, 201-202, 204-205, 239, 331-332, 343, 345
(lacks) 206, 279
Jung, Carl 309
Jupiter 33, 60, 75, 143, **151-154**, 156, **161**, **163**, 236, 320, 327, 332-333
aspects **152-153**, 171-173
focalized **153-154**
G-planet (occupies plus zone) 123, 125, **151**, 154, **161**, 287, 294, 299, 302
handle or leading planet 112, **153-154**
in or ruling the sixth house or in Virgo **153**
in or ruling the tenth house or in Capricorn **153**, 237
interdependent personality function/ vocationally significant **91**, **152**
singleton **153-154**
(See also trait 9)

K
Kant, Immanuel 315
Karajan, Herbert Von 139, 162
"Kathy" **70-71 (chart)**
Keaton, Diane 95, 98, 117, 162, 264, 275, 287, 329
Kennedy, Caroline 95, 103, 112, 139, 147, 158, 162, 262, 266, 275, 278, 290
Kennedy, John F. 162, 329
Kennedy, Ted 267
Kent, Rockwell 109, 166, 255, 347
Kepler, Johannes 269
Kerouac, Jack 143, 162
Killy, Jean Claude 95, 109, 131
King, Morgana 97, 103, 114, 131, 139, 158, 166, 255, 260, 274, 294, 340
Kissinger, Henry 131
kite pattern **174**
Knievel, Evel 150, 309, 347
know-it-all 86, 197-198, 201-203, 210, 237, 331
knowledge, knowledgeable 11, 52, 74, 111, 185, 188, 202, 204, 208-209, 212, 216, 232, 237-239, 241, 252, 254, 264, 275, **302-304**, 331
(See also facts)
Koch, Dr. Walter 150
Koufax, Sandy 251
Kraft, Karl 253

L
labor, See manual labor
laid off 225
Laing, R. D. 96, 101, 272, **294-295 (chart)**, 297
La Laurie, Maria 166
Lalo, Edouard 143, 278
language, languages (job involves) 52, 203, 208
Lanza, Mario 143, 309, 347

large scale (projects, undertakings) 223, 232, 234, 239
Last Quarter Moon phase, See trait 10
Laughton, Charles 329
law (the) 81, 151, 153
lawyer 311
Lawrence, D. H. 329
lazy, laziness, lackadaisical **49**, 99, 130, 180, 182, 190, 192-194, 196, 198, 212, 220, 225-226, 228, 231, 238, 262, 326
(See also slack)
leader, leads, leadership **43-44**, **46**, **57**, **69**, 94, 104, 112-113, 119, 129, 130, 133, 179, 182-183, 187, 205, 213, 215, 218-219, 232, 234, 237, 249-250, 265, 272, 285, 303, 321, 323, 333
leading planet 36, **105**, 109-110, 112, 115, 122, 126, 128
in Aries or first house **129**
in Taurus or second house **133**
in Gemini or third house **138**
in Cancer or fourth house **142**
in Leo or fifth house **146**
in Virgo or sixth house **138**
in Libra or seventh house **133**
in Scorpio or eighth house **150**
in Sagittarius or ninth house **153**
in Capricorn or tenth house **157**
in Aquarius or eleventh house **162**
in Pisces or twelfth house **166**
learn (desire to) 340
learning **52**, 180, 197-199, 201, 238
learns (by doing) **44**, **247-248**, 251, 284, 333
(by observation) 197, **329**
(from mistakes) **44**
(quickly) 203, 238
lecturer, lectures, lecturing 12, 58, **75**, **87**, 154, 172, 180, 190, 197, 201, 223, 228, 240, 254, 271
Lee, Bruce 147
Leger, Fernand 162
Leigh, Vivien 93, 98, 143, 147, 154, 163, 166, 253, 269, 278, 280, 290, 336, 340
Leo, Alan 131, 166, 253, 278, 305, 329, 336
Leo, See trait 5
Leopold, Nathan 297
Le Petomane 166
"Les" **19-21 (chart)**, 59, 146
Level I **36-38**, 44, 47, 51, 54, 57, 61, 65, 69, 74, 77-78, 80, 83, 85-87, 105, **122**, **128-166**, **176**, 178, 317, 332-333, 344
Level II **37-38**, **126**, 178, **246**, **248**, **283-315**, **321-347**
Level III **37-38**, **92-120**, 178
Liberace 139, 143, 278
Libra, See trait 7
license (needs a) 200
limitations, limits (issue of) 74, **78**, **86**, **258**, **326-328**
Lincoln, Abraham 143, 147
"Linda" **62-63 (chart)**
listener 197, 199-200, 207
livelihood, See income
lives (in one's head/own world) 187, 197, 199, 204, **254**
(off others) **253**, 265
locomotive pattern, See traits 1 and 8
Lodge, Henry Cabot 108, 154
logic, logical 204, 243, 253, 278, 329, 331, 340, 342, 345
longings **88**, **311-312**
Love, Michael 255
love (of work) **14-15**, 147
loved one (works with a) **58**, **67**, 99, 191, 213-214, 229, 297
(See also family, partner, spouse)
Lovell, James 158
loyal 217, 229, 233
lunation birthday **281**
luck **29**, **151**, 172, 185, 209, 216, 238, 267, 275
lucky 216, 223, 238-239
lunar personality, See trait 4
Lundsted, Betty **345**, 347
Luther, Martin 142, 150
Lynde, Paul 154

M

machinery (works with) 45
Mahara Ji 143
mail (work involves) **51**
major configurations **174**
management, managerial, See business
Mancini, Henry 121
Manet, Edouard 150
manipulation, manipulative **71-72**, **95**, **147**, 185, 201, 215, 232, 236, 262, 264
manipulator 233, **327**
manual (dexterity), See dexterity
(labor) **44-45**, 184
(skills) **179**, 188
Marconi, Guglielmo 95, 344
"Margot" **8-10 (chart)**, 25, 86-87
marriage 207, 231, 293
married (to career) 100, 229
Mars 32-33, 35, 37, **128-131**, 143, 152, 161, 179, 321, 323, 327, 333
aspects 129, 131, 153, 172-173, 323
G-planet (primary plus zones) **44-46**, **123-127**, **129**, 131, 323
(secondary plus zone) **124**, 127, 129, 131, 133
handle or leading planet 112, 115, **129**, 131, 284, 306, 320
in or ruling the sixth house or in Virgo **129-130**, 183
in or ruling the tenth house or in Capricorn **129-131**, 186

M (cont.)
Mars (cont.)
singleton **129**, 131, 284
undeveloped personality function **129-131**
vocationally significant, interdependent personality function **91**, **129**
(See also trait 1)
martial arts 45
Martin, Dean 154
martyr 240
(See also savior, victim)
mate, See spouse
Marx, Karl 131, 163, 266
masochism, macochist 212, **264**
master, mastery of (an activity, subject, occupation) **69**, **81**, **149**, **160**, 203, 211, 218, 299, 312, 325
(appetites, self) **72**, 148, 184-185, 192, 215, 263
material (rewards) 195, 229
materialistic 274, 337
maternal (motherly) 107, 344, 346
Matisse, Henri 162, 253
math, mathematical 62, 162, 164, 187, 203, 211, 243, 302
Mathias, Robert 114
mature (approach to work) 78, 308, 313
Maurois, Andre 143
May, Rollo 131, 266
McLoughlin, Tom 134, 154
McNamara, Robert S. 154
meaning, meaningful (pursuits, work) **1-2**, **4**, **12-15**, **23**, **26**, **29**, 270
meaningless (job, work) **1-2**, **29**, 157
"measure up" **62**, 183, 199, 213, **279**, 296
mechanically inclined 43, **45**, 129
mechanic 53
meditation 35, 270
Mehta, Zubin 154, 272, **291-292 (chart)**, 294
Melville, Herman 135, 253, 294
memory (retentive) 197-198
menial (work) **86**, 271
mental (activity, energy, faculties) **51-52**, 108, **135**, 186, 198, 202, 249, 253, 275, 285-286, 295, 317, 321, 329, 332
(mastery) 80, 243
mental health care, See psychology
mentally active, alert **51**, **135**, 180, 185, 198, 201, 330-331, 340
mentors 186, 276
Mercury 32-33, 52, **135-139**, 146, 157, 197, 220, 340
aspects 137, **173**, 320
focalized planet **138**
in Level I **255**, 332
in or ruling sixth house or in Virgo 135, **137**, 199
in or ruling tenth house or in Capricorn 135, **137**
leading planet 105, **138-139**
near angles (within six degrees) **139**
singleton **137**
vocationally significant function **137**
(See also traits 3 and 6)
messenger 135-136
messiah complex **311**
metaphysical, metaphysics **55**, **160-161**, 193, 201, 208, 211, 219, 232, 238, 243, 266, 270, 304, 311, 346
Meyer, Michael **174**, 244
Middlecoff, Gary 150
Midheaven (MC) 33, 37, **246-249**, 272
(ruler) 37, **249**
midpoints **173**
Miller, Henry 119
Millet, Jean Francois 158
mind games **72**
Minnelli, Liza 267
mission (on a) **111**, **164**, **268**
Modigliani, Amadeo 143
Mondale, Walter 131, 135, 158, 272, 297, 329
Moon 32, 34, 37, **139-144**, 149, 164, 204, 247, 282, 291, 294, 298-299, 301, 305, 317, 333, 336, 340, 344
aspects 142, **173**
G-planet (occupies plus zone) 123, **140-141**, 143, 164, 287, 294, 306
handle or leading planet 105, **141-143**
in or ruling the sixth house or in Virgo **141**, 206
in or ruling the tenth house or in Capricorn **141-142**, 210
interdependent personality, vocationally significant function **91**, **139**
phases, See phases
singleton **142**
"water planet" **317**, 321
(See also trait 4)
Moore, Robin 255
mother, motherhood 140, 144
motivated, motivation **125**, **176**
(lacks) **101**, 190
moves (from birth place) **151**, 208
movie studios (works in) 219, 226
multicapable (aptitudes) **179-187**, 197, 201-204, 209-210, 213, 215, 217, 225, 229, 236, 238-240
music, musician 128, 132, 164
(ability for) 234, 239
Mussolini, Benito 109, 162, 260
mutability 320, **329-333**
(diminished representation) 197, **332-333**
(preponderance) 109, 197, 328, **330-333**, 340
mysteries 164, 235, 243
mystical 232, 281

N
naive, naivete **44**, 69, 201, 204, 286
name (makes a) 209, 308
national guard 46
needed (need to be) **55**, 111, **141**, 145, 205-207, 212, 276, 297
Neptune 33, 89, 156, **163-166**, 244, 317, 332, 344
aspects **164**, 320
focalized **166**
handle or leading planet 105, **166**
in or ruling the sixth house or in Virgo **164-165**
in or ruling the tenth house or in Capricorn **165-166**, 242
near angles (within six degrees) **166**, 287
singleton **166**
"water planet" **317**
(See also trait 12)
nervous, nervousness 109, 130, 152, 197, 199, 201, 203, 209, 256, 260, 322, 330-331, 340
(breakdowns) 102, 296
neuroses, neurotic 125, 152, 247, 297
new age 2, 75, **81**, 83, 160-161, 211, 218, 225, 238-239
Newman, Paul 135, 158, 264
New Moon phase, See trait 1
Nicholson, Jack 252
"Nick" **24-25**
Nicklaus, Jack 93, 100, 117, 135, 139, 260, 264, 273, 294
Nietzsche, Friedrich 131, 134, 260
nine-to-five (job, world) 83, 86, 238
nit-picking 260, 279
Nixon, Pat 93, 98, 114, 154, 158, 162, 166, 264, 269, 273, 315, 329, 344
nodes (Moon) 37, 91, 97, 103, 246, **272-280**
in Aries/Libra-first/seventh house 184, **272-273**
in Taurus/Scorpio-second/eighth house 193, **273-275**
in Gemini/Sagittarius-third/ninth house 202, **275-276**
in Cancer/Capricorn-fourth/tenth house 210, **276-277**
in Leo/Aquarius-fifth/eleventh house 219, **277-278**
in Virgo/Pisces-sixth/twelfth house 226, **278-280**
"number one" (to be) **250**
noncommital 8, **116**, **120**
nonprofit organizations 83, 196, 219
nonworker, nonworking 25, 165, 191, 219, 240
(See also work personality type E)
North, Jay Waverly 154
northern hemisphere emphasis, See trait 4
notoriety, See fame
novelist, See writer (creative)
nurturing 82, 181, 205, 209, 346
(early experience of) **56**, **139**, 210-211

O
objective (reasoning), objectivity **50**, 188, 197, 200, 203, 234-235, 243, 249, **253**, **261**, 278, 310, 340, 342
objects (works with) 191, 231
obsess, obsessed, obsessive (about work) **115**, **149**, 184, 208, 215, 222, 227, 235, **263**
obstancy, obstinate 152, 159, 230
occult **69**, 200, 227, 232, 263
occupations (associated with trait pairs) **180-244**
off-the-cuff, See extemporaneous
offbeat (approach, occupations) **81**, **83**, 238
office politics **69**, 150, 215, 221-222
office practice (occupations) 51, 62, **136**
O'Henry 253, 269
Olivier, Sir Lawrence 255, 269
O'Neal, Ryan 131, 272
O'Neill, John J. 143
on the go (needs to be) **51**, 136, 180, 198-199, 203, 332, 342
"on the line" **8**, 98, 137, **156**, **162**, 186, 252, 286
open-minded 278, 284
ophthalmologist 38, 52
opinionated 325
opportunities (job) 208, 237
optimism, optimistic **74**, 237-238, 265
orbs 169-170, **174-175**
(major aspects) 37, 170, **174-175**
(minor aspects) 37, 170, **174-175**
(progressed major/minor aspects) **177**
organizational (skills) 213
organizations (works for) 110, 211, 226, 312
(professional) 119
organized, organizes, organization 158, 193, 207, 209, 212, 217-218, 223, 233, 238, 259
original, originality **81**, 110, 187, 195, 218, 224-225, 240, **312**
others (easily influenced by) 344
"otherworldly" (interests, occupations) **85**, 117, **160**, **164**, 219, 270, 310
outer planets **148-149**, 158, **173**
(See also transpersonal forces, planets)
out of doors (works) 44
out-of-the-ordinary (work, work places) **81**, **83**, **102**, 161-162, 195, 211, 230
"out-of-this-world" (occupations), See otherworldly
outgoing 183, 217, 239
overachieves 199
overestimates (abilities, self) 185, 188, 209, 217, 219, 223-224, 231

P
Packard, Vance 162
Pagan, Isabelle 96, 100, 117, 143, 154, 158, 163, 257, 272, 276, 280, **299-300 (chart)**, 344, 347
"pain" **346**
painting 48, 55
paperwork **50-51**, **53**, 197, 199
paranoia, paranoid 262, 296, 312
parental (abuse) 208
(approval) **23**, 296
(control) 263, 291
(disputes, separations) 82, 108, 288, 300
(expectations) 24, **55**, **144**, **289**
(figures) **70**, **110**, 258
(footsteps [follows in]) **55**, **256**, **291**
(influence), See family influence
(jealousy) 49
(manipulation) 208
(values) 291
(See also family)
parenthood **291-292**, **297**
parenting (seeks) 156, 205, 257
parents 23, 139, **155-156**, 212, 256, 276, 289, 307, 310, 327, 338, 345
Parr, Jack 131
part-time (works) 49, **83**, 161, 195, 211, 224, 230, 240
partner, partnership **64-65**, **67**, 99-101, 107, 134, 183, 191, 207, 214, 221, 227-230, 261-262, 273, 292-293, 298, 300
(resources of) 232, 235
passion, passionate (about work) **69**, **115-116**, 133, 149, 166
passive, passivity 56, **67**, **71**, 95, 125, 132-133, 140, 147, 184, 192, 227, 232, 242, 262
passive/aggressive 208, 215
passive parental behavior **72**, 256
Pasteur, Louis 139, 259, 297
paternalism (fatherly) 107, 344, 346
patience, patient 78, 157, 194, 217, 223, 229, 250
(lacks) 224
patients (works with) **61**, **81-82**, 109, 134, 180, 207, 230
pattern focal points, See handle, leading, focalized planets
Patton, George 166, 272
"Paul" **2-4 (chart)**, 10, 14, 21, 29, 46, 75, 83
paying dues 78, 259
Peckinpah, Sam 252, 257
peers (relationship to) 82
(recognition of) 225, 238, 268
(See also colleague recognition)
"Peggy" **23-24**
perceptive 241
perfection (strives for) 206, 236
perfectionism, perfectionist **62**, 198, 213, 236, 296
"perfect" (career, job) 196, 226, 332
(one should be) 279
perform (needs to), See audience
(ability to) **62**, 182, 214-215, 217, 295
performing arts **55**, **65**, 107, 110, 117, 121, 127, 141, 149, 154, 172, 179, 231, 320
Perls, Fritz 112, 143, 252, 259, 273, 277, 309
"Perry" **38-41 (chart)**, **52-53**, **75**, **81**, 109, 122
Perry, Troy 143
persecution (complex, fears) **70**, 242, 251, 269
perserverance (lacks) 330
personal development/growth (needs) **70**, 98
(See also self-development, psychological repair)
personality **6**, **316-317**
(drives) **90**, **103**, **105**, 128-129, 155
(formation), See ego, identity formation
(functions [the five interdependent]) **65**, **91**, **93**, **103**, 129
(See also vocationally significant functions)
(needs) **4**, **13**, 29, 105, 128
(traits) **28**, 32, 43, 103, 124, 129, 131, 141
(See also traits)
persuasiveness 261
pessimism 330
"Peter" **11-12 (chart)**, 14, 27, 45, 49
phases (of the Moon) 36-37, **281-316**
Phillips, Wendell 257
philosopher 294
philosophical 23, 185, 193, 201, 208, 237, 243, 265-266, 302, 304
philosophy 75, 151
phone (uses) **51**
phony 242
photography 128, 164
physical (abuse) 72
(activity) **45**, 184, 285-286, 317, 333, 346
(contact [needs]) 227, 338
(exertion) **45**, 68-69
(education) 45
(prowess) 44
(senses [the five]) **48**, 50, 65, 135
physically active **45**, **51**, 185-186, 201
physician 52, 123, 129, 284, 311
physics 203, 302
pioneer, pioneering (in an occupation) **129**, **250**, **284**
pipe dreamer, pipe dreams **7-8**, **10**, 19, **24-25**, **46**, 75, 86, 102, **118**, 156, 165, 209, 216, 219, 239, 242, 312, 331
Pisces, See trait 12
Placidus house cusps/system **123**, **177**
(See also cadent houses)
planets 34
("prominent") **36**, 45
(See also Level I)
(six degrees from angles) **36**, 122

Planets in Combination 173
planner (poor) 267
plays fair, See fair play
playwright 16, 56, 287, 306
pleasure **48**, 274, 278
plus zones 6-7, **122-126**, 129, 132, 140-141, 143, 151-152, 155, 161, 299
(primary) **123**, 125-126
(rising) **123**, 148, 294, 306
(secondary) **123-124**, 306, 320
(setting) **124**
Pluto 33, 140, **147-150**, 232, 284, 328
as fixed water **148**, **344**
aspects **147-148**, 328
focalized **150**
handle or leading planet 114, **150**
in or ruling the sixth house or in Virgo **149-150**
in or ruling the tenth house or in Capricorn **150**, 234
near angles (within six degrees) **150**
retrograde 175
singleton **150**
(See also trait 8)
poet 132, 140
Poitier, Sidney 257
police artist 133
political, politics 65, 75, 80, 119, 133, 154, 200, 232
politician **123**, 151
pompous 220
popular, popularity 58, 238
Pottenger, Maritha 329
Power, Tyrone 142, 280
power 17, **68-69**, **115-116**, **147**, **150**, 184, 201, 215, 222, 227, 232-233, 250, 302, 304, 308, 324
(abuses) **69**, 262
(behind the throne) **62**
(different forms of) **69**, 192, 207, 221, 263, 263
(fears, suppresses) **116**, **147-148**, 184, 236, 264
(gains) 234
(inner) **69-70**, **72-73**, **116-117**, **148**, **150**, 185, 192, 215, 222, 227, 235-236, 263-264, 274
(of persuasion) 227
(players) **71**, **149**, 185, 215
(shares) **72**, **148-149**, 192, 215, 221
(staying) 214
(struggles) 222, 227, 235-236, **327**
powerful personality (needs to develop a more) **70**
practical **48**, **65**, **96-97**, 192, 194, 209, 217, 240-241, 252, 341
(jobs) 189, **290**
(necessities) **47-48**, 50, 195
practicality **48**, **86**, 179, 224-225, 237, 241, 277, 336
(See also conventional, financial concerns)
pragmatic 62, 92, 186, 198, 209, 276
praise (needs) **59**
preacher, preaching 75, 302
precise, precision 213, 221, 225-226, 242
Presley, Elvis 260
pressure (endures) 207, 215, 327
prestige 78, **96**, 190, 229, 237, **266-267**, 296, **308**, 310
pretentious 204, 212, 217, 220
Price, Leontyne 93, 98, 114, 131, 147, 158, 264, 269, 277-278, 294, 323, 340
Price, Vincent 114, 154, 315
pride **58-59**, **152**, 204, 217, 278, 326
primary vocational functions/planets **129**, **137**, **153**
(See also personality functions, vocationally significant traits)
Prince Charles 143
Princess Anne 97, 131, 135, 154, 166, 259, 262, 278, 287
private tutoring 66
procrastinate 328
production (tangible) **77**, **330**, 337
productive (needs to be) 206
productivity **48**, 200, 214
product (produces a tangible) **48-49**, **78**
products (of the earth) **48**, 65
(See also agriculture)
professional, professional approach 139, 142, 155, 172, 205, 218, 223, 307, 346
(practice [creates a]) 208-209, 240
(See also business, builds a)
professionalism **77**, 217, 229, **252**, **266**
profession, the professions 52, 78, 81, 179, 240, 243, 276, 278, 309
profound thinker 207
Progoff, Ira 114, 134
progressed (aspects) **177**
progressions **175**
prominence (rises to, seeks) **58**, 184, 240
prominent (positions) 276
(tendencies in a chart) **32**, **34**
promotion (job) **67**, 224, **326**
promotional campaigns 58
prove self (needs to) **17**, **19**, **58**, **144**
Proust, Marcel 114, 158, 166, 251
psychic **55**, **87**, 203-204, 207, 212, 219, 231-232, 234-235, 239, 243, **271**, **344**
(investigation) 160
psychoanalysis 284
psychological repair (needs) **56**, **99**
(See also psychotherapy, personal development)
psychological, psychologist, psychology 81, 115,

P (cont.)
psychological, psychologist, psychology (cont.) 149, 153, 158, 165, 200-201, 207, 211, 232
psychosomatic 10, **304**
psychotherapy (needs) **70**, **98**, 113, 208, 236, 260, 263-264, 271, 297, 301, 303, 311
(See also counseling, psychological repair)
public (attracts attention of) 199, 207, 214, 217, 229-230, 307
(deals, interacts with) **66**, 101, 107, 183, 191, 206-207, 227-228, 261
(relations) 65
public opinion (influences) 232
public office 304
publishing 2, 29, 75, 151
Puccini, Giacamo 134, 301
purpose (sense of) 4, **12-13**, **29**, 96, 98, 103, 109, 118-119, 146-147, 153, 184-185, 187, 250, 253, 259, 270-271, 275, 279, 281-282, 298, 300, 309, 325
(lacks) **23**, **26**, 94, 271

Q
quadrant focus 37, 90, **97-103**
qualities (the) 37, **316-333**
(diminished representation) 37
("lack of" [by sign only]) **317-318**
(preponderance) 37, 317
See also cardinality, fixity, mutability
quit (a job), See job

R
race 35
racing 45
radio 160
Rafael 260
rational 242, 244, 345
Ravel, Maurice 264
Reagan, Ronald 117, 290
realistic 78, 85, 87, 155-156, 185-186, 193, 196, 202, 209, 212, 216, 223, 241
reality 77, 86, 196, 211-212, 218, 225, 236-238, 241-242, 249, 254, 271, 316-317, 331, 337
(quotient) **4**, **59**, **86-87**, 102, 117-118, 130, 153, 163, 311
rebellion, rebellious 159, 218, 225, 230, 235, 238, 278
rebuilding (job entails) 69
reclusiveness 269, 335
recognition, recognized (seeks, needs to be) 24, 44, 46, 58-60, 74, 102, 112, 182, 184, 205, 213, 217-218, 229, 250, 265, 278, 285, 291, 309, 322-323, **333**, **335**
(insufficient, lack of) 101, 216, **335**
record industry 160
recreation, recreational activities **57-58**, 182, 213, 217-218, 277
(See also hobbies)
recruiting 261
recycling (of goods) 150
Reddy, Helen 96, 101, 117, 131, 143, 252, 278, 280, 290, 333, 347
Redford, Robert 119, 272
Reeves, Christopher 150, 154
references material (relies on) **52**
referrals 230
refined, refinement 107, 131, 133
reforms 232, 234
relationships 23, 67, 72, 95, 100, 131, 134, 183-185, 191-192, 200, 207-208, 227-231, 261-262, 263, 274, 293, 295-297, 300-302, 304, 312
religion 151, 232, 238
(eastern) 231, 270
religious 23, 117, 163, 193, 208, 228, 235, 243, 265-266, 270
(ideology) 75
(instruction) 275
Renoir, Pierre 131, 269
renovates 234
renown (seeks) 263, 303
(See also fame)
reorganizes 234
repair work 62
repress, repressed 35, 70
respresentative 261
reputation 101, 142, 194, 202, 210, 237, 241, 248, 267
research, researcher 48, 52, **62**, **68**, **78**, 115, 137, 149-150, 184, 200, 222, 234-235
resourceful 116, 148, 185, 221-222, 263
(needs to become more) 70
resources 132, 196, 274
(joint) 236
respect (needs) **59**, 146, 217, 256, 267, 276
responsible **96**, **100**, **155**, 186, 209, 217, 223, 313
responsibilities, responsibility (accepts, assumes) **24**, 41, 67, **78-79**, 94, 146, **155-156**, 179, 223, 229, 251, 260, 265, 276, 306
(abuses) 233
(evades, fears) 142, **165**, 186, 194, 210, 224, 229, 233, 241, 251, 256, 258, 267, 308, 328
restless 211, 330
retirement 26
retrogradation **175-176**
revolutionary **150**, 284
rewarding (work) 183, 220, 223, 337
(See also fulfillment)
rewards (measureable, tangible) **15**, 21, **78**, 249, 259
Reynolds, Burt 121, 139, 255, 275, 305
rich, See wealth
rigidity 337
"rim" (of chart pattern) **110**, **114**
Rimbaud, Arthur 143
risk, risk-taking, risks **44-45**, **58**, **69**, 150, 179, 182, 185-186, 190, 215-216, 218, 232, 234, 237, 250-251, 285-286, 333
Robertson, Marc 281, 315
Rockefeller, Nelson 294

Rodden, Lois M. 89, 294
Rogers, Roy 143
role (models) **55**, **62**, **93**, **99**, 181, 198, 206, 213, 254, 263, 275, 288, 290, 296
(playing) 293
romantic (attachments, inclinations) 182, 220, 236, 214-215, 258-259, 297
Rooney, Mickey 150
Roosevelt, Franklin 119
Roosevelt, Theodore 121
Rostand, Edmond 139
routinized 337
Rudhyar, Dane **281**, 307, 315
Ruskin, John 143
Russell, Bertrand 158, 344
Ruth, Babe 119
ruthless 147, 149, 201, 215, 232-233

S
sacrifice 163, 271
sadomasochistic **71**
"safe" (jobs, livelihood) **48**, 187, 253, 271, 337-338, 346
Sagittarius, See trait 9
Saint-Saens, Camille 301
sales 58, 65-66, 70, 81, 161, 179, 225, 231, 261
Sandburg, Carl 278
Sanders, George 252, 297
Satie, Eric 252
Saturn 10, 33, 37, 41, 80, 86, 137, **154-158**, **163-164**, **171**, 177, 240, 247, 269, 285-286, 306, 313, 322-323, 328, 333, 336, 340, 344
aspects 146, **171-173**, 320, 328
focalized **158**
G-planet (occupies plus zone) 123, 125, **154-155**, **158**, 328
handle or leading planet 112, **157-158**, 313, 320
in or ruling the sixth house or in Virgo **156-157**
in or ruling the tenth house or in Capricorn **157**
interdependent personality function, vocationally significant planet **91**
retrograde **175**
singleton 139, **157-158**
(See also trait 10)
Saturn Return **24-25**
savior (martyr, victim) 165, 188, 212, 231, 251, 279, 310, 315
scandals 242
scattered, scatter energies **52**, 109, 159, 330, 340
scholarly, scholastic 85, **87**, **164**, 187, 202, 204, 239, 270-271
(See also academic)
Schubert, Franz Peter 257, 272, 280
science, the sciences **78**, **81**, 139, 164, 166, 179, 203, 211, 229, 235, 241, 243
scientific 34, **158**, **160-161**, 209, 217, 219, 270, 308
(achievements) 119, 223
(research) 35, 234
scientist 38, **52**, 123, 155, 160
Scorpio, See trait 8
Scott, David R. 158
second fiddle (playing) 104, 113
second quadrant focus **99-100**, 207
secretary 62-63, 99, 134, 136, 191, 285
secretive 69
security 234, 256, 293
(-conscious) 159, 233, 337
(-oriented) **69**, 322
seesaw pattern, See traits 2 and 7
self, selfhood (sense of) **14**, **26**, **71-72**, **86**, **94-95**, 185, 248, 258, 285, 295-296, 310, 321
self-
absorbed 250, 254, 257, 334
acceptance 279
aggrandizement 181, 211, 286
appreciation 274
assertion, assertive 35, **43-46**, **67**, **95-96**, **128**, 172, 181, 183-184, 187, 250-251, 255, 271, 273, 286, 300, 317, **321-322**, **333**
awareness 282
centered 300
concept **251**, **308-309**
confidence 8, 10, 58, 61, 152, 182, 185, 214, 247, **257-258**, **333**
conscious 146, 182, 210, 258, 309
contained **108**, 112, **153**, **324**
control **72**, 209
(lacks) 215
critical 206, 214
deceived, deluded 211-212, 220
deprecating **274**
development **56**, **263**
directing **45**, 112, 130, **248**, **286**
discipline 266, 286
(lacks) 276
discovery 262, 264, 266-268, 270
driving **69**, **115**
doubts **49**, **133**, **148**, 190-191, 194, 208, 252, **263**
effacing 190, 205, 210, 217, 258
employed, employment 3, 14, **45**, 67, **81**, **130**, **145**, 161-162, 180-183, 186, 189, 195, 209, 213, 215, 217, 223, 225, 230, 256-257, 346
esteem 1-2, 57, **59**, 113, 172, 182, 213, 215-219, **257-258**, **260**, 277-278
(lacks) **3**, 182, 190, 205, 218
expression, expressive 33, 46, **57-58**, **60**, **93-94**, 104, 109, 113, 130, 159, 172, 177, 183, 190, 204-205, 213-215, 217, 247-248, 250, 258, 261, 263-264, 269, 272, 277, **286**, 306

S (cont.)
self- (cont.)
(work) **13-14**, **17**, **23**, 27-28, **145**, 182, 216, 257
focus 282
image (appropriate, grounded, healthy, positive, solid) **56**, **92**, **98**, **111-112**, **148**, **165**, 206, 212, 256, 260, 285, 302, 311
(See also adequacy)
(diminished, false, faulty, grandiose, inaccurate, inadequate, limited, poor, etc.) **8**, **10-11**, **13**, **27**, **55-56**, **76**, **90**, 93-95, 97, 100, 118, 139, 152, 185, 210, 212, 246, 257, 265, 267, 271, 276, 287, 296, 304, 309, 344
importance 205, 258, 278
indulgent **48-50**, 182, 184, 189-190, 192, 209, 228, 239, 252, 274
interest 269
involved **44**, **58**, 285
limiting **92**, **98**, **111-112**, **142**
love **147**, **260**, 274
made **98**
motivation **14**, **44**, **98**, 155, 175, 187, 286, 335
pitying 220
projection 33, 181, 184, **247**
promoting **44**, **58**, 94, 104, 250, 334
protection, protective **69**, **94**, 98, 344
reliance, reliant 205, 215, 237, 250, 257, 263
repressed, repressive **147**, **149**, 264
restricting 210, 217, 267
satisfied 216
secure **69-70**
sufficient 292, 306
taught **160**, 201, 224, 275
validation 294
willed 211, 325
worth 47, **49**, 58, 61, **67**, **72**, 132, 166, 180, 189-194, 196, **252-253**, 273, 290, 339
selfish 325
seminars (work involves) 110, 211, 218, 230
sensitive, sensitivity, (emotional) sensitivities **54-55**, **87**, **110**, 127, **139-142**, 153, **164**, 166, 196-197, 249, 255, 270, 276-278, **344**, **346**
sensual (pleasures) **47-48**, **132**, 191-192, 194
serious 51, **62**, **78**, 109, 112, 135, **154-155**, 186, 193, 202, 209, 223, 226, 233, 241, 259
serves, in service of (others) 99, 179, 191, 220, 278, 297, 308, 312
service (to be of, work as a) **61-62**, 110, 113, 130, 137, 141, 145, 171, 183, 206, 213, 221, 224, 226, 239, 243, 278, 296
"serving" (in highest sense) **166**
sex, sexual, sexuality 35, 72, **128**, **149**, **184**, 227, 232-234, 236, 263-264, 304, 322, 324, 327
(occupations related to) 69
shared (activity, efforts) **119**, 195, 227, 229, 312
(See also teamwork, partner)
Shaw, George Bernard 131, 269, **306-307 (chart)**, 309
Shelly, Percy 253, 267, 301
Sheppard, Sam 150
Shields, Brooke 97, 101, 131, 135, 143, 150, 154, 158, 255, 260, 276, 287, 333, 336
"shocking" 110, **160**, 187, 268
"shoulds" 86, 144, 205, 217
shy, shyness 101, 147, 181-182, 217, 256, 258, 300, 344
sibling rivalry **255**, **289**
siblings 70, 82, 202-203, **255**, **289**
sick **61-62**, **72**, 183
(See also health disorders, illness)
(works with the) 212
silent (backers, partners) 196
Simpson, O.J. 143, 347
singer, singing 9, 128
(See also performing arts)
singleton (planet) 37, 122, **126**
skill development 21, 23, **78**, 137, **147**, 177, 183, 206, 214, 220-221, 253, 260, 295, 302, 330
(inadequate) 59, **61**, **162**, 187, 191, 199, 220, 223-224, 226
skills (fails to develop) **86**, 221-222, 226, 229, 258, 279, **295-296**
(perfects) **62**, 109, 198, 221, 223, 266, 270, 278, **312**
(productive, rewarding, self-expressive) **61**, **137**, 159, 183, 190, 213, 225, 260
(special, specialized) 223, **296**, 306
(See also craft, service, talent, technical skills)
slack, slackness (on the job) **56**, **132**, 191, 214, 221
(See also lazy)
smothering, smother-love **72**, **155**, 205, 208
sneaky 215
snob, snobbery **140-141**
Snow, Phoebe 95, 98, 134, 139, 147, 154, 252, 257, 276, 287
sociable 56, 107, 191, 199, 340
social (consciousness) **306-307**
(service) 196, 212
(skills) 300
social contacts (needs) **330**, **332**
socially taboo activities (occupations related to) **69**
soft angles, See aspects, harmonious
soldier 123, 129

"somebody" (needs to be) **1**, **4**, 8, **13**, **18**, 86, 102, 296, 308-309, 311
(See also fame, important, special)
Somers, Suzanne 96, 100, 112, 143, 154, 162, 253, 268, 274, 276, 305, 324, 344
southern hemisphere emphasis, See trait 10
space (needs) **51**, 109, 180, 187, 254, 304
space exploration 160
speaker (public speaking) **56**, 110, 198, 201, 203, 218, 234, **256**, 299
"special" (wants to be) 29, **59**, **76**, **144**, **146-147**, 182, 216, 218, 258, 277, 296
(See also fame, important, "somebody")
specialize (in an occupation) **109**, **174**, 191
Speck, Richard 301
speculation, speculative ventures, speculator **58**, 190, 198, 218, 257
speech (use of) **52**, **136-137**, 252
spiritual (interests, quests) 25, 117, **163-164**, 166, 188, 201, 235, 239, 243, 251, **271**, **304-305**
splash pattern, See traits 10 and 11
splay pattern, See traits 9 and 12
spontaneity, spontaneous **57**, 214, 217, 219
sports 15, **45-46**, 58, 113, 190, 201, 216, 228
(See also athlete)
spouse (works with) **67**, 101, 134, 214, 220, 228, 231, 261, 285
stable, stability **47-48**, 241, 290, 335-336
staff 56, 183, 207, 213-214, 221, 223, 230, 261
stage fright 215
stagnate, stagnation **324-325**, 328
stamina **43**, 72, **128**, **179**, 185, 187, 234, 249, 263, 324
stand for something (needs to) **149-150**
"star" 104, 113
Starr, Ringo 109, 329
stationary planets 37, 122, **176**
statistics 199
status, See prestige
status conscious 266
Steinmetz, Charles 259
stellium **174**
stimulation (needs) 80, **82**, **84**, **161**, 186, 195, 210-211, 218, 224-225, 230, 234, 241, 325, 328, 330
(excessive needs for) 187, 238
(represses needs for) 195, 211, 218, 225, 238
stock options 58
Stokowski, Leopold 139
Stone, Bobby 332
Stravinsky, Igor 109
Streisand, Barbra 93, 98, 112, **126-128 (chart)**, 131, **133-134**, 252, 268, 280, 294, 324, 329, 336, 347
stress 62, **172-173**, 207, 213, 238, 260, 289, 296
(endures, works well under) 215, 233, 238
(-producing aspects), See aspects, inharmonious
strive, striver, striving 33, **43-44**, 94, 102-104, **112**, **129-130**, 216, 249-250, 276, 278, 285-286, 290-291, 335
stubborn 211, 238, 325, **327**
student (perpetual) 267, 275
students (works with) 61, **81**, **109**, **134**, 203, 207, 221, 230
studious **51**
succeed (ability to) 74, 186, 327
(determined to) 211, 326, 337
success, success-oriented **7**, 17, **28**, 41, **75**, **77**, 86, 95, 97, 124, 132, 143, 156, 165, 172-173, 185, 198, 209, 211, 214, 218, 231-232, 237, 239-240, 250, 258, 262, 270, 285-286, 290
successful **29**, **124-125**, **144**, 174, 289, 291, 298, 310
sudden (changes) 80, **83**, **158**, **325**
Sun 33, 37, 59, **143-147**, 152, 213, 282, 291, 294, 298, 301, 305, 333, 340, 344
aspects 32, 146, 153, **171-173**, 320, 336
focalized **147**
in Leo **147**, 306
in or ruling the sixth house or in Virgo **145**
in or ruling the tenth house or in Capricorn 32-33, **145-146**, 218
leading planet 105, **146-147**
near angles (within six degrees) **147**
singleton **146-147**
"sign" 8, **32**, **143**
(See also trait 5)
Sun/Moon phase, See phases
sun sign columns **32**
superficial 340
superiority complex 238, 269, 271, 304, 312
superiors 58, 70, 116, 130, 134, 156, 186, 193, 210-211, 217, 229-230, 264, 286
(See also boss, supervisors)
supernatural (confronts the) 236
supervision (dislikes) 113, 233, 308
(free of) 44, 183, 222, 240
(requires) 101, 186, 276
supervisors 46, 83-84
(See also boss, superiors)
support (attracts) 215, 243
surgeon, surgery 52, 82
sympathetic, sympathy 164, 212, 219, 231, 276, **344**
synastry 169

S (cont.)
system (to weigh "planets") **92**, 97
(of thought) **75**, 81, 153, 195, 201, 208, 211, 222

T
take charge **44**, 262
"takes one places" (work that) **74**, 201, 216, 222
talent, talented, talents 11, 21, **29**, **47-49**, 91, 98, 100, 111, **125**, 130, **132-134**, 141, 145, 152, 177, 180, 183, 193-194, 196, 206, 217, 228, 230, 232, 252, 270, 273, 274, 290, 296, 304, 306, 327, 339
talking (relies on) **51**, 109, 136
(See also voice)
Taurus, See trait 2
tax problems 232
teacher, teaches, teaching **58**, **75**, 113, **138-139**, 172, 179-180, 189-190, 197, 205, 223, 228, 231, 240, 254, 257, 275, 302
team (player) 218
(spirit) 215, 243
teamwork **64-65**, 67, 101, 191, 195, 199, 214, 220, 230, 238, 240, 261, 268, 298
(See also partner)
technical (craft, expertise, flair, know-how, skill, talent) **61-62**, 78, **80-81**, 99, 134, **136-137**, 141, 145, 153, 157, **160-161**, 165, 179, 187, 191, 193, 195, 202-203, 206, 211, 213, 218, 225, 243, 257, 259, 299
technically proficient 220, 223, 277
technology 81
telecommunications 331
telephone (relies on) **51**, 180, 199, **343**
television **81**, 149, 160, 162
Telsa, Nikola 253, 268
tension (developmental) **246**, **272**, 276-277
Theosophical Society 300
therapist, See counselor
therapy, See psychotherapy
thieves, thievery 165, 236
thinking (relies on) **51**
thinks on one's feet 44
third quadrant focus **100-101**, 134, 229
Thomas, Billy Joe 109
Thomas, Michael Tilson 264, 267
thorough **78**, 209, **326**
threatening (appears) 70
Tierney, Bil 244
timid, timidity **70-72**, **147**, 215
tools (uses) **45**, 180
Torn, Rip 108
Toscanini, Arturo 119, 267, 329
trades (the) 62, 69, 78, 276
trainer (works with a) 67, 99, 134, 191, 285
training (job entails advanced) 179
(needs additional, advanced) 75, 153-154, 216, 224
trait (grid) 35-37, **41-42**, 178
(pairs) 36, 41, 97, **178-244**
trait 1 32-33, 35-36, **43-47**, 55, 58, 61, 69, 91, **93-96**, 98, 102, 113, **115-117**, **128-131**, 177, **179**, 182-185, 188, **246-252**, **272-273**, **283-287**, 298, 303, 306, **321-324**, **333-336**
Aries 32, **321-322**
(on Ascendant or Midheaven) 179, 186, **250-252**
attitudinal approach **333**
cardinality 46, 140, **321-324**
(diminished representation) 179, **323-324**
("lack of" [by sign only]) **320**
(preponderance) 179, **321-324**, 333
eastern hemisphere emphasis 36, 91, **94-95**, 103, 179
fire element 58, 62, 79, 143, 152, 161, 265, 285-286, 326, 329, 330, **333-336**, 342
(diminished representation) 179, **333-334**, 336
("lack of" [by sign only]) **333**
(preponderance) 75, 179, 323, **333-336**, 346
locomotive pattern 105, **115-117**, 133, 142, 154, 157
New Moon phase 44, 126, 179, **283-287**, 291, 298, 307, 323
occupations (associated with) **46-47**
trait pair 1/1 **179**
(See also Mars)
trait 2 32, **47-50**, 55, 65, 67, **106-108**, **131-135**, 159, **188**, 192, 202, **252-253**, **273-274**, 289-290, 306, 320, **324-329**, **336-340**
earth element 77, 259, 266, 317, 322, 324, 326-330, **336-340**
(diminished representation) 188, **336-341**
("lack of" [by sign only]) **336**
(preponderance) 188, 320, 336, **338-341**
occupations (associated with) **50**
seesaw pattern **106-108**, 192, 294, 299
Taurus 32, 37, 131-132, 178, **324**, **328**
(on Ascendant or Midheaven) 180, 194, **252-253**
trait pair 2/2 **188**
(See also Venus)
trait 3 32, **50-54**, 62, 66, **108-109**, **135-139**, **197-198**, 200, **253-255**, **275-276**, 289, **329-333**, **340-344**
air element 82, 161, 261, 269, 310, 325-326, 328, 330, **340-344**
(diminished representation) 197, **340**
("lack of" [by sign only]) **340**

trait 3 (cont.)
(preponderance) 109, 197, **341-342**, 346
bundle pattern **108-109**, 142, 154, 158, 183, 199
Gemini 32, 37, 135, 178, **330**
(on Ascendant or Midheaven) 181, 203, **253-255**
occupations (associated with) **53**
trait pair 3/3 **197**
(See also Mercury)
trait 4 32, **54-57**, 65, 87, **92-96**, **98-100**, **110-112**, **139-143**, 159, 165, **204**, 206-209, 211-212, **255-257**, **276-277**, 285, 287, **291-294**, 298-300, 303, 306, 317, **344-347**
bowl pattern **110-112**, 126, 133, 142, 153, 182, 287
Cancer 32, 140, **321-322**
(on Ascendant or Midheaven) 182, 210, **255-257**
First Quarter Moon phase 56, 204, 282, **291-294**, 321
northern hemisphere emphasis **91-93**, 204
occupations (associated with) **56-57**, 69
trait pair 4/4 **204**
water element 86, 140, 263, 270, 292, 310, 317, 321-322, 324-327, **344-347**
(diminished representation) 204, 342, **344-347**
(preponderance) 204, **344-347**
(See also Moon)
trait 5 33-34, **57-62**, **112-114**, **143-147**, 157, 172-173, 182, 205, **213** 215-219, **257-259**, **277-278**, 295-296, 306, 326
bucket pattern 103-104, **112-114**, 138, 142, 154, 157, 182, 284, 302, 306, 313, 320
Leo 33, **325-326**, 328
(on Ascendant or Midheaven) 146, 182, 218, **257-259**
occupations (associated with) **60**
trait pair 5/5 **213**
(See also Sun)
trait 6 33, 52, **61-64**, **108-109**, **135-139**, 165, 177, 191, 206, 213, **220**, 226, **259-260**, **278-280**, 295-296, 330
bundle pattern **108-109**, 142, 154, 158, 183, 199, 278
occupations (associated with) **64**
trait pair 6/6 **220**
Virgo 33, 37, 135, 178, **330**
(on Ascendant or Midheaven) 183, 224, **259-260**
(See also Mercury)
trait 7 33, 49, 55, **64-68**, **95-96**, **100**, **106-108**, **131-135**, 183, **226**, 227-228, 230, **261-262**, **272-273**, 289, 294, **298-301**, 303, 306, 320
Full Moon phase 227, 282-283, **298-301**, 306
Libra 33, 37, 132, 178, 251, **322**
(on Ascendant or Midheaven) 184, 229, **261-262**
occupations (associated with) **68**
seesaw pattern **106-108**, 192, 294, 299
trait pair 7/7 **226**
western hemisphere emphasis 91-92, **95-96**, 107, 227
(See also Venus)
trait 8 33, 55, **68-73**, **115-117**, **147-150**, 184, 192, 200, 207, 215, 221, 227, **232**, 235, **262-264**, **273-275**, 301-305, **324-329**, 333
locomotive pattern 105, **115-117**, 133, 142, 154, 157, 185
occupations (associated with) **73**
Scorpio 33, **324-325**, 328
(on Ascendant or Midheaven) 185, 234, **262-264**
trait pair 8/8 **232**
(See also Pluto)
trait 9 33, **74-77**, 86, 97, 113, **117-119**, **151-154**, 164, 185, 201, 208, 216, 222, 228, **236-238**, **264-266**, **275-276**, 285, 287, 294, 299-305
occupations (associated with) **76**
Sagittarius 33, 75, **330-331**
(on Ascendant or Midheaven) 186, 237, **264-266**, 320
splay pattern 105, **117-119**, 240
trait pair 9/9 **236**
(See also Jupiter)
trait 10 33-34, 45, 61, **77-79**, 81, 87, **96-97**, **100**, **119-121**, 151, **154-158**, 165, 172-173, 177, 209, 217, 237, **240-242**, 248, **266-268**, **276-277**, 285, 303, **305-309**, 313, 333
Capricorn 33, 322, 339
(on Ascendant or Midheaven) 186, 240, **266-268**
Last Quarter Moon phase 240, 283, **305-309**
occupations (associated with) **79**
southern hemisphere emphasis 91, **96-97**, 240
splash pattern **119-121**, 186-187, 241
trait pair 10/10 **240**
(See also Saturn)
trait 11 33, 41, **80-85**, **119-121**, **158-163**, 187, 203, 211, 218, 225, 230, 235, 238, **241-243**, **268-269**, **277-278**, 294, 300, 302, 309-315, 325-326, 328
Aquarius 33, 81, 269, **325**, 328
(on Ascendant or Midheaven) 187, 241, **268-269**

T (cont.)
trait 11 (cont.)
occupations (associated with) **84**
splash pattern **119-121**, 186-187, 241
trait pair 11/11 41, **242**
(See also Uranus)
trait 12 33, 35, 55, 75, 79, **85-88**, **117-119**, **163-166**, **175-176**, 188, 196, 204, 212, 219, 226, 242, **244**, **270-272**, **278-280**, 285, 287, 300, 309-315, 337
occupations (associated with) **88**
Pisces 33, 320, **331**
(on Ascendant or Midheaven) 188, 242, **270-272**
splay pattern 105, **117-119**, 240
trait pair 12/12 **244**
(See also Neptune)
transformation, transforms 185, 215, 221, 233, 264
(princple of) **148**
transpersonal (forces, issues) **148**, 270
(See also outer planets)
transpersonal psychology 163
transportation (of objects) 50, **136**
travel (long/short trips) 12, 15, **51**, **74-75**, 109, 151, 180, 199, 201, 208, 228, 238-239, 266, 331
(fears) 193, 209, 237
traveler 275
Travolta, John 257
Trevino, Lee 119
troubled career/job life **1**, **13**, **17**, **27**, **29**, **59**, **79**, **91**, **96**, 155, 157, 163, 186, 229, 249, 251, 256, 262, 269, 277, 287, 309, 311, 334
truck driver 53
Truman, Harry 147, **325**
trust (lacks) 263
truths (higher) 238-239, 243
Tuna, Charlie 143
turbulence, turbulent 133, **148**, 150
Tyl, Noel 31, **120-121 (chart)**, 305

U
unambitious 196
unapproachable 263-264
unassuming 239, 271
uncommitted 205
unconscious (the) 5, 148, 158
(dependency) 56
(habits) 56
unconventionality **159**
uncovers flaws **62**, 279
underdog (assists the) 235
under par (works) 213
underestimates (capabilities, self) 185, 188, 209, 217, 219, 223, **258**, 285
understanding 11, 265, 275, 278, 299, 310, 344
"underworld" (occupations involving the) 69
undisciplined, See discipline, lacks
unemployment 156, 194, 213, 222, 224, 226, 233
(compensation) 196
unethical 242
unfulfilling (career, employment, job, vocation, work) **27-29**, 46, 56, 61, 78, 90-91, 94, 99, 115, 143, 145, 186, 199, 206, 213, 223-224, 251, 254, 256, 260, 289, 296
unions 195
universal themes **97**
universities (works for) 219, 226
unpredictable **84**
unrealistic **7**, 76, 219-220, 240, 242, 258
(about life, self, success) **8**, **153**, 176, 185, 193, 226, 241, 302
(about others) **95**, 192, 243
(goal expectations) **18-19**, **25**, 75, 86, 102, 186, 209, 216, 237, 239, 244, 275, 304, 309, 331
unstable 244
unusual hours (works) **83**, 161
up to par (fails to work) 224, 238
Uranus 33, 80, 140, **158-163**, 242, 299, 320, 340
aspects **158**, 320
handle or leading planet 109-110, 114, **160**, **162**, 302
in eleventh house 121
in or ruling the sixth house or in Virgo **161**
in or ruling the tenth house or in Capricorn **161-162**, 241
near angles (within six degrees) **162-163**, 294, 314
repressed Uranian urges **162**
singleton **162**
(See also trait 11)
used (feels) 279
useful (needs to be) **62-63**, 141, 198-199, 206, 220-221, 297, 308
uses (others, usury) **21**, **72**, **100**, 253, 267, 308
Ustinov, Peter 162

V
value (personal, stable sense of) **132**, 196
Van Gogh, Vincent
variety (needs) 198-199, **254**
Venus 32-33, **131-135**, 146, 149, 188, 227, 320, 336, 340
aspects **173**
focalized planet **107**, 133
G-Planet (occupies plus zone) 107, 123, 126-127, **132**, 135, 314, 320
interdependent personality function **91**
in or ruling the sixth house or in Virgo **133-134**, 191, 299, 313
in or ruling the tenth house or in Capricorn **134**, 143, 194, 229
leading planet 126-127, **133-134**
singleton 126-127, **133-134**
(See also traits 2 and 7)

verbal (abilities/faculties) **51**, 188, 202, 253, 330
(exchanges) 254
verbally (active, expressive) **51**, 135, 198-199, 201
versatile, verstility 173, 199, 220, 329
"vicarious" (experiencing) **329**
victim, victimized 165-166, 212, 279, 310, 315
Virgo, See trait 6
visionary **85**, 164, 219, 239, 243, 270, 300
visions 241, 278
(See also dreams)
visual (appreciation) 65
visualization **29**, **87**, 204, 212
vocally active **135**
vocation, See career
vocational (See also career, job, work)
(analysis) **31**, **38**
(approach) **28**, **43**, 126, 128, 136, 250, 252-253, 255, 257, 259, 261-262, 264, 266, 268, 270, 310
(aptitudes), See aptitude
(astrology), See astrology
(choice, direction) **4-6**, **13**, 32 117, 123, 176, 178
(See also direction)
(dissatisfaction), See unfulfilling
(expression) **45**, **65**, **74**, 253, 256-257, 260, 312
(satisfaction), See fulfillment
(indicators [traditional]) **26**
(needs) **15**, 21, **23**, 32, 35, 43, 66
(needs analysis form) **36-37**, 178
vocationally significant (factors) **37**
(functions, traits, planets) **56**, **74**, **103**, **129**, **137**, **139**, 149, 151-152, 155, 157
(See also primary personality/vocational functions)
voice (relies on speaking) 50, 180, 204, 253, 275, 343
volunteer work 15, 26
Von Klocker, H. Baron **27-28**, 30, 45, 248
Von Strahl, Lotte 97, 103, 108, 135, 139, 147, 158, 163, 264, 267, 274, 280, 297
vulnerable, vulnerabilities **56**, 69, 242, 344

W

waitperson 138
walking (job entails) **51**, 109, 136
waning (Moon phases) **282**, 302, 305
Warren, Earl 134
wasteful 239
water element, See trait 4
(planets/signs) 164, **317**
waxing (Moon phases) **282**, 297-298
wealth, wealthy 5, **74**, **115**, **118**, 152, 185, 205, 208, 215-216, 220, 228, 232, 237, 239, 243, 251, 270-271, 275, 304, 311
weak, weakness 35, 67, 86, 236
weight (gains) 185, 207, 228
Weismuller, Johnny 264
welfare 196
Welles, Orson **110-112 (chart)**
Wells, H. G. 119
western hemisphere emphasis, See trait 7
Whitman, Walt 143
Wilde, Oscar 260
willful 208, 327
wimp, wimpy 185, 215, **264**
win (needs to) **44**, **128**, 181, 186, 214-215, 272
wishful thinking 239
wit, witty **135-136**, **138**, 152, 253, 343
withdrawn 70, 227
Wood, Natalie 97, 103, 135, 154, 257, 262, 274, 309
work (as service) **61**, 206, 217, 224, 335
(See also career, employment, job, service)
(as art form) 259
(ethic) **15**, **79**, 156, 171, 188, 194, 206, 219-220, 226, 260, 262, 289
(background, experience, history) **28-29**, 178, 223
(importance of) 206, 259
(lack of satisfying), See unfulfilling
(lack of willingness to, prefers not to) **27-28**, **59**, **61**, 78, 180, 188, 237-238, 267
(See also effort [lack of], work personality type E)
(satisfying), See fulfillment
work environment 48, 58, 65, 98-100, 131, 136, 218, 220-221, 263, 321, 332
work personalities **13-26**
type A **14-15**, 17, 20, **28**, 44, 62, 74, 77
type B **15-17**, **28**, 44, 62, 74, 77
type C **17-21**, **23-26**, **28**, 44, 55, 59, 62, 74-75, 77
type D **21-23**, **25-26**, **28**, 45, 48-49, 52, 59, 61, 75, 78, 86, 296
type E **25-26**, **28**, 45, 49, 56, 59, 62, 75, 78, 86, 165, 296
workaholic, workaholism **14-15**, **62**, **149**, 183, 198-199, 213, 224, 226, 233, 242, 279, **297**
works (closely with/through others) **65**, **95**, 100, 107, 179, 191-192, 207, 214, 220, 227
(See also clients, customers, friends, loved one, spouse, students, partners, patients)
worthlessness (feelings of) 5, 10, 156, 242, 309

W (cont.)
writer, writing 9, 11, **52**, **56**, 75, 115, 121, 123, **132**, **135**, **140**, **155**,**180**, 189, 240, 254, 256, 268, 271, 290, 294, 299-300, 306, 320, 341
(creative) **55**, 110, 121, 136, **140-141**, 149, 154

Y
yearnings 75, **88**, **163**, **270**, 312
Yeats, William Butler **282**
youthful 136, 254